Indian Foreign Policy in a Unipolar World

War and International Politics in South Asia

Series Editor: **Srinath Raghavan**
Senior Fellow, Centre for Policy Research, New Delhi.

This Series seeks to foster original and rigorous scholarship on the dynamics of war and international politics in South Asia. Following Clausewitz, war is understood as both a political and a social phenomenon which manifests itself in a variety of forms ranging from total wars to armed insurrections. International politics is closely intertwined with it, for war not only plays an important role in the formation of an international order but also a threat to its continued existence. The Series will therefore focus on the international as well as domestic dimensions of war and security in South Asia. Comparative studies with other geographical areas are also of interest.

A fundamental premise of this Series is that we cannot do justice to the complexities of war by studying it from any single, privileged academic standpoint; the phenomenon is best explained in a multidisciplinary framework. The Series welcomes a wide array of approaches, paradigms and methodologies, and is interested in historical, theoretical, and policy-oriented scholarship. In addition to monographs, the Series will from time to time publish collections of essays.

Also in this Series

Fighting Like a Guerrilla: The Indian Army and Counterinsurgency
Rajesh Rajagopalan
ISBN 978-0-415-45684-5

India's Nuclear Debate: Exceptionalism and the Bomb
Priyanjali Malik
ISBN 978-0-415-56312-3

Interrogating International Relations: India's Strategic Practice and the Return of History
Jayashree Vivekanandan
ISBN 978-0-415-59812-5

Indian Foreign Policy in a Unipolar World

Editor

Harsh V. Pant

Routledge
Taylor & Francis Group
LONDON NEW YORK NEW DELHI

First published 2009 in India
by Routledge
912 Tolstoy House, 15–17 Tolstoy Marg, Connaught Place,
New Delhi 110 001

Simultaneously published in the UK
by Routledge
4 Park Square, Milton Park, Abingdon, Oxon OX14 4RN

Routledge is an imprint of the Taylor & Francis Group, an informa business

© 2009 Harsh V. Pant

Paperback edition published 2013

Typeset by
Star Compugraphics Private Limited
5–CSC, First Floor, Near City Apartments
Vasundhara Enclave
Delhi 110 096

All rights reserved. No part of this book may be reproduced or utilised in any form or by any electronic, mechanical or other means, now known or hereafter invented, including photocopying and recording, or in any information storage and retrieval system without permission in writing from the publishers.

Notice:
Product or corporate names may be trademarks or registered trademarks and are used only for identification and explanation without intent to infringe.

British Library Cataloguing-in-Publication Data
A catalogue record of this book is available from the British Library

ISBN 13: 978-0-415-84306-5 (pbk)

To the students and practitioners of Indian foreign policy

Contents

Preface   ix

1. Introduction   1
   Harsh V. Pant

PART I: Major Themes in Indian Foreign Policy

2. India and the Global Balance of Power:
   A Neorealist Snapshot   23
   Devin T. Hagerty

3. India and the Emerging Non-Proliferation Order:
   The Second Nuclear Age   43
   C. Raja Mohan

4. India and the Challenge of Global Terrorism:
   The 'Long War' and Competing Domestic Visions   73
   Timothy D. Hoyt

5. India and Energy Security: A Foreign Policy Priority   99
   Manjeet S. Pardesi and *Sumit Ganguly*

PART II: India and Major Global Powers

6. India and the US: Embracing a New Paradigm   131
   C. Christine Fair

7. India and China: As China Rises, India Stirs   163
   Mohan Malik

8. India and Russia: Renewing the Relationship   192
   Deepa M. Ollapally

9. India and the EU: A Long Road Ahead   209
   Fraser Cameron

PART III: India's Regional Policy

10. India and South Asia: Towards a Benign Hegemony   231
    Stephen F. Burgess

11. India and the Middle East: A Re-Assessment of Priorities?   251
    Harsh V. Pant

12. India and Central Asia: Part of the New Great Game   277
    Stephen Blank

13. India and East Asia: A Region 'Rediscovered'   305
    Manish Dabhade

Afterword by Harsh V. Pant   323
Bibliography   336
Notes on Contributors   371
Index   377

Preface

This book is an attempt at exploring the multidimensional nature of the Indian foreign policy at this critical juncture in its trajectory when India is being talked about as a rising power in the international system, almost in the same league as China. The project was very ambitious in scale, given the desire to examine Indian foreign policy not only along various conceptual axes but also empirically, especially in the light of India's engagement with the US on various issues and across regions. It was only with the help, support and encouragement of a number of people that this project could come to fruition.

*

First of all, I would like to express my deep sense of gratitude to all the contributors who, despite their busy schedules, took time off to be a part of this volume, being edited by a very junior colleague of theirs. Most of them are senior scholars of South Asia and I have learnt a lot from their work. So it was a privilege for me when they agreed to be a part of this project. I hope they will not be disappointed with the final product.

Special thanks to Srinath Raghavan, and Nilanjan Sarkar at Routledge, New Delhi. It was Srinath who encouraged me to do the project with Routledge when I mentioned the idea of the volume to him. I am also deeply grateful for the support, assistance and good cheer of Sreenath Sreedharan of Routledge India without whose patience, understanding and great work at copy-editing this book would not have materialised in its present form.

Finally, a special note of thanks to my family and to Chotu, in particular, without whose support none of this would have been possible.

I can only hope that the abiding faith of all those who have been involved with this project in one form or another will be suitably rewarded. Hopefully, more systematic studies of Indian foreign policy will emerge very soon and will enrich this field of study.

1

Introduction

HARSH V. PANT

By all reckoning, India has arrived on the world stage. No longer a mere bystander to the actions of other powers, India is gradually coming to terms with its increasing weight in contemporary international politics. It is being viewed as a major pole in the configuration of the emerging global balance of power by outsiders as well as Indians themselves. The US Secretary of State Condoleezza Rice boldly declaims that the US is 'willing and ready to assist in the growth of India's global power ... which [the US] sees as largely positive'.[1] And Indian strategists are no longer shy in proclaiming India to be one of the six members of the emerging global balance of power.[2]

If the global balance of power is indeed shifting from the Atlantic to the Pacific, then the rise of India, along with China, is clearly an indisputable reality that few can dare to dismiss any longer. As a consequence, India is now being invited to the G-8 summits, is being called upon to shoulder global responsibilities—from the challenges of nuclear proliferation to the instability in the Persian Gulf and is increasingly being viewed as more than merely a 'South Asian' power. From a nation that was mortgaging its gold reserves in 1990 to one whose foreign exchange reserves are overfull, from a nation that was marginal in the global distribution of economic might to one that is steadily emerging as one of the centres of modern global economy, India has indeed come a long way. Its economy is one of the fastest growing in the world; it is a nuclear weapon state, a status that is being grudgingly accepted by the world; its armed forces are highly professional, on their way towards rapid modernisation; and its vibrant democratic institutions, with the world's second-largest

---

[1] 'India a Growing Global Power', *The Times of India* (New Delhi), May 29, 2005.
[2] K. Subrahmanyam, 'Wanted Leaders with a Vision', *The Tribune* (Chandigarh), September 24, 2005.

Muslim population, are attracting global attention at a time when promotion of democracy is being viewed as a remedy for much of what is wrong with a large part of the world. However, the most significant attribute of today's India is its attempt to carve out a foreign policy that is much more confident about India's rising stature in the international system.

According to the US National Intelligence Council report, 'Mapping the Global Future', by 2020, the international community will have to confront the military, political and economic dimensions of the rise of China and India.[3] This report has likened the emergence of these countries in the early 21st century to the rise of Germany in the 19th and America in the 20th, with impacts potentially as dramatic. The CIA has labelled India the key 'swing state' in international politics and predicts that, by 2015, India will emerge as the fourth most important power in the international system. According to the assessment of Goldman Sachs, by 2040, the four largest economies will be China, the US, India and Japan.[4] India will overtake the G-6 economies faster than previously expected and its GDP, in all likelihood, will surpass that of the US before 2050, making it the second-largest economy after China. After decades of marginalisation due to the vagaries of Cold War, its own obsolescent model of economic management and the seemingly never-ending tensions with Pakistan, India is finally coming into its own with a self-confidence that comes with growing capabilities. Its global and regional ambitions are rising and it is showing an aggressiveness in its foreign policy, which had not been its forte before.

This transformation since the end of the Cold War has been the result of a number of factors. All through the Cold War years, India saw itself as the leader of the Third World, even as the Third World group of states existed more in myth than in reality. While the idea of a non-aligned foreign policy may have been devised to prevent Indian foreign policy from becoming hostage to the Cold War rivalry between the US and the former Soviet Union, in practical terms it led to a certain ideological rigidity that prevented India from protecting and enhancing its vital interests in an

---

[3] The report is available at http://www.cia.gov/nic/NIC_globaltrend2020.html (accessed on December 20, 2007).
[4] The report is available at http://www2.goldmansachs.com/insight/research/reports/99.pdf (accessed on December 20, 2007).

anarchical international environment. As the Cold War drew to a close, India was forced to reorient its economic and foreign policies to the changing global realities and in less than two decades seems on the cusp of achieving the status of a 'great power'.

While some proclaimed the end of history with the fall of the Berlin Wall, in many ways it was the beginning of history for Indian foreign policy, free as it was from the structural constraints of a bipolar world order. It lost its political, diplomatic and military ally with the demise of the Soviet Union and its economy was on the threshold of bankruptcy. There was domestic political uncertainty with weak governments unable to last for a full five-year term as the plethora of internal security challenges were becoming more prominent. The ignominy of having to physically lift bullion to obtain credit pushed India against the ropes and the national psyche was at its most vulnerable. It was against this background that the minority government of late P.V. Narasimha Rao had to formulate its economic and foreign policy, to preserve Indian interests in a radically new global environment. And slowly, but surely, began the process that continues to unfold till date as India tries to redefine its place in the international system in consonance with its existing and potential power capabilities.

Both India and the international system are undergoing profound changes, complicating the interplay between them. On the one hand, the rise of India is bound to alter the international structure in the near future, while on the other, external systemic constraints are increasingly becoming central in shaping India's international behaviour. As in the case of most other nations, the sources of Indian foreign policy are manifold, ranging from the international system to economic interests and to domestic political pressures and institutions. This volume, while taking into account all the sources, focuses primarily on the impact of emerging structural realities of the international system on Indian foreign policy. As India moves from the periphery of the international system to its centre, India's structural position in the international system will be the most important variable in defining the trajectory of its foreign policy.

RISING POWERS AND THEIR FOREIGN POLICIES

According to the realist tradition in International Relations, it is the international systemic constraints that determine the foreign policy behaviour of states. While individual or domestic political variables may influence the policy at the margins, it is the structure of the international system that sets the terms for its conduct across time and space. Realists contend that 'the pressures of [international] competition weigh more heavily than ideological preferences or internal political pressures'.[5] In his seminal work on structural realism, Kenneth Waltz has argued that his is a theory of international politics, not of foreign policy, because structural realism tries to explain the outcomes of state interactions. Theories of foreign policy would seek to explain the behaviour of individual states in the external realm.[6] According to Waltz, foreign policy does not constitute an autonomous realm, because it is driven by both external and internal factors and so there is no point in trying to find a theoretical explanation for foreign policy. A theory of international politics shows how the interaction of states generates a structure which then constrains states, rewarding or punishing them for taking certain actions. Thus it explains why states similarly placed in the system behave similarly despite the differences among them. For Waltz, to explain how any single state will respond to the constraints imposed by the international structure requires a theory of foreign policy. A theory of foreign policy, therefore, explains why states similarly placed in the international system do not behave similarly, thereby underlining the differences in the internal make-up of states as explanations for the differences.[7]

However, despite his emphatic rejection of the use of structural realism as a theory of foreign policy, he has proceeded to explain specific foreign policy behaviour of states using his theoretical framework. He has argued, for example, that the 'foreign policies of nations are affected in important ways by the placement of countries in the international–political system or more simply by their relative power'.[8] Others have also pointed out that his work contains a number of examples of specific foreign policies attributable to

---

[5] Kenneth N. Waltz, 'A Response to My Critics', in Robert O. Keohane, ed., *Neorealism and its Critics* (New York: Columbia University Press, 1986), p. 329.

[6] Kenneth N. Waltz, *Theory of International Politics* (Reading, Mass.: Addison-Wesley, 1979), pp. 71–72.

[7] Kenneth N. Waltz, 'International Politics is Not Foreign Policy', *Security Studies* 6:1 (Autumn 1996), pp. 54–55.

[8] Kenneth N. Waltz, 'America as a Model for the World? A Foreign Policy Perspective', *PS: Political Science and Politics* 24:4 (December 1991), p. 667.

systemic factors and have concluded that neo-realist theories can be employed as theories of foreign policy.[9] As a consequence, various scholars have explained foreign policy bahaviour of states by updating and systematising Waltz's basic argument, concluding that a state's position in the international system and its relative material power capabilities are the most important drivers of its foreign policy.[10] In the words of Fareed Zakaria, 'a good theory of foreign policy should first ask what effect the international system has on national behaviour, because the most powerful generalisable characteristic of a state in international relations is its relative position in the international system'.[11]

How states respond to relative material rise or decline has long been central to understanding the forces that shape international politics. As has been argued, 'similar security policies recur throughout history and across the international system in states that, whatever their differences, occupy similar positions in the international system [...] The security policies of very strong states are different from those of very weak ones, and both differ from those of states that are neither very strong nor very weak'.[12] Structural constraints, in other words, force states towards a particular set of foreign policies in line with their relative position in the international system. And as that position undergoes a change, so will change the foreign policy of that state changes as well. As Robert Gilpin explains, 'a more wealthy and a more powerful state…will select a larger bundle of security and welfare goals than

---

[9] Colin Elman, 'Horses for Courses: Why Not Neorealist Theories of Foreign Policy', *Security Studies* 6:1 (Autumn 1996), p. 10.

[10] See, for example, Thomas J. Christenson, *Useful Adversaries: Grand Strategy, Domestic Mobilisation, and Sino-American Conflict, 1947–1958* (Princeton: Princeton University Press, 1996); Randall L. Schweller, *Deadly Imbalances: Tripolarity and Hitler's Strategy of World Conquest* (New York: Columbia University Press, 1998); William C. Wohlforth, *The Elusive Balance: Power and Perceptions during the Cold War* (Ithaca, NY: Cornell University Press, 1993); and Fareed Zakaria, *From Wealth to Power: The Unusual Origins of America's World Role* (Princeton: Princeton University Press, 1998).

[11] Fareed Zakaria, 'Realism and Domestic Politics: A Review Essay', *International Security* 17:1 (Summer 1992), p. 197.

[12] Michael Mandelbaum, *The Fates of Nations:The Search for National Security in the Nineteenth and Twentieth Centuries* (Cambridge: Cambridge University Press, 1988), pp. 2, 4.

a less wealthy and less powerful state',[13] thereby trying to use the tools at its disposal to gain control over its strategic environment. A state, therefore, will become more ambitious in defining the scale and scope of its foreign policy as its relative material power capabilities increase and vice versa.

According to Hans Morgenthau, the interests of a state are shaped by its power.[14] An increase in a state's relative power capabilities will result in a concomitant increase in its interests in the realm of foreign policy. And as it will rise in inter-state hierarchy, it will 'try to expand its economic, political and territorial control; it will try to change the international system in accordance with its own interests'.[15] Rising powers in the international system will try to change the status quo and establish new institutions and arrangements that reflect more accurately their own conception of their place in the world. Rising powers seek to enhance their security by increasing their capabilities and their control over the external environment.

As states become economically and militarily more powerful, they not only seek greater global influence over international political and economic institutions and the behaviour of other states in consonance with their rising capabilities, but they are also more capable of expanding their interests by changing the established order. A redistribution of power always poses a threat to the stability of the international system and the fundamental problem of international relations continues to be the resolution of the consequences of uneven growth of power among states.[16] Change for the realists is the result of the rise and fall of the state's relative power, conditioned by the nature of the overall distribution of capabilities. With the gradual accretion of power by states such as China and India, the world may now be witnessing a major shift in power dynamics. Given the significance of the changes in the structure of the international system, it is not surprising that scholars and policy-makers have examined closely the evolution of the international system in the last few years.

---

[13] Robert Gilpin, *War and Change in World Politics* (Cambridge: Cambridge University Press, 1981), pp. 22–23, 94–95.
[14] Hans Morgenthau, *Politics Among Nations*, 5 edn (New York: Knopf, 1973), p. 75.
[15] Gilpin, *War and Change in World Politics*, pp. 94–95.
[16] This is the central argument of Gilpin, *War and Change in World Politics*.

THE EMERGING INTERNATIONAL ORDER

The debate on the emerging structure of the international system that commenced soon after the demise of the former Soviet Union continues unabated, often reflecting a diversity of assumptions about the way the world works. Though scholars by and large accept that the US is the dominant power in the world today, there are differences with regard to how far ahead the US is relative to the other states and how long this dominance will last. Also, some question whether the US is clearly ahead in all dimensions of power.

Christopher Layne has argued that the victory of the US in the Cold War gave the world a 'unipolar moment' and even though the US might try to maintain its hegemony through benevolence rather than coercion, states will eventually balance it.[17] Taking issue with this proposition, William Wohlforth has claimed that not only is the international system unambiguously unipolar but also that it is more peaceful and durable. This is because today no state exists which can seriously challenge the US in any domain of power—military, economic, technological, and cultural—and because of its special geographical position other states will find it difficult to counterbalance the US.[18] Underlying this argument is the claim of the US being the only 'comprehensive global superpower' á la Brzezinski.[19]

A slightly different position is taken by Joseph Nye who argues that it is the transformation in the nature of power, from hard power to soft power, that gives the US unique advantages in the present international system. With political leadership and strategic vision, he claims, the US can maintain its hegemony in world politics.[20] For Huntington, it is a 'uni-multipolar' system, where a single superpower, the US, exists with several major powers and this system will lead to a clearly multipolar system in the coming years.[21]

---

[17] Christopher Layne, 'The Unipolar Illusion', *International Security* 17:4 (Spring 1993), pp. 5–51.
[18] William C. Wohlforth, 'The Stability of a Unipolar World', *International Security* 24:1 (Summer 1999), pp. 5–41.
[19] Zbigniew Brzezinski, *The Grand Chessboard: American Primacy and Its Geostrategic Imperatives* (New York: Basic Books, 1997), p. 24.
[20] Joseph S. Nye, Jr., *Bound to Lead: The Changing Nature of American Power* (New York: Basic Books, 1990), pp. 173–201.
[21] Samuel P. Huntington, 'The Lonely Superpower', *Foreign Affairs* 78:2 (March/April 1999), pp. 35–49.

Despite these differing perspectives, it is clear that as of today the US remains *the* dominant power in the system. The current war on terror and the surprisingly swift defeat of the Iraqi army has also driven home the fact that it will be extremely difficult, if not impossible, for any nation to challenge the military might of the US in the near future. As has been argued, 'the larger lesson', of this war 'and one stupefying to the Russian and Chinese military, worrying to the Indians, and disturbing to proponents of a common European Defence Policy, is that in military terms there is only one player on the field that counts'.[22] But the Iraq war and its aftermath have also made clear the limits of US power and its unilateral approach in international affairs.

The US penchant for unilateral actions has also been clear for quite some time now to the other states, especially after the US air strikes in Iraq in 1998 and the US-led North Atlantic Treaty Organization (NATO) air strikes on former Yugoslavia in 1999. For many nations this tendency has got aggravated under the current US administration with its emphasis on pre-emptive strategies and a distinct lack of respect for even its closest allies. The recent dispute over Iraq has also demonstrated that most of the major global powers do not share American perspectives on major problems in the international system and the appropriate means for resolving them. Many countries, therefore, see a need to balance the US might in the global system, but there is little that they are capable of doing given the enormous differentials in capabilities. This desire to balance the US and the opposition to so complete a US dominance of the international system are shared by major global powers such as France, Russia, China and India, though perhaps to different degrees. But what is interesting about the present international environment is that we do not see these major powers making any serious effort to counterbalance the US dominance. While it is possible that balancing tendencies may already be taking place and that, as some have suggested, it may only be a matter of time before other major powers found a serious balancing coalition,[23] major powers have so far refrained from posing any serious challenge to the US. There is, as of now, no

---

[22] Paul Kennedy, 'The Eagle has Landed', *The Financial Times* (London), February 2, 2002.

[23] Kenneth Waltz, 'Structural Realism after the Cold War', *International Security* 25:1 (Summer 2000), pp. 5–41.

theoretical consensus among scholars as to whether the balancing is taking place at all vis-à-vis the US preponderance and, if it is occurring, what form is it taking.[24]

Even as another decade comes to a close in the so-called post-Cold War period, the most remarkable, and to some the most troublesome, characteristic of the present international system remains the overwhelming power of the US. The US accounts for about 30 per cent of the world's GDP,[25] its defence budget is almost half of global defence expenditures,[26] it is on the verge of achieving nuclear superiority over its nearest nuclear rival,[27] Russia, all giving it almost an unheard of freedom to project its power globally. Though it is in vogue these days to talk about an America in decline, given its relative economic decline in the last few years, overextension of its military commitments and its diminishing soft power, few are arguing that the US will not continue to dominate the international system in the policy-relevant future.[28]

It is the primacy of the US in the international system, as the one singular structural reality, that the Indian foreign policy has been

---

[24] On this debate, see Robert A. Pape, 'Soft Balancing Against the United States', *International Security* 30:1 (Summer 2005), pp. 7–45; T.V. Paul, 'Soft Balancing in the Age of US Primacy', *International Security* 30:1 (Summer 2005), pp. 46–71; Stephen G. Brooks and William C. Wohlforth, 'Hard Times for Soft Balancing', *International Security* 30:1 (Summer 2005), pp. 72–108; and Keir A. Lieber and Gerard Alexander, 'Waiting for Balancing: Why the World is Not Pushing Back', *International Security* 30:1 (Summer 2005), pp. 109–39.
[25] The US GDP was 30.2 per cent of the global GDP in 2005. For details, see World Bank, 'World Bank Indicators 2006', (Washington, DC: World Bank, 2006).
[26] US defence expenditure is approximately ten times that of the second-largest defence spender, the UK. See, Stockholm International Peace Research Institute, *SIPRI Yearbook 2005: Armaments, Disarmament and International Security* (Oxford: Oxford University Press, 2005), p. 318, Table 8.3.
[27] Keir A. Lieber and Daryl G. Press, 'The End of Mad? The Nuclear Dimension of US Primacy', *International Security* 30:4 (Spring 2006), pp. 7–44.
[28] On the growing literature on America's decline, see Charles Kupchan, *The End of the American Era* (New York: Alfred A. Knopf, 2003); Roger Bhrbach and Jim Tarbell, *Imperial Overstretch* (London: Zed Books, 2004); Nancy Soderbeg, *The Superpower Myth* (New Jersey: John Wiley & Sons, 2005); Fred Kaplan, *Daydream Believers* (New Jersey: John Wiley & Sons, 2008). For a succinct argument as to why the US will remain the predominant power in the policy-relevant future, see Ashley J. Tellis, 'India in Asian Geopolitics', in Prakash Nanda, ed, *Rising India* (New Delhi: Lancer Publishers, 2007), pp. 119–21.

trying to come to grips with, ever since the end of the Cold War. While some might object to the use of the term 'unipolar' in the title of this volume, given the recent setbacks that the US foreign policy seems to be facing across the globe, the fact remains that all major powers continue to shape their foreign policies as a response to American preponderance. The Chinese and the Russians may talk of the desirability of a 'multipolar' world and the Europeans may be irritated by the American 'hyperpuissance', but there is no escaping the reality of American pre-eminence in global politics at the present juncture. India is no exception and, in recent years, it has engaged with the US more deeply and fruitfully than ever before. As it has begun to craft a more confident foreign policy, the role of the US has emerged as a central factor in the shaping of that policy.

One cannot but agree with the formulation that 'great powers are like divas; they enter and exit the stage with great tumult'.[29] India is not yet a great power. In fact, it is a long way from achieving that status. But it is a rising power and will have to make some consequential foreign policy choices in the near future. It has been suggested that 'rising states have choices about whether to become great powers. However, a state's freedom to choose whether to seek great power status is in reality tightly constrained by structural factors. Eligible states that fail to attain great power status are predictably punished. If policy-makers of eligible states are socialised to the international system's constraints, they understand that attaining great power is a pre-requisite if their states are to be secure and autonomous'.[30] There is little doubt that policy-makers of a rising India would like the country to attain the status of a great power and are aware of the constraints that the structural realities of the international system impose on their country's future trajectory.

India is rising rapidly but with a certain ambivalence about the present global order, which it feels does not give it the attention and honour which it deserves. Historically, international power redistribution has been a source of conflict as old powers tend to

---

[29] Fareed Zakaria, 'Speak Softly, Carry a Veiled Threat', *New York Times*, February 18, 1996.
[30] Layne, 'The Unipolar Illusion', pp. 9–10.

defend the existing international order that have underpinned their power, while rising powers seek to establish a new order on their own terms. As India begins to assert itself in the global political arena, both the ability of the present international order to integrate India into its fold and India's commitment to current world order will come into sharp relief.

INDIAN FOREIGN POLICY: EMERGING THEMES AND ISSUES

The case of India raises some very interesting theoretical and policy issues. The most significant of them is, how does a rising power shape its foreign policy that enhances its interests in a changing international context? This book is aimed at examining the forces that have shaped the Indian response to the emerging international security environment since the end of the Cold War. Since 'a first-cut theory of foreign policy should begin by looking at the effect of [a state's] relative standing [in the international system] on a state's preferences', most contributors start from the basic premise that the distribution of power in the international system is the most critical variable in foreign policy behaviour. This does not imply that other sources of Indian foreign policy have been ignored by the contributors. In fact, most contributors have gone beyond the first-cut and have identified how domestic, political and ideational constraints continue to shape Indian foreign policy, even as the structural imperatives continue to push India towards a more expansive definition of its foreign policy priorities and interests. Though not designed to cover the entire spectrum of Indian foreign policy, the contributors of this volume were asked to address some of the essential and enduring questions in Indian foreign policy:

1. What is India's perception of various issue areas and regions in crafting its foreign policy? How does it view its role and its interests? How has it gone about configuring its foreign policy towards meeting those ends?
2. How is it interacting with the US in all those issue areas as well as in various parts of the world? Are its interests compatible with US interests? Where and how do they diverge? How is India negotiating those divergences with the US?

The first section of this volume is organised along thematic lines. It examines four major influences that have shaped Indian foreign policy in recent years: the changing global balance of power, the emerging global nuclear order, the challenge of global terrorism and India's pursuit of energy security. In his analysis of the emerging balance of power in the international system, Devin Hagerty, using a neo-realist frame of reference, argues that India is on the path to achieving the status of a great economic and military power and, in all likelihood, will emerge one by 2020. Moreover, India will be the world's third-greatest power, though much behind the US and China in material terms. Given the shift in the locus of global politics from the Atlantic to the Pacific, India, along with the US and China, will define the emerging global balance of power. For Hagerty, this triangular relationship between the US, China and India will be the most significant aspect of the emerging international system. Despite a number of changes, the international system, according to Hagerty, remains decidedly unipolar and therefore India's burgeoning relationship with the world's most powerful state, the US, will bring enormous advantages to India on a whole range of issues.

The most important benefit that has accrued to India by virtue of this relationship is its gradual acceptance as a responsible nuclear state by the global nuclear order, best exemplified by the recently signed US–India civilian nuclear cooperation agreement that has virtually rewritten the rules of the global nuclear regime by underlining India's credentials as a responsible nuclear state that should be integrated into the global nuclear order. The nuclear agreement creates a major exception to the US prohibition of nuclear assistance to any country that does not accept international monitoring of all its nuclear facilities. As C. Raja Mohan points out, this 'nuclear reconciliation between the global nuclear order and India must be seen as a consequence of the changes in the international distribution of power as well as the perceived need to adapt to the changing dynamics of nuclear politics in the post-Cold War period'. The main challenge facing the global nuclear order has been its inability to integrate emerging powers and the emergence of a second nuclear age, according to Mohan, forced the hegemonic power, the US, to restructure the prevailing nuclear order. Given India's revisionist aspirations vis-à-vis the global nuclear order, it was more than willing to go along.

Mohan underlines the crucial role of India in the emerging balance of power in Asia, something also highlighted by Hagerty, and its impact on the Bush administration's attitudes towards the reconfiguration of the nuclear non-proliferation regime.

The single-most important foreign policy challenge confronting the US today is the challenge of global terrorism which the US policy-makers have interpreted as a protracted ideological struggle, the 'Long War'. India has been a victim of terrorism long before it reached the American shores and today both states share a complementarity of views on this issue. Timothy Hoyt points out that 'India will take an increasing role in managing the challenge of global terror, as its relative power and extra-regional and global influence increases'. While India will have to consider how its world-view conforms with the US preferences and priorities, as Hoyt makes clear, its future policy regarding global terrorism will be driven not simply by its growing ties with the US but also by 'India's competing domestic visions of India's role in the world and by gradual shifts in India's perception of the terrorist threat'. This is reflected in the fact that while the Indian government agrees with the US on the threat posed by terrorism, there is little agreement on the definition of key state sponsors of terrorism. India's own threat perception and domestic considerations will make it unlikely that India will follow US lead on global terrorist issues.

India's rapidly rising rates of economic growth can only be sustained by making adequate provisions for energy resources and energy security remains a major constraining factor in its emergence as a major global player. The Indian prime minister himself has made it clear that energy security is the second most important priority of his government after food security. Not surprisingly, Indian foreign policy is being shaped by this quest for energy. As Sumit Ganguly and Manjeet Pardesi argue, 'buoyed by high economic growth rates and learning from its past experiences and contemporary developments, India is being more proactive in the international arena to secure its energy requirements'. They point out that India's energy strategy will, in all likelihood, 'confirm New Delhi's centrality in South Asia…, increase India's influence in Central Asia, promote amicable diplomatic relations with China, enhance strategic congruence with the United States, and enhance India's military profile in Central Asia and the Indian Ocean region'. While India's relations with China remain competitive in so far as exploitation of energy resources around the world is concerned, its pursuit of energy can promote strategic congruity between New Delhi and Washington.

Section two and three of this volume build on the first one, in so far as the four broad thematic issues examined in the first section continue to reappear in almost all the following chapters, thereby providing a framework with which to examine the Indian foreign policy. Section two of this volume examines India's relations with four major global powers: the US, China, Russia and the European Union (EU). The evolution of India's ties with the US has probably been the biggest success story of Indian foreign policy in recent years. Christine Fair delineates the significant security challenges that confront both states and the complementarity between Indian and American threat assessments in South Asia and beyond. She also raises the broader issues, discussed in the first section of the volume, that seem to be bringing the two states closer: the emerging global balance of power with the emergence of China, the global war on terror and the pursuit of energy security. Fair underlines the unique role that the US plays in the Indian security policy primarily 'because its assistance to India is critical in enabling India to become a regional or even extra-regional military power'. The US, on its part, has declared its new India policy with the goal of helping India become a major world power in the 21st century. But, as Fair also makes clear, India's growing closeness to the US does not come cost free and due to the complex domestic political milieu, India will find it hard to fulfil the expectations that the US would have from a close ally, especially in the realm of military/strategic issues.

India's ties with the US will be crucial in determining its relations with the other major global players. This is particularly true of Sino-Indian ties which remain inherently competitive in nature. As Mohan Malik points out, despite some recent helpful developments in bilateral relations, Sino-Indian relations remain 'fragile, and as vulnerable as ever to sudden deterioration as a result of misperceptions, unrealistic expectations, accidents, and eruption of unresolved issues'. The same structural changes that are bringing India closer to the US are also raising the possibility of a gradual increase in the tempo of the competition between the two Asian giants, China and India. It is not surprising therefore that 'the US factor' should play an influential role in how India–China ties shape up in the future. Malik reiterates that the issues of global nuclear order, energy security and global balance of power, among others, will determine the dynamics of the US–India–China triangular relationship. India's China policy is evolving in a context in which India is pursuing what Malik calls a 'multi-dimensional multi-alignment' with the world, to not only meet the challenge of a rising China but also to facilitate its own rise to the status of a great power. According to Malik, 'strained US–China relations would make India the pivotal power in the US–China–India triangle but tense India–China relations would put the US in a pivotal position', thereby underlining the crucial roles of the US, China and India in the emerging configuration of the balance of power, an aspect also identified by Hagerty in his discussion of India's role in the emerging global balance of power. Malik's conclusion that India will neither join the US to contain China nor align with Beijing against Washington reinforces the point made by Fair in her contribution that India will find it difficult to emerge as a 'future Australia' given the high value it places on charting 'an independent' course in its foreign policy.

The changing contours of the global balance of power are also central to understanding the evolution of traditionally close India–Russia ties since the end of the Cold War. Deepa Ollapally contends that after the turbulent 1990s, India–Russia relations seem to have reached 'a new equilibrium point' and she underlines the role that both realist and ideational factors have played in the process. Indian interests converge with that of Russia on a whole range of issues: both are sceptical of the unipolarity of the current global order and have openly expressed their desire to restrain US hegemony; the two nations are also worried about China's growing influence around their periphery; the recent US policy shift in allowing India access to the global nuclear market provides massive opportunities to Russia who is viewed as a more reliable partner and Russia, with its second largest reserves of oil and largest reserves of natural gas, remains key to India's energy security. Even on confronting terrorism, the Indian approach seems much closer to the Russian one, with both states being opposed to outside interference in Kashmir and Chechnya respectively. As Ollapally points out, 'Russia's resurgence and greater consolidation is a favourable outcome for New Delhi' and, given the emerging tensions between Russia and the West, 'a robust relationship with a democratic and plural India, whose global influence is rising, is symbolically attractive [to Moscow]'.

The emergence of the EU has been one of the most remarkable developments in global politics since the end of the Second World War. It is more than 50 years since the signing of the Treaty of Rome that established what has turned out to be an exemplary model of building peace, prosperity, stability and solidarity within a single entity with 27 member states, many of whom ravaged by bloody wars or separated by ideological divisions. Some argue that Europe today is a global superpower of world-historical importance, second to none in economic clout, increasingly held up as a role model for the rest of the world. This may very well be true but, as Fraser Cameron argues, for India 'the EU ranks far behind the US and China as a strategic actor', though both the EU and India have started engaging each other more substantively in recent years. Cameron also underlines the differences in worldviews of the two sides, with India's emphasis on hard security issues and the EU's own strength in the projection of its soft power. India's relations with the US and China also play an important role in the shaping of India–EU ties. The emerging 'strategic partnership' between India and the US and the EU's fixation with China can be the inhibiting factors as India and the EU decide to deepen their ties. But Cameron concludes that a India–EU partnership based on common values and interests makes sense, especially given the setbacks that the US is currently facing in its foreign policy and China's rise in the global order.

The third section of the volume explicates Indian foreign policy in the context of various regions around the globe. India's rise as a global power is inextricably linked to peace and stability in its immediate neighbourhood in South Asia. India is surrounded by 'weak states' that view India's hegemonic status in the region with suspicion. The conundrum that India faces is that, while it is seen as unresponsive to the concerns of its neighbours, any diplomatic aggressiveness on its part is also viewed with suspicion and often resentment. The structural position of India in the region makes it highly likely that Indian predominance will continue to be resented by its smaller neighbours, even as instability in its immediate neighbourhood continues to have the potential of upsetting its own delicate political balance. However, a policy of 'splendid isolation' is not an option for India and India's desire to emerge as a major global player will remain just that, a desire, unless it engages with its immediate neighbourhood more meaningfully. Stephen Burgess points out that India has traditionally exercised hegemony in South Asia using hard power so as to be able to 'consolidate its territorial sovereignty, oppose regional and global adversaries and ensure access to water and other resources for a very large and expanding population'. In recent years, however, India's approach has shifted towards the use of soft power and development of trust with neighbouring states. According to Burgess, 'India's emergence as a strategic and economic power in the 1990s enabled it to assume a regional leadership and promote economic cooperation as well as dispute resolution'. While the US opposed India's hegemonic approach towards its South Asian neighbours during the Cold War years, the emerging US–India entente is playing an enabling role for India to assert its leadership in South Asia. For Burgess, 'as India's international expansion and cooperation with the US continues, the opposing Pakistan–China partnership becomes less able to resist the growing Indian leadership in the South Asian sub-continent'.

India's interests are growing beyond South Asia and it views Central Asia as a region of prime importance, investing a lot of diplomatic energy in the region. Examining India's increasing engagement with the Central Asian region, Stephen Blank argues that 'India's growing interests and capabilities in regard to Central Asia are fully accepted as normal by all the major powers'. Moreover, he claims that the US and Indian interests converge in the region as the US would not like Central Asia to fall under the exclusive influence of either Russia or China. Therefore, 'the growth of India's presence in Central Asia and its ability to influence key economic and political decisions there are decidedly in the US interest'. The interests of India in Central Asia range from preventing the region from becoming dominated by China and ensuring regional stability to satisfying its energy needs and curtailing the growing influence of radical Islam. Central Asia is also becoming a region where India is gradually asserting its power and influence. Blank points out that India's 'rising capacities and expanding interests' are driving India 'to assume a greater role as security provider and partner in and around Central Asia'.

India is also charting a new course in the Middle East with a more ambitious foreign policy than before. As I argue, it is striking to note that, today, Indian foreign policy in the Middle East is revolving around Iran, Saudi Arabia and Israel, the three states that were virtually ignored by India in the last several decades. Though domestic constraints continue to exert a significant influence on Indian foreign policy towards the Middle East, the structural changes in the international system after the end of the Cold War have allowed India to define its interests in the Middle East in more 'realistic' terms and to aggressively pursue them. Other important factors that are shaping India's new approach towards the Middle East are India's burgeoning demand for energy, 65 per cent of which is met by the Middle East, India's growing wariness about the impact of global Islamist networks on its domestic Muslim populace, China's growing reach in the Middle East and growing Indo-US convergence. The shadow of the US will continue to loom large over Indian foreign policy vis-à-vis the Middle East in the years to come, most significantly as India tries to balance its ties with Iran and the US.

If there is one region where the consequences of the changing balance of power are being felt with the most immediacy, it is East Asia where not only are major powers such as China and Japan on the ascendant but also the growing economies of South East Asia are making their presence felt. The 'Look East' factor in the Indian foreign policy has been very prominent since early 1990s. During the Cold War, India's perceived national interests placed it at odds with the larger US-backed ASEAN grouping but, after the end of the Cold War, India reached out to the South East Asian nations and quickly redressed this estrangement. Manish Dabhade points out the centrality of the systemic factors in the Indian foreign policy towards East Asia as India has tried to increase its power and influence in the region. According to Dabhade, India's 'rediscovery' of East Asia in the post-Cold War period has been a consequence of not simply the dissolution of the structural constraints imposed by the Cold War but also of growing Indian ambitions to play a more influential role in global politics. With this in mind, Indian foreign policy, as per Dabhade, has focussed on 'congaing China'; increasing political engagement, economic integration and defence linkages with regional powers and participation in regional and multilateral initiatives. India's complicated relationship with China has become the backdrop against which India has defined its foreign policy priorities in East Asia, an issue also highlighted by Malik in his chapter in Sino-Indian bilateral ties. Dabhade argues that 'Indian perceptions and grand strategy in East Asia since 1991 reveal a growing convergence of priorities and policies between the US and India', though he also points out some significant differences between the two states. Dabhade is in agreement with the views propounded by Malik and Christine Fair in their respective chapters that India would be reluctant to form an explicit alliance against China. And in line with the conclusion reached by Tim Hoyt, Dabhade also underlines the differences between India and the US on the global 'war on terror'.

As various contributions to this volume make clear, the Indian foreign policy, out of the structural confines of the Cold War strategic framework, has become more expansive in defining its priorities over the last few years. If a state's interests are defined by its power capabilities and power drives a state towards an expansive interpretation of its interests abroad, then it follows that the more powerful a nation becomes its aspirations to play a more significant role in global politics also increase.[31] As India's economic and military capabilities have increased, so has its strategic interests, shaping a diplomacy that is much more aggressive in the pursuit of those interests.

Indian foreign policy is clearly multidimensional with an ability to pursue a range of interests at the same time but the four variables that seem to be having the most significant impact on its present direction are India's search for its due place in the emerging international balance of power which continues to be dominated by the US even as China is gearing up to challenge that pre-eminence; an accommodation with the global nuclear order as the international system comes to terms with a 'nuclear' India; India's balancing act between tackling the challenge of global terrorism while not alienating its Islamic minority; and India's search for energy security to guarantee that the current trajectory of its economic growth can be maintained. It is these factors that shape India's definition of its strategic interests in various regions of the globe and, in terms of its bilateral ties, with major powers in the international system.

---

[31] Zakaria, *From Wealth to Power: The Unusual Origins of America's World Role*.

Given that the single greatest challenge in international relations is for nations to adjust peacefully to changes in relative power among states, India's rise will inevitably have an impact on other major states, the most important of which is the US. As a consequence, India's relations with the US remain crucial in determining its foreign policy on a range of issues and with various other powers. While Indo-US interests converge on a host of issues, India is trying to balance this convergence within a domestic political context where a vocal and powerful minority continues to resist close ties with the US. India will continue to forge close political and economic ties with the US even as its desire for 'strategic autonomy' will make it a difficult partner for the US. How adroitly India manages to find this balance will, to a large extent, determine the success of the Indian foreign policy in the years to come.

In line with the suggestion that a good explanation of foreign policy 'must separate the effects of the various levels of international politics',[32] this volume has largely focused on the impact of the systemic constraints in shaping the contours of the foreign policy of a rising India, though most contributors have also underlined the domestic political and normative sources of Indian foreign policy in so far as they limit the impact of structural factors. The next logical step for scholars would be to analyse not only the domestic sources of the Indian foreign policy but also the linkages between domestic and external variables, as 'a good account of a nation's foreign policy should include systemic, domestic and other influences, specifying what aspects of the policy can be explained by what factors'.[33] Hopefully, this volume will make the transition to the next level a little bit easier.

---

[32] Zakaria, 'Realism and Domestic Politics', p. 197.
[33] Ibid., p. 198.

PART I
Major Themes in Indian Foreign Policy

2

India and the Global Balance of Power: A Neorealist Snapshot

DEVIN T. HAGERTY

India's on-going ascent to the ranks of the world's major powers is one of the most significant developments in post-Cold War international relations. The programme of liberalising economic reforms begun by New Delhi in the early 1990s has unleashed the Indian economy, bringing about rates of growth that are double and triple those of the Cold War era. New Delhi's nuclear tests of 1998 established India as an unambiguous and unapologetic nuclear-weapon state, a posture that has been gradually accepted by the international community, led by the US.[1] Now in its seventh decade as an independent country, India is widely considered to be on the brink of achieving its enormous potential for global influence.[2] In this regard, observers point to India's large size and population, resilient democracy, rapidly growing economy, booming information-technology sector, scientific and technological sophistication, fast-expanding middle class, nuclear and conventional military strength, the important role that it plays in global governance, and its geostrategic position as the most powerful state along the Indian Ocean littoral and the sea lanes between East Asia

---

[1] See Devin T. Hagerty, 'Are We Present at the Creation? Alliance Theory and the Indo-US Strategic Convergence', in Sumit Ganguly, Brian Shoup and Andrew Scobell, eds, *US-Indian Strategic Cooperation into the 20th Century: More than Words* (London: Routledge, 2006), pp. 11–37.

[2] Symbolic of this perception is the July/August 2006 issue of *Foreign Affairs*, which on its cover trumpets 'The Rise of India' and contains four lead articles examining various dimensions of New Delhi's new prominence in global affairs. See *Foreign Affairs* 85:4 (July/August 2006), pp. 2–56. Also see, Teresita C. Schaffer, 'India on the Move' *Survival* 49:1 (March 2007), pp. 229–34.

and the Middle East.³ Increasingly, analysts of both South Asian international affairs, and great-power politics more generally, will have to turn their attention to India's emergence as a major power and its relationship to the evolving global balance of power.

This essay is a preliminary attempt to undertake such an analysis. In this essay, I ask several interrelated questions: what is India's potential to become a great power in the near future, between now and roughly 2020? What is the nature of India's relations with other major powers in the international system and how is that posture likely to evolve? What are the prospects for New Delhi's great-power aspirations? My larger argument is that in material, 'hard-power' terms, India is rapidly achieving great-power status and will almost certainly qualify as a military and economic great power by 2020. However, I also maintain that India's real weaknesses lie, and will continue to lie, in the non-material, 'softer' dimensions of power that also contribute to a well-rounded great-power status in today's international system. In particular, the sprawling, overbearing Indian state persists in clogging India's economic arteries with protectionism, overregulation and bureaucratic bloat.

The essay unfolds in the following way. Section two presents a conceptual framework for analysing contemporary international power and power relationships. Drawing primarily on the work of the neorealist theorist Kenneth N. Waltz, it combines traditional 'hard' dimensions of power, principally military and economic capabilities, with 'softer' elements of power like domestic political stability and competence. In section three, I situate India within this conceptual framework, comparing it along various dimensions with other great-power aspirants. Section four analyses India's developing relations with the two most important players in the global balance of power, the US and China. In the concluding section, I briefly discuss the likelihood that India will soon emerge as a global great power.

---

[3] For examples, see Teresita C. Schaffer and Pramit Mitra, 'India as a Global Power?' *Deutsche Bank Research*, Frankfurt am Main, Germany, December 16, 2005; Ashley J. Tellis, *India as a New Global Power: An Action Agenda for the US* (Washington, DC: Carnegie Endowment for International Peace, 2005); and US National Intelligence Council, *Mapping the Global Future: Report of the National Intelligence Council's 2020 Project*, NIC 2004–13 (Washington, DC: US Government Printing Office, December 2004).

Elements of Power: A Conceptual Framework

Students of great-power politics, realist and otherwise, have often observed that neorealism—or 'structural realism'—provides a useful starting point for the analysis of evolving power configurations in international affairs.[4] In Waltz's model, the international political system is 'composed of a structure and of interacting units'. The units are states, 'unitary actors who, at a minimum, seek their own preservation and, at a maximum, drive for universal domination'. For Waltz, 'so long as the major states are the major actors, the structure of international politics is defined in terms of them. That theoretical statement is of course borne out in practice. States set the scene in which they, along with non-state actors, stage their dramas or carry on their humdrum affairs.' He continues:

> International-political systems, like economic markets, are formed by the coaction of self-regarding units. International structures are defined in terms of the primary political units of an era, be they city states, empires, or nations. Structures emerge from the coexistence of states.

The structure is an 'abstraction'. The 'system-wide component that makes it possible to think of the system as a whole'.[5]

International Political Structure

The two distinguishing characteristics of Waltz's model of international political structure are its ordering principle—anarchy—and the distribution of capabilities across the units. Anarchy, in this sense, denotes not chaos or disorder, but simply the absence of a world government. As Waltz puts it, 'whatever elements of authority emerge internationally are barely once removed from the capability that provides the foundation for the appearance of

---

[4] It would be difficult to exaggerate the importance of Waltz's *Theory of International Politics* (New York: Random House, 1979) for international relations scholarship. The book launched the school of neorealism, which draws on the core insights of the centuries-old classical realist perspective while putting them on a social–scientific basis which classical realism is said to lack. For nearly three decades, Waltz's theory has anchored many of the major debates in the theory of international relations.
[5] Waltz, *Theory of International Politics*, pp. 79, 118, 94, 91, 79–80.

those elements'. The main implication of this anarchic condition is that international politics is a 'self-help' system:

> Whether or not by force, each state plots the course it thinks will best serve its interests. If force is used by one state or its use is expected, the recourse of other states is to use force or be prepared to use it singly or in combination. No appeal can be made to a higher entity clothed with the authority and equipped with the ability to act on its own initiative.

In Waltz's view, 'the enduring anarchic character of international politics accounts for the striking sameness in the quality of international life through the millennia'. The second characteristic of his international political structure is the distribution of capabilities across the units, i.e., the balance of power. In bipolar systems capabilities are distributed roughly evenly between two great powers, while multipolar systems evidence a rough equality of capabilities between more than two great powers. Waltz cautions against counting poles of power based on any one type of capability:

> The economic, military, and other capabilities of nations cannot be sectored and separately weighed. States are not placed in the top rank because they excel in one way or another. Their rank depends on how they score on *all* of the following items: size of population and territory, resource endowment, economic capability, military strength, political stability and competence.

International political structures 'vary only through a change of organising principle or, failing that, through variations in the capabilities of units'. Writing in 1979, Waltz argued that 'in all of modern history the structure of international politics has changed but once'—from multipolarity to bipolarity in 1945.[6]

The Emergence of a New Balance of Power

The structure of international politics changed in 1991, with the demise of the Soviet Union—and, therefore, of bipolarity. When two states make up a balance of power and one of them goes out of business, the system's structure ceases to be bipolar. According

---

[6] Ibid., pp. 66, 88–93, 102, 111, 113, 131, 163.

to Waltz's balance-of-power theory, when an existing balance of power shatters, a new one will eventually form: 'The expectation is not that a balance, once achieved, will be maintained, but that a balance, once disrupted, will be restored in one way or another.' There is a 'strong tendency toward balance in the system'.[7]

Waltz's theory also specifies *how* balances of power will be restored: the weaker will tend to balance the stronger. Regarding internal balancing efforts, he argues that 'within a given arena and over a number of years, we should find the military power of weaker and smaller states or groupings of states growing more rapidly, or shrinking more slowly, than that of stronger and larger ones'. Concerning external balancing, or making alliances, he writes that 'we do not expect the strong to combine with the strong in order to increase the extent of their power over others, but rather to square off and look for allies who might help them'. Elaborating further on this, Waltz argues that 'in self-help systems, external forces propel the weaker parties toward one another. Weaker parties, our theory predicts, incline to combine to offset the strength of the stronger.' This behaviour contrasts with that of domestic political systems, where 'bandwagoning' (the opposite of balancing) is common:

> Externally, states work harder to increase their own strength, or they combine with others, if they are falling behind. In a competition for the position of leader, balancing is sensible behavior where the victory of one coalition over another leaves weaker members of the winning coalition at the mercy of the stronger ones. Nobody wants anyone else to win; none of the great powers wants one of their number to emerge as the leader.

If the first priority of states were to maximise power, rather than to survive, they would 'join the stronger side, and we would see not balances forming but a world hegemony forged. This does not happen because balancing, not bandwagoning, is the behavior induced by the system.' Summarising this fundamental dynamics of international politics, he writes, 'In anarchy, security is the highest end. Only if survival is assured can states safely seek

---

[7] Ibid., p. 128.

such other goals as tranquility, profit, and power. Because power is a means and not an end, states prefer to join the weaker of two coalitions.'[8]

In Waltz's conception, the only sustainable alternative to bipolarity is multipolarity: an international political system with more than two great powers. Put another way, his theory treats unipolarity — a situation in which one great power towers above the rest for any appreciable length of time — as a theoretical impossibility: two 'is the smallest number possible in a self-help system'. Waltz does discuss the possibility of a world hegemony arising, but then dismisses it on historical grounds: 'To promote a change of system, whether by building a world hegemony or by promoting an area to great power status by helping it find political unity, is one of history's grandiose projects. We should be neither surprised nor sad that it failed.'[9]

The New Balancers

As for the post-bipolar era, Waltz early on suggested that, 'for some years to come . . ., the United States will be the leading country economically as well as militarily'. Inevitably, though, new challengers will arise: 'balance-of-power theory leads one to predict that other countries, alone or in concert, will try to bring American power into balance'. He elaborates on this logic: 'Even if the powerful state's

---

[8] Ibid., pp. 124, 126, 127, 201, 202.

[9] Ibid., pp. 136, 145, 201. Here Waltz was referring to US efforts to construct an 'Atlantic imperium' during the Cold War. Unlike the terms 'polarity', 'bipolarity', 'multipolarity', and 'tripolarity', the terms 'unipolarity' and 'hegemony' do not appear in the index to *Theory of International Politics*. For the purposes of my analysis, it is necessary to distinguish between the concepts of unipolarity and hegemony. As used herein, unipolarity refers simply to a given distribution of power in the international system. It is agnostic as to the intentions of the system's sole great power. Hegemony has many meanings in the literature, some of which are value-loaded. Because of that, I avoid using the term. John Mearsheimer's definition will suffice to illustrate the importance of the great power's *intentions* in the concept of hegemony as I understand it: 'Under a hegemony there is only one major power in the system. The rest are minor powers that cannot challenge the major power, *but must act in accordance with the dictates of the major power.*' (emphasis added) See his 'Back to the Future: Instability in Europe After the Cold War', *International Security* 15:1 (Summer 1990), p. 13. My use of the term 'unipolarity' should not be construed to mean that I think the US can impose its will on secondary states. All hegemons are unipolar great powers, but not all unipolar great powers are hegemons.

intentions are wholly benign, less powerful states will, from their different historical experiences, geographic locations, and economic interests, interpret events differently and often prefer different policies.' This, then, is the universal logic of all international politics: 'The response of other countries to one among them seeking or gaining preponderant power is to try to balance against it. Hegemony leads to balance, which is easy to see historically and to understand theoretically.' With respect to the post-bipolar world, this is 'happening, but haltingly so because the US still has benefits to offer and many other countries have become accustomed to their easy lives with the US bearing many of their burdens'. That said, Waltz's ultimate expectation about post-bipolar international politics is unambiguous. In 1993, he wrote, 'in the fairly near future, say ten to twenty years, three political units may rise to great-power rank: Germany or a West European state, Japan, and China'. Adding the US and Russia, 'the emerging world will [. . .] be one of four or five great powers'.[10]

A fundamental premise of this chapter is that, owing to the developments since Waltz first made his prediction in 1993, India should be added to this list of potential future great powers, meaning that six countries in the near future will vie for great-power status: China, Germany, India, Japan, Russia and the US. (I discount the possibility of a 'West European state' becoming a significant pole of power within the time frame under consideration. The European Union (EU) does not constitute such a state today and, even if it did, its paltry military forces would not allow it to be a true, well-rounded great power.) To reiterate Waltz's view of the dimensions of power, 'great powers do not gain and retain their rank by excelling in one way or another. Their rank depends on how they score on a combination of the following items: size of population and territory, resource endowment, economic capability, military strength, political stability and competence.'[11]

---

[10] Kenneth N. Waltz, 'The Emerging Structure of International Politics', *International Security* 18:2 (Autumn 1993), pp. 71, 53, 74, 77, 50, 70. Waltz reiterated this prediction in his 'Structural Realism after the Cold War', *International Security* 25:1 (Summer 2000), pp. 5–41.

[11] Ibid., p. 50. It bears noting that in this chapter I am not assessing the validity of Waltz's theory; rather, I am using his underlying model and adding India to the empirical mix.

COMPARING THE POTENTIAL GREAT POWERS
Indices of Power

In the next section, I compare India's power to that of the other five states under consideration.[12] First, it is necessary to refine some of Waltz's categories, to allow for more precise measurement. To measure countries' 'resource endowment', I use two indices: proven oil reserves and proven natural gas reserves. While admittedly providing only a limited picture, these capabilities allow a snapshot of how countries fare in terms of these vital natural resources. Concerning 'economic capability', I look at two metrics: Gross Domestic Product or GDP (purchasing power parity method) and the 2007 Heritage Foundation/*Wall Street Journal* 'Index of Economic Freedom', which 'is a simple average of 10 individual freedoms, each of which is vital to the development of personal and national prosperity'. These ten variables are business freedom, trade freedom, monetary freedom, freedom from government, fiscal freedom, property rights, investment freedom, financial freedom, freedom from corruption and labour freedom. The index defines the 'highest form of economic freedom' as 'an absolute right of property ownership, fully realised freedoms of movement for labor, capital, and goods, and an absolute absence of coercion or constraint of economic liberty beyond the extent necessary for citizens to protect and maintain liberty itself'. Simply put, 'individuals are free to work, produce, consume, and invest in any way they please, and that freedom is both protected by the state and unconstrained by the state'. The highest possible score is 100 and the lowest is zero.[13] I measure 'Military strength' by reference to the overall defence spending and whether or not the country in question is a nuclear-weapon state.[14] Lastly, to assess 'political stability' and 'competence', I use the data from the World Bank's 'Worldwide Governance Indicators: 1996–2005', which ranks countries in terms

---

[12] Unless otherwise specified, my source of data is the online version of the CIA's 2007 *World Factbook*, updated on November 15, 2007 and accessed on November 19, 2007. See https://www.cia.gov/library/publications/the-world-factbook/index.html.

[13] See http://www.heritage.org/index/ (accessed on November 19, 2007).

[14] In doing so, I give countries credit for having a secure second-strike nuclear deterrence capability, but not for having redundant but arguably useless accretions of that capability. This stance accords with Waltz's views. See Kenneth N. Waltz, 'Nuclear Myths and Political Realities', *American Political Science Review* 84:3 (September 1990), pp. 731–45.

of the quality of their governance. More specifically, I use two of the six indicators: 'Political Stability and Absence of Violence' and 'Government Effectiveness', as measures of, respectively, political stability and competence. Countries are ranked by percentile, which indicates the 'percentage of countries worldwide that rate below the selected country . . . Higher values indicate better governance ratings'.[15] Taken together, these ten categories create a first-cut 'big picture' of how the six countries compare along various dimensions of power.

Table 2.1
Size of Territory

Country	Area (sq km)	Rank
Russia	17,075,200	1
US	9,826,630	3
China	9,596,960	4
India	3,287,590	7
Japan	377,835	60
Germany	357,021	61

Source: CIA World Factbook, 2007

Table 2.2
Population

Country	Population	Rank
China	1,321,851,888	1
India	1,129,866,154	2
US	301,139,947	3
Russia	141,377,752	8
Japan	127,433,494	10
Germany	82,400,996	14

Source: CIA World Factbook, 2007

Table 2.3
Resource Endowment: Proven Oil Reserves

Country	Oil Reserves (bbl)	Rank
Russia	74,400,000,000	8
US	21,370,000,000	11
China	16,300,000,000	12
India	5,600,000,000	20
Germany	394,400,000	49
Japan	58,500,000	72

Source: CIA World Factbook, 2007

---

[15] See http://info.worldbank.org/governance/kkz2005/ (accessed on January 11, 2007).

Table 2.4
Resource Endowment: Proven Natural Gas Reserves

Country	Nat. Gas Reserves (cu m)	Rank
Russia	45,630,000,000,000	1
US	5,551,000,000,000	6
China	1,448,000,000,000	21
India	1,056,000,000,000	24
Germany	246,500,000,000	41
Japan	38,020,000,000	66

Source: CIA World Factbook, 2007

Table 2.5
Gross Domestic Product (GDP)

Country	GDP (ppp in US$)	Rank
US	13,060,000,000,000	1
China	10,210,000,000,000	2
Japan	4,218,000,000,000	3
India	4,164,000,000,000	4
Germany	2,632,000,000,000	5
Russia	1,746,000,000,000	9

Source: CIA World Factbook, 2007

Table 2.6
Economic Freedom

Country	Score	Rank
US	82	4
Japan	73.6	18
Germany	73.5	19
India	55.6	104
China	54	119
Russia	54	119

Source: 2007 Heritage Foundation/Wall Street Journal 'Index of Economic Freedom'

Table 2.7
Military Expenditures and Nuclear-weapon Status

Country	Military Spending (US$)	Rank	Nuclear-weapon State
US	518,100,000,000	1	Yes
China	81,480,000,000	2	Yes
Japan	44,310,000,000	4	No
Germany	35,063,000,000	6	No

(Continued)

(Continued)

Country	Military Spending (US$)	Rank	Nuclear-weapon State
Russia*	24,000,000,000	8	Yes
India	19,040,000,000	10	Yes

*Congressional Research Service Estimate[16]
Source: CIA World Factbook, 2006

Table 2.8
Political Stability

Country	Percentile Rank
Japan	80.2
Germany	67.0
US	48.6
China	39.2
India	22.2
Russia	18.9

Source: World Bank World Governance Indicators, 1996–2005: 'Political Stability and Absence of Violence'

Table 2.9
Competence

Country	Percentile Rank
US	91.9
Germany	90.4
Japan	84.7
China	52.2
India	51.7
Russia	38.8

Source: World Bank World Gvernance Indicators, 1996–2005: 'Government Effectiveness'

Table 2.10
A Snapshot of the Global Balance of Power:
The Six Powers' Rankings vis-à-vis One Another in Ten Categories

Country	Size	Pop.	Oil	Nat. Gas	GDP	Economic Freedom	Military Spending	Pol. Stab.	Comp.
China	3	1	3	3	2	5	2*	4	4
Germany	6	6	5	5	5	3	4	2	2

(Continued)

---

[16] 'Russian Political, Economic, and Security Issues and US Interests', CRS Report for Congress (RL 33407), Congressional Research Service, Washington, DC, October 19, 2006, p. 14.

(Continued)

Country	Size	Pop.	Oil	Nat. Gas	GDP	Economic Freedom	Military Spending	Pol. Stab.	Comp.
India	4	2	4	4	4	4	6*	5	5
Japan	5	5	6	6	3	2	3	1	3
Russia	1	4	1	1	6	5	5*	6	6
USA	2	3	2	2	1	1	1*	3	1

*Nuclear-weapon state
Sources: See previous tables

The Six Countries Compared

What do these ten indicators tell us about the emerging 21st-century global balance of power?

The main conclusion to be drawn from this snapshot is that, some 17 years into the post-bipolar era, the international system remains unambiguously unipolar. If the great powers of any era are those countries that rank roughly equally at the top of the power tables, the US today faces no peer competitor; it is the world's only true great power. In military terms, the US is far and away the world's most capable nuclear-weapon state, and it spends more than six times as much on defence as China, the second-ranking military spender. Indeed, US defence spending is more than two and one-half times that of the other five states combined. The US also ranks first in economic terms, with a GDP that amounts to slightly less than 20 per cent of total world output, as well as an economy that by one measure is the most free of the six under consideration. In every other respect—size, population, resource endowment, political stability and competence—the US ranks no lower than third among the 'big six'.

The data also strongly suggest that China is, by a fairly wide margin, the world's second-ranking power today. China is a mature nuclear-weapon state with secure second-strike capabilities and rapidly modernising conventional military forces. Its defence spending and GDP are second only to those of the US, and in both of these categories, China far outpaces the third-ranking state, Japan. China's GDP is 2.4 times the size of Japan's and its military spending is 1.84 times the size of Japan's. After thirty years of economic reforms, China's GDP represents 15 per cent of the global economic output. Of the six countries under study, China ranks third in size, first in population and third in oil and natural gas reserves. However, as might be expected with a liberalising economy but a one-party authoritarian political system, China ranks lower in terms of economic freedom, political stability and competence.

A final broad implication of the data is that four of these countries—Germany, India, Japan and Russia—are more 'lopsided' powers, but, nonetheless, certain contenders for future great-power status. Unlike the US and China, each of these states has more pronounced strengths and weaknesses across the various dimensions of power. Perhaps most important in simple existential security terms is that Russia and India are both nuclear-weapon states whose second-strike capabilities would almost certainly deter any potential aggressor from either a nuclear or major conventional attack. For that reason, their lower spending on overall military capabilities, relative to Germany and Japan, is less consequential than it might otherwise be. Both countries' size also gives them greater strategic depth than that enjoyed by either Germany or Japan. The existential security of Germany and Japan rests more on their alliance commitments from the US than on internal military capabilities, clear or conventional—a fact that in norealist terms makes them more vulnerable than states with their own nuclear deterrents and/or large conventional military forces.

In terms of individual strengths, Russia's strengths lie in its bountiful reserves of oil and natural gas, while India's rest on its large population and economic dynamism. India's economy is now the world's fourth-largest, after those of the US, China and Japan. In 2002, the size of India's economy was 73 per cent that of Japan. By 2006, that figure had grown to 99 per cent.[17] If prevailing trends persist, India's economy will overtake Japan's this year. On the negative side of the ledger, both Russia and India rank relatively low in the categories of economic freedom, political stability and competence. As would be expected with mature, capitalist democracies, Germany and Japan's strengths lie exactly in those areas. Their weaknesses, in addition to those discussed in the previous paragraph, are relatively small land areas and populations as well as relatively meager resource endowments.

With respect to India specifically, the data support CIA analyses indicating that 'when countries are ranked by composite measures

---

[17] 'CIA World Factbook', 2003 and 2007.

of national power—that is, weighted combinations of . . . GDP
. . . defense spending, population, and technology growth—India
is projected to possess the fourth most capable concentration of
power by 2015—after the United States, the European Union, and
China . . .'.[18] Again, I exclude the EU as a 'country' or 'national'
actor at this point in time, meaning that—according to the CIA's
projections—India is on the verge of becoming the world's third-
greatest power, albeit one that substantially trails the two countries
ahead of it, the US and China.

INDIA AND POST-COLD WAR ASIAN TRIPOLARITY[19]

While it is destined to become a global great power, India's immediate interests and aspirations lie within the Asia–Pacific region.
In either an Asian or a global context—and these are increasingly
converging, owing to the ongoing shift in global power from Europe
to Asia—the two most important states in India's foreign relations
are, and will continue to be, the US and China. The disintegration
of the Soviet Union, the evolution of global unipolarity and China's
impressive rise to power have forced a reappraisal of the grand
strategy in every world capital. New Delhi is no exception. Indian
policy-makers concluded from the realignments of the 1990s that
they must cast aside their nuclear ambivalence and make India an
overt nuclear-weapon state. In turn, the US has come to respect
a newly confident India—more so today than at any time since
1947. This shift in US perceptions was evident in the National
Intelligence Council's late 2004 forecast of global trends over the
next 15 years:

> The likely emergence of China and India as new major players—similar
> to the rise of Germany in the 19th century and the US in the early 20th
> century—will transform the geopolitical landscape, with impacts
> potentially as dramatic as those of the previous two centuries . . .
> The[se] 'arriviste' powers—China [and] India . . . could usher in a new

---

[18] Tellis, *India as a New Global Power*, p. 30.
[19] Parts of this section draw upon my 'Alliance Theory and the Indo-US Strategic Convergence', pp. 24–28. Space constraints preclude a more comprehensive discussion of India's relations with all of the other five powers under consideration. For such an analysis, see C. Raja Mohan, 'India and the Balance of Power', *Foreign Affairs* 85:4 (July/August 2006), pp. 17–32.

set of international alignments, potentially marking a definitive break with some of the post-World War II institutions and practices . . . how China and India exercise their growing power and whether they relate cooperatively or competitively to other powers in the international system are key uncertainties.[20]

After 17 years of unipolarity, the outlines of a new international system are visible. In the Asia–Pacific, major-power relations increasingly will be structured by the triangular interaction between the US, China and India. Again, these states' economies will soon rank first, second and third in the world, respectively. In military spending, India ranks far below the US, China and Japan. However, India vaults ahead of every other Asian state, except for China, by virtue of its modernising nuclear-weapon and ballistic missile capabilities and the secure second-strike deterrence they afford New Delhi. Japan's economic muscle and substantial military spending might otherwise qualify it as an Asian great power, but its lack of nuclear-weapon, its continuing strategic dependence on the US, and its constitutional restrictions on the use of force render it less powerful than its relative military spending and economic size would suggest.

Qualitatively, relations along the three legs of the US–India–China triangle are generally harmonious. Washington, Beijing and New Delhi are each working hard to develop strong relations with the other two governments. The quality of Indo-US ties has improved enormously over the last two decades. In 1987, Washington and New Delhi were essentially on opposing sides in the Cold War. Despite its professions of nonalignment, India was closely tied to the Soviet Union. Ten years later, the Cold War was over, but Indo-US ties were still strained, with Washington badgering New Delhi on non-proliferation and annoying Indians with its equivocal stand on the Kashmir dispute. Today, Washington has accepted the reality of India's nuclear weaponisation, and the two countries are in the process of finalising agreement that will allow the US to provide India with civilian nuclear technology and fuel.[21] Furthermore, Washington has significantly eased its restrictions on transfers to

---

[20] *Mapping the Global Future*, p. 47.
[21] Somini Sengupta, 'Indian Coalition Wins Dispute Over Nuclear Pact', *New York Times*, November 17, 2007.

India of both advanced weapon systems and sophisticated dual-use technologies. All said, on every important grand-strategic issue in Asia–Pacific affairs, New Delhi and Washington share common interests, if not always identical solutions to day-to-day challenges.

In the meantime, Sino-Indian relations have been slowly warming since 1988 and they continue their gradual upward trajectory, even though conflicting boundary claims remain formally unreconciled. Moreover, because of their sensitivities to internal secessionist threats—particularly in Kashmir and Xinjiang, respectively—India and China are as committed to the war against jihadi terrorism as the US. Lastly, unlike in previous decades, both Washington and Beijing now endorse India's position on the Kashmir dispute, i.e., that the conflict should be resolved peacefully and bilaterally, as per the Indo-Pakistani Simla Agreement of 1972.

At the same time, India and the US are creating a relationship with each other whose warmth is not matched along the other two legs of the Asia–Pacific strategic triangle. New Delhi and Washington have a similar strategic vision for Asia–Pacific stability and they now collaborate, politically and militarily, in preparing for a variety of regional contingencies. Although India and the US go out of their way not to portray China as a threat, they clearly view it as a *potential* threat. As one analyst has argued, New Delhi and Washington 'share a convergence of interests in seeing that China does not become a "non status quo power" or try to "radically alter" the balance of power in Asia'.[22] Historically, although the US and India have had cold relations, they have never viewed each other as direct strategic adversaries. On the other hand, India and China share a long and contested border and have fought a war with one another. China has pursued a policy of strategic encirclement vis-à-vis India, the most menacing aspect of which was the transfer in the 1980s and 1990s of nuclear-weapon and ballistic missile technology to India's main South Asian adversary, Pakistan. For its part, the US tends to perceive China as more of a long-term threat than India, and is therefore pursuing a strategy of helping India to become a 'major world power'.[23]

---

[22] Jonah Blank, 'Bridging US-India: A Defence Perspective', Panel Discussion, Center for Strategic and International Studies, Washington, DC, December 9, 2003, at http://chennai.usconsulate.gov/wwwhpr031216a (accessed on April 19, 2007).
[23] David C. Mulford, 'US-India Relationship to Reach New Heights', *Times of India*, March 31, 2005.

Although structural considerations are important, the matter of why India and the US view China as more threatening than either views the other also requires an examination of domestic factors. In the realm of common identities, the US and India are democracies, while China continues to be a Communist state in theory and an authoritarian one in practice. Equally important is that Washington and New Delhi increasingly see themselves as partners in the global 'establishment', as status quo, rather than revisionist, states. Establishment states today are free-market, liberal democracies that do not support terrorism or transfer nuclear-weapon or ballistic missile capabilities to other states. India and the US fall into this category, while China does not. China's economy is liberalising, but its political system remains dictatorial. And, notwithstanding its de jure status as a member of the non-proliferation regime and recent indications of its more rigorous application of non-proliferation norms to Chinese policy, Beijing has contributed significantly to the nuclearisation of Pakistan and, indirectly, Iran—two of today's most worrisome proliferants.

The lessons of the past have also influenced the warming of Indo-US relations. India's most painful formative strategic experience was its humiliation in the 1962 Sino-Indian war. The bitter experience taught New Delhi that while nonalignment might be ideologically satisfying, national borders cannot be defended by ideology alone. Since 1962, India has followed a grand strategy of 'tilted nonalignment', by which it seeks great-power security reassurance vis-à-vis China. The US briefly played this role in the early-to mid-1960s. In the late 1960s, and especially with the Indo-Soviet treaty of 1971, Moscow became New Delhi's main security guarantor. With the collapse of the Soviet Union in 1991 and the post-Cold War thaw between India and the US, New Delhi is again tilting toward Washington.

This is not to say, of course, that there are no limits to the nascent Indo-US entente. The contemporary international security environment is less conducive to the formation of formal military alliances than it was in the 20th century. Today's security threats are more diffused and less bound to states. The jihadi insurgency that both India and the US identify as their primary threat is a shadowy, transnational phenomenon. Unlike a stationary enemy, it assumes different manifestations in different places at different times. This requires countries to maintain a greater degree of flexibility in their alignment policies. Because ententes are more malleable than alliances, the US—with interests in every part of the world—can be expected to prefer them as security institutions. New Delhi's views on this complement Washington's. India's strategic culture is such that it prefers to avoid formal alignments; 'strategic autonomy' has long been a post-colonial rallying cry. At the same time, India aspires to become a great power and feels that its moment is at hand. The Indo-US entente offers it faster economic progress and a degree of psychological protection against China, while avoiding the negative costs of a more formal alliance commitment: the perception of compromised Indian sovereignty, domestic political upheaval rooted in the Indian left's residual anti-Americanism and a strategically irritated China.

The gruelling process of formalising the US–India nuclear agreement illustrates that in international affairs, even close friendships will face knotty problems. This is particularly true when the friends are democracies with plural, competitive domestic interests. Despite their newly forged entente, US and Indian views will occasionally diverge. For example, as India rapidly grows, its thirst for oil and natural gas imports from Iran will increasingly chafe against New Delhi's maturing relationship with Washington. As noted in tables 2.3–2.4, India ranks 20th in the world in oil reserves and 24th in natural gas reserves. These would be respectable figures were it not for the fact that India is projected by 2010 to 'emerge as the fourth-largest consumer of energy, after the US, China, and Japan'.[24] Regarding the policy towards Iran, India's rising energy demand will conflict with New Delhi's interest in being a responsible stakeholder in the non-proliferation regime and, more broadly, the global establishment. This dilemma poses the greatest challenge to Indian foreign policy-makers over the next several years.

CONCLUSION: INDIA'S GREAT-POWER PROSPECTS

This essay has argued that, from a neorealist perspective, India is, in most respects, poised to become a global great power within the next decade or two. India's economy, which is expected to grow at an annual rate of 7.5 per cent over the next five years,[25] will soon be the

---

[24] Schaffer and Mitra, 'India as a Global Power?', p. 11.
[25] 'India', *Economist Intelligence Unit Country Briefing*, November 7, 2007, at http://www.economist.com/countries/India/profile.cfm?folder=Profile%2DEconomic%20Data (accessed on November 18, 2007).

world's third-largest, after those of the US and China. Although its military spending ranks only 10th in the world, India's modernising nuclear deterrent and ample conventional forces make it highly unlikely to suffer a major attack by even the most determined of adversaries. In order to project its military power into regions neighbouring South Asia, New Delhi would need to significantly increase its defence spending, but India's national interests evince little need for such a capability. Indeed, by Waltzian standards, efforts by India to achieve more lethal and expansive offensive capabilities would be wasteful and potentially counterproductive, considering its potential foes' likely responses. India's status as the world's seventh-largest and second most-populous country also augur well for its great-power aspirations.

New Delhi is well-positioned, too, in terms of its relationships with the world's other major powers. Most importantly, Indian diplomacy has succeeded in engineering an entente with the world's superpower, the US, that will over time garner New Delhi a range of benefits. Among them are advanced weapon systems, civilian nuclear equipment and fuel, dual-use technologies to enhance India's scientific and technological prowess, increased investment in India's booming economy and the security reassurance accruing from a relationship with the world's most powerful state.

In the meantime, India's relationship with the globe's second-ranking power, China, has also improved in recent years. New Delhi's increased power has enabled it to seek a territorial 'settlement with Beijing on a political basis, rather than on the basis of legal or historical claims', a shift that is now allowing the two sides to explore 'the contours of mutually satisfactory territorial compromises'.[26] Bilateral trade between India and China has grown from less than $200 million to more than $20 billion since the early 1990s, and China may soon become India's primary trading partner.[27] In addition, New Delhi has warm relations with all of the other great-power aspirants, leading one commentator to remark that 'never before has India had such expansive relations with all the major powers at the same time—a result not only of India's increasing weight in the global economy and its growing power potential, but also of New Delhi's savvy and persistent diplomacy'.[28]

---

[26] Mohan, 'India and the Balance of Power', pp. 21–22.
[27] Ibid., p. 24.
[28] Ibid., pp. 23–24.

Of course, New Delhi also faces significant hurdles in its attempt to join the world's most exclusive club. Foremost among these is that, while India has made great economic strides in the post-bipolar era, its economic potential is constrained by an 'old centralised bureaucratic Indian state . . . in steady decline'.[29] According to the data presented in tables 2.6, 2.8 and 2.9, India ranks 104th in the world in economic freedom, and its percentiles in the areas of political stability and government effectiveness are 22.2 and 51.7, respectively. These figures lend convincing empirical support to the contention that, 'rather than rising with the help of the state, India is in many ways rising despite the state'.[30] For this reason, India's arrival as a true great power is at least a decade off.

---

[29] Gurcharan Das, 'The India Model', *Foreign Affairs* 85:4 (July/August 2006), p. 9.
[30] Ibid., p. 3.

3

India and the Emerging Non-Proliferation Order: The Second Nuclear Age

C. RAJA MOHAN

The agreement to resume civilian nuclear cooperation, signed by the US President George W. Bush and India's Prime Minister Manmohan Singh on July 18, 2005 at the White House, is arguably the single most important development in the rapid evolution of Indo-US relations during the early years of the 21st century.[1] The agreement, greeted with enthusiasm from some sections in both the countries, for its potential to transform the Indo-US relations, has also met equally strong criticism for departing from the past nuclear policies of both the nations. It was also seen as undermining the essence of the global non-proliferation regime built around the Nuclear Non-Proliferation Treaty (NPT).[2] There was doubt that the deal marked a historic departure for both the US and India. Under the deal, the Bush administration agreed to change the three and half decades-old domestic law on non-proliferation and persuade the international community to modify its rules to facilitate civilian nuclear energy cooperation with India. The Manmohan Singh government in turn agreed to separate India's military and civilian nuclear programmes and place the latter under international safeguards and undertake substantive global non-proliferation commitments. In essence, the agreement sought to accommodate India into the global nuclear order, without demanding that India give up its nuclear-weapons programme. Given India's unwillingness and inability to join the NPT, which cannot by the

---

[1] For a comprehensive account of the origins and evolution of the negotiations that led to the July 18, 2005 agreement, see, C. Raja Mohan, *Impossible Allies: Nuclear India, United States and the Global Order* (New Delhi: Indian Research Press, 2006).
[2] For the pithiest critique that covers all controversial elements of the deal, see, Strobe Talbott, *Engaging India: Diplomacy, Democracy and the Bomb* (Washington, DC: Brookings Institution, 2004).

very nature of its provisions accept India as a nuclear-weapon state, the Indo-US agreement makes a significant modification to the international nuclear order, to bring just one country into it. The agreement necessarily involved far-reaching changes in the nuclear policies of both Washington and New Delhi and an acceptance of the change by the international community. Not surprisingly, the deal has courted controversy across the world.

While much of the debate in the US, India and the world has focused on the relative merits and problems of the agreement, there has been little discussion of the reasons for the change in the attitude of the international community between 1998 and 2005. In the wake of nuclear tests by India and Pakistan in May 1998, the G-8, P-5 and the UN Security Council had unanimously castigated the defiance of the two subcontinental rivals and demanded they roll back their nuclear and missile programmes and submit to the nuclear order. Since July 2005, the international system has been debating the terms for accommodating India, and India alone, into the global nuclear order. This essay argues that the nuclear reconciliation between the global nuclear order and India must be seen as a consequence of the changes in the international distribution of power as well as the perceived need to adapt to the changing dynamics of nuclear politics in the post-Cold War world. The willingness of the hegemonic power to restructure the extant nuclear order and a revisionist India's willingness to overhaul the organisation of its own nuclear programme, the essay suggests, can be best understood in terms of the unfolding of a second nuclear age. It begins with an assessment of the notion of the second nuclear age that is centred around Asia, explains the Asian nuclear power spread in terms of changes in the distribution of regional power and examines the implications for the Asian balance of power. It concludes with a brief assessment of the terms of nuclear reconciliation between India and the global nuclear order.

THE SECOND NUCLEAR AGE

Since the mid-1990s, the idea of a second nuclear age had begun to gain intellectual ground.[3] It was Bracken, however, who offered

---

[3] See, Fred Charles Ikle, 'The Second Coming of the Nuclear Age', *Foreign Affairs* 75:1 (January/February 1996), pp. 119–28; Keith B. Payne, *Deterrence in the Second Nuclear Age* (Lexington: University of Kentucky Press, 1996); and Colin S. Gray, *The Second Nuclear Age* (Boulder, CO: Lynne Reinner, 1999).

a structural examination of the second nuclear age.[4] He located the 'roots' of the second nuclear age in Asia. The other factors identified by Bracken are the multiplicity of players in the new nuclear game, the special role of the state in the second nuclear age, the constraints posed by the extant nuclear order, the inability of new nuclear players to build costly command and control systems and the 'second mover advantage' in technological development. To that list of factors we could now add the rise of non-state actors in the nuclear game, and the renewed importance of civilian nuclear power in addressing the energy security requirements of major powers and the consequent difficulties of building a firewall between peaceful and military uses of the atom.[5]

The dramatic expansion of Asian military capabilities, including in the field of weapons of mass destruction (WMD), Bracken rightly underlines, is part of the relative decline of Western dominance of the international system. He also argues that despite the reluctance of the West to come to terms with it, the global security order will inevitably have to evolve amidst the rise of Asia. Notwithstanding Bracken's valuable assessment of the Asian factor in the second nuclear age, one could easily quibble with the residual ethnocentrism in his arguments. Bracken's insistence that Asian nationalism, which drives the nuclear proliferation in Asia, is at once dangerous and stands in contrast to the spirit of enlightenment that pervaded the US–Soviet rivalry is indeed questionable. Nationalism was certainly an important factor in the nuclearisation of Britain and France. It was not absent in the nuclear policies of Moscow and Washington. Behind the veneer of communist ideology, it was Russian nationalism that drove Moscow to compete with the US and the West during the Cold War. Nationalism remains

---

[4] See, Paul Bracken, *Fire in the East: The rise of Asian Military Power and the Second Nuclear Age* (New York: Harper Collins, 1999); Paul Bracken, 'The Second Nuclear Age', *Foreign Affairs* 79:1 (January/February 2000), pp. 146–56; Paul Bracken, 'The Structure of the Second Nuclear Age', *Orbis* 47:3 (Summer 2003), pp. 399–413.

[5] See, Nobuyasu Abe, 'Challenges of the Second Nuclear Age: Preserving Multilateralism, Advancing Disarmament', Keynote address at the Middle Powers Forum, New York, October 6, 2003; Donald Berlin, 'The Indian Ocean and the Second Nuclear Age', *Orbis* 48 (2004), pp. 55–70; William J. Broad, 'Facing the Second Nuclear Age', *New York Times*, August 3, 2003; William J. Broad and David E. Sanger 'Officials Fear a Second Nuclear Age with Spread of Technology', *International Herald Tribune*, October 14, 2006; and Noah Feldman, 'Islam, Terror and the Second Nuclear Age', *New York Times Magazine*, October 29, 2006.

an enduring factor in the current Russian emphasis on nuclear weapons. In the early years of the Cold War, nationalism played an important role in mobilising Americans in favour of a nuclear confrontation with the USSR. Bracken's argument that nationalism drives Asian states into 'absurd behaviour and strange decisions' applies equally well to the US. One can quickly recall President Kennedy's decision to land a man on the moon. Equally universal is Bracken's sense that the passions of nationalism preclude informed discourse on nuclear policy in Asian states. The American debate on the 'missile gap' and the extended debate on the 'window of vulnerability' easily come to mind. There is no doubt that nationalism has been a powerful factor in driving India's nuclear policy.[6] However, the nuclear behaviour of India and other Asian actors could be explained in more generic notions such as 'balance of power' rather than exclusively in terms of an 'Asian strategic culture'. While national peculiarities and cultural specificities do matter in the discourse on the security policies of key Asian powers, they need not necessarily be the defining elements in thinking about the second nuclear age. For example, India's critique of the international order has been articulated in moral and normative terms from the very moment independent India joined the global nuclear debate in the middle of the 20th century, and in its strong support to the notion of total and comprehensive global nuclear disarmament. But that emphasis on ideals and norms, which often took a quixotic turn—for example in proclaiming its first nuclear test in 1974 as a 'peaceful nuclear explosion'—did not prevent India from pursuing slowly but relentlessly the ambition of becoming a full fledged nuclear-weapon power. If one judges India by what it did, rather than what it said, it should not be difficult to see the enduring realist elements of India's nuclear policy and its running battles with normative considerations.[7]

EXPLAINING THE NUCLEAR PROLIFERATION IN ASIA

The acquisition of nuclear weapons in Asia by China, Pakistan, India and North Korea can be explained with some credibility in

---

[6] See, T.T. Poulose, *The CTBT and the Rise of Nuclear Nationalism in India* (New Delhi: Lancer Books, 1996).
[7] See, Rajesh M. Basrur, 'Nuclear Weapons and Indian Strategic Culture', *Journal of Peace Research* 38:2 (March 2001), pp. 181–98.

terms of balance of power. Although ideology was an important factor in the Russian decision to assist China in its nuclear quest, it also had to do with the notion of nuclear balance between the East and the West. Sino-Soviet differences in the late 1950s put an end to this assistance. China's necessary search for a national nuclear deterrent was driven by Beijing's own sense of its destiny as a natural great power in the world and, more immediately, by the need to redress the military imbalance with two powerful adversaries—Washington and Moscow.

Pakistan's quest for nuclear weapons was a classic response to the failure of the system of regional balance of power to protect the territorial integrity of the nation in 1971. It was not a response to the acquisition of nuclear weapons by India. There is enough evidence now to suggest that Pakistan's nuclear programme was driven less by the 1974 nuclear test by India, but by New Delhi's ability to successfully vivisect Pakistan. As India, backed by the USSR, embarked on the project to divide Pakistan, the US and China failed to stand up for Islamabad. Recognising that without nuclear weapons Pakistan will not be secure against India's conventional power capabilities, Zulfiqar Ali Bhutto ordered the nuclear weapons programme as the first order of business in early 1972. It did not really matter to Pakistan, whether India had nuclear weapons or not. Pakistan believed it needed them to balance India and preserve its nationhood. Considerations of balance of power (against India) were part of China's active assistance to Pakistan's nuclear weapons programme in the 1970s and 1980s and the missile development programme in the 1990s. It was also the considerations of balance, against the USSR, that made the US turn a blind eye to the nuclearisation of Pakistan in the 1980s.

The acceleration of the North Korean nuclear weapons programme and its culmination in the nuclear test of October 9, 2006, too, could be attributed to the change in the East Asian balance of power. As it saw South Korea draw closer to Moscow and Beijing, its long-standing partners, and worried about its own survival as a state, North Korea responded with its decision to withdraw from the NPT. The international nuclear diplomacy towards North Korea, which eventually conducted a nuclear test at the end of 2006, had repeatedly come down to the questions relating to the security of the regime in Pyongyang. Adequate security guarantees might well prove to be instrumental in reversing the North Korean proliferation.

Balance of power and regime survival are equally important factors in the Iranian search for a nuclear-weapon option. It is interesting to recall that Ayatollah Khomeini, the founder of the Islamic Republic, with his ideological bravado about people's power, had dismantled a fairly well-advanced nuclear power programme, put in place by the Shah of Iran. Yet, within years, Iran was confronted with the Western support for Iraq's Saddam Hussein, the international refusal to condemn the use of WMD by Iraq and the reality of a nuclear Pakistan on its eastern borders. Thus, the revival of the nuclear option became an inevitability for Iran. What is not settled, however, is whether Iran's proliferation is driven by immediate security considerations or long-term ambitions of becoming a regional power. The former motivation could indeed be addressed by the international system, while the latter will not be easy to accept.

India's own debate on nuclear weapons started immediately after the first Chinese nuclear test in 1964. The 1974 test was, in many ways, a delayed response to Chinese nuclear weapons programme. Yet, a noteworthy feature of the Indian nuclear policy was its reluctance to weaponise its nuclear option, despite the 1974 test. This has been attributed to the strength of an idealist and normative strain in Indian politics.[8] Undoubtedly, the inheritance from a century-long national movement that was built around liberal norms and on the commitment to non-violence, this strain was an important factor in delaying the Indian response to the introduction of nuclear weapons by China, soon after the 1962 war between the two nations. That alone, however, does not adequately explain India's nuclear restraint during much of the 1970s and 1980s. I would argue that an alternative explanation might lie in the fact that India's security alliance with the USSR, unveiled in the 1971 treaty of peace and friendship, had reduced the imperatives for an immediate acquisition of nuclear weapons. The treaty gave India the confidence that the balance against the US strategic cooperation with China and Pakistan had been established. The strong economic, military and political partnership with Moscow reduced India's incentive in acquiring its own nuclear weapons,

---

[8] George Perkovich, *India's Nuclear Bomb: The Impact on Global Proliferation* (Berkeley, CA: University of California Press,1999) captures the tension between realpolitik and moralpolitik in the Indian nuclear debate, after the Chinese nuclear test in October 1964.

despite the fact that China, its rival in the region and the third world as a whole, was a fully recognised nuclear-weapon power. It was only when the USSR collapsed, the Cold War ended and the global balance shattered that pressures mounted on India to exercise its nuclear-weapon option. Having lost its only international ally, the major source of its military equipment, and confronted with a rising China and unable to build a new partnership with the sole super power, India was compelled to recast its strategic framework in the 1990s. The decision to become an overt nuclear-weapon power in 1998 was a consequence of the fundamental change in the balance of power around India. If many in India and outside tended to attribute the change to the arrival of the right-wing Hindu nationalist BJP to power or to the continuing rivalry with Pakistan, Some Chinese analysts were willing to see it in systemic terms.[9]

The stability of the Cold War, or the first nuclear age, hinged on the central military/nuclear balance between the US and USSR and its extension into such key regions as Europe and Asia. Although the credibility of 'extended deterrence' was often questioned, it largely held. It offered security to the allies of the two great powers and prevented them from acquiring their own nuclear weapons. While the end of the Cold War saw a broader reconciliation in Europe and its accelerated integration, a similar process has not emerged in Asia. The end of the Cold War forced many Asian nations to reconsider their nuclear options.[10] But where long-standing alliances were reinforced as in the case of Japan, there was no rush towards nuclear weapons. But if Japan finds that the credibility of US-extended deterrence is in doubt or that China might replace Japan as the principal partner of the US or the attractions of autonomy overwhelm those of the alliance, Tokyo could well reconsider its nuclear-weapon options.

NUCLEAR PROLIFERATION AND THE ASIAN BALANCE

The literature on nuclear proliferation, especially after 1991, has tended to debate the problems merely as the difficulties of

---

[9] See, Weixing Hu, 'New Delhi's Nuclear Bomb: A Systematic Analysis', *World Affairs* 163:1 (Summer 2000), pp. 28–38.
[10] Victor D. Cha, 'The Second Nuclear Age: Proliferation Pessimism versus Soviet Optimism in South Asia and East Asia', *Journal of Strategic Studies* 24:4 (December 2001), pp. 79–120.

implementing a regime that had the endorsement and support of all the great powers. It was merely a question of dealing with the deviants and the legal loopholes sharpened by technological change, the problems resulting from the break-up of the USSR and the difficulties of implementation and verification. But the extant non-proliferation regime built around the NPT was, however, just a reflection of the balance of power system that was codified in 1970. In many ways, it was an extension of the Yalta system. The victorious allies of the Second World War—the US, the USSR and the UK—through a series of steps in the 1960s, moved towards the NPT. France and China were offered their rightful places, which were taken up fully after the end of the Cold War. The second nuclear age, in essence, is about the break-up of the old system of balance of power. In the first nuclear age, the structure of the global balance was more important than regional rivalry in inducing Asian proliferation. In the second nuclear age, marked by the resurgence of Asia, the regional imperative has become more predominant. With most of the great global struggles shifting from Europe to Asia, the regional is close to becoming global.

There are a number of factors that shape this new dynamics in Asia. First and foremost, the improbability of an Asian collective security order. Despite a growing regional economic interdependence, and the new talk of an Asian economic union and a single currency, a stable Asia-wide security architecture is not within reach in the near future. Although the East Asia Summit and the Shanghai Cooperation Organisation are the first attempts to create such an order, it is unlikely that other powers within the region and outside see them as the answers to Asia's security problems. The reliance on national power and alliances is most likely to endure in the region and lay the basis for a prolonged competitive military/nuclear dynamics in the region. India's own security policies are often masked by its rhetoric in favour of multilateralism and collective security. Yet the fact remains that India opposed all previous attempts by its friend and ally USSR to construct a collective security system for Asia.[11] India is today extremely wary of Chinese attempts to construct a regional security system in Central Asia and East Asia. India is not too enthusiastic

---

[11] See, A. G. Noorani, 'Soviet Ambitions in South Asia', *International Security* 4:1 (Winter 1979–80), pp. 31–59.

about endorsing the Chinese and Russian agenda in Central Asia,[12] and is fully conscious of the Chinese attempts to keep it out of the East Asia Summit.[13]

Second, there is a debate among the American Sinologists on whether a Chinese preponderance is the natural order of things in Asia and whether the US should contest the region's acceptance of a Sino-centric order.[14] But logic might be compelling in the other direction. Despite their expansive economic ties with China, neither Japan nor India are likely to accept a regional security order based on Beijing's primacy. Fears about the rise of China are already propelling Tokyo and New Delhi closer to each other and to the US. Japan and India will not satisfy themselves with a mere balancing of China, but they will also vigorously contest Beijing's attempts at establishing its dominance in various parts of Asia. It has been well-established that balancing China has been an enduring feature of India's foreign policy.[15] There is nothing to suggest that this rivalry has abated despite the significant improvement in bilateral relations in the early years of the 21st century. In many ways, the rise of China has intensified India's efforts to catch up in a range of areas such as energy diplomacy, seeking influence in Africa, competing for leverage in Burma, and in the civilian and military space domains, to mention a few.

Third, it is widely understood that Bush administration's motivation in expanding defence cooperation with India and in agreeing to change the global non-proliferation regime rested in part on the objective of balancing China.[16] Although no decision

---

[12] See, Sudha Ramachandran, 'India Gives Shanghai the Cold Shoulder', *Asia Times Online*, June 17, 2006, at http://www.atimes.com/atimes/South_Asia/HF17Df01.html (accessed on April 10, 2008).

[13] See, Mohan Malik, 'China and East Asian Summit: More Discord than Accord', *Asia Pacific Center for Security Studies* (Honolulu), February 2006, at http://www.apcss.org/Publications/APSSS/ChinaandEastAsiaSummit.pdf (accessed on April 10, 2008).

[14] David Shambaugh, ed, *Power Shift: China and Asia's New Dynamics* (Berkeley,CA: University of California Press, 2006).

[15] John Graver, *Protected Contest: Sino-Indian Rivalry in the 20th Century* (Seattle: University of Washington Press, 2006).

[16] Gwynne Dyer, 'Containing China', *Walrus*, October, 2005, at http://www.walnrusmagazine.com/articles/2005.10-international-affairs-containing-china/ (accessed on April 10, 2008); and Strobe Talbott, 'Good Day for India, Bad Day for Non-Proliferation', *Yale Global Online*, July 21, 2005, at http://yaleglobal.yale.edu/display.article?id=6042 (accessed on April 10, 2008).

has been made in the US either on a strategy of containing China or drafting India into that exercise, it is quite reasonable to assume that even a prudent strategy in Washington on hedging against China's rise will necessarily have to put some weight on the India factor. The Bush administration's assertion early on in the second term on 'assisting India's rise as a great power' is critical in understanding the logic behind the controversial decision to resume civilian nuclear cooperation with India. This decision came on top of a review that saw fundamental changes in the global distribution of power and the emergence of new powers like India and more rapid ascent of China in the international system. This change was instinctively sensed during the first presidential campaign of George W. Bush, which promised greater attention to India.[17] Although the events of 9/11 drew away most of American energies to West and South West Asia, the administration kept an eye on the relationship with India and was keen to treat it as a potential great power in the international system and go beyond the traditional view of India as a South Asian power.[18] With its focus on India as a rising power and its likely contribution to the construction of a new balance of power in Asia amidst the rapid rise of China, the Bush administration was determined to find a way of resolving the long-standing nuclear differences with India.

Besides China, the question of the balance between India and Pakistan too appears to have figured in the Bush administration's decision to accommodate India, and only India, into the global nuclear order. This involved an interesting paradox. If the Indo-US civil nuclear initiative resulted in a historic nuclear differentiation between India and Pakistan, one of the immediate triggers for the decision was the perceived need in Washington to compensate New Delhi for the renewed arms sales to Pakistan in 2005. One of the main purposes of the US Secretary of State Condoleezza Rice's visit to India in March 2005, in the very first weeks of President Bush's second term, was to inform New Delhi that the administration had made up its mind to begin selling arms to Pakistan, seek Indian understanding for this decision and offer to advance the Indo-US

---

[17] Condoleezza Rice, 'Promoting National Interest', *Foreign Affairs* 79:1 (January/February 2000), pp. 45–62.

[18] For a review of the Bush administration's assessments on India, reflected in the national security strategy reports, see, Mohan, *Impossible Allies*.

relations to even a higher plane. It was in Rice's discussions in New Delhi that the proposal for nuclear and other high technology cooperation was given a new weight in bilateral relations. Further, Rice also promised in New Delhi to remove all impediments to American sale of advanced conventional weaponry to India. When the Bush administration announced the resumption of arms sales to Pakistan at the end of March 2005, it combined the announcement with the formal commitment to elevate relations with India to the highest possible level. The Indian government held in check its habit, nurtured over five decades, of automatically condemning US arms sales to Pakistan. While the Indian Prime Minister expressed his 'disappointment' at the US decision, the Indian Government highlighted the new areas of cooperation, including civil nuclear, that were now on the table.[19] It is indeed possible to argue that without the pressure to alter the arms sales policy towards Pakistan, the civil nuclear initiative and the commitment to 'assist India's rise' might not have acquired bureaucratic urgency for the Bush administration.

With the prospect of the US selling advanced conventional arms to both Pakistan and India, the Bush administration turned on its head the traditional paradigm of US policy towards South Asia. For the first time, Washington had broken the zero-sum game dynamics of US relations with India and Pakistan, and had simultaneously improved relations with the subcontinental rivals. Until 9/11, in the first term of the Bush administration, Washington was focussing on the presumed China threat, was prepared to build a new South Asia policy centred around India and largely ignore Pakistan.[20] The events of 9/11, however, facilitated the return of Pakistan to the front and centre of American foreign policy. To its credit, the Bush administration did not let the South Asian policy drift back to the old pattern and managed to sustain the new forward movement in the relationship with India. The Bush administration's refusal to extend the civil nuclear deal to Pakistan, while deepening cooperation with it in other areas,

---

[19] For a comprehensive discussion of the Rice visit and its consequences see, Mohan, *Impossible Allies*, pp. 53–72.
[20] See, Ben Barber, 'US Plays the India Card', *Salon.com*, August 11, 2001, at http://archive.salon.com/news/feature /2001/08/11/india/index.html (accessed on April 10, 2006).

seemed to achieve the impossible—the real dehyphenation of US policies towards New Delhi and Islamabad. As Pakistan sank into a political abyss in the final years of President Bush's second term, the prospect of a future administration reaffirming nuclear parity between India and Pakistan appears remote. For the real and perceived gap between the strategic futures of India and Pakistan has increased in the first decade of the 21st century.

Fourth, non-nuclear developments, too, might have an impact on the future nuclear dynamics in Asia. If the US and its Asian allies focus on missile defence as the principal response to further proliferation, its impact on China's nuclear arsenal has long been debated. Would a rapid modernisation of the Chinese nuclear arsenal eventually produce a similar response in India? And would changes in Indian nuclear posture produce a reaction in Pakistan? While some would answer in the affirmative, others would argue that, for a nation like India, getting missile defence capabilities might be more important than merely responding symmetrically to the size and sophistication of the Chinese nuclear arsenal. Traditional arms control literature has focussed exclusively on the nature of stability among the new nuclear powers and on the consequences of the introduction of missile defences. But some Asian powers have demonstrated new and extraordinary possibilities for exploiting the strategic options that come with the possession of nuclear weapons. Pakistan's emphasis has been less on maintaining a nuclear balance with India and more on fomenting a low intensity conflict within the territory of its regional adversary. India's problem with Pakistan since the late 1980s, when the latter acquired nuclear weapons, has been less about the character of Pakistan's arsenal but Pakistan's new freedom to conduct a sub-conventional conflict under conditions of nuclear parity. India, as a consequence, instinctively turned towards options of missile defence by reaching out to Israel and examining missile-interceptor options from Russia. The NDA government ended the absence of a larger Indian doctrine on missile defence by seizing the political opportunity presented by the Bush administration, when it announced its controversial missile defence initiative in May 2001.[21] The US, in turn, welcomed India's positive response

---

[21] For a discussion of the domestic politics on missile defence, see, Raja Mohan, *Crossing the Rubicon: The Shaping of India's New Foreign policy* (New York: Palgrave, 2004).

and has made cooperation in missile defence a critical element in its defence engagement with India.[22] Although the Congress-led UPA government in New Delhi was initially sceptical about missile defence, it authorised India's first missile defence test at the end of 2006.[23] After a second round of tests at the end of 2007, Indian scientists suggested the possibility of the deployment of a system by 2010.[24] Despite denials by New Delhi and Washington, concerns about Chinese nuclear-weapon potential is an important element driving Indo-US cooperation on missile defence.[25]

THE EMERGING NUCLEAR ORDER

As the world began to cope with new challenges arising from the proliferation of WMD after the Cold War, a number of alternatives came into view, in terms of the future of the global nuclear order. One option for the world would be to simply disband the NPT, given its failure to prevent the proliferation of nuclear weapons. There are few takers for this radical proposition. Pragmatists, familiar with the origins of the NPT, argue that the treaty was never meant to completely halt nuclear proliferation. It was aimed at slowing down rather than eliminating proliferation. In that sense, the NPT has worked remarkably well since it came into force in 1970. The second option is to revise the NPT system. This is easier said than done. Given the complexity of developing an international consensus around a new treaty or modifying the NPT, such an exercise is not in the realm of possibility. The third is for a vigorous defence of the current order centred around the NPT, irrespective of its weaknesses and its flaws. Literal interpretation of the NPT is no longer possible, given the new awareness of the

---

[22] See, Ashley J. Tellis, 'Evolution of US-Indian Defence Ties: Missile Defence in an Emerging Strategic Relationship', *International Security* 30:4 (Spring 2006), pp. 113–51.

[23] Martin Seiff, 'A Giant Leap for Indian Missile Defense', December 1, 2006, at http://www.spacewar.com/reports/A_Giant_Leap_Forward_For_Indian_Missile_Defense_999.html (accessed on April 10, 2008).

[24] Y.P. Rajesh, 'India Says to Have Missile Defence System in Three Years', *Reuters* (New Delhi), December 12, 2007, at http://www.reuters.com/article/latestCrisis/idUSDEL331120 (accessed on December 13, 2007).

[25] Tellis, 'Evolution of US-Indian Defence Ties'.

possibilities of misusing its provisions by certain states. Fourth, despite the desire of many to uphold the NPT as it is, the very policy practice, as it has evolved since the end of the Cold War, has underlined the importance of changing the interpretation of the NPT to make it more effective. As a result, important changes have begun to take place in its implementation. For example, most supporters of the NPT today argue that the Article IV of the treaty—promising comprehensive civilian nuclear cooperation with non-nuclear-weapon states party to the treaty—must not be treated as an unconditional right. Given the threat of the misuse of Article IV provisions, there is a growing consensus that it can only be considered in the broader political context. The calls for the restriction on the transfer of uranium enrichment and plutonium reprocessing technologies, which are critical for the manufacture of nuclear weapons, have gathered considerable political support. Along with the proposition for circumscribing the interpretation of Article IV, considerable effort in the last few years has gone into strengthening Article III, which is about verifying the obligations of the non-nuclear states under the NPT. Recognising the weaknesses of the International Atomic Energy Agency (IAEA) safeguards and the potential for states to cheat on it, the international community has transformed the entire technical and operational basis of the verification mechanisms since the end of the Cold War. A number of other provisions of the NPT, such as total abolition of nuclear weapons (Article VI) and international cooperation in the use of Peaceful Nuclear Explosions (Article V), have long become irrelevant.

Meanwhile, the US has adopted a different approach to the strengthening of the non-proliferation system. Many in the US establishment have lost faith in the power of arms-control treaties.[26] The argument that states will cheat on treaties and that the US needs a whole range of unilateral methods and ad hoc multilateral arrangements to prevent states from acquiring nuclear weapons has

---

[26] For an insightful description of the loss of faith in arms control, see, Steven E. Miller, 'Skepticism Triumphant: The Bush Administration and the Waning of Arms-Control', May 2003, at http://bcsia.ksg.harvard.edu/BCSIA_content/documents/Miller_Paris.pdf (accessed on April 10, 2008). See also, George Perkovich, 'Bush's Nuclear Proliferation: A Regime Change in Non-Proliferation?', *Foreign Affairs* 82:2 (March/April 2003), pp. 2–8.

acquired a new salience in Washington. Many of these approaches go beyond those of the NPT. While the US sees them as a way of supplementing the NPT, others find it deeply disconcerting that Washington is adopting a strategy that might in fact jeopardise the whole system. Among these measures are one—the missile defence—which fundamentally redefines the nature of nuclear deterrence. During the Cold War, the effectiveness of nuclear deterrence was premised on the centrality of offensive nuclear forces. The US policy now demands the introduction of defences into the nuclear calculus. While the US insists that defences are necessary to maintain deterrence against 'rogue states' and terrorist groups armed with WMD, the critics fear a renewed arms race among major powers. Second, both the Clinton and Bush administrations underlined the importance of 'counter-proliferation'. This strategy presumes the ineffectiveness of treaties in preventing proliferation and the need to have military capacities to deal with the challenge of the spread of WMD. This involves developing unilaterally, military capacities to deal with WMD use on the battlefield as well as multilateral efforts, like the Proliferation Security Initiative (PSI), to interdict illegal traffic in WMD materials between states. Many have argued that the former is a recipe for disaster and the latter a violation of international law. In its National Security Strategy document of September 2002, the Bush administration went one step ahead in suggesting the importance of 'pre-emption' in neutralising the WMD capacities of rogue states and terrorist groups. The Bush administration's argument that Washington cannot wait for nuclear threats to materialise before dealing with them, however, has generated a storm of protest within and beyond the US. The administration has also emphasised 'regime change' in dealing with WMD proliferation. Underlying this is an important argument that the nature of the regime is more important than the technical features of proliferation in a particular state. Critics, however, point to the disastrous consequences of attempting regime change by citing to the experience in Iraq of overthrowing Saddam Hussein in the name of preventing the proliferation of WMD.

Even as it initiated new approaches to non-proliferation, the Bush administration also sought to change the global thinking on the relationship between the use of nuclear energy and proliferation. For nearly three decades since the mid-1970s the bipartisan consensus in the US was in favour of discouraging the use of nuclear energy for electric power generation at home and abroad. Reversing this approach, amidst rising oil prices and growing concerns about global warming, the Bush administration has come out strongly in favour of expanded use of nuclear power. Besides altering domestic laws in favour of the use of nuclear energy, it is now in favour of promoting nuclear power abroad, within a new framework. This involves the development of nuclear technologies that reduce the risk of proliferation through international cooperation, a new commitment to reprocess plutonium for commercial use under international safeguards, limiting the transfer of uranium enrichment and plutonium reprocessing technologies and assurances of fuel supply to nations that want to develop nuclear power. Although all the new non-proliferation initiatives from the US have been controversial, they have moved forward at varying speeds and some of them, like the PSI, have garnered considerable international support. Put simply, irrespective of the current debate, the global non-proliferation order has already undergone considerable change and has begun to look very different from the accepted international consensus in the mid-1970s.

Although defining the nature of the new nuclear order will remain contentious, we could outline a set of factors necessary for its success. First, such an order must meet the aspirations and interests of all the great powers, current as well as rising. Among the traditional powers, despite the huge arguments across the Atlantic on the future of arms control, a broad consensus has indeed begun to emerge on the next steps towards non-proliferation. The North Atlantic Treaty Organization (NATO) has already accepted many, if not all, new American precepts on non-proliferation. Russia, too, has been supportive of some new non-proliferation measures, but remains opposed to missile defence. But Moscow has often differed on the tactics to be used in dealing with such proliferation threats, for example, in Iran.

Second, the real challenge, however, lies in integrating the rising powers of Asia as stakeholders in the construction and implementation of the new nuclear order. For far too long, the debate on nuclear non-proliferation has been conducted within an American framework and in recent years in a more Atlantic framework. Asia has largely been marginal to these debates. The US and Europe have tended to be the *demandeurs* and the Asian powers the *repondeurs*. Since the early 1990s, China has steadily become a part of the non-proliferation system. It has tended to modify some of its cavalier non-proliferation policies in the past. Although deeply concerned about missile defence and suspicious about the PSI, China has recognised the importance of cooperation with the other powers in preventing further proliferation of WMD. The Bush administration has taken a big step in bringing India, one of the three important non-signatories to the NPT, into the non-proliferation order through the July 18, 2005 nuclear agreement. Despite widespread criticism of the agreement within the non-proliferation community, key practitioners like the IAEA Director General Mohammed El Baradei has welcomed it as a major gain for non-proliferation. More importantly, all the major powers, with the exception of China, have extended political support. This again is rooted in the calculus of the changing distribution of power. Russia, France and Britain have nothing to lose by the accommodation of India into the international system and the former two have much to gain. China clearly has problems. It has reasons to be concerned about the recognition of India's nuclear exceptionalism as well as the new strategic warmth between Washington and New Delhi, which is at the source of the Indo-US civil nuclear initiative and could alter the future balance of power in Asia.

Third, if new technologies hold the key to managing the second nuclear age, the role of Asian powers as both consumers of technology and its generators will have to be factored in. China and to a lesser extent India are both in the position to influence nuclear technology flows to non-nuclear countries and, as a consequence, the prospects for proliferation of WMD. The technological capabilities of both are likely to expand further in the coming years. Therefore, their full participation in drafting the rules, and not merely in adhering to them, is important. Fourth, the Western attitudes to the rising powers and their role will ultimately be shaped by enduring assessments on whether they are allies or adversaries in the construction of global security. If they are treated as adversaries, and if their specific security interests are not taken into account in constructing the new nuclear order, it stands to reason that the regime would get progressively weaker. The attempt to integrate India into the global nuclear order, however, runs the risk of sharpening tension between the two rising powers. That probably is the reason why India has gone out of the way to engage China and limit its incentives in disrupting the prospect of a reconciliation with the international system.

The Terms of Indo-US Nuclear Reconciliation

Although many structural factors facilitated the Indo-US nuclear rapprochement after Pokharan II, it was neither easy arriving at the framework announced in July 2005 nor interpreting and implementing it to the satisfaction of relevant institutions in both Washington and New Delhi. For the US, principal question was the importance of preventing any real or perceived damage to the global non-proliferation regime while accommodating India's nuclear aspirations. For New Delhi, the problem was always the price—political and technological—that had to be paid for getting the international rules changed in its favour. Reconciling this divergence was at the heart of the Indo-US nuclear dialogue that began in earnest in the early 1990s, when Washington began to address the consequences of undeclared acquisition of nuclear weapons by Islamabad and New Delhi from the late 1980s.

Two factors shaped the bilateral Indo-US nuclear negotiation. First, the growing mutual stakes in the bilateral relationship. Since the end of the Cold War and the collapse of the USSR, improving relations with the US became one of the central bipartisan priorities of the Indian political establishment. The US too had to—slowly and over an extended period—come to terms with the promise of India's new economic policies since 1991 and their implications for India's emergence as a major power. The post-Cold War enthusiasm in Washington for the promotion of democracy worldwide, and the recognition that the world's largest democracy could not be punished for possessing nuclear weapons, added some urgency to a nuclear reconciliation with India. Second, both recognised the urgent imperative of overcoming the nuclear dispute, that originated from the implementation of the NPT in 1970 and India's first nuclear test in May 1974. Besides differences over Jammu and Kashmir and the historic role of the US in Indo-Pak disputes, the nuclear question remained the major obstacle to improving bilateral relations.

The Indo-US nuclear negotiations might be divided into four phases—one, the Clinton Administration's nuclear dialogue with India before Pokharan II (1993–98); two, the post-Pokharan II engagement under President Clinton (1998–2000); three, the first term of the Bush administration (2001–04); and the negotiation and implementation of the 2005 Indo–US nuclear initiative in the second term of the Bush administration that began in January 2005. In each of these phases, the two sides sought to preserve their core interests; inevitably, though the definition and relative weight of these interests began to alter. The US had to balance its defence of the nuclear regime with the need to build a partnership with India. New Delhi, in turn, had to balance its traditional emphasis on nuclear autonomy with the need to find a modus vivendi with the global non-proliferation order.

In the first phase, there was little prospect for any reconciliation.[27] After the end of the Cold War and the collapse of the USSR, there was a liberal triumphalism in the US. It was reflected in the domination of the Clinton administration's first term by groups that were focused on specific issues—for example, non-proliferation and human rights. The early 1990s were also one of the weakest moments of independent India's history, as the political establishment had to come to terms with weaker federal governments, inflamed frontier regions, collapse of state socialism, the challenges of globalisation and the disappearance of the trusted international ally, the USSR. This period saw the US expanding high technology sanctions against India as part of a general tightening of the non-proliferation regime, pressurising the USSR to stop civilian nuclear and space cooperation with India and proclaiming the objective of bringing legal constraints on India's strategic programmes. It was the proclaimed objective of the Clinton administration to cap, roll-back and eventually eliminate the nuclear and missile programmes of India (and Pakistan).[28]

Although rolling back and eliminating India's nuclear and missile capabilities were never credible policy options in Washington, the declaratory approaches of the Clinton administration fed into the Indian apprehensions and nuclear policy-making. The Indian diplomatic strategy in the 1990s was about 'buying time' for a

---

[27] For a discussion among Indian and American scholars and policy-makers on the nuclear issues in the mid-1990s, see Francine Frankel, ed, *Bridging the Nonproliferation Divide, The United States and India* (Lanham, Md.: University Press of America, 1995).

[28] 'The United States has engaged India and Pakistan in seeking agreement on steps to cap, reduce, and ultimately eliminate their weapons of mass destruction and ballistic missile capabilities.' The White House, *A National Strategy of Engagement amd Enlargement* (Washington DC, 1995), p. 31.

putative overt exercise of the Indian nuclear option and avoid a direct confrontation with Washington. India deeply resented the Clinton administration's framing of the issues within the regional framework that equated India with Pakistan and sought to avoid any arms-control commitments within such a framework. New Delhi, in turn, suggested a more acceptable multilateral or international framework of arms-control that would provide some diplomatic room for India. It was within this context that India supported the active negotiations on the Comprehensive Test Ban Treaty (CTBT) and the proposals for similar talks on the Fissile Materials Cut-off Treaty (FMCT) in the early 1990s. As the drafting of the CTBT came to a closure in 1995, there was strong backlash against the possibility that the treaty might undo the prospects for the credibility of India's nuclear arsenal. The stronger the US pressure to accept a legal constraint on India's nuclear programme, the greater the internal pressures on New Delhi to conduct a test. Although the Congress government led by P.V. Narasimha Rao succumbed to US pressures against a nuclear test in December 1995, the ground had been cleared for the demonstration of India's nuclear-weapon capabilities. More importantly, the US pressure on signing the CTBT became a rallying cry for renewed nuclear nationalism in India and a strong insurance against external pressures on the testing of nuclear weapons.[29]

India's nuclear tests in May 1998 angered the Clinton administration, but also provided the shock necessary for a more substantive security dialogue between the two countries. India, on its part signalled restraint by announcing a voluntary moratorium on further testing on May 13. This opened the space for a dialogue which began within a month of the nuclear tests. The two interlocutors, US Under Secretary of State Strobe Talbott and the Indian Foreign Minister Jaswant Singh, met more than ten times during 1998–99.[30] The principal objective of the dialogue was to reconcile American non-proliferation interests with the Indian security imperatives. Having applied the mandatory sanctions under the US non-proliferation law and mobilised international pressure, especially

---

[29] Arundhati Ghose, 'Negotiating the CTBT: India's Security Concerns and Nuclear Disarmament', *Journal of International Affairs* 51:1 (Summer 1997), pp. 239–62; and Poulose, *The CTBT and the Rise of Nuclear Nationalism in India*.
[30] For a first hand account of the dialogue see, Talbott, 'Engaging India'.

from Japan, India's largest donor, Washington offered to ease these if India was prepared to abide by the five benchmarks it had laid down. These were: signing the CTBT, accepting a freeze on the production of nuclear material, strengthening export controls, restraining its nuclear-weapons posture and negotiating peace with Pakistan. India was quite happy to respond to these broad ideas. It had no problem with modernising its export controls over sensitive technologies, support the negotiations on the FMCT and engage Pakistan in a dialogue. India, however, was unwilling to accept any specific restraints on its nuclear weapons programme. As the Clinton administration eventually focussed on the CTBT signature as the single most important condition for ending the post-1998 sanctions, India's domestic nuclear discourse became deeply divisive. Jaswant Singh promised Talbott that India would sign the CTBT, while holding back on its ratification. His attempt to sell the idea at home collapsed amidst the opposition within the government as well as outside. The US Senate's failure to ratify the CTBT made it even more difficult to mobilise support within India in favour of the treaty.

That left the Singh–Talbott dialogue inconclusive. President Clinton was keen to improve relations with India as the tests had woken him to both India's power potential as well as its future role as the world's largest democracy. Clinton discarded the advice from the bureaucracy to condition his India visit (in March 2000) to a prior Indian signature on the CTBT. While he reached out to the Indian people and successfully removed much of the accumulated poison in bilateral relations, he was not prepared to put the future of the relationship with India above his administration's non-proliferation goals. Until the last day, Clinton officials insisted that the full potential of Indo-US relations cannot be realised without India meeting the administration's benchmarks, especially the CTBT.[31] The Clinton administration was unwilling to elevate the bilateral relationship above the presumed imperatives of the US non-proliferation policy.

The third phase saw President Bush coming to power and signalling a new change in the hierarchy of interests in dealing

---

[31] Thomas Pickering, 'US Policy in South Asia: The Road Ahead', Address to the Foreign Policy Institute, Johns Hopkins University, Washington DC, April 27, 2000.

with India. Besides its willingness to see India in the larger perspective of the Asian balance of power, rather than a mere South Asian one, the Bush administration believed that the US non-proliferation policy towards India was both unrealistic and misplaced. India's enthusiasm for the US missile defence initiative seemed to justify the unprecedented interest in Washington to transform relations with India. Unlike the Clinton administration which sought to leverage the post-May 1998 sanctions for nuclear concessions from India, the Bush administration dismantled these sanctions on its own. Bush took a step further and put the question of civilian and other high technology cooperation with India on the table. Although preoccupied with Afghanistan and Iraq, Bush's effort culminated in the Next Steps in Strategic Partnership (NSSP) with India that was announced in January 2004.[32] The statement underlined a set of reciprocal obligations by both sides. The US promised to expand its cooperation with India in civilian nuclear, space, high technology trade and missile defence. New Delhi, in turn, agreed to strengthen its controls on both inward proliferation (diversion for military uses) and outward proliferation (exports to other countries).

Although the NSSP was a breakthrough in the history of the nuclear engagement between Washington and New Delhi, it was limited by the fact that it was fundamentally constrained by its provision that 'these cooperative efforts will be undertaken in accordance with our respective laws and international obligations'.[33] In Washington, the bureaucracy used this provision to narrowly interpret the possibilities of high technology cooperation with New Delhi. India was disappointed that real cooperation in the field of nuclear cooperation remained elusive. This in turn led to a slow-down in the implementation of the terms of the NSSP in India. It was left to the new Congress government that came to power in 2004 to complete the implementation of the NSSP at the end of that year.

The final phase of reconciliation began in the first months of the second Bush administration in 2005, when the White House signalled its commitment to go beyond the NSSP and think more

---

[32] Atal Bihari Vajpayee, 'Next Steps in Strategic Partnership with USA', New Delhi, January 14, 2004, at http://www.mea.gov.in (accessed on April 10, 2008).
[33] Ibid.

boldly about future nuclear cooperation with India. Bush and Manmohan Singh, in July 2005, produced that breakthrough and both sides gave unprecedented commitments.[34] Bush Agreed to change American domestic non-proliferation law and persuade the international community to change the extant guidelines on nuclear commerce to facilitate full civilian nuclear cooperation with India. Singh, in turn, agreed to fundamentally reorganise the national nuclear programme by separating civilian and military nuclear facilities and place the former under international safeguards. India also agreed to strengthen its commitment to the global non-proliferation regime by maintaining its unilateral moratorium on nuclear testing, working with the US to draft a fissile materials cut-off treaty, banning exports of enrichment and reprocessing technologies and harmonising its export controls with the existing international regimes. Every phrase and word, including the use of articles 'an' and 'the' (with reference to the IAEA additional protocol), in the July 18, 2005 statement, were negotiated with such intensity that the talks often broke down. The US and India were trying to square a circle by bending the existing non-proliferation regime to facilitate nuclear cooperation with India.

If it was a miracle that a mutually satisfactory agreement was finally crafted, it needed many more to sell its controversial terms to sections of the bureaucracy and the political classes in both the capitals. In the US the arms controllers were aghast at what they thought was the easy pass Washington was giving New Delhi. In India, even the limited arms-control concessions that the government had made were attacked as an abandonment of India's 'nuclear autonomy'. Every one of the six steps[35] involved in implementing the agreement would draw relentless protests in both countries and from the rest of the world. There were three central

---

[34] Manmohan Singh, 'PM's Address at the China Academy of Social Sciences' Beijing, January 15, 2005, at http://www.pmindia.nic.in/lspeech.asp?id=644 (accessed on April 10, 2008).

[35] These six steps, to be taken in sequence, were the following: 1. India produces a separation plan that was acceptable to the US; 2. Washington gets the US Congress to change the domestic non-proliferation law; 3. the two governments would negotiate the so-called 123 Agreement to define the terms of future bilateral nuclear cooperation; 4. India signs a safeguards agreement with the IAEA; 5. The Nuclear Suppliers Group modifies the export guidelines; 6. The US Congress endorses the 123 Agreement.

contentions in the US domestic and internal debates: whether it was worth changing the regime to favour one country; whether India had given enough arms-control concessions to deserve a change of rules and whether the nuclear accommodation of India undermined the global non-proliferation regime.

The Bush administration has answered all the above questions with an 'yes' and has successfully mobilised a broad bipartisan support for the nuclear accommodation of a rising India[36] despite the widespread criticism of the deal by arms controllers in the US. The political classes in the US, unlike the vocal non-proliferation activists, saw the rise of a democratic India as a positive development and were prepared to pay the price of nuclear accommodation in return for a new partnership. Similar political arguments prevailed in Paris, Moscow and London, resulting in the three nuclear-weapon powers supporting the Indo-US nuclear deal. Beijing, which had reasons to suspect that the nuclear deal might be the thin-end of the wedge of a putative Indo-US alliance against China, expressed reservations.[37] However, Beijing too had to calculate the costs of opposing the Indo-US nuclear deal and eventually signalled its neutrality during Prime Minister Manmohan Singh's visit to China in January 2008.[38] While most of the major powers are expected to support the Indo-US nuclear deal, when it comes up before the Nuclear Suppliers Group (NSG), a small group of Western countries, echoing the US non-proliferation community, might insist on stronger Indian arms-control commitments—in signing the CTBT and accepting a freeze on its production of nuclear material.

---

[36] The Hyde Act, which allowed the US renew nuclear cooperation with India, was passed in December 2006 by the US Congress with nearly 80 per cent of the members of the House and Senate, including a large number of Democrats, voting in favour.

[37] For an Indian view of China's response to the Indo-US nuclear deal, see, B. Raman, 'China and the 123 Agreement: An Update', Paper No. 2330, South Asia Analysis Group, August 12, 2007, at http://www.southasiaanalysis.org/56papers2456paper2330.html (accessed on April 10, 2008).

[38] 'As two countries with advanced scientific capabilities, the two sides pledge to promote bilateral cooperation in civil nuclear energy, consistent with their respective international commitments'. See Joint Statement, Manmohan Singh and Wen Jiabao, 'A shared vision for the 21st Century of the Republic of India and the People's Republic of China', Beijing, January 14, 2008. pp. 3–4, at http://www.pmindia.nic.in/speech_14jan2k8-1.pdf (accessed on April 10, 2008).

They might also insist on the condition that civilian nuclear cooperation with India will cease in the event of a nuclear test. India, however, is unlikely to accept such conditions and has managed to get American understanding that in the event of a future Indian test, there will be political consultations on the nature and circumstances of the test.[39] The extraordinary political commitment of President Bush for the transformation of political relations with India and the willingness of the Democrats to rally behind him on this issue have helped overcome many technical difficulties that would have paralysed any agreement of the kind signed in July 2005.

CONCLUSION: DOMESTIC POLITICS AND NUCLEAR DIPLOMACY IN A UNIPOLAR WORLD

As the weaker of the two parties, and a country that is burdened by its past fears and anxieties, India's debate on the nuclear deal was entirely different. In India, the questions were two: whether India was giving away too much, in terms of its technological and foreign policy autonomy, to regain access to international nuclear energy cooperation; and how to balance restraints and rewards that come with becoming a part of the international order. Despite the widespread perception that the Indo-US civil nuclear initiative was loaded in favour of India, New Delhi has had greater difficulty in mobilising domestic political support for the nuclear deal. The opposition initially came from the atomic energy community, which for two generations had experienced nothing but sanctions from the US, and was deeply suspicious of American motivations and fearful that the foreign policy strategists were driving the agenda of nuclear reconciliation.

After he painstakingly succeeded in getting the atomic energy establishment on board, Prime Minister Manmohan Singh found himself ambushed by the right-wing BJP and the Communist partners of his ruling coalition. The BJP's opposition, framed in terms of the potential constraints on India's nuclear weapons programme, was entirely opportunistic. When in power, the BJP

---

[39] See Article 13 of the of the 123 Agreement, Agreement 2007, 'Agreement between the Government of India and the Government of the United States of America Concerning Peaceful Uses of Nuclear Energy', released by the Mnistry of External Affairs, New Delhi, August 1, 2007, http://www.mea.gov.in (accessed on April 10, 2008).

government led by Atal Bihari Vajpayee, immediately after conducting the tests, sought a nuclear reconciliation with the US. For the Communist left, the problem was ideological. They saw the nuclear deal with the US as a stepping stone for a new alliance with the US and the abandonment of India's traditional policy of non-alignment and were not going to let this happen under their watch. Although technical questions dominated India's domestic debate on the nuclear deal, the problem was essentially political. It was rooted in the fundamental weakness of the Congress-led government that depended on the Communist support for political survival. The fact that Manmohan Singh was not a political figure and was a nominee of the Congress leader Sonia Gandhi for prime ministership had limited his ability to effectively manage the government and the coalition. A stronger government would have easily pushed through the nuclear deal, without the angst that dogged the Manmohan Singh government.

Manmohan Singh obtained from Bush, on July 18, 2005, a goal that India had striven for since the emergence of the NPT left India in a nuclear limbo—neither a nuclear-weapons state nor a non-nuclear-weapons state. Perceptive scholarship had argued the essential revisionism of the Indian state on nuclear issues.[40] Yet, India's critique of the international order and its consistent support for the elimination of nuclear weapons have often been mistaken for a normative opposition to a 'discriminatory' global nuclear order. A closer reading of India's behaviour, however, suggests that considerations of realpolitik and a determination to retain its nuclear option to ensure a favourable balance of power have been the enduring features of the Indian policy. India's real concern was about ending the discrimination against itself rather than finding a genuinely equitable nuclear order. This was quite evident in the controversial Indian decision to vote against Iran at the IAEA Board of Governors in September 2005 and March 2006. India understood that a vote in favour of Iran or even an abstention would have doomed or limited the prospects of the nuclear deal being approved in the US Congress. In any case, contrary to the

---

[40] T.V. Paul, 'The Systematic Bases of India's Challenge to the Global Nuclear Order', *The Nonproliferation Review* 6:1 (Fall 1998), pp. 1–11; and D.R. Sardesai and Raju Thomas, eds, *Nuclear India in the 21st Century* (New York: Palgrave Macmillan, 2002).

many ideological criticism of the decision at home, India had no incentive in defending Iran's proliferation at the cost of its nuclear interests. Ever since it conducted the nuclear tests and proclaimed itself a nuclear-weapons power, India had doggedly pursued the objective of a nuclear reconciliation. From the outset, India understood that, in order to gain acceptance, it needed to alter its traditional nuclear defiance of the international system and offer support to various global non-proliferation measures. India's willingness to change many aspects of its traditional nuclear policy in the wake of 1998, reflected in the approach of two very diverse political coalitions that have governed from New Delhi since, demonstrated that realist considerations have tended to prevail over idealist arguments. The post-Pokharan changes in India's nuclear diplomacy have involved the endorsement of the basic objectives of the NPT after decades of demonising it, support to the non-proliferation regime in the form of stronger export control, tighter domestic law against proliferators, accepting regional arms-control through military/ nuclear CBMs with Pakistan and support to nuclear weapons free zones in Southeast Asia and Africa. Even on the controversial PSI, the problem has never been the principles relating to its legality but the management of domestic politics.[41] India's changing attitude to nuclear arms-control and non-proliferation were summed up by Jaswant Singh, the former external affairs minister, when he used the metaphor of getting into a crowded train on the Indian Railway system. The attitudes are very different when you are inside the train. India's shift in the attitude towards global nuclear arms control was not very different from that seen in China—which castigated the non-proliferation system in the 1960s and 1970s and was quite happy to support it as part of its own integration into the global order under Deng Xiaoping in the 1980s.[42] Unlike China, however, India's place as a nuclear-weapon state was not predetermined in the NPT; it had to find its way into the system through an extraordinary arrangement.

---

[41] For a comprehensive review of India's adaptation to the global arms-control regime after 1998, see, C. Raja Mohan, 'India's Nuclear Exceptionalism', in Sverre Lodgaard and Maerli, eds, *Nuclear Proliferation and International Security* (Abingdon: Routledge, 2007), pp. 152–71.
[42] Wendy Frieman, *China, Arms Control and Non-Proliferation* (London: Routledge Curzon, 2004).

India's problem was about finding the right terms, or put another way, of paying the least possible entry-price for joining the nuclear club. This depended on the circumstance and conditions of the negotiation rather than an inherent hostility to international arms-control arrangements. India's many flip-flops on the CTBT underscore this point. Under pressure to support regional arms control, India offered in the early 1990s to support the negotiations on the CTBT. When it confronted the question of testing nuclear weapons, it backed off from the CTBT. India put it back on the negotiating table after the nuclear tests as a bargaining chip with the Clinton administration. After the US Senate refused to ratify it at the end of 1999, India was unwilling to join the CTBT. Aware of the Bush administration's lack of enthusiasm for the treaty, India had no reason to go beyond a promise to maintain its unilateral moratorium on testing.

India's hard negotiating stance on nuclear issues can be seen as a part of its enduring strategic culture. India's tendency to overnegotiate, often at the cost to its own longer term interests has been noted.[43] Others have pointed to a notion of cultural superiority that 'holds India's importance to be singular and self-evident, an entitlement that does not need to be earned, proved or demonstrated'.[44] The sense that India deserves to be at the nuclear high table, that it had been discriminated unfairly all these years and that it will not accept any unfair conditions on its accommodation with the world are very much part of India's own national narrative on nuclear issues. The fractious domestic debates on nuclear policy at home and the pressure on the governments of the day to be seen as standing up to external pressure on nuclear issues have in fact helped India to negotiate for better terms with its international interlocutors. In negotiating with India, the US had to come to terms with the difficulties of coercing a large democracy into accepting difficult terms. This democracy effect, in fact, has meant that the Bush administration had to show extraordinary sensitivity to the political concerns of the Indian government in

---

[43] Amrita Narlikar, 'Peculiar Chauvinism or Strategic Calculation: Explaining the Negotiating Strategy of a Rising India', *International Affairs* 82:1 (January 2006), pp. 59–76.
[44] See, Rodney Jones, 'India's Strategic Culture', *Science Applications International Corporation* (Washington DC), October 31, 2006, p. 7.

the nuclear negotiations. India's ability to extract the best possible terms, or the least possible constraints on its nuclear programme, could not have been possible without the rapid economic growth in the first decade of the 21st century and the growing international perceptions of India's rise.

If India was a revisionist nuclear power, it needed a revolutionary hegemonic power to change the rules of the regime in its favour. While the nuclear empathy from Russia and France was welcome, India realised that the regime can be changed only through an initiative of the sole superpower, the US. Only an administration in the US that was willing to question the fundamentals of the global order and take political risks in changing the domestic laws could embark on such a venture. The Bush administration's readiness to rethink the nuclear system had a number of sources, especially the recognition that the old order was no longer capable of dealing with the new threats to international peace and security. But in terms of the attitude to India, it was the acknowledgement of an unfolding change in the global distribution of power and the value of a new relationship with a rising India in managing the future Asian balance that encouraged the Bush administration to break the mold.

If sustained empathy from President Bush was critical for the forward movement of the nuclear negotiations between India and the US, the new warmth in the Indo-US relationship would also turn out to be a domestic political problem in India. The framing of India's civilian nuclear initiative as part of a new partnership with the US saw the eventual political backlash from the Indian communists. As the Communists threatened to pull down the government if the Congress government implemented the nuclear deal, the Manmohan Singh government, at the end of 2007 and in 2008, had to demonstrate that the nuclear initiative was about cooperation with the international system as a whole and not just the US. During his visit to Beijing in January 2008, Singh had to reassure his Chinese audience as well as his communist partners at home that India will continue to pursue an independent foreign policy and will not align against China.[45] In a paradox, to implement the Indo-US nuclear deal, India had to signal a measure of distance

---

[45] Manmohan Singh, 'PM's Address at the China Academy of Social Sciences'.

from the US and downplay the significance of the strategic partnership with Washington. In that sense, the more Indian foreign policy changes, it largely remains the same. If and when India implements the nuclear initiative, it will be largely on its own terms and with least possible concessions to the global nuclear order and minimal adjustments to its vaunted independent foreign policy. By any measure, that will go down as a huge diplomatic triumph for India's foreign policy.

4

India and the Challenge of Global Terrorism: The 'Long War' and Competing Domestic Visions*

TIMOTHY D. HOYT

> *Terrorism is the greatest national security threat our country faces today. Combating this threat presents unique and unprecedented challenges. The tactics adopted by terrorists, often with the assistance of State-sponsors, require constant study and analysis.*
> —Indian Prime Minister, Manmohan Singh.[1]

India, like the US, confronts terrorist threats from a wide range of sources. While considering how it will manage the threat of global terrorism, however, India also must deal with a fundamental problem—the definition of and response to this threat is driven primarily by US policy and operations in the aftermath of 9/11. India's future policies regarding global terrorism will be shaped by its emerging relationship with the US, by competing domestic visions of India's role in the world and by gradual shifts in India's perception of the terrorist threat.

India has, regrettably, abundant experience with terrorist threats. These threats emerge from a variety of sources—ethnic and religious intolerance, competing nationalist visions, economic disparities, rejection of caste and older forms of social order, revolutionary ideologies and transnational or international support.[2] As a result

---

* The views expressed in this essay are those of the author and are not the policies of the US Navy, the Department of Defense, or any other branch of the US government.
[1] Dr. Manmohan Singh, Prime Minister of India, cited in *Doctrine for Sub Conventional Operations* (Shimla: Headquarters Army Training Command, December 2006), p. 1.
[2] An earlier perspective on this problem is Timothy D. Hoyt, 'The War on Terrorism: Implications for South Asia', in Devin T. Hagerty, ed, *South Asia in World Politics* (Lanham, MD: Rowman & Littlefield, 2005), pp. 281–300. For an extensive database of terrorist problems in India and its region, see the South Asia Terrorism Portal, http://www.satp.org (accessed on November 23, 2007).

of its experience with jihadist groups in Kashmir, for example, Indians could legitimately argue that they had been fighting some manifestation of a global terrorist movement literally since their independence.[3] Since 1989, India has confronted a terrorist threat actively assisted by both Pakistan and transnational non-state actors affiliated with Al Qaeda and Associated Movements (AQAM) in Kashmir.[4] India's perspective on the challenge of global terrorism, therefore, pre-dates US concerns with this issue and it differs substantially from American policy.

Nevertheless, because the current American struggle with global terrorist threats is a dominant issue in the international arena, India must consider and adapt to US perspectives. This chapter, therefore, is laid out in three sections. Section one contains a brief discussion of US perspectives on the war on global terror (increasingly known as 'The Long War').[5] Section two will examine three different Indian approaches to the emerging international system. Section three will assess the potential impact of these approaches on Indo-US relations in the context of the 'Long War'. The conclusion will re-address the likelihood and level of Indo-US cooperation, based on recent events and trends and the possibility for a gradual shift towards a more collaborative definition of the war on terror and a greater level of mutual accommodation and support.

---

[3] See Praveen Swami, *India, Pakistan and the Secret Jihad* (London: Routledge, 2006).

[4] On Pakistani assistance to Taliban and AQAM and links to Kashmir, see Ahmed Rashid, *Taliban* (New Haven: Yale University Press, 2000); Steve Coll, *Ghost Wars* (New York: Penguin, 2004); Owen Bennett Jones, *Pakistan: Eye of the Storm* (New Haven: Yale University Press, 2002); Mary Anne Weaver, *Pakistan: In the Shadow of Jihad and Afghanistan* (New York: Farrar, Straus & Geroux, 2002). Pakistani accounts include Husain Haqqani, *Pakistan: Between Mosque and Military* (Washington, DC: Carnegie Endowment for International Peace, 2005) and Hassan Abbas, *Pakistan's Drift into Extremism: Allah, the Army, and America's War on Terror* (London: M.E. Sharpe, 2005).

[5] This discussion is distilled from an ongoing series of US National Security documents, including (among others), *The National Security Strategy of the United States of America* (September 2002), *National Strategy for Combating Terrorism* (February 2003), *National Military Strategy of the US of America* (2004), *The National Defense Strategy of the US of America* (March 2005), *The National Counterintelligence Strategy of the US* (March 2005), *Victory in Iraq* (Washington, DC: National Security Council, November 2005), *Quadrennial Defense Review Report* (Washington, DC: Department of Defence, 6 February 2006), *The National Security Strategy of the US of America* (March 2006), *National Strategy for Combating Terrorism* (September 2006).

'THE LONG WAR': AMERICA'S WAR AGAINST GLOBAL TERRORISM

The September 11, 2001 terrorist attacks on New York and Washington shattered the complacent assumptions of a generation of policy-makers and analysts. The apparent vulnerability of the American homeland to sophisticated attacks forced terrorism to the top of the US national security agenda. Within days, President Bush had declared a 'war on terror'—a concept that continues to shape US national security policy today, even as the core notions of that conflict have evolved and been refined.

Other nations expressed sympathy, bewilderment and amazement at the rapidity and scale of the US response. Many states had experienced the wave of terror, both transnational and domestic, that emerged in the 1970s and 1980s. Their experiences, in many cases, suggested that treating the threat as a war was an inappropriate reaction.[6] For the US, however, 9/11 was not a domestic terrorist act, but an act of external aggression, launched from foreign soil. In this respect, it *was* a war—and required retaliation by military instruments and the other tools of foreign policy.[7] Operation Enduring Freedom, the liberation of Afghanistan from Taliban rule, constituted the opening salvo in the war on terror and received broad international support.

International support for the conflict declined significantly in 2002 as US strategy and policy evolved. President Bush's declaration of the 'axis of evil' identified states as the primary malefactors in the international system.[8] His speech at West Point in June 2002 articulated a new emphasis on preventive or pre-emptive military operations.[9] By August 2002, administration officials were publicly mulling the possibility of war with Iraq and the

---

[6] Michael Howard, 'What's in a Name? How to Fight Terrorism', *Foreign Affairs* 81:4 (January/February 2002), pp. 8–13.
[7] Timothy D. Hoyt, 'Military Force', in Audrey Kurth Cronin and James M. Ludes, eds, *Attacking Terrorism: Elements of a Grand Strategy* (Washington, DC: Georgetown University Press, 2004), pp. 162–85.
[8] State of the Union Address, January 2002, at http://www.whitehouse.gov/news/releases/2002/01/20020129-11.html (accessed on November 23, 2007).
[9] President George W. Bush, Graduation Speech at West Point, June 2002, at http://www.whitehouse.gov/news/releases/2002/06/20020601-3.html (accessed on November 23, 2007).

September 2002 *National Security Strategy of the United States* emphasised preventive war and identified the nexus of terrorists, rogue states and weapons of mass destruction (WMD) as the primary targets for the war on terror.[10] Iraq became a major target for US efforts, given its thirteen-year record of noncompliance with UN resolutions. The US arranged for UN Security Council Resolution 1441, calling for renewed inspections of suspected Iraqi WMD facilities, to be passed in November 2002.[11] A subsequent effort to get the UN Security Council to approve military action failed in February 2003 and US military operations against Iraq were initiated without a UN resolution.[12] Operation Iraqi Freedom (OIF), launched in March 2003, generated significant international opposition and, over time, a profound evolution in US definitions of what was still (at that time) called the 'GWOT' (Global War on Terror, or Terrorism).

The suspected nexus between Iraq, terrorist networks and WMD remains inconclusive at best.[13] The on-going multi-dimensional insurgency in Iraq continues to shape US definitions of the war on terror. Iraq became the central front in the war on terror in the eyes of both the US and Al Qaeda—a conclusion that has not been widely accepted in the international community.[14] Although unilateral preventive operations have not been eliminated from the US list of options, they have been publicly de-emphasised and

---

[10] *National Security Strategy of the United States*, September 2002, at http://www.whitehouse.gov/nsc/nss.pdf (accessed on November 23, 2007).

[11] See United Nations Security Council Resolution 1441 (November 2002), at http://daccessdds.un.org/doc/UNDOC/GEN/N02/682/26/PDF/N0268226.pdf (accessed on November 23, 2007).

[12] See the speech of Secretary of State Colin Powell to the UN Security Council, February 5, 2003, at http://www.whitehouse.gov/news/releases/2003/02/20030205-1.html (accessed on November 23, 2007).

[13] The most comprehensive evaluation of Iraq's WMD programmes remains the *Comprehensive Revised Report with Addendums on Iraq's Weapons of Mass Destruction (Duelfer Report)* (Washington, DC: Government Printing Office, September 2004), available at http://www.gpoaccess.gov/duelfer/index.html (accessed on December 5, 2007).

[14] See, for example, President Bush's speech of June 28, 2005, at http://www.whitehouse.gov/news/releases/2005/06/20050628-7.html (accessed on November 23, 2007). Some statements from Al Qaeda suggest that their leadership agrees. See the comments of White House Press Secretary Tony Snow, May 3, 2007, at http://www.whitehouse.gov/news/releases/2007/05/20070503-6.html (accessed on November 23, 2007).

are limited in practice by the on-going requirements for a heavy US ground presence in Iraq.

What, then, are the defining elements of the constantly evolving US war on terror? For the purposes of this analysis, they will be deliberately oversimplified into two key concerns. First, what are the core threats to both the US and the international community? If it is, as the US now calls it, a 'Long War', why is it long and what is the nature of the threat? Second, who are the actors involved? Who are the primary adversaries and how does the US plan to oppose and defeat them? These will be the key elements in any discussion of India's response to global terrorism, because US visions will tend to shape, if not drive, the definition of the problem.

INDIA AND AMERICA'S 'LONG WAR': EARLY REVIEWS

Many states, India not the least among them, may have viewed America's sudden obsession with global terrorism with a certain degree of irony. As mentioned above, India (like other states) had suffered from terrorism in various forms for decades before 9/11. Nevertheless, India's response reflects not only its interpretation of the nature of the problem and its seriousness, but also its willingness to work with the US against potentially common problems on a regional or global scale.

Given the history of Indo-US relations, close cooperation between these two states should not be taken for granted.[15] Indian elites view India as a significant power and viewed the US with suspicion both during and immediately after the Cold War (this will be discussed further below). Early in the Cold War, India rebuffed American and British efforts to bring it into an anti-Communist alliance. It opted instead for non-alignment, which took an increasingly pro-Soviet tilt with the 1971 Treaty of Peace, Friendship and Cooperation and the more embarrassing refusal to condemn the Soviet invasion of Afghanistan at the United

---

[15] An excellent account of the Indo-US relationship is Dennix Kux, *India and the United States: Estranged Democracies, 1941–1991* (Wahington, DC: National Defense University Press, 1992). A more up-to-date account is Stephen P. Cohen, *India: Emerging Power* (Washington, DC: Brookings, 2001). For a complimentary account of US policy in the region focusing on India's primary regional adversary, see Dennis Kux, *The US and Pakistan, 1947–2000: Disenchanted Allies* (Baltimore: The Johns Hopkins University Press, 2001).

Nations in 1979–80. India regarded US non-proliferation efforts, including the Nuclear Non-Proliferation Treaty (NPT), as 'nuclear apartheid', and bristled at what it considered unfair sanctions after its nuclear test in 1974.[16] The only truly warm period in Indo-US relations was during the Kennedy administration, but even this was partly the result of Indian desire for US military assistance after its disastrous defeat at the hands of China in the 1962 Sino-Indian War.

In the post-Cold War environment, however, there were signs of a possible thaw on both sides of the relationship. Joint military exercises began in the 1990s. President Clinton was determined to create a more positive relationship, but ran afoul of domestic political distractions, Indian opposition to US international non-proliferation efforts, and also the attempted (in late 1995) and successful (in 1998) nuclear tests conducted by India. Nevertheless, before the end of his final year in office, he enjoyed an extended visit to India culminating in a Joint Vision Statement on March 21, 2000.[17] During the Presidential Campaign in the year 2000, Bush advisor Condoleeza Rice made a point of singling out India as a key great power with whom the US must have closer relations.[18] Indo-US cooperation has accelerated under the Bush administration. It included a major Presidential visit in 2006 and a new nuclear agreement which circumvents non-proliferation efforts that would limit India's civilian nuclear sector.[19]

---

[16] This concept was most famously articulated after the 1998 nuclear tests in the very influential journal *Foreign Affairs* by the Senior Advisor on Defence and Foreign Affairs to Prime Minister Vajpayee. See Jaswant Singh, 'Against Nuclear Apartheid', *Foreign Affairs* 77:5 (September/October 1998), pp. 41–52, at http://www.foreignaffairs.org/19980901faessay1416/jaswant-singh/against-nuclear-apartheid.html (accessed on November 23, 2007).

[17] See *Joint India–US Statement* (March 21, 2000), at http://www.indianembassy.org/indusrel/clinton_india/joint_india_us_statement_mar_21_2000.htm (accessed on November 23, 2007).

[18] See Condoleeza Rice, 'Campaign 2000: Promoting the American Interest', *Foreign Affairs* 79:1 (January/February 2000), pp. 45–62, at http://www.foreignaffairs.org/20000101faessay5/condoleezza-rice/campaign-2000-promoting-the-national-interest.html (accessed on November 23, 2007).

[19] For an up-to-date account of the evolution of the Indo-US relationship, see K. Alan Kronstadt, *CRS Report for Congress: India–US Relations*, RL 33529 (Washington, DC: Library of Congress, Congressional Research Service, updated October 2, 2007), at http://italy.usembassy.gov/pdf/other/RL33529.pdf (accessed on November 23, 2007).

Despite the positive direction of Indo-US relations, however, Indian cooperation with the US war on terror—defined in terms acceptable to the US—has been selective. India offered the use of several military bases to the US in September 2001, to be used for carrying out military operations against Afghanistan. This offer was literally unprecedented—an indication of profound Indian sympathy as well as a demonstration of continued intent to improve the relationship. In November 2001, President Bush and Prime Minister Vajpayee agreed that terrorism constituted a major threat to both countries and to efforts to build freedom and democracy around the world.[20] More recently, both states agreed that defeating terrorism and religious extremism is a major shared interest.[21]

However, India has proven more reluctant to take part in coalitions supporting US military action in the war on terror. India did not join the coalition against Iraq, although it reportedly considered sending a contingent of ground forces to Iraq for post-conflict stability and peacekeeping.[22] India has not been strongly supportive of US efforts to pressure Iran in 2006–07. Indian firms have been allowed to transfer chemical and possibly nuclear technology to Iranian weapons programmes and there are reportedly low-level links between the Indian and Iranian armed forces.[23] Iran remains an important source of energy for India, which has shown itself unwilling to endanger traditional ties to the Middle East (including Iraq, before 2003) to support America's more aggressive efforts to prosecute the war on terror.

---

[20] See 'Joint Statement of US, India on Terrorism, Bilateral Ties', November 9, 2001, at http://www.globalsecurity.org/military/library/news/2001/11/mil-011109-usia05c.htm (accessed on November 23, 2007).
[21] See 'New Framework for the US–India Defence Relationship', (June 28, 2005), at http://www.indianembassy.org/press_release/2005/June/31.htm (accessed on November 23, 2007).
[22] See, for example, 'India: No troops to Iraq', July 14, 2003, 7:58 a.m. EDT, at http://www.cnn.com/2003/WORLD/asiapcf/south/07/14/india.iraq/; 'Iraq is not Vietnam, But…', *Time Magazine*, June 24, 2003, at http://www.time.com/time/columnist/karon/article/0,9565,460834,00.html (both accessed on November 23, 2007). For an acerbic Indian perspective, see 'And the Boys Go to Babylon', *Indian Express*, June 22, 2003, at http://www.indianexpress.com/india-news/full_story.php?content_id=26225 (accessed on November 23, 2007).
[23] *CRS Report for Congress: India–US Relations*, pp. 39–41. See also K. Alan Kronstadt, *India–Iran Relations and US Interests* (August 2, 2006), at http://italy.usembassy.gov/pdf/other/RS22486.pdf (accessed on November 23, 2007).

One might conclude, therefore, that the Indian governments to date have agreed with the US that terrorism poses a threat. Indian governments have not necessarily agreed with the US definition of the key state supporters of terrorism, on crucial proliferation issues, or with the broader concept of a 'war on terror'. These issues are particularly important to India as it manages both its emergence as a growing power in the international community and its emergence as a US partner in that international community. Next section of this chapter will examine the perspectives of Indian foreign policy elites regarding the emerging international environment and potential opportunities or constraints on closer collaboration in the near term.

INDIAN VISIONS OF THE EMERGING WORLD ORDER

As India emerges as a more significant political and economic actor, it must confront and adapt to an international system still dominated by a single superpower—the US. India is a revisionist power—as it rises, it will seek an increasing role in the international system. How Indian elites view the international system and the US role, will profoundly affect both Indo-US relations and India's participation in the global war on terror.

Understanding the leading domestic and intellectual approaches to Indian foreign and security policy, therefore, is important in anticipating both emerging Indian policy and potential conflicts with the US and other key actors. A leading Indian scholar has identified three schools of thought among Indian elites and academics—Nehruvianism, neoliberalism and hyperrealism. Each will be discussed briefly below and then used as a tool to examine possible Indian responses and preferences in the effort to combat global terrorism.[24]

---

[24] This method is intended to be illustrative rather than comprehensive, demonstrating the range of elite opinions in India today. These elite approaches are found in the writings of Kanti Bajpai, specifically 'Indian Strategic Culture', in Michael R. Chambers, ed, *South Asia in 2020: Future Strategic Balances and Alliances* (Carlisle, PA: Strategic Studies Institute, November 2002), pp. 245–303. For other approaches to Indian strategic culture and elite perception, see T. V. Paul, ed, *The Indo-Pakistan Conflict: An Enduring Rivalry* (Cambridge: Cambridge University Press, 2005); and Baldev Raj Nayar and T.V. Paul, *India in the World Order: Searching for Major-Power Status* (Cambridge: Cambridge University Press, 2003).

Nehruvianism

This approach is rooted in the unique and highly moralistic Indian struggle for independence, led by Mohandas Gandhi, Jawaharlal Nehru and the Indian Congress Party. Nehruvians accept that large-scale conflict and violence are a regular part of international affairs, in the absence of some overarching global authority, but believe that war should be the last resort. They believe that the state of anarchy and mistrust that characterises international relations can be mitigated through international organisations and agreements, through negotiations and cooperation and, most of all, through mutual understanding. Nehruvians believe that premising policy on the balance of power and the acquisition of military capabilities are wasteful and futile—the resources spent on the military would be better utilised for more positive aims and balances of power do not prevent catastrophic war. Nehruvians see communication, contact and negotiation as the keys to the transformation of the international system.[25]

Nehruvianism was the dominant world-view of post-Independence India—a view shaped by the colonial experience, by the Indian National Congress' decision not to fully endorse the Allies in the Second World War and by a fundamentally idealistic view of international politics. Nehruvianism was antagonistic towards the US, which it saw as the heir of European colonial attitudes, and suspicious of US leadership. This viewpoint is no longer the predominant view of Indian policy-makers, but remains entrenched in both Indian academic writings and also in the bureaucracy and intelligentsia that are the products of Indian academe. As a result, this perspective continues to have some influence on Indian policy formulation.

Neoliberalism

This approach is well represented in Western theoretical literature. Neoliberals believe that both economic power and military power are vital to national security and well-being and that economic power can substitute for military power in many respects. The role of force, in this view, is declining in the international system, as globalised economies drive states to levels of interdependence that

---
[25] Bajpai, 'Indian Strategic Culture', pp. 251–52.

make war less likely. Free markets, mutual gain and globalisation are seen as the driving forces to transform the international system into one of greater cooperation and less anarchy.[26]

Neoliberalism now represents the dominant policy perspective of Indian policy-makers in all major parties. The Bharatiya Janata Party (BJP) initially opposed globalisation in the early 1990s, but gradually accepted neoliberalism as the Indian economy boomed. Neoliberalism is not reflexively antagonistic to the US, but is concerned about US decisions to act in non-neoliberal ways (preventive war being an obvious example). Neoliberals make a distinction between the US as a global economic enabler, an Indian partner and a hegemonic leader—the last being an issue of relatively greater concern.

Hyperrealism

Hyperrealists form a small but influential group in Indian society, often grounded in a rejection of Nehruvianism or a justification for the development of Indian nuclear-weapon capabilities. Hyperrealists see international relations as an ongoing cycle of conflict and violence. Good relations with states are simply transitory phenomena—the only guarantee of safety is through military strength and the threat or use of violence. Hyperrealists reject the reliability of international law, agreements and organisations and support increased defence spending as a means both of stimulating the domestic economy and of assuring national security. They argue that military power and especially nuclear capability, is more important than economic power, because a strong military will set the conditions for the economy to grow, but a strong economy cannot be depended on to defend the state.

Hyperrealism is *not* related to a particular political party, although it is sometimes associated with the more nationalistic elements of the BJP. It *is* often associated with a distrust of the US, which is suspected of encircling India, enabling its enemies and containing its 'natural' growth. Hyperrealism is an insular, limited, but still influential perspective on Indian security matters. It has not been significantly defused, either by the open development of an Indian nuclear arsenal or by the recent US-Indian nuclear agreement—which hyperrealists view with great suspicion.

---

[26] Bajpai, 'Indian Strategic Culture', pp. 252–53.

Although most hyperrealists view China as a long-term competitor and serious threat, many argue that India requires a nuclear deterrent against the US, and some even argue in favour of a India–China–Russia axis to balance US power.[27]

THE CHALLENGE OF GLOBAL TERROR: THREATS AND THE NATURE OF THE WAR

Using a deliberately simplified framework for assessing the Long War, the two key elements driving US policy were identified earlier as the nature of the threat and the nature of the actors. These elements shape US objectives or ends in the Long War and also the ways and means used to pursue those objectives.

Nature of the Threat

The critical elements shaping the US response in the war on terror are the proliferation of WMD—chemical, biological, nuclear and radiological weapons—and the fanatical ideology driving those who wish the US and its allies ill. Although the threat of nuclear annihilation is relatively much lower than during the Cold War, the potential threat of nuclear use on US or allied soil—by a state or non-state actor (see below)—may actually be higher than it was in the Cold War. This emerging WMD threat to US territory was highlighted by the World Trade Center attacks—a 'weapon of mass effect' that killed 3000 people and had the equivalent effect of a one kiloton nuclear detonation. The WMD threat is thus a major driver in US policy and strategy for this conflict.

An additional element in US decision making is the interpretation of the conflict as a protracted ideological struggle—hence the new title of 'Long War',[28] US analysts liken the struggle to the Cold War or the Second World War, even going so far as to (briefly) refer to radical Islamists as 'Islamofascists'. The assumption that the

---
[27] Bajpai, 'Indian Strategic Culture', p. 256. A volume with a wide range of perspectives, including those of some hyperrealists, is Bharat Karnad, ed, *Future Imperilled: India's Security in the 1990s and Beyond* (New Delhi: Viking, 1994).
[28] See *Quadrennial Defense Review Report 2006* (26 February 2006), at http://www.defenselink.mil/qdr/report/Report20060203.pdf (accessed on November 23, 2007).

ideology driving the enemy is fanatic, highly motivational (justifying suicide attacks) and based on religious commitments suggest that any conflict will be protracted and difficult. Some refer to Samuel Huntington's *Clash of Civilisations* (1996) to describe the conflict, but others might argue that this is what the US wants to avoid—that a clever strategy will disarm radical Islamist extremists without further polarising Islam and the West.[29]

Potential Actors

The actors in this struggle can be divided into two categories—potential adversaries and potential allies. The initial US response to the attacks of 9/11—'You are either with us or against us'—has become more nuanced, especially with the difficulties of maintaining coalition forces in Iraq and Afghanistan. This has been achieved, at least in part, by a more flexible attitude regarding adversaries and allies, narrowing the definition of the former and expanding the definition of the latter.

Potential Adversaries: The term covers a range of possible non-state and state candidates. They could include some or all terrorist groups (hence the early use of the term 'war on terrorism'); a smaller subset of particular groups based on targets, ideology or transnational links; or even a range of states—those passively supporting terrorism; those with WMD and suspect motives and those actively linked with particular groups. Not surprisingly, different definitions of the primary adversaries will produce different strategies to combat the challenge. They will also pose different obstacles to Indian cooperation.

Potential Allies: This term includes states actively supporting US military efforts abroad; those providing support for specific operations; those providing access and/or logistic support and those supporting the war on terror through non-military means

---

[29] Huntington's argument about the importance of civilisational differences in shaping future international conflict is available in both article and book form. See Samuel P. Huntington, 'The Clash of Civilisations?', *Foreign Affairs* 72:3 (Summer 1993), pp. 22–49, at http://www.foreignaffairs.org/19930601faessay5188/samuel-p-huntington/the-clash-of-civilisations.html (accessed on November 23, 2007). The argument is expanded in Samuel P. Huntington, *The Clash of Civilisations and the Remaking of World Order* (New York: Touchstone, 1997).

(including intelligence and law enforcement cooperation, diplomatic support, economic assistance to areas of concern, etc.). To complicate matters further, some states exist in both camps. Pakistan and Saudi Arabia, for example, are both traditional sources of radical Islamist extremists and also vital sources of assistance in pursuing Al Qaeda and similar groups.

THE 'LONG WAR' THROUGH INDIAN EYES
Nehruvianism

Like many Europeans, Nehruvians would be perplexed by the US decision to declare war on terror. Nehruvians view terror as a tactic—an unacceptable tactic, given its frequent focus on non-combatants—and ultimately a sign of weakness. After all, organisations turn to violence when they are frustrated and cannot achieve their aims through legitimate means. Declaring war on them gives them stature—a reward for illegitimate activity—and also leads to organised violence and invasion, which inevitably leads to unacceptable levels of non-combatant suffering.

Nehruvians take a very different approach to the major threats—ideology and WMD. The radical ideology of Islamist movements could be undermined by a concerted effort at cooperation—after all, Islam is derived from both Judaism and Christianity and has co-existed with Hinduism and Zoroastrianism in the Indian subcontinent and Persia, respectively. Declaring war on 'Islamists' veers dangerously close, from the Nehruvian perspective, to declaring war on Islam—essentially enacting the clash of civilisations. Nehruvians would see the roots of the current terrorist activity in other causes—social, economic and political—which are inherently more amenable to negotiation, cooperation and peaceful resolution. The WMD issue can be resolved by peaceful cooperation—starting with the West's fulfilling its obligation of nuclear disarmament under the NPT. The Chemical Weapons Convention and Biological Weapons Convention are more certain means of eliminating a WMD threat than any pre-emptive or preventive military activity. This is an area rich with possibilities for international cooperation—a perspective shared by many idealists in the US.[30]

---

[30] See, for example, Graham Allison, *Nuclear Terrorism: The Ultimate Preventable Catastrophe* (New York: Henry Holt, 2004), which suggests a ten-step programme for keeping nuclear weapons out of the hands of terrorists.

A Nehruvian approach to adversaries would focus on the distinction between state and non-state actors. States are amenable to diplomacy, negotiation and cooperation—it is all a matter of finding what they want to stop supporting terrorism, and making a deal. States that provide soft support for terrorism, like sanctuary or rhetorical support, clearly also have agendas that are resolvable through other means. In some cases, economic assistance may be necessary to help create good governance and a more robust infrastructure to deny terrorists sympathy and support. Economic instruments will also be fundamental to resolving dissatisfaction and resentments that lead young men and women into terrorism. Non-state actors that persist in terrorist activities can be dealt with as a law enforcement problem, and the historical evidence of successful cooperation in this field is quite strong.

Nehruvians would focus on cooperation and common approaches as the easiest and most effective means of resolving the terrorist problem. They would view the US with some concern, because of its insistence on military options, its violent unilateralist tendencies, its apparent rejection of international organisations and commitments and its use of 'preventive war'—a contradiction in terms to a Nehruvian mindset. A particular issue of concern would be the indications that the US sought to create or maintain a role of global military and economic predominance.[31]

Neoliberalism

Neoliberalism represents the largest portion of the Indian elite's view of the world today. As India rises economically, it also rises on the international stage, shedding the diplomatic detritus of the Cold War. Economic power converts into social stability and security, allowing India to represent itself not only as an ancient civilisation, but also as a model for other developing countries

---

[31] This was a major international concern with *The National Security Strategy of the United States 2002*. Other US studies have raised similar concerns, particularly the Defence Planning Guidance of 1992. See 'US Strategy Plan Calls for Insuring No Rivals Develop a One Superpower World', *New York Times*, March 8, 1992, at http://work.colum.edu/~amiller/wolfowitz1992.htm (accessed on November 24, 2007). See also James Mann, *Rise of the Vulcans: The History of Bush's War Cabinet* (New York: Viking, 2004) for a discussion of US policy aims in the early 21st century.

and, in particular, as a model for moderating and co-existing with Islam (since India has the third-largest Muslim population in the world).[32] As a result, neoliberals view the rise of radical Islam with concern but not alarm. Some of India's most booming economic sectors, including information technology, are emerging in areas with heavy Muslim populations, like Hyderabad. Despite an eighteen-year struggle in Kashmir, militant forces there still rely heavily on foreign fighters and violence has not spread more broadly into the Indian Muslim population. Islamist extremism, neoliberals might argue, is best combated through economic development. Military responses will antagonise Muslims, justify violent resistance and increase recruiting efforts.

Neoliberal approaches to WMD will also look at the problem as one of cooperation and of economic importance. India's civilian nuclear programme is closely linked to its nuclear weapons programme (although the US–India nuclear deal will begin to separate these sectors) because of India's desperate need for energy.[33] Non-proliferation must be non-discriminatory and cannot disadvantage India economically. Neoliberals will focus on some proliferation threats more than others. Pakistan's uncertain nuclear control capabilities must be enhanced as they are the most likely source of terrorist WMD (and the most serious threat of a terrorist WMD strike on India).[34] China's notorious reluctance to abide by non-proliferation norms must be brought under control. Both may be amenable to economic persuasion—China may soon become India's

---

[32] There remain, however, substantial obstacles to India's use as a global economic model. See Gurchuran Das, 'Unshackling the Economy', *Foreign Affairs* 85:4 (July/August 2006), pp. 2–16.
[33] For pessimistic perspectives on India's civilian nuclear energy programme, see John Stephenson and Peter Tynan, 'Will the US–India Civil Nuclear Cooperation Initiative Light India?', pp. 15–70, and M. V. Ramanna, 'Nuclear Power in India: Failed Past, Dubious Future', pp. 71–98, both in Henry Sokolski, ed, *Gauging US-Indian Strategic Cooperation* (Carlisel, PA: Strategic Studies Institute, March 2007).
[34] See Peter R. Lavoy, 'Pakistan's Nuclear Posture: Security and Survivability', at http://www.npec-web.org/Frameset.asp?PageType=Single&PDFFile=20070121–Lavoy-PakistanNuclearPosture&PDFFolder=Essays (accessed on November 23, 2007). See also *Oxford Analytica*, 'Pakistan: Instability Raises Nuclear Concerns' (August 31, 2007), at http://www.belfercenter.org/files/Pakistan%20Nuclear%20Hassan%20Abbas.pdf (accessed on November 23, 2007).

largest trading partner, which has helped improve relations, and neoliberals would hope that economic development and, perhaps, democratisation of Pakistan would contribute to put an end to anti-Indian feelings and terrorist support.

Neoliberals would reject the concept of the 'axis of evil' and US-identified rogue regimes. North Korea is a concern, but clearly is not ideologically connected with Islamist terrorists. The North Korean threat lies more in its proliferation of missiles and WMD to Pakistan—an issue which might be addressed as part of the Agreed Framework and other efforts to buy off North Korean WMD capability. Iran is an important trading partner for India and a source of energy. Unlike Afghanistan, which actively harboured Al Qaeda until 2002, and Pakistan, which facilitated training and support of AQAM groups in return for a steady supply of militants to infiltrate into Kashmir, Iran is not easily linked to AQAM. While it does support terrorist movements and even terrorist movements that attack India's friend Israel, it is a more manageable threat amenable to negotiation and trade. After all, Iran has significant quantities of WMD—chemical weapons—and could easily have transferred them to terrorist groups if it desired.

From a neoliberal perspective, the war in Iraq is unrelated to the war on terror. Iraq, again, had been a friend to India and had provided no justifiable rationale for US preventive war. India did consider providing peacekeeping troops for post-OIF operations, which is compatible with neoliberal thinking (especially if they were under UN command), but the bloody aftermath of OIF only verifies the wisdom of avoiding involvement. The major state supporter of terrorism from a neoliberal point of view is Pakistan. While neoliberals accept the US rationale for not prosecuting the war on terror in Islamabad, they view both Pakistan and Afghanistan as key sources of Islamic extremism and the logical focus of coalition counter-terror efforts.

Neoliberal views of allies, again, focus on non-military concerns. Neoliberals see the US as an indispensable player in India's emergence in the international system but they remain unwilling to commit military forces to US adventures or create a formal alliance. They view India as a partner to the US, view preventive war and unilateral military activity as destabilising and dangerous and are suspicious of conspicuous efforts to assert or proclaim US predominance in the international system—something they see as a temporary phenomenon that will be superseded by a shift towards a more multilateral balance of power in the future.[35] As a result, while neoliberals are unlikely to be antagonistic towards the US, it would not be surprising to find them in significant disagreement with the US on certain core issues.

Hyperrealism

Hyperrealists share many common ideas with American policy makers, particularly regarding the utility of military force in the international system and the potential value of preventive war. They also, however, viscerally reject ideas of a 'natural strategic partnership'. Hyperrealists see Islamic fundamentalism as a major ideological threat to India and to world order and argue that India has in fact been engaged in a 'long war' of its own for decades (some might argue centuries). They would point to Islamist terrorism in Bangladesh, Kashmir, Mumbai and Delhi as evidence that the focus of this threat may be directed primarily at India and South Asia. WMD is a particularly touchy issue for hyperrealists, who demand an expanded Indian nuclear weapons programme. While no hyperrealist would want a terrorist to procure WMD, they also would not want to see any limits placed on India's ability to procure and utilise the necessary technologies in sufficient amount. They see the source of 'bad' WMD as two-fold—Pakistan but, most particularly, China (which is responsible for Pakistan's arsenal).

This leads to significant differences with US policy regarding the adversary. The US sees Pakistan as part of the solution. Hyperrealists see Pakistan as a very significant part of the problem. They would question why the US identifies only four Pakistani militant groups as 'Foreign Terrorist Organisations' when Indian sources identify at least 32 Pakistani terrorist groups.[36] They would point to Pakistani links with Islamist militants in Kashmir, terrorists in Punjab in the 1980s and 1990s, terrorist movements in Bangladesh and the attempted decapitation attack on India's Parliament on December 13, 2001. They would note Pakistan's Inter-Service

---

[35] An excellent assessment of rising India is C. Raja Mohan, 'India and the Balance of Power', *Foreign Affairs* 85: 4 (July/August 2006), pp. 17–32.
[36] *Foreign Terrorist Organisations (FTOs)* (Fact Sheet, Office of Counterterrorism, Washington, DC, October 11, 2005); South Asia Terrorism Portal http://www.satp.org (accessed on May 12, 2008).

Intelligence (ISI) links with known AQAM groups through 9/11 and the continuing presence of AQAM and Taliban militants on the Afghan-Pakistan border. Hyperrealists would, in fact, argue strongly that Pakistan was a more reasonable target for American preventive or pre-emptive assault in 2003, given its proven nuclear arsenal and close ties to AQAM groups. They identify the 'axis of evil' very differently from the US—they would see it as China, Pakistan and, perhaps, North Korea.

Hyperrealists reject US notions of global hegemony or military predominance and place a high priority on acquiring a robust nuclear force that will deter the US as well as regional adversaries. US unilateral activity is not seen as anything out of the ordinary, but it also suggests that India could be a target and, therefore, requires a nuclear deterrent capability against potential US hostility. Hyperrealists would reserve for India the same right to act unilaterally and indeed to launch a preventive war against Pakistan if necessary—a possibility the Indian government considered seriously on several occasions during the 2001–02 crisis.[37] They might consider working in coalition with the US, but would only begin to trust US promises and commitments if India were in a position of both economic and military strength.

INDIA, THE US AND THE WAR ON TERROR

Like many other nations, India views the US war on terror with a combination of sympathy and concern. For the US, 9/11 came as a brutal surprise—a literal paradigm shift in the nature of threats and the danger to the homeland. For Indians, terrorism and insurgency have been constants in the region for almost thirty years—ethnic and religious terror in Punjab, caste based terror in Bihar, on-going ethnic and religious troubles in the Northeast and a brutal and protracted struggle with Muslim separatists in Kashmir, to name just a few.[38]

---

[37] See, for example, Rahul Bedi, 'The Military Dynamics', *Frontline* 19:12 (June 8–21, 2002), at http://www.hinduonnet.com/fline/fl1912/19120100.htm (accessed on November 24, 2007).

[38] For an extensive database of terrorist problems in India and its region, see the South Asia Terrorism Portal, http://www.satp.org (accessed on May 12, 2008)

All three Indian world-views reflect the concern over the ideology of Islamic extremism and recognise that resolving the issues behind Islamist terror will take years, if not decades. This suggests an intellectual base of support for some involvement in confronting the global challenge of terror. Each world-view, however, disagrees with the US approach in fundamental ways— ways which may affect Indo-US cooperation in that struggle.

Predominant Indian intellectual and policy frameworks are at variance with US policy preferences on the appropriate response to the key elements of the threat. Indian elite views on WMD differ widely—as demonstrated in the long evolution of India's nuclear weapons programme and the cognitive dissonance in India's draft nuclear doctrine released shortly after the 1998 tests.[39] Nehruvians believe the problem can be resolved through international cooperation and that this is the best way to remove a threat of terrorist-delivered WMD from the international scene. Neoliberals also believe in negotiation but recognise the value of nuclear deterrence as well—a concept that US analysts regularly suggest is less relevant in the 21st century.[40] Hyperrealists see WMD as an absolute essential for Indian security and a prerequisite for acceptance as a great power. While hyperrealists sympathise with US concerns regarding state transfer of WMD to terrorist organisations, they have more trouble understanding America's embrace of Pakistan, given its poor record on proliferation.

Because of India's long history of regional terror and multifaceted approach to resolving domestic and regional terrorist problems, it is not surprising that Indian elites broadly disagree with the US approach. Nehruvians reject the use of military force as a solution, neoliberals understand the use of force but think the root causes

---

[39] Perkovich, *India's Nuclear Bomb*; Raj Chengappa, *Weapons of Peace* (New Delhi: HarperCollins Publishers India Pvt Ltd, 2000); *Draft Nuclear Doctrine*, August 17, 1999, at http://www.indianembassy.org/policy/CTBT/nuclear_doctrine_aug_17_1999.html (accessed on November 24, 2007); and commentary by R.Ramachandran, 'Unclear nuclear identity', *Frontline* 16:18 (August 28–September 10, 1999), at http://www.frontlineonnet.com/fl1618/16180160.htm (accessed on November 24, 2007).

[40] *US National Security and Nuclear Weapons: Maintaining Deterrence in the 21st Century* (July 2007), at http://www.nnsa.doe.gov/docs/factsheets/2007/NA-07-FS-04.pdf (accessed on November 24, 2007); Keith B. Payne, *The Fallacies of Cold War Deterrence and a New Direction* (Lexington, KY: University of Kentucky Press, 2001).

of terrorism must be addressed through economic means and hyperrealists accept the use of force but feel it has been misapplied, as the obvious source of the problem is Pakistan. In addition, Indian elites perceive the threat of transnational terror differently from the US. For the US, the rise of transnational terror is a recent phenomenon and Americans focus on the Islamist threat to allies in the Middle East (including Israel), Europe and the homeland. For all practical purposes, the US perceives radical Islamist threats emerging in Southwest Asia directed primarily westward into the Middle East and Europe. India's long struggle with Pakistani-supported insurgents (including Afghan and foreign fighters in Kashmir) demonstrates to India that the threat of radical Islam is pointed EAST at India—a concept supported by at least some statements by AQAM leaders and affiliates.[41]

Nehruvians would deal with adversaries, however defined, primarily through contact, cooperation and discussion of the grievances and concerns that drive them to violence. They might even see US policy as the core grievance—an approach that might find sympathisers in the US as well. Neoliberals would address underlying problems through economics. Although not necessarily persuaded that democracy will resolve the problems of the Islamic world, neoliberals would certainly contend that open markets, greater economic interdependence and multinational cooperation are critical to resolving the long-term threat of Islamist violence. They would see the transnational nature of the threat as arising from a combination of economic deprivation and political marginalisation—issues which can be addressed in the context of transformation of the regional economic order. Hyperrealists see the root of the transnational problem as residing firmly in the Pakistani Army Headquarters in Rawalpindi and in the Saudi-backed madrassas. There, proxy forces of radical Islamists have been raised both to export troublemakers and to spread a virulent

---

[41] 'Al Qaeda Claim of Kashmir Link Worries India', *International Herald Tribune*, July 14, 2006, at http://www.iht.com/articles/2006/07/13/news/india.php (accessed on November 24, 2007); 'Al Qaeda Statement: Full Text', *British Broadcasting Corporation*, November 17, 2003, at http://news.bbc.co.uk/2/hi/in_depth/3276859.stm (accessed on November 24, 2007); 'Al-Qaeda declares war, calls Kashmir "gateway of Jihad against India"', *The Daily Excelsior*, June 8, 2007, at http://www.jammu-kashmir.com/archives/archives2007/kashmir20070608d.html (accessed on November 24, 2007).

form of Islam in pursuit of a notional caliphate that will destroy the Indian state.

Each of these Indian visions of the global terrorist threat recognises the protracted, ideological nature of the current struggle. Each supports a different mix of the elements of national power—diplomatic, information, military and economic—and a different policy approach to resolve this protracted struggle. Each world-view is congruent with some aspects of US policy but conflicts significantly in others. Nehruvianism sees the importance of what the military would call strategic communications and information operations in resolving the conflict, but rejects the use of the military or the involvement of the military in these efforts, and suspects that many of the terrorists' motivations come from unjust US policies. Neoliberalism probably comes closest to accepting the American world-view, but rejects the use of unilateral and preventive war. It also, perhaps with good reason, sees the US as fixated on the Middle East and overly-supportive of Pakistan despite its obvious regional misbehaviour. Hyperrealism views the US with suspicion because of its aggregate power and its continuing tilt towards Pakistan.

All three of these visions will complicate Indo-US relations and greater Indian involvement in the global struggle against terror, because each conflicts at some level with US national security priorities. Strident claims of a 'natural strategic partnership' from Indian policy-makers (mostly in the neoliberal camp) and American advocates (frequently tagged with the much abused 'neo-conservative' label) must be viewed with suspicion. They are certainly premature, may be misleading and could actually lead to significant problems later in the relationship, if it does not evolve at a rapid pace.

Conclusions

India will be tempted to take an increasingly important role in managing the challenge of global terror, as its relative power and extra-regional and global influence increase. That role, however, may not align closely with US policy preferences. Domestic considerations—manifested in the three foreign policy visions discusses above—will drive Indian policy in directions that are not easily compatible with US desires. The dissonance will be particularly pronounced where the US identifies state sponsors that historically have good relations with India (particularly Iran),[42] *and vice versa* (with particular reference to Pakistan).[43]

Indian foreign policy will continue to be driven by the debate between these three visions. While the leading political parties appear to have embraced neoliberalism, they must still form coalitions with more parochial or locally-focussed parties to govern. While the Nehruvian perspective is no longer dominant in Indian policy, it retains considerable influence in the bureaucracy and the intelligentsia, ensuring that it will still have some impact on Indian policy choices in the future. Hyperrealism has even fewer supporters in leading policy positions. It remains influential in security affairs, however, because of the importance of hyperrealist thinkers on nuclear issues—several participated in creating India's Draft Nuclear Doctrine in 1999.[44] In addition, India still lacks a robust national security debate and the density of expertise found in some, but not all, Western powers. As a result, hyperrealist thought continues to exercise a disproportionate impact on Indian security affairs.

The ramifications of this domestic debate on Indian policy regarding global terrorism are not yet clear. It does appear, however, that India is unlikely to readily follow the US lead on global terrorism issues. The prevailing neoliberal view disagrees with America's 'war on terror', while the other two perspectives are viscerally distrustful of American exercise of power and leadership.

This disagreement, however, is neither sharp nor hostile. It is also buffered by a wide range of bilateral working groups, committees and contacts between the India and the US, discussing issues of mutual interest.[45] The emergence of strong institutional

---

[42] See, for example, Harsh V. Pant, 'A Fine Balance: India Walks a Tightrope between Iran and the United States', *Orbis* 51: 3 (summer 2007), pp. 495–509; and C. Christine Fair, 'India and Iran: New Delhi's Balancing Act', *The Washington Quarterly* 30:3 (Summer 2007), pp. 145–59.

[43] A joint anti-terrorism mechanism between India and Pakistan was proposed in September 2006 and met for the first time in March 2007. It is far from perfect—Pakistan insists that Kashmir not be included in the framework—but does suggest the potential for meaningful progress.

[44] Two particularly well-known nuclear 'hawks', Dr Bharat Karnad and Dr Brahma Chellaney, were both members of the National Security Advisory Board that drafted India's nuclear doctrine after the 1998 nuclear tests.

[45] In recent talks in New Delhi, for example, one expert noted that there were over thirty working groups discussing defence and security issues.

contacts may, over time, identify areas where both states can cooperate on issues related to the war on terror, even if they do not agree completely on either the definition or the appropriate strategy to prosecute that conflict. This will not be easy, however. Overcoming the legacy of the past will take time, even with a promising institutional base.

Military-to-military and particularly naval, contacts are viewed as the most promising area of Indo-US cooperation.[46] The US and India are already engaged in joint training and exercises across a wide range of military capabilities, including counterinsurgency, mountain warfare, aerial combat and maritime operations. These exercises are vital to building the relationship and they raise expectations of much closer cooperation between both security communities in the future. A particularly important facet of this policy is the US-India Joint Working Group on Counterterrorism, founded in January 2000.[47]

Both the US and India have announced new maritime strategies which emphasise multiple areas for bilateral and multilateral cooperation on issues related to the war on terror.[48] These new strategies incorporate and expand on previous announcements.[49] They raise the possibility of further collaboration on issues of great

---

[46] The findings of Juli MacDonald, *Indo-US Military Relationship: Expectations and Perceptions* (Washington, DC: Director, Net Assessment, Office of the Secretary of Defense, October 2002) remain entirely valid. See p. XXXIII in the Executive Summary for a five-point summary of the particular promise of naval cooperation.

[47] See 'US, India Continue Cooperation Against Terrorism: US-India Joint Working Group on Counterterrorism meets in Washington', April 22, 2006, at http://usinfo.state.gov/xarchives/display.html?p=washfile english&y=2006&m=April&x=200 60422113511ABretnuH0.1901972 (accessed on May 12, 2008).

[48] See *Freedom to Use the Seas: India's Maritime Military Strategy* (New Delhi: Indian Ministry of Defence (Navy), May 2007) and 'A Cooperative Strategy for 21st Century Seapower' (October 2007), at http://www.defenselink.mil/Blog_files/MaritimeStrategy.pdf (accessed on November 24, 2007).

[49] *Indian Maritime Doctrine INBR* 8 (New Delhi: Integrated Headquarters, Ministry of defence (Navy), 2004) and the 'Thousand Ship Navy'/Global Maritime Partnership concept first articulated in John G. Morgan Jr. and Charles W. Martolgio, 'The 1,000 Ship Navy: Global Maritime Network', *Proceedings* (November 2005), at http://www.usni.org/magazines/proceedings/archive/issues.asp?issue_year=2005 (accessed on November 24, 2007), and discussed in Amy Klamper, 'The Thousand Ship Navy', *Sea Power*, February 13, 2007 at http://www.military.com/forums/0,15240,125158,00.html (accessed on November 24, 2007).

importance, including WMD proliferation at sea. Recent domestic political disagreement in India, however, has affected the pace and scope of naval cooperation.[50] The Indian domestic debate over the Indo-US Agreed Framework continues to pose obstacles to cooperation.[51] A promising area of potential cooperation, including joint action on issues of concern that are related to the war on terror, is therefore currently constrained by Indian domestic political debates.[52]

Efforts to curb state sponsorship of terror may also be impeded by domestic politics, particularly regarding the Persian Gulf and the Middle East. On the one hand, India's evolving relationship with the US and, equally important in some respects, Israel may drive it to a greater appreciation of the problems of terrorism in the Middle East. On the other hand, India has traditionally maintained good relations (both diplomatic and economic) with all the regimes in the Middle East and Persian Gulf. This dichotomy of interests is already emerging in policy its towards Iran. If India chooses relative passivity in the face of significant competing interests, it may forfeit the chance to exercise meaningful leadership in an area of global importance and in areas which, again, are of mutual interest but fall under the US definition of the war on terror.

---

[50] Indian Communists, Muslims and intellectuals protested the port call of the USS Nimitz—a nuclear-powered aircraft carrier—in the summer of 2007, reflecting in part a left-wing, Nehruvian distrust of US political motives. See, for example, 'USS Nimitz Go Back!', *People's Democracy* XXI:27 (July 8, 2007), at http://www.cpim.org/pd/2007/0708/07082007_aanainar.htm (accessed on November 24, 2007); and 'Muslims protest docking of USS Nimitz off Chennai port', *Yahoo India News*, July 4, 2007, at http://in.news.yahoo.com/070704/139/6hojm.html (accessed on November 24, 2007).

[51] Indian reports note that the agreement remains a significant political issue. See 'AFP: Indo-US nuclear pact not out of the woods: analysts', November 17, 2007 at http://afp.google.com/article/ALeqM5hB6CRtEOKNYNoBjfzYoIi0AGwT9w (accessed on November 24, 2007). Regional reports note that the debate over the nuclear deal forced the government to postpone both planned elections in October 2007, for fear of a significant defeat, and the implementation of the deal itself. See 'Current status of the Indo-US nuclear deal', *The Daily Star* (Bangladesh), November 24, 2007, at http://www.thedailystar.net/story.php?nid=12753 (accessed on November 24, 2007).

[52] In recent meetings with Indian officials in New Delhi (April and September 2007), both civilians and military officers expressed suspicion about cooperation in the Proliferation Security Initiative and suggested that the pace of military cooperation be ratcheted back until the domestic political environment settles.

Pakistan continues to loom as a potential problem in the Indo-US relationship and in any reasonable definition of the threat of global terrorism. The more India focuses on Pakistan as a key state sponsor of global terrorism, the more friction can be anticipated with the US which still views Pakistan as a necessary partner against AQAM and the Taliban. Pakistan's on-going interest in a revisionist solution in Kashmir, despite the apparent warming of Indo-Pakistani relations, is almost certain to remain a point of contention.[53] India also maintains an interest in Afghanistan, providing significant quantities of economic assistance but refusing to provide troops in the absence of a UN mandate.[54] Although this might seem a fertile area for cooperation, Indian troops in Afghanistan would surely provoke significant Pakistani opposition. Pakistan's activities and domestic politics will determine, in large part, the potential difficulties in resolving US and Indian definitions of the global terrorist threat.

In confronting the challenge of global terrorism, India may make its greatest contribution (in the near term) on the margins—in South East Asia and, perhaps, the Horn of Africa. These are areas that have always been of some interest to India, due to both diaspora populations and historical ties. One of India's foremost strategic analysts defines the Indian Ocean littoral as India's second 'strategic circle'.[55] Here, India benefits from not having core interests at stake, from being perceived as a fairly benign external power in the region and from US bureaucratic politics. Because India falls in the Department of Defense's Pacific Command and Pakistan in Central Command (a deliberate choice to separate two potentially hostile powers), the US tends *not* to encourage an Indian role in the Middle East—unintentionally avoiding some of the problems noted above. India has, instead, taken on anti-piracy missions in the Straits of Malacca and humanitarian operations in South East Asia-areas of clear national interest for India. These activities contribute to combating the ideological support for terrorism and radical extremism. They raise India's profile in an important neighbouring

---

[53] See, for example, *Annual Report 2006–2007* (New Delhi: Ministry of Defence, 2007), pp. 4–5, at http://mod.nic.in/reports/welcome.html (accessed on November 24, 2007).

[54] Ibid., p. 7. India has provided $750 million in reconstruction efforts in Afghanistan and aid is increasing. *India–US Relations*, p. 18.

[55] C. Raja Mohan, 'India and the Balance of Power', p. 18.

region without provoking significant domestic opposition. In fact, these missions correspond with some key element or elements of each of the three foreign policy visions detailed above. As the US creates AFRICOM—a new Africa Command—India will again be a natural player, due not only to the existence of local Indian population but also because of its previous participation in UN peacekeeping operations in this part of the world.

Working the margins in these areas enhances Indo-US cooperation, engages India in fighting extra-regional terrorist problems and still avoids the key area of potential policy dissonance in the Middle East and Persian Gulf. In the short term, this approach offers the greatest opportunities for India to collaborate, in its own national interest, in the broader US concept of the war on terror. At relatively low domestic and international cost, it can improve co-operation with the US, increase its international role and profile and leverage its history and traditions of secularism and tolerance while serving as a successful role model of a post-colonial state and emerging global power. Relying on 'satisficing' in the global war on terror might not meet the expectations of the most vigorous US advocates of the 'natural strategic partnership'. It may prove the best way, over time, of securing closer Indo-US cooperation on crucial issues in the war on terror with a minimal adverse impact on Indian domestic politics.

5

India and Energy Security: A Foreign Policy Priority

MANJEET S. PARDESI AND SUMIT GANGULY

Indian economy has emerged as one of the fastest growing economies in the world in recent years. It registered an average growth rate of 5.5 per cent p.a. in the period 1980–91 and a slightly higher average growth rate of 6 per cent p.a. in the following decade, 1992–2001.[1] In the years 2004 and 2005, the Indian economy grew at a still higher rate of 8.5 per cent[2] and registered 9.4 per cent growth rate in 2006.[3] As a result, India has emerged as the twelfth-largest global economy when measured by the size of its GDP at market rate and the fifth-largest global economy when measured by the size of its GDP adjusted for purchasing power parity.[4] At the same time, with a population of 1.05 billion, India is the second-largest nation in the world and is projected to become the world's largest over the next half century.[5] As a result, India faces daunting challenges in meeting its energy needs to feed its fast-growing economy and to meet the developmental goals of its rising population. For India, the elasticity for energy (i.e., percentage change

---

[1] Arvind Virmani, *India's Economic Growth: From Socialist Rate of Growth to Bhartiya Rate of Growth*, Indian Council for Research on International Economic Relations, Working Paper No. 122, February 2004, p. 15, at http://www.icrier.org/pdf/wp122.pdf (accessed on October 26, 2006).
[2] *India Data Profile* (World Development Indicators database), April 2007, at http://devdata.worldbank.org/external/CPProfile.asp?PTYPE=CP&CCODE=IND (accessed on October 26, 2006).
[3] *CIA: The World Factbook 2006: India*, 2006, at https://www.cia.gov/library/publications/the-world-factbook/geos/in.html (accessed on December 23, 2007).
[4] *2005 International Comparison Programme: Preliminary Global Report Compares Sizes of Economies* (The World Bank), December 17, 2007, at http://go.worldbank.org/3YLCQ7L9K0 (accessed on December 23, 2007).
[5] *India Population 'to be Biggest'*, August 18, 2004, at http://news.bbc.co.uk/2/hi/in_depth/3575994.stm (accessed on October 26, 2006).

in per capita energy for every percentage change in per capita GDP) is close to unity for both total commercial primary energy consumption and electricity.[6] This fact has given a sense of urgency to India's energy policy. According to Prime Minister Manmohan Singh, 'the quest for energy security is second only in our [India's] scheme of things to food security'.[7] To further highlight the thrust that the search for energy was providing to India's foreign and security policy, Prime Minister Manmohan Singh mentioned that the quest for energy security had 'become an important element of Indian diplomacy and ... [was] shaping . . . [India's] relations with a range of countries across the globe'.[8]

Noting the above, this essay analyses how this quest for energy is affecting India's foreign and security policy. It also attempts to understand the impact of India's foreign and security policy on its energy security. Importantly, it does not deal with India's overall energy strategy which has domestic, foreign policy, technological, environmental, developmental and economic dimensions, amongst others. It will address the domestic dimension of India's energy security strategy in as much as it has an impact on New Delhi's foreign policy. Furthermore, the impact of specifics such as the fluctuation in the price of energy resources (whether in the price of oil in international markets or the pricing policies of energy within India) on India's energy security are not discussed from an economic standpoint. In as much as these economic issues are discussed, they are focussed on the foreign policy choices and the strategic imperatives they create for India. Finally, the links between energy and environmental security are not discussed in this essay. The focus of this essay is on the two-way links between India's energy security and foreign/security policy. To this end, the next section will define the concept of energy security and the need to integrate energy security and foreign policy imperatives. This will

---

[6] *Draft Report of Expert Committee on Integrated Energy Policy* (Planning Commission, Government of India), December 2005, pp. 21–26, at http://planningcommission. nic.in/reports/genrep/intengpol.pdf (accessed on October 26, 2006). Hereinafter referred to as the *Draft Report*.

[7] 'Prime Minister Dr Manmohan Singh's Interview with Financial Times', May 11, 2004, at http://meaindia.nic.in/interview/2004/11/05in01.htm (accessed on October 26, 2006).

[8] Manmohan Singh, 'The New India', *The Wall Street Journal* (Eastern edition), May 19, 2005.

be followed by a detailed discussion of India's energy needs and the strategies being pursued by India to address these needs. The final section will discuss the strategic implications at the regional and global levels as well as the military implications of the energy strategies being pursued by India.

ENERGY SECURITY AND FOREIGN/SECURITY POLICY

Energy security has been an integral part of foreign and security policy objectives of all nations, ever since the British navy converted its ships from coal to oil propulsion, on the eve of the First World War, to gain advantage over German ships powered by coal. Several major battles fought during the Second World War, including the 1941 German attack on Russia and Japan's decision to attack the US naval base in Pearl Harbor at the end of that year, were directly or indirectly related to issues of energy security. There has always been a close relationship between energy and military security as all major weapon systems—tanks, aircraft and ships—run on oil. As a result, the oil-rich Middle East was a major arena of Cold War power politics where the US and the former USSR built up relationships and alliances with energy-rich states to reduce one another's influence. The links between energy security on the one hand and economic growth and stability on the other became stark during the 1973–74 global 'oil shocks'.[9]

Furthermore, even though oil reserves are finite, there is a high degree of uncertainty about how long the global oil reserves will last. However, what is certain is that the global oil production will be dominated by the twin imperatives of economics and technology for the foreseeable future, as opposed to the limitations of geology. Consequently, oil will continue to dominate global politics and economics.[10] Noting this, Daniel Yergin has commented that 'it must be recognised that energy security does not stand by itself

---

[9] For an excellent discussion of the political and economic history of oil and the oil market, see Leonardo Maugeri, *The Age of Oil: The Mythology, History and Future of the World's Most Controversial Resource* (Westport, Conn.: Praeger Publishers, 2006); and Daniel Yergin, *The Prize: The Epic Quest for Oil, Money and Power* (New York: Simon and Schuster, 1991).

[10] Leonardo Maugeri, 'Oil: Never Cry Wolf—Why the Petroleum Age is Far from Over', *Science* 304:5674 (May 2004), pp. 1114–15.

but is lodged in the larger relations among nations and how they interact with one another'.[11]

Due to a number of important developments, energy security has come to dominate the global agenda in recent years. In addition to the traditional focus on political instability in the Middle East and the security of oil and gas supplies from that region (including the Persian Gulf), a number of new concerns have emerged. These include an exceedingly tight oil market, the crisis in Iraq and the Iranian nuclear issue, Russia's emergence as an energy superpower, political crises in oil-rich countries outside the Middle East (e.g., Venezuela and Nigeria), the rising demands for oil from the rising powers of China and India and the geopolitical competition among the world's major and emerging powers as energy security has the potential to reshape the security architecture of the international system.

Given these factors and the geographical mismatch between the major centres of oil and gas production (primarily in the Middle East, Central Asia and the Caucasus) and consumption (the US, Europe, China, Japan and India), the large consuming nations are pursuing foreign and security policies in the energy-rich regions with an aim of increasing their political, economic and military influence there. Through such proactive foreign policies, these large consuming states hope to reduce their 'energy/security dilemma'. According to Michael Klare, reliable access to energy makes a given country economically and militarily strong. However, overseas dependency due to geographical mismatch between sources of supply and demand introduces vulnerability and weakness. This dependence on overseas sources creates an 'energy/security dilemma' as states often try to secure their sources of energy and their supply routes from political and military instability.[12]

This dependency dilemma and the fact that energy security is lodged within the wider international context lead states to integrate their quest for energy security with their foreign policy objectives. Importantly, energy security is a much wider concept that

---

[11] Daniel Yergin, 'Ensuring Energy Security', *Foreign Affairs* 65:2 (March/April 2006), p. 69.

[12] For a description of the 'energy/security dilemma', see Michael T. Klare, *Blood and Oil: The Dangers and Consequences of America's Growing Petroleum Dependency* (New York: Metropolitan Books, 2004), pp. 10–11.

has been broadly defined as the 'assurance of the ability to access energy resources required for the continued development of national power'.[13] In India, energy security has been defined as follows:

> The country is energy secure when we can supply lifeline energy to all our citizens as well as meet their effective demand for safe and convenient energy to satisfy various needs at affordable costs at all times with a prescribed confidence level considering shocks and disruptions that can be reasonably expected.[14]

These notions of energy security represent a very broad concept that includes a host of factors including national security, technology, good governance, sustainable development, energy pricing, environmental considerations and the security of the sources of energy and their supplies. However, this essay approaches energy security from a narrow perspective that represents the 'intersection of energy, security and foreign policy'.[15]

India's Energy Security: A Foreign Policy Priority

Energy security has always been a foreign policy concern for India as the country has been traditionally dependent on imports of oil (primarily from the Middle East and the Persian Gulf) for its energy needs. India was adversely hit during the 1973–74 oil shocks, a period during which New Delhi had to significantly increase its exports to the oil-rich countries to prevent a balance-of-payments crisis. Later, during the 1991 Gulf War, India had to step up its imports from Saudi Arabia and some other Gulf states to make up for the loss of its imports from Iraq and Kuwait, countries that then supplied nearly two-fifths of India's total oil imports.[16] Interestingly, it

---

[13] Jan H. Kalicki and David L. Goldwyn, 'Introduction: The Need to Integrate Energy and Foreign Policy' in Jan H. Kalicki and David L. Goldwyn, ed, *Energy and Security: Toward a New Foreign Policy Strategy* (Washington, D.C: Woodrow Wilson Center Press and The Johns Hopkins University Press, 2005), p. 9.
[14] *Draft Report*, p. 56.
[15] Kalicki and Goldwyn, 'Introduction', p. 9.
[16] For a brief but excellent overview of the impact of these crises on India's energy strategy, see the section titled 'Energy Politics in India' in Raju G C Thomas, 'India's Energy Policy and Nuclear Weapons Programme', in D R SarDesai and Raju G. C. Thomas ed, *Nuclear India in the Twenty-First Century* (New York: Palgrave-Macmillan, 2002), pp. 282–87.

was in the midst of the 1991 crisis when the Congress-led government in India (under Prime Minister Narasimha Rao and the then Finance Minister Manmohan Singh) implemented major structural reforms in the Indian economy that led the country towards marketisation and high growth rates.[17]

However, in these earlier crises, India's responses were largely reactive. During these crises India was neither a major global economy nor amongst the largest energy consuming countries in the world (even though India's energy import dependence was high). However, over the past fifteen years or so (i.e., after implementing structural economic reforms), India has emerged as one of the fastest-growing, major economies in the world. In turn, this has led to increased energy consumption.[18] By the Indian economy which was the fifth-largest primary energy consumer in the world in 2006.[19] The growth of the Indian economy, accompanied by increased energy consumption, has increased India's dependence on foreign sources of oil and gas. However, buoyed by high economic growth rates and learning from its past experiences and contemporary developments, India is becoming more proactive in the international arena to secure its energy requirements. As a result, energy security has emerged high on India's foreign policy agenda.[20] We now turn to India's energy profile and the energy security policies being pursued by New Delhi. The strategic implications of these policies will be discussed in the subsequent section.

---

[17] Sumit Ganguly, 'Between Iraq and a Hard Place: The Developing World and the New Oil Crisis', *International Executive* 31:4 (January–February 1991), pp. 37–38.

[18] For an overview of the impact of the structural economic reforms on India's energy needs (and greenhouse gas emissions), see Subir Gokarn, 'Economic Policy Reforms: Implications for Energy Consumption', in Michael A. Toman, Ujjayant Chakravorty and Shreekant Gupta, ed, in *India and Global Climate Change: Perspectives on Economics and Policy from a Developing Country* (Washington, D.C.: Resources For the Future Press, 2003).

[19] *BP Statistical Review of World Energy June 2007*, 2007, at http://www.bp.com/liveassets/bp_internet/globalbp/globalbp_uk_english/reports_and_publications/statistical_energy_review_2007/STAGING/local_assets/downloads/pdf/statistical_review_of_world_energy_full_report_2007.pdf (accessed on December 23, 2007), p. 40.

[20] Edward Luce and Ray Marcelo, 'Diplomacy: Why Energy Security is Top Priority?', *The Financial Times*, January 17, 2005.

INDIA'S ENERGY PROFILE

Table 5.1 provides an overview of India's energy profile. Coal, oil, natural gas, nuclear power and hydroelectricity account for the bulk of the total primary commercial energy (including electricity) consumed within India.[21] As a result of its rapidly growing economy and growing population, the total primary energy consumption in India increased by 55.87 per cent in the decade 1996–2006. Together with an increase in the overall consumption of energy, the level of imports in India's total primary commercial energy consumption increased from 17.85 per cent in 1991 to 30 per cent in 2003.[22] Furthermore, it is clear from Table 5.2 that India's total primary commercial energy consumption is likely to increase by a third every five years. This will only increase India's dependence on foreign sources of energy with important implications for New Delhi's foreign and security policy.

Table 5.1
India's Primary Commercial Energy Consumption Profile in 1996 and 2006
(Million tonnes oil equivalent)

	1996	2006	% increase (1995–2005)
Coal	154.4 (56.87%)	237.7 (56.17%)	53.95%
Oil	81.1 (29.87%)	120.3 (28.43%)	48.33%
Natural Gas	18.5 (6.81%)	35.8 (8.46%)	93.51%
Nuclear Energy	1.9 (0.70%)	4.0 (0.95%)	110.53%
Hydroelectricity	15.6 (5.75%)	25.4 (6.00%)	62.82%
Total Primary Commercial Energy	271.5	423.2	55.87%

Source: BP Statistical Review of World Energy June 2007.
The BP Statistics document defines primary energy as commercially traded fuels. As a result, fuels such as wood, peat, animal waste, wind, thermal and solar power are excluded. Figures within parenthesis indicate the percentage contribution of a particular energy source to the total primary energy consumed in the given year.

---

[21] Leena Srivastava and Megha Shukla, 'The Present Status and Future Prospects of Energy in India', in *Asian Energy Markets: Dynamics and Trends* (Abu Dhabi: The Emirates Center for Strategic Studies and Research, 2004), pp. 311–40.
[22] *Draft Report*, p. 57.

Table 5.2
Projections for Total Commercial Primary Energy
Requirements for 7 per cent & 8 per cent
GDP growth rates

(Million tonnes oil equivalent)

	7% GDP growth	8% GDP growth
2006–07	375	381
2011–12	483	508
	(28.80%)	(33.33%)
2016–17	625	684
	(29.40%)	(34.65%)
2021–22	797	901
	(27.52%)	(31.73%)
2026–27	1051	1234
	(31.87%)	(36.96%)
2031–32	1344	1633
	(27.88%)	(32.33%)

Source: Draft Report, p. 30.
Figures within brackets indicate the percentage increase over the previous five-year period for the same percentage GDP growth.

Coal

Coal is the most important source of energy for India and accounts for slightly more than half of the total commercial primary energy consumption (see Table 5.1). Coal is also the single most important fuel for electricity generation in India, accounting for 60 per cent of the total power generated in the country.[23] With 10.17 per cent of the world's proven coal reserves at the end of 2005, India is home to the fourth-largest reserves of coal.[24] As a result, coal is likely to remain the principal source of energy for the foreseeable future.[25] Earlier estimates expected coal reserves of the country to last for over 200 years. However, a recent study done by the Central Mine Planning and Design Institute of India estimates that the country's coal reserves may only last another four to five decades.[26] Added to this is the problem of regional concentration of domestic coal

---
[23] Ibid., p. 13.
[24] BP Statistical Review of World Energy June 2007, p. 32.
[25] R. K. Pachauri, 'Living with Coal: India's Energy Policy in the 21st Century', Journal of International Affairs 53:1 (Fall 1999), pp. 101–15.
[26] Defining an Integrated Energy Strategy for India: Ensuring Security, Sufficiency and Sustainability (New Delhi: The Energy and Resources Institute Press, 2005), pp. 8–9. This report was published in 2002 by the same organisation (then known as Tata Energy Research Institute).

supplies in the central-eastern regions of the country—Bengal, Bihar, Orissa and Madhya Pradesh—and the issues associated with its mining and domestic transportation and distribution throughout India.[27] Furthermore, Indian coal suffers from low calorific value and causes considerable environmental degradation as it possesses a high content of sulfur and ash. As a consequence, India has already become a coal-importing nation, especially to meet the coking coal requirements of its steel industry.[28]

Oil

Oil consumption accounts for about 30 per cent of the total primary commercial energy consumed in India (see Table 5.1). The total demand for petroleum products, petrol and diesel grew at the rates of 5.4 per cent p.a., 7.4 per cent p.a. and 5.7 per cent p.a. respectively between 1980 and 1981 and between 2003 and 2004.[29] There have been no major oil discoveries in India since the offshore Bombay High fields were discovered roughly three decades ago. India has onshore oil fields in Assam and recently the British firm Cairns Energy discovered oil in Rajasthan.[30] In spite of this, India has a very small supply of crude oil reserves that can be sustained for barely two decades at the current level of production.[31] This factor, coupled with limited domestic production of oil, means that oil imports constitute 72 per cent of India's total consumption.[32] India currently imports oil from over two dozen countries and the Middle East accounts for more than two-thirds of India's oil imports. At the same time, a collection of just five countries in Saudi Arabia (24.96 per cent), Nigeria (15.73 per cent), Kuwait (11.85 per cent), Iran (10.03 per cent) and Iraq (8.69 per cent)—accounted for

---

[27] Thomas, 'India's Energy Policy and Nuclear Weapons Programme', p. 285.
[28] India's total imported coal requirement increased from 5.93 million tonnes in 1990–91 to 22.47 million tonnes in 2001–02 and is further projected to increase. See Amit Mitra, 'Rising Coal Imports—Ports Need to Ramp Up Infrastructure', *The Hindu Business Line*, April 21, 2003. On the need for imported coking coal by India's steel industry, see Amit Mitra, 'Global Coal Supplier Bullish on Indian Market', *The Hindu Business Line*, February 15, 2003.
[29] *Draft Report*, p. 11.
[30] *Oil Find in India's Desert State*, February 4, 2003, at http://news.bbc.co.uk/2/hi/business/2725969.stm (accessed on October 28, 2006).
[31] *Draft Report*, p. 36.
[32] Ibid., p. 57.

more than 70 per cent of India's imported oil in 2004–05.[33] India's demand for oil consumption has been steadily growing and given the limited prospects for domestic oil discoveries, India's dependence on foreign supplies of oil is likely to increase further. India's dependence on oil imports is estimated to account for 91–93 per cent of its total oil consumption by 2021–22.[34] The Middle East will continue to provide the bulk of India's oil imports that will be supplemented by imports from Africa and Central Asia.

Natural Gas

Natural gas currently accounts for 8–9 per cent of the total commercial primary energy consumption in India (see Table 5.1). Natural gas consumption in India has grown at a rate of 2.7 per cent p.a. in the period 1999–2005.[35] The share of natural gas is likely to increase further in India's energy matrix as it is fast emerging as a major alternative to India's poor quality coal, especially for producing electricity. At the same time, it is also emerging as an alternative to oil in the transportation sector in the form of compressed natural gas (CNG), both for environmental reasons and to reduce India's increasing dependence on oil. The prospects of gas discoveries in India look promising with gas fields discovered offshore in the Krishna–Godavari basin, the Bay of Bengal region and the Andaman Sea area and onshore in Rajasthan. In spite of this, India began importing significant quantities of gas in the form of liquefied natural gas (LNG) in 2004.[36] It is estimated that India will be dependent on imported gas for more than 10–11 per cent of its total gas needs by 2031–32.[37] India is currently dependent on the Persian Gulf region—Qatar, Oman, Iran, etc.—for most of its imported gas needs. India is looking towards Myanmar, Bangladesh and Central Asia, among other regions, to fulfil its future requirements for imported gas.

---

[33] Ibid., p. 63.
[34] Ibid., p. 47. This estimate assumes 8 per cent GDP growth p.a.
[35] 'Oil and Gas', India Brand Equity Foundation, January 2006, p. 3, at http://ibef.org/download/OilandGas_sectoral.pdf (accessed on October 28, 2006).
[36] Sushma Ramachandran, 'Dahej LNG terminal commissioned', *The Hindu*, February 10, 2004.
[37] *Draft Report*, p. 47. This estimate assumes 8 per cent GDP growth p.a.

Nuclear Power

Nuclear power accounts for a small fraction of the total commercial primary energy consumed within India (see Table 5.1). Used for generating electricity, nuclear power accounted for 2.84 per cent of the total electricity generated within India in 2003–04.[38] In spite of its small current contribution, nuclear power has the potential to offer India 'energy independence' beyond 2050[39] and hence its development is seen as crucial.[40] However, India is endowed with low concentrations of poor quality uranium ores but with large quantities of thorium ores. Consequently, India's nuclear-generation programme is based on a three-stage plan—(1) Pressurised Heavy Water Reactors, (2) Fast Breeder Reactors and (3) Reactors based on the Uranium 233–Thorium 232 cycle—aimed eventually at the exploitation of the country's vast thorium reserves. However, as a non-signatory to the nuclear Non-Proliferation Treaty (NPT) and having conducted nuclear tests in 1974 and 1998, India has been under international sanctions that have denied it access to nuclear materials and technology from abroad.[41] The future development of nuclear power within India is dependent on civilian nuclear commerce with the international community. In this regard, the Indo-US civil nuclear cooperation deal (that still needs a formal approval from both the Indian and American governments)[42]

---

[38] Ibid., p. 25.
[39] Ibid., p. viii.
[40] For a strong case for nuclear power for India, see Thomas, 'India's Energy Policy and Nuclear Weapons Programme'. Also see Anil Kakodkar, 'Energy in India for the Coming Decades', paper presented at the *Inter-Ministerial Conference on 'Nuclear Power for the 21st Century'*, organised by the International Atomic Energy Agency, Paris, France, March 21–22, 2005. For a useful discussion on the applicability and viability of nuclear power for India's energy security, see the various articles published in the following journal by The Energy and Resources Institute. *Energy Security Insights* 1:1 (March 2006), at http://www.teriin.org/div/esiissue1march06.pdf (accessed on October 29, 2006).
[41] For an excellent overview of India's three-stage nuclear power generation plan and the effects of nuclear sanctions, see A Gopalakrishnan, 'Evolution of the Indian Nuclear Programme', *Annual Review of Energy and the Environment* 27 (November 2002), pp. 369–95.
[42] For the exact statement of this deal, see 'Joint Statement Between President George W. Bush and Prime Minister Manmohan Singh', July 18, 2005, at http://www.whitehouse.gov/news/releases/2005/07/20050718-6.html (accessed on October 29, 2006).

is crucial for India's energy security and also has important global strategic implications.

Hydroelectricity

Hydroelectricity accounts for 5–6 per cent of the total commercial primary energy consumption in India (see Table 5.1). In 2003–04, hydroelectricity contributed 11.85 per cent of the total electricity generated in India.[43] Endowed with many large rivers, India has substantial hydroelectricity potential. However, India has thus far exploited barely a quarter of its total estimated hydel power capacity.[44] As the controversy over the Narmada project indicates, India faces serious ecological, social and political challenges in developing its hydel power potential.[45] Even if India were able to exploit its full hydel power potential, India's fast-growing energy needs indicate that the contribution of hydroelectricity to India's energy mix will be around 5–6 per cent only.[46] However, as will be seen in the next section, hydroelectricity cooperation at the regional level in South Asia is crucial for its energy security and has important implications for its foreign policy goals.

INDIA'S ENERGY SECURITY STRATEGY

An important domestic structural change that India must implement to address its energy needs is the creation of an apex body in the country that addresses India's overall energy strategy (including its foreign/security policy implications). Currently, India's energy sector is governed by five different ministries and departments: the departments of Power, Petroleum and Natural Gas, Coal, Non-Conventional Energy Sources and the Department of Atomic Energy. In addition to these, the foreign/security policy dimension of India's energy security also involves policy coordination across the Ministry of External Affairs, the Ministry of Defence and the Ministry

---

[43] *Draft Report*, p. 25.
[44] *Hydropower Development in India*, 2006, at http://www.worldbank.org.in/WBSITE/EXTERNAL/COUNTRIES/SOUTHASIAEXT/INDIAEXTN/0,,contentMDK:20660353~pagePK:141137~piPK:141127~theSitePK:295584,00.html (accessed on October 29, 2006).
[45] On the Narmada project controversy, see Vandana Shiva, *Water Wars: Privatisation, Pollution and Profit* (Boston: South End Press, 2002). Shiva's analysis should be read while recognising that she is a social activist.
[46] *Draft Report*, p. viii.

of Finance. As a result, India is unable to make bold choices needed to conduct a coherent energy strategy. In this regard, the creation of an inter-ministerial Energy Coordination Committee (ECC) has been a step in the right direction.[47] Chaired by the prime minister himself, the ECC will include the ministers of Finance, Power, Petroleum and Natural Gas, Coal, Non-Conventional Energy Sources, the National Security Advisor and a number of other senior officials. However, it is not yet clear how often the ECC will meet. Moreover, it is also not clear whether its purpose is to make and implement policy or if it will simply coordinate policy among the various ministries involved.

There are several other dimensions to India's energy security strategy. India has stepped up the search to tap its domestic coal, gas and oil reserves. India is also contemplating the introduction of market mechanisms in its energy sector (especially for pricing). Structural and technical reforms in India's electricity sector are also a major priority for New Delhi.[48] However, those aspects of India's energy security that have foreign policy and strategic implications include diversification of suppliers, diversification of the sources of energy, the purchase of equity stakes overseas, the security of its hydrocarbon supplies, ensuring adequate storage of energy and cooperation with countries in India's immediate neighbourhood (both in and just outside South Asia). In addition to this, India is also pursuing a strategy that avoids head-on commercial competition with China, Asia's other rising power. Finally, the Indo-US civil nuclear cooperation deal has the potential to end India's nuclear isolation.[49]

---

[47] *PM Constitutes Energy Coordination Committee* (Prime Minister's Office), July 13, 2005, at http://pib.nic.in/release/release.asp?relid=10163 (accessed on November 2, 2006).

[48] For more on this important domestic aspect of India's energy security, see Hubert H Reineberg, 'India's Electricity Sector in Transition: Can Its Giant Goals Be Met?,' *The Electricity Journal* 19:1 (January–February 2006), pp. 77–84; and Sunila S Kale, 'Current Reforms: The Politics of Policy Change in India's Electricity Sector', *Pacific Affairs* 77:3 (Fall 2004), pp. 467–91.

[49] Some of these strategies are discussed in Vibhuti Haté, 'India's Energy Dilemma', *CSIS South Asia Monitor* No. 98 (September 2006), pp. 1–4; *Defining an Integrated Energy Strategy for India*, pp. 15, 22–26; and Shebonti Ray Dadwal, 'Energy Security: India's Options', *Strategic Analysis* XXIII: 4 (July 1999), pp. 653–70. On the civil nuclear cooperation with the US, see Sumit Ganguly and Dinshaw Mistry, 'The Case for the US–India Nuclear Agreement', *World Policy Journal* 23:2 (Summer 2006), pp. 11–19.

Diversification of Suppliers and Sources of Energy

A major priority for India is the diversification of its sources of oil. In 2004–05, India imported oil from 25 different countries, including those from the Middle East, Africa, South America and Southeast Asia.[50] However, India's overwhelming dependency on the Middle East is likely to continue for reasons of geography and cost. India is also pursuing the diversification of fuels to reduce its high dependence on oil. In this regard, the consumption of natural gas in the country is set to increase dramatically in the years ahead. In addition to spot purchases of LNG, India has already been importing LNG through a long-term contract with Qatar and discussions to do the same from Iran and Oman are already underway.[51] India is also contemplating the import of gas through pipelines from gas-rich states in India's neighbourhood. These states include Bangladesh, Myanmar, Iran and countries in Central Asia.[52] Since a pipeline traverses through several countries, it entails a complex contractual framework and has an important bearing on geopolitics. This is in stark contrast to energy transportation via tankers, contracts that have a comparatively limited impact of geopolitics.[53]

India is actively trying to harness hydroelectricity to reduce its dependence on fossil fuels for electricity generation. Given the domestic problems associated with the generation of hydro-electricity, India is very keen on purchasing hydroelectricity from the Himalayan states of Bhutan and Nepal.[54] Currently, Nepal and Bhutan exploit merely 1.2 per cent and 2.6 per cent respectively of

---

[50] For a list of these countries, see *Draft Report*, p. 63.

[51] Arijit Barman, 'India Strikes LNG Import Deal with Qatar', 2003, at http://www.ndtvprofit.com/homepage/storybusinessnew.asp?id=15342&frmsrch=1&txtsrch=LNG per cent2CQatar (accessed on October 30, 2006); 'Iran Wants to Renegotiate 5-mt LNG deal with India', *The Hindu Business Line*, August 5, 2006; and 'Ratnagiri Gas: India looks to Oman for fuel supply', *The Hindu*, January 28, 2006.

[52] For the details of some of the pipelines that India is considering, see Najeeb Jung, 'Natural Gas in India', in Ian Wybrew-Bond and Jonathan Stren, ed, *Natural Gas in Asia: The Challenges of Growth in China, India, Japan and Korea* (New York: Oxford University Press, 2002), pp. 78–79.

[53] Furthermore, compared to LNG imports, pipelines represent a comparatively cheaper mode of supply.

[54] Stanley A Weiss, 'The Untapped Might of the Himalayas', *International Herald Tribune*, May 11, 2005.

their total hydroelectricity potential.[55] The size of their domestic markets as well as technological and financial imperatives makes hydroelectricity cooperation with India a very important consideration for both Bhutan and Nepal. India already imports a small quantity of hydroelectricity from Bhutan and Nepal to supply its northern states.[56] At present, India is discussing almost 15 joint hydroelectric power projects with four of its neighbouring countries—Bhutan, Nepal, Myanmar and Afghanistan.[57]

Purchase of Equity Stakes Overseas

India is also actively seeking equity coal, oil and gas abroad. As a recognition of India's increasing imported coal requirements, the Planning Commission[58] has recommended the promotion of imported coal (and obtaining equity coal abroad) as a major policy recommendation to the government.[59] Indian public and private sector firms are already planning or buying stakes in coal mines abroad, in places as diverse as Indonesia, Australia, Bangladesh and South Africa.[60] The Indian government has already invested in excess of US$3 billion in acquiring oil and gas fields abroad and further plans on investing US$1 billion per annum until 2015 'with a view to meet 15 per cent of its demand'.[61] ONGC Videsh Limited (OVL), the overseas arm of India's Oil and Natural Gas

---

[55] South Asia Regional Initiative for Energy Cooperation and Development, *Hydropower in South Asia—Potential Resource for Energy Exports*, at http://www.sari-energy.org/successdocs/IStudy_SouthAsianHydroResources.pdf (accessed on November 2, 2006).

[56] Anil Sasi, 'India Gets Power from Bhutan's Tala Project', *The Hindu Business Line*, August 17, 2006; and Santa B. Pun, 'Trading Off a Jewel', *Himal South Asian*, November 2003.

[57] Anil Sasi, 'India to Wheel in Power from Abroad', *The Hindu Business Line*, August 12, 2006.

[58] The Planning Commission is the apex institution of the Government of India responsible for formulating and implementing policy, including the country's Five-Year plans.

[59] *Draft Report*, pp. 70, 124.

[60] For example, see 'Tata Steel to buy 5 % Stake in Australian Coal Mine', *The Hindu Business Line*, July 19, 2005; and Amit Chaudhary, 'NTPC Scouts for Partners to Acquire Coal Mines Abroad', *The Hindu Business Line*, May 2, 2005.

[61] 'India to invest US$1bln in Foreign Oil Equity', May 25, 2004, at http://www.atimes.com/atimes/South_Asia/FE25Df03.html (accessed onOctober 30, 2006).

Corporation has purchased exploration and production blocks in a dozen countries in the Middle East, Asia–Pacific, Africa and Latin America.[62] The Indian private sector, led by Reliance Industries, the Tata Group and Videocon Industries, is in the process of purchasing oil and gas exploration and production blocks in a range of countries from Yemen, Oman, Australia and East Timor to Colombia.[63] The production of oil and gas from these blocks, if successful, is likely to provide India with a source of energy far cheaper than the prevailing international market price.[64]

India as an 'Energy Outsourcing Hub'

The demand for imported oil and gas as well as the need to purchase energy equity abroad is creating a huge demand for foreign exchange for India. In the financial year 2005–06, India's oil import bill alone was US$44.64 billion.[65] While a part of this was a result of an increase in the international market price of oil, India's growing energy needs were the major cause behind the huge bill. By comparison, India's total exports amounted to US$123.2 billion in 2006.[66] India is pursuing several financial options like participating in futures trading in oil to alleviate some of the challenges associated with its huge energy import bill. The Planning Commission has also recommended New Delhi to purchase buying options from large oil storages in neighbouring states with well-developed infrastructure, like Singapore.[67] But the most important strategy that India is pursuing to reduce its energy import bill (and to earn

---

[62] The details of OVL's operations in these countries can be found at www.ongcvidesh.com under 'Operations' (accessed on November 2, 2006).

[63] For example, see 'Reliance in Pact for Oman Drill', *The Telegraph*, 13 March 2005; 'Tata Arm on Oil, Gas Hunt Abroad', *Business Standard*, April 10, 2006; and Vinod Matthew, 'Videocon Bags Australian Offshore Exploration Block', *The Hindu Business Line*, April 04, 2006.

[64] Shebonti Ray Dadwal and Uttam Kumar Sinha, 'Equity Oil and India's Energy Security', *Strategic Analysis* 29:3 (July–September 2005), pp. 521–29.

[65] 'India's oil import bill shoots to $44.64 bn', May 10, 2006, at http://us.rediff.com/money/2006/may/10oil.htm?q=bp&file=.htm (accessed on October 30, 2006).

[66] *CIA: The World Factbook 2007, India*, 2007, at https://www.cia.gov/library/publications/the-world-factbook/geos/in.html (accessed on December 23, 2007).

[67] *Draft Report*, p. x.

a significant amount of foreign exchange in the process) is the promotion of investment in oil refining infrastructure in the country. With recent investments in a special economic zone at Jamnagar in Gujarat, India is all set to emerge as an 'energy outsourcing hub' by the end of the year 2008. Jamnagar already boasts of the world's third-largest oil refining capacity and is further set to emerge as the world's largest when Reliance Petroleum Limited begins its operations there in December 2008. India has already become a net exporter of petroleum products and is especially targeting markets in Europe and North America.[68]

Creation of Strategic Reserves

New Delhi is also concerned about the uncertainty regarding the availability of oil, especially at the time of a crisis, and about the possibility of a sudden increase in oil price and its negative impact on the Indian economy. As a result, the Indian government decided to establish strategic petroleum reserves for 15 days of consumption in 2004. It was also decided that this stock of reserves would be over and above the existing storage with the country's oil companies.[69] The Planning Commission has recently recommended that New Delhi should build and maintain a strategic reserve for 90 days of oil imports.[70] The Indian government is also studying the possibility of a strategic reserve for natural gas. India's storage capacity is expected to conform to the standards set by the International Energy Agency (IEA). However, in spite of its growing dependency on energy imports and its efforts to build strategic reserves, India is not yet a member of the IEA.

---

[68] See Siddharth Srivastava, *India Bets Big on Refining*, May 5, 2006, at http://www.atimes.com/atimes/South_Asia/HE05Df03.html (accessed on October 30, 2006); Amy Yee, *Fuel for a Nation's Ambitions*, October 17, 2006, at http://www.ft.com/cms/s/6b21da38–5dfd–11db–82d4–0000779e2340.html (accessed on October 30, 2006); and Joe Leahy, 'Refining Hub will be the Largest in the World,' *Financial Times*, November 23, 2007.

[69] Happymon Jacob, *Building a 'Strategic Oil Reserve' for India 2005*, at http://www.observerindia.com/analysis/A018.htm (accessed on October 30, 2006); 'Strategic Crude Reserve Gets Nod', *The Hindu*, January 7, 2006; and Richa Mishra, 'Strategic Oil Reserves to Come Directly under Govt', *The Hindu Business Line*, April 2, 2006.

[70] *Draft Report*, p. x.

China, US and India's Quest for Energy

As India has entered the global energy market, it has encountered an important competitor—the People's Republic of China.[71] China is one of the fastest-growing economies in the world and is also a rising military power with a vast appetite for oil and other raw materials. Both India and China view each other as a major competitor in their global quest for energy. The vast foreign-exchange reserves available to China's state-owned oil firms have enabled the Chinese to undercut India's efforts to acquire energy assets overseas (in Angola, Nigeria, Ecuador and Kazakhstan). In each of these instances, the Chinese firms ended up acquiring oil and gas blocks only after substantially increasing their proposed bid.[72] However, efforts have been made by India and China to reduce the commercial/financial aspect of their competition over energy security. In 2005, the two countries signed several Memorandums of Understanding (MoUs) to promote energy cooperation.[73] These MoUs have essentially been guided by tactical financial/commercial logic and cooperation between the two countries thus far has been limited in nature and scope (even as they have jointly bid for oil assets in places like Syria and Colombia). Furthermore, International Relations theory tells us that as a result of the 'relative gains' problem, these agreements are unlikely to have any significant impact.[74] As far as energy is concerned, India is in a fundamentally competitive, if not conflictual relationship, with China.[75]

---

[71] For a comprehensive overview of the Sino-Indian energy dynamics, see Stein Tønnesson and Åshild Kolås, *Energy Security in Asia: China, India, Oil and Peace* (Report to the Norwegian Ministry of Foreign Affairs), April 2006, at http://www.prio.no/files/file47777_060420_energy_security_in_asia__final_.pdf?PHPSESSID=b8a30ac (accessed on November 1, 2006).

[72] 'China and India: A Rage for Oil', August 25, 2005, at http://www.businessweek.com/bwdaily/dnflash/aug2005/nf20050825_4692_db016.htm?chan=gb (accessed on November 1, 2006).

[73] Richard McGregor, Jo Johnson and Carola Hoyos, 'China and India Forge Alliance on Oil', *Financial Times*, January 12, 2006; and John Larkin, 'India and China Forge an Energy Tie: National Oil Companies to Work Together to Bid For Select Assets Abroad', *The Wall Street Journal* (Eastern Edition), August 18, 2005.

[74] Joseph Grieco, 'The Relative-Gains Problem for International Cooperation', in the Controversies section of *The American Political Science Review* 87:3 (September 1993). pp. 727–43.

[75] Sumit Ganguly, *Energy Trends in India and China: Implications for the United States* (US Senate Foreign Relations Committee Testimony), 2005, at http://www.indiana.edu/~isp/media/sfr_7-26-05.doc (accessed on November 1, 2006).

India's policy-makers are also keen to expand the role of nuclear power to meet the country's growing appetite for energy. India's meager uranium reserves and the poor quality of its ores mean that India's nuclear reactors are operating at sub-optimal levels and barely contribute about 3 per cent of India's electricity needs (as mentioned above). In the long-term, India's substantial thorium reserves can make significant contributions to electricity production. This process can be accelerated if New Delhi is allowed to access uranium and other civil nuclear technologies from foreign sources. This will enable India to accelerate the conversion of its vast thorium supplies into fissile material fit for electricity production. But these technologies are currently barred to New Delhi as it is not a signatory to the nuclear NPT.

However, in July 2005, the US and India agreed to a broad framework that can potentially establish civil nuclear commerce between the two states if agreed to by the Indian government and ratified by the US Congress. India would also need the approval from the 44-member Nuclear Suppliers Group (NSG) to engage in civil nuclear commerce with the international community. In return, India has agreed to separate the civil and strategic (including military) aspects of its nuclear programme in a phased manner by 2014 and bring the former under special International Atomic Energy Agency (IAEA) safeguards.[76] This quest, if successful, will not only address India's energy needs but will also accommodate India in the international nuclear order. As such, the quest to end India's nuclear isolation has emerged as a foreign policy priority for New Delhi in its relations with not only the US but other important players like Russia, France, UK, Brazil, South Africa, Australia and other important members of the NSG.

The Military Dimension

Finally, India's quest for energy security also has a military dimension as a result of its reliance on foreign sources for the supplies of oil and gas and to guarantee the security of its overseas energy assets. The Indian air force and navy are likely to play critical role in

---

[76] For a comprehensive overview of the various dimensions of this complicated deal, see 'US–India Nuclear Energy Cooperation: Requirements and Implications', *IISS Strategic Comments* 11:10 (December 2005), pp. 3–4; and Teresita Schafer and Pramit Mitra, 'The Bush Visit and the Nuclear Deal', *CSIS South Asia Monitor* 93 (April 2006), pp. 1–3.

ensuring energy security for the country. According to Indian Air Chief Marshall S. P. Tyagi, the Indian military is poised to play a crucial role in providing energy trade security to ensure the country's economic resurgence.[77] As early as 1995, India had emphasised the need to project power—long-range aircrafts with greater loiter time, AWACS and mid-air refueling—in its first-ever airpower doctrine.[78] And recently, Air Chief Marshal Tyagi highlighted the need to expand the Indian air force to ensure greater energy security. He also emphasised that India's expanded reach would be 'strategic and defensive in nature'.[79]

In its first-ever maritime doctrine published in 2004, the Indian navy explicitly highlighted energy security of the country as a context that required the application of maritime power in both offensive and defensive operations conducted to protect the country's maritime trade.[80] India's maritime doctrine also highlights the importance of the Gulf region and Central Asia for India's energy security.[81] It further mentions the '[s]afeguarding [of] Indian energy assets outside territorial India' and the preservation of 'international SLOCs [Sea Lines of Communication] through the Indian Ocean on a permanent basis' amongst the several scenarios of conflict in which the Indian navy may find itself.[82]

STRATEGIC IMPLICATIONS

India's quest for energy sources and related technologies is likely to have profound regional and geopolitical consequences—both political and military. India's energy strategy is likely to,

---

[77] For a report on Air Chief Marshal Tyagi's views about the role of the Indian military in its security environment, see 'India's Strategic Environment and the Role of Military Power', August 22, 2006, at http://www.carnegieendowment.org/events/index.cfm?fa=eventDetail&id=908&&prog=zgp&proj=zsa (accessed on November 1, 2006).
[78] Pravin Sawhney, 'India's First Airpower Doctrine Takes Shape', *Jane's International Defence Review* 30:6 (June 1997), pp. 33–38.
[79] Sanjeev Srivastava, 'India's Air Force "Needs to Grow"', April 18, 2006, at http://news.bbc.co.uk/2/hi/south_asia/4919420.stm (accessed on November 1, 2006).
[80] *Indian Maritime Doctrine INBR 8* (New Delhi: Integrated Headquarters, Ministry of Defence (Navy), 2004), p. 93.
[81] Ibid., pp. 63–68.
[82] Ibid., p. 59.

(1) confirm New Delhi's centrality in South Asia while allowing India to exercise its influence in the region,
(2) increase India's influence in Central Asia,
(3) promote limited cooperative relations with China,
(4) enhance strategic congruence with the US, and,
(5) enhance India's military profile in Central Asia and the Indian Ocean region.

If India is able to exploit the full hydroelectricity potential of its smaller South Asian neighbours by taking the technical and financial lead in generating and distributing hydroelectricity, Bhutan and Nepal are likely to become more dependent on New Delhi than they already are. According to one leading analyst of the region, hydroelectricity cooperation between India and its smaller Himalayan neighbours would not only promote energy security for New Delhi, it would also limit Beijing's influence in Bhutan and Nepal. Moreover, it would consolidate the ties between India and its smaller neighbours more effectively than any political treaty.[83]

Gas pipelines from the Persian Gulf region, for example, Iran–Pakistan–India (IPI) pipeline, or from Central Asia, for example, the Turkmenistan–Afghanistan–Pakistan–India (TAPI) pipeline, would need to traverse through Pakistani territory before supplying India. However, very little progress has been made on these pipelines due to the tensions between New Delhi and Islamabad. Given the limited trade complementarities between India and Pakistan, many analysts are of the view that energy pipelines such as the IPI pipeline can effectively end the 'economic partition' of the sub-continent and give each country a stake in the other's economy.[84] A pipeline from Iran to India via Pakistan would lower the cost of gas for Islamabad due to economies of scale. At the same time, Pakistan would also earn a significant transit fee for the pipeline. On the other hand, some Indian strategists are against the idea of

---

[83] Frederic Grare, 'Energy Security for India', in Brahma Chellaney, ed, *Securing India's Future in the New Millennium* (New Delhi: Orient Longman Limited, 1999), pp. 49–80.
[84] For a strong advocacy of trans-border energy projects in South Asia, see C. Raja Mohan, *Crossing the Rubicon: The Shaping of India's New Foreign Policy* (New Delhi: Viking, 2003), p. 252. Also see, C. Raja Mohan, 'Pipeline Diplomacy in South Asia', *Gulf News*, March 7, 2005.

such a pipeline traversing through Pakistan territory as it would enable Islamabad to stop supplies to India in the event of a military stand-off.[85]

Apart from the uneasy political relations between India and Pakistan, an important factor impeding progress over the IPI pipeline is political instability in Pakistan's Baluchistan province through which this pipeline is expected to pass through.[86] Geopolitical tensions between the US and Iran over the latter's nuclear programme have further complicated the IPI pipeline. The US has signalled that it would not like to see New Delhi or Islamabad cooperating with Tehran over this pipeline as it would not only end Tehran's geopolitical isolation but will also allow Iran to use the revenues thus generated for its nuclear programme.[87] The US is interested in extending the Tajikistan–Afghanistan–Pakistan pipeline to India.[88] However, this pipeline would face the same set of political problems between New Delhi and Islamabad, while adding an unstable Afghanistan to the equation.

India is further interested in a gas pipeline from Burma.[89] With the 1993 visit of the then Indian Foreign Secretary J. N. Dixit to Rangoon (now Yangon), India began engaging the Burmese military junta in order to address its own strategic needs: to access Burmese gas, to counter Beijing's growing influence in Yangon and to seek the help of the Burmese military in fighting insurgents in India's northeast operating out of bases in northern Burma. The US has some concerns regarding New Delhi's engagement with the Burmese

---

[85] For a view that argues that there is a lack of congruence in the politico-economic and strategic objectives of India, Pakistan and Iran as far as the IPI pipeline is concerned, see S. Pandian, 'The Political Economy of Trans-Pakistan Gas Pipeline Project: Assessing the Political and Economic Risks for India', *Energy Policy* 33:5 (March 2005), pp. 659–70.

[86] Gal Luft, *Iran–Pakistan–India Pipeline: The Baloch Wildcard* (Energy Security), January 12, 2005, at http://www.iags.org/n0115042.htm (accessed on November 2, 2006).

[87] For a comprehensive overview of American concerns over India's relations with Iran, including India's energy relations with Iran, see K. Alan Kronstadt, *India–Iran Relations and US Interests* (CRS Report for Congress), August 2, 2006, at http://fpc.state.gov/documents/organisation/70294.pdf (accessed on November 2, 2006).

[88] 'India to Join US-Backed Gas Pipeline Project', *The Hindu*, May 19, 2006.

[89] 'Natural Gas Deal may Link Iran, India and Burma', *Alexander's Gas & Oil Connections*, June 29, 2004.

military junta.[90] New Delhi would ideally like this pipeline to pass through northeastern India and Bangladesh before reentering India in West Bengal. New Delhi's aim is to tap the gas reserves in India's northeast as well as those of Bangladesh. However, progress on this front has been stalled by Dhaka's unwillingness to export gas to India as well as India's unwillingness to link trade-related issues in its negotiations with Bangladesh. This is largely a product of the uneasy political relations between the two countries.[91] India is currently studying the feasibility of a longer and more expensive pipeline that bypasses Bangladesh altogether.[92]

India's energy security is interlocked with the energy complementarities (whether in terms of energy sources or energy supply routes) that it shares with its immediate South Asian neighbours. As far as energy is concerned, the US, Europe, China and Japan are all moving towards 'regional sources of supply, buttressed by long-term political and economic relationships'.[93] This regional dimension is important for India's energy security needs too. Energy cooperation with its South Asian neighbours, including Pakistan, would tie the economies of these states with India's much larger and fast-growing economy. Several initiatives such as the creation of a regional energy market and that of regional energy (electricity and natural gas) grids have been proposed to promote energy cooperation in South Asia. It has also been proposed that India's strategic petroleum reserves should be set up as a regional facility with New Delhi taking the lead.[94]

---

[90] For a comprehensive discussion of India's interests in Myanmar, see Renaud Egreteau, *Wooing the Generals: India's New Burma Policy* (New Delhi: Authors Press, 2003).

[91] Sushma Ramachandran, 'Myanmar–India Gas Pipeline Proposal Runs into Problems', *The Hindu*, July 7, 2005.

[92] 'India, Myanmar may Bypass Bangladesh for Gas Pipeline—Other Options to be Explored', *The Hindu Business Line*, July 7, 2005.

[93] Sudha Mahalingam, 'Diversification and Energy Security', *The Hindu*, March 30, 2006. In this article, Mahalingam makes a strong case for regional energy cooperation for India's energy security.

[94] For example, see Vladislav Vucetic, *South Asia Regional Energy Trade Opportunities and Challenges*, October 1, 2004, at http://siteresources.worldbank.org/INTSOUTHASIA/Resources/Energy_a.pdf (accessed on November 2, 2006); *Regional Energy Security for South Asia: Regional Report* (USAID's South Asia Initiative for Energy), at http://www.sari-energy.org/ProjectReports/RegionalEnergySecurity_RegionalReport_Complete.pdf (accessed on November 2, 2006); and 'Energy Cooperation in South Asia: Potential and Prospects', *RIS Policy Briefs* No. 8 (December 2003).

Cooperation on energy with India would allow the other countries of the region to partake of India's economic resurgence that, in turn, will be dependent on energy cooperation with its neighbours. Furthermore, given India's sheer size, energy cooperation with its South Asian neighbours would only confirm New Delhi's regional centrality as its neighbours would develop considerable financial and commercial stakes in ensuring India's economic success. Proactive energy diplomacy in its neighbourhood would allow India to transform into an important actor that shapes its regional security environment, as opposed to being a victim of what New Delhi perceives to be a hostile environment.[95]

India is also interested in tapping the vast Central Asian gas and oil markets. Even though India has not yet entered into long-term energy import agreements with countries of Central Asia, New Delhi is closely monitoring the strategic developments in this energy-rich region, while enhancing its own political, economic and military influence there.[96] In addition to accessing Central Asia's hydrocarbons, India is also interested in accessing hydroelectricity from Tajikistan and Kyrgyzstan to supply states in northern India.[97] India hopes to access oil and gas from the Caucasus and the Caspian Sea region by cooperating with the Central Asian states. For example, Kazakhstan is interested in selling oil to India via the Caspian Sea and Iran.[98] Furthermore, India hopes that the TAPI pipeline, if and when successful, would be able to supply gas from other Central Asian states and the Caucasus region to India through an interlinked network connecting these regions with Turkmenistan. In a related development, India has also expressed its interest in accessing Caspian oil through the Baku–Tbilisi–Ceyhan oil pipeline that was inaugurated in 2005.[99]

However, India faces a strategic competition with China in Central Asia and the South Caucasus regions. On the other hand,

---

[95] Grare, 'Energy Security for India', p. 79.
[96] For a discussion of the geopolitical, geographic and economic aspects of India's energy trade with Central Asia, see Barnali Rag, 'Issues Related to India's Energy Trading with Central Asian Countries', *RIS Discussion Essays* No. 69 (March 2004).
[97] Siddharth Varadrajan, 'Power Grids and the New Silk Road in Asia', *The Hindu*, July 11, 2005.
[98] Ibid.
[99] Soma Banerjee, 'High on Energy, India Goes for Caspian Coup', *The Economic Times*, June 11, 2005.

Washington and New Delhi see a convergence of their strategic interests in this part of Eurasia.[100] In early 2006, the US put forth the idea of an electricity grid fed by oil and gas from Kazakhstan and Turkmenistan and hydroelectricity from Tajikistan and Kyrgyzstan to supply Afghanistan, Pakistan and India.[101] The US is interested in bringing the economies of Central Asian states close to South Asian states in order to reduce the influence of Russia and China in that critical region. Even though such an ambitious project needs to overcome several technical, financial and political difficulties to be successful, India's influence in Central Asia is likely to increase as a result of its own economic rise and its growing strategic congruence with the US.

India's emergence as a major international energy player has brought the country into a strategic competition with Asia's other rising power—China. India's former Minister for Petroleum and Natural Gas, Mani Shankar Aiyar, a strong proponent of energy cooperation in Asia, enthusiastically proposed Sino-Indian energy cooperation to avoid the prospects of a conflict in their competition over sources of energy.[102] Indeed, many serious Indian commentators have proposed the creation of ambitious projects, including an 'Asian Energy Union' through Sino-Indian partnership.[103] Under Aiyar's leadership, the possibility of extending the IPI pipeline to southern China was also discussed.[104] Indian analysts have entertained the idea of extending the Siberia–China gas pipelines to India and of accessing Central Asian gas deposits through pipelines

---

[100] For a view that India faces a strategic competition with China (and not Pakistan) in Central Asia and the South Caucasus regions and that there is strategic congruity between New Delhi and Washington in these regions, see Juli A. MacDonald, 'Rethinking India's and Pakistan's Regional Intent', in *Regional Power Plays in the Caucasus and Central Asia*, NBR Analysis 14:4 (November 2003), pp. 5–26.

[101] Richard A. Boucher (Assistant Secretary of State for South and Central Asian Affairs), *US Policy in Central Asia: Balancing Priorities (Part II)* (Statement to the House International Relations Committee, Subcommittee on the Middle East and Central Asia), April 26, 2006, at http://www.state.gov/p/sca/rls/rm/2006/65292.htm (accessed on November 2, 2006).

[102] Mani Shankar Aiyar, 'Asia's Quest for Energy Security', *Frontline* 23:3 (January 28—February 10, 2006), at http://www.frontlineonnet.com/fl2303/stories/20060224002309000.htm (accessed on April 2, 2008).

[103] Siddharth Varadrajan, 'India, China and the Asian Axis of Oil', *The Hindu*, January 24, 2006.

[104] Atul Aneja, 'Gas Pipeline Could be Extended to China', *The Hindu*, June 13, 2005.

via China's Xinjiang province.[105] However, Chinese analysts have been less enthusiastic about these grand proposals. Moreover, it is not clear if India and China would entrust the passage of their respective energy supplies through the other's territory as they view one another as strategic competitors in Asia in the long-run.[106] In an attempt to reduce the mutual suspicion, India and China signed several MoUs on energy cooperation in early 2006. However, being primarily of commercial nature, these MoUs are devoid of any strategic logic. Moreover, as mentioned earlier, as a result of the problem of 'relative gains', even the commercial dimension of Sino-Indian energy cooperation is unlikely to be of any significance. These MoUs are important symbolically and diplomatically in as much as they promote amicable relations between Asia's two rising powers that are in a fundamentally competitive relationship.

The end of the Cold War, India's economic rise and the presence of a successful Indian-American community have all transformed Indo-US bilateral relations.[107] To be sure, there are several sticking points in their relations, including India's relations with Iran and the proposed IPI pipeline as well as America's relations with Pakistan. However, it has been argued that India's pursuit of energy can promote strategic congruity between New Delhi and Washington. In this regard, it has been suggested that India's energy relations with Iran, its energy ties with important regions like the Middle East and Central Asia, its limited energy cooperation with China and its energy links with states like Myanmar, where the US presence is minimal or non-existent, can emerge as arenas where India and US can engage in joint strategy building for mutual benefit.[108] Interestingly, in a bid to strengthen their relationship, the US and India are already engaged in three high-level dialogues on energy

---

[105] M. K. Bhadrakumar, 'India Plays Catch-Up with China, Russia', March 28, 2006, at http://www.atimes.com/atimes/South_Asia/HC28Df04.html (accessed on November 2, 2006).

[106] Mohan Malik, 'China's Strategy of Containing India', February 6, 2006, at http://www.pinr.com/report.php?ac=view_report&report_id=434&language_id=1 (accessed on November 2, 2006).

[107] For example, see Eric Lober and Pramit Mitra, 'US–India Relations: Convergence of Interests', *CSIS South Asia Monitor* Number 84 (July 2005), pp. 1–4.

[108] Juli A. MacDonald and Bethany Danyluk, 'Pursuit of Energy Security can Enhance its Relationship with the US', *Force*, September 2006.

security, strategic coordination and economic engagement.[109] In other words, the bilateral mechanism to promote energy security and enhance strategic congruity is already in place, and is evolving further. The Indo-US civil nuclear cooperation agreement, if successful, will further promote their strategic relationship, while also addressing India's energy security needs.[110]

However, the Indo-US civil nuclear deal is being hampered by the left-wing allies of the present Congress-led government in India as a result of their reflexively anti-American posture. The main opposition party, the Bharatiya Janata Party (BJP), is also opposing the deal out of opportunism as the successful passage of the agreement in India will give the Congress Party the credit for cementing strategic ties with the US. The BJP-led National Democratic Alliance (NDA) that governed India from 1998 to 2004 had played an important role in laying down the framework within which the civil nuclear deal has emerged.[111] The failure of the Indo-US civil nuclear deal will adversely impact both India's energy security and its rising strategic profile.[112]

The military dimension of India's energy security also has important implications. Given its reliance on the Middle East for its oil supplies and the Persian Gulf for its gas needs, India is serious about the security of its energy sources and the security of its sea lanes in the Indian Ocean region. India has identified the maritime region stretching from the Straits of Hormuz in the Persian Gulf to the Straits of Malacca in Southeast Asia as a region of vital concern for India's energy security. India is keen on building a blue-water navy to protect its trade and energy interests in this region. In the eastern Indian Ocean region, India has already established its first tri-service base in the Andaman and Nicobar Islands at the mouth of the Straits of Malacca. The Indian government also plans

---

[109] Ashley J. Tellis, *India as a New Global Power: An Action Agenda for the United States* (Washington, D.C: Carnegie Endowment for International Peace, 2005), pp. 19–54.

[110] Dinshaw Mistry and Sumit Ganguly, 'The US–India Nuclear Pact: A Good Deal', *Current History*, November 2006.

[111] On these issues, see Sumit Ganguly, 'Save the Nuclear Deal', *The Times of India*, October 26, 2007.

[112] Nicolas Blarel and Manjeet S. Pardesi, 'Price of Failure,' *Daily News & Analysis*, November 13, 2007.

on setting up a full-fledged air base on the Nicobar Islands.[113] In future, New Delhi may seek a naval access facility in Singapore.[114] In the western Indian Ocean region, India's ambitious Project Seabird, which consists of the Karwar naval base in Karnataka state together with an air force station and missile silos, is already operational in part. When fully ready in five years time, it is expected to be Asia's largest naval base.[115] India is acutely aware of its geographic location which connects the Middle East and East Asia in the Indian Ocean region and as such is keen to play an important security role in this region as it emerges as a great power in Asia and beyond. At the same time, given its interest in Central Asian oil and gas, India has reportedly acquired a military airbase at Ayni in Tajikistan. According to several media reports, New Delhi is likely to deploy a fleet of Mi-17 helicopters and some Kiran trainer aircrafts to train Tajik pilots there by the end of 2007. However, both New Delhi and Dushanbe have officially denied these reports.[116]

CONCLUSION

Promoting energy security is crucial for India as the country is estimated to increase its annual GDP growth rate by 2 per cent p.a., if its energy sector were to reach international levels of performance.[117] Energy security is India's Achilles' heel in its economic resurgence and in its path to becoming an Asian and global player.[118] Even though it needs to make difficult choices and huge financial and technological investments to ensure its energy security, India can potentially attain its strategic goals by adequately addressing

---

[113] See 'Andaman and Nicobar Command', in Lt Gen. (Retd) Jasbir Singh, PVSM, ed, *Indian Defense Yearbook 2002* (New Delhi: Natraj Publishers, 2002), pp. 303–07.
[114] David Boey, 'Sky's the Limit with S'pore–India Defence Pact', *The Straits Times*, October 17, 2003.
[115] 'Sea Bird Poised to Become Largest Naval Base: Officer', *The Hindu*, December 5, 2005.
[116] Stephen Blank, *India: The New Central Asian Player* (Eurasia Insight), June 26, 2006, at http://www.eurasianet.org/departments/insight/articles/eav062606a.shtml (accessed on November 13, 2006). Also see Rajat Pandit, 'Indian Forces Get Foothold in Central Asia', *The Times of India*, July 17, 2007.
[117] *Defining an Integrated Energy Strategy for India*, p. vi.
[118] Samrat, 'No Superpower if there is No Power', *Hindustan Times*, October 6, 2006.

its energy security requirements. The pursuit of energy security has the potential to consolidate India's dominant position in South Asia, enhance New Delhi's influence in Central Asia, promote limited cooperative relations with China, enhance strategic congruence with the US and enable New Delhi to emerge as a major military player in Central Asia and the Indian Ocean region.

PART II
India and Major Global Powers

6

India and the US: Embracing a New Paradigm

C. CHRISTINE FAIR[*]

Since 2000, the US and India have worked to fundamentally reorder the strategic underpinnings of their bilateral ties as well as the substance of their engagement. While US President Bill Clinton and Indian Prime Minister Atal Bihari Vajpayee initiated this transformation process, both leaders held orthogonal positions on the issue of India's nuclear weapons programme—even though both leaders understood the mutual value of more robust relations. India's nuclear tests in May 1998 enervated the 'Strategic Dialogue' that had Clinton launched to reach out to India.[1]

Ironically, those tests hastened a genuine strategic dialogue between New Delhi and Washington. In this dialogue, then Deputy Secretary of State Strobe Talbott represented the US and then Indian External Affairs Minister Jaswant Singh represented India. Talbot and Singh met 14 times in seven countries in an effort to resolve the extant bilateral differences over India's nuclear weapons programme and develop the means to manage those

---

[*] C. Christine Fair, at the time of writing this essay, was a Senior Research Fellow at the United States Institute of Peace (USIP). She is currently a Senior Political Scientist for the RAND Corporation. This essay reflects the views of the author only and not those of USIP or RAND. The information cut-off for this essay is November 30, 2006. It was minimally updated in November 2007, following external review. Many events with respect to Pakistan could not be clarified at that juncture, given the recent decision of President and General Musharraf to declare what was tantamount to emergency rule.

[1] For more details about the Strategic Dialogue, see C. Christine Fair, *The Counterterror Coalitions Cooperation with India and Pakistan*. (Santa Monica: RAND, 2004) and C. Christine Fair, 'Learning to Think the Unthinkable: Lessons from India's Nuclear Test', *India Review* 4:1 (January 2005), pp. 23–58.

differences that could not be resolved. The Talbott–Singh dialogue constituted what was at the time the most prolonged engagement between high-level American and Indian officials in their bilateral history. These meetings laid the foundation for the on-going evolution in US–India strategic relations.[2]

While Clinton and Vajpayee made tremendous progress in changing the structure and substance of the US–India relationship, Clinton's commitment to global non-proliferation norms precluded elemental changes during his presidency. In contrast to Clinton, President George W. Bush's administration prioritised getting the Indo-US relationship 'right' and, unhindered by the non-proliferation commitments of past presidencies, Bush embraced a new paradigm for relating to the major power in South Asia. Unlike past administrations that pursued policies towards India or Pakistan with an implicit calculation as to how the other would respond, under Bush the US sought to de-couple its relations with India and Pakistan, in a process that has become known as 'de-hyphenation' in New Delhi, Islamabad and Washington.

Ashley Tellis authored this new approach in an influential RAND (Research and Development) report for the new administration in 2000. In the report, he recommended that the Bush administration pursue a differentiated set of policies with respect to India and Pakistan and called for 'deepened engagement with India' and a 'soft landing for Pakistan'.[3] According to this course, 'US relations with each state [would be] governed by an objective assessment of the intrinsic value of each country to US interests rather than by fears of how US relations with one would affect relations with the other'. Moreover, it was Tellis' view that '. . . India is on its way to becoming a major Asian power of some consequence and, therefore, that it warrants a level of engagement far greater than the previous norm and also an appreciation of its potential for both collaboration and resistance across a much larger canvas than simply South Asia'.[4]

---

[2] For Strobe Talbott's account of this engagement, see Strobe Talbott, *Engaging India: Diplomacy, Democracy, and the Bomb* (Revised Edition) (Washington, DC: Brookings Institution Press, 2006).

[3] Ashley J. Tellis, 'South Asia: US Policy Choices', in Frank Carlucci, Robert Hunter and Zalmay Khalilzad, eds, *Taking Charge: A Bipartisan Report to the President-Elect on Foreign Policy and National Security—Discussion Papers* (Santa Monica: RAND, 2000), p. 88.

[4] Ibid.

Since early 2001, relations between India and the US have expanded both in terms of the kinds of engagements pursued and in terms of the depth of those engagements. They have made great strides in the areas of military-to-military engagement, civilian space and nuclear cooperation, and in high-technology exchanges and collaboration. Furthermore, while these areas have advanced faster than what the most optimistic observers had surmised possible, both countries have assembled a number of private sector ventures that have created important stakeholders with vested interests in the relationship. These bilateral efforts have been buttressed and even galvanised by the financially well-off and numerically strong Indo-American community.

Notwithstanding these important accomplishments, it is worth interrogating the durability of, and long-term prospects for, this bilateral partnership. This query animates the substance of this essay. Since the recent and distant history of the Indo-US relationship has been extensively covered elsewhere, it focusses on the contemporary dynamics of the Indo-US relationship, referencing the past only as it directly impinges upon the present.[5] To evaluate the robustness of this relationship, this essay poses and answers the following set of key questions:

- What do India and the US hope to achieve from their relations with states generally and from this dyad in particular? To what degree are these goals and objectives complementary?
- What are their threat perceptions and how do these perceptions complement or, alternatively, conflict with each other?
- How do they assess the costs and benefits of engaging each other?
- What import does these questions and concomitant answers have for a sustained US–India relations?

The remainder of this essay will attempt to answer each of these questions in its next six sections. Section two lays out the states' expectations of their security relationships generally and their

---

[5] See, inter alia, Dennis Kux, *Estranged Democracies: India and the United States 1941–1991* (Washington, DC: National Defense University Press, 1993); Fair, *The Counterterror Coalitions Cooperation with India and Pakistan*, pp. 66–79; Satu Limaye, *US-Indian Relations: The Pursuit of Accommodation* (Boulder, CO: Westview Press, 1993).

bilateral ties in particular. Section three exposits New Delhi's main security challenges and section four examines the US evaluation and appreciation of those perceptions. This twin assessment yields some insight into the complimentarity between Indian and US threat assessments in South Asia and beyond. It also explicates both states' expectations of security partnerships generally and of this dyad in particular. Section five lays out both states' cost–benefit calculus with respect to their bilateral ties. Section six, the final section, concludes with a discussion of the key challenges that both the states will confront as they forge ahead.

INDIAN PERSPECTIVES ON STRATEGIC PARTNERSHIPS: WHAT ROLE FOR THE US–INDIA RELATIONSHIP?

India contends that it is the pre-eminent power in South Asia and an emergent global power. Consequently, New Delhi values those security partnerships that both confirm this world-view and increase the likelihood of the US and the wider international community accepting India's belief about its natural strategic role in the world.[6] The US occupies a privileged place within the Indian national security establishment because US assistance to India is critical to India's emergence as an extra-regional military power in a politically relevant timeframe. Strides in the Indo-US relationship have accelerated since July 2005, when the Bush administration explicitly stated its intention to further India's growth as a global power. Since then, the US has done much to make this happen.[7]

---

[6] See Fair, *The Counterterror Coalitions Cooperation with India and Pakistan*, pp. 86–89.

[7] Achievements of note include the March 2006 agreement on civilian nuclear cooperation; the July 2005 Joint Statement signed by President Bush and Prime Minister Manmohan Singh to establish a 'global partnership' as well as subsidiary commitments, including a ten-year defence framework agreement, the January 2004 Next Step Strategic Partnership, unprecedented military-to-military ties, technological sales and commitment to ballistic missile development. For details of these and other milestones, see Ashley J. Tellis, *India as a New Global Power: An Action Agenda for the United States* (Washington, DC: Carnegie Endovment for International Peace, 2005); Stephen J. Blank, *Natural Allies: Regional Security in Asia and Prospects for Indo-American Strategic Cooperation* (Carlisle, PA: Strategic Studies Institute, 2005); K. Alan Kronstadt, *US–India Bilateral Agreements*, in 2005 Congressional Research Service Report RL33072, September 8, 2005; C. Christine Fair, 'US-Indian Army-to-Army Relations', *Asian Security* 1:2 (April 2005), pp. 157–73

While US officials have proclaimed India's rise as a potential great power, Indian strategic thinkers have been slow to articulate what it means to be a regional or extra-regional military power and how this aspiration squares with Indian claim that its armed forces are not likely to be a conventionally-considered 'global power projection' military in the near future. While opacity persists around India's force projection objectives, it is moving towards consolidating its military presence outside its own borders (e.g., it now has access to two airfields in Tajikistan, and it has a military and intelligence presence in Iran and Afghanistan, among other locales). India's blue-water naval aspirations and the armed forces' participation in peace-keeping operations are notable exceptions, as is India's expected role in disaster relief (as witnessed during the 2005 Asian tsunami).

While India surely values its political and military engagement with the US, the most significant confirmation that Washington sees India differently is the former's willingness to sell high-end defence-related technologies to India and to grant India permission to produce such technologies under licence. More important yet is Washington's willingness to explore co-development of such technologies. Previous efforts by New Delhi and Washington to forge robust security ties failed time and again because they disagreed about the role of technology transfers in their nascent bilateral relations. Whereas Washington saw such transfers as the apex of a pyramidal structured bilateral relationship, sitting atop a robust base of political, diplomatic and economic ties, New Delhi, conditioned on the modalities of its relations with the former USSR, expected such transfers as an 'up front' commitment to a serious partnership.[8]

While New Delhi seeks relations with the US for reasons noted above, India has been very active over the last decade cultivating numerous significant relations with a complex mix of states—many of whom share adversarial relations with one another. India maintains a sophisticated portfolio of foreign policies with Israel, Iran, Saudi Arabia, China, Russia, the Central Asian Republics as well as

---

[8] See discussion of historical US-Indian relations in Fair, *The Counterterror Coalitions Cooperation with India and Pakistan*, pp. 66–79; and Satu Limaye, *US-Indian Relations: The Pursuit of Accommodation*.

several states in Southeast Asia (India's so-called 'look east' strategy).[9] Throughout India's extended strategic environment, New Delhi relies upon 'soft power' aspects of its military establishment, including the provision of military training to personnel of regional armies, contribution to peace-keeping forces as well as training peace-keepers. In addition, India trains police and paramilitary personnel from a number of countries throughout Africa and Asia, and believes that such training is a major tool for expanding its military and intelligence presence throughout its extended neighbourhood. While India focusses upon these softer aspects of power projection, in recent years it has established two airbases in Tajikistan, which is the foothold of India's military and intelligence presence in Central Asia.[10]

India's other important relationship is with Israel and their security ties predate formal diplomatic recognition in 1991. Recently, Israel has surpassed Russia and has become the largest arms supplier to India and this defence supply relationship will continue to grow in scope and sophistication of products. Israel is seen as a reliable supplier of affordable, high-quality equipment without moral or political strings attached, unlike the US.

Consonant with India's perception of itself as an extra-regional power and aspiring global power, it seeks alternatives to the current monopolar global power structure, in which the US is pre-eminent. Instead, New Delhi favours a multipolar structure that features India, China and the EU, as well the US. In the Ministry of Defence's *Annual Report 2005–06*, the government of India notes the success of this goal: 'Progress towards a truly multi-polar world, with India

---

[9] See Sushil J. Aaron, *Straddling Faultlines: India's Foreign Policy Towards the Greater Middle East*, Centre de Sciences Humaine, New Delhi, Occasional Paper No. 7, 2003; Frederic Grare and Amitabh Mattoo, eds, *India and ASEAN: The Politics of India's Look East Policy* (New Delhi: Manohar, 2001); Stephen Blank, 'India's Rising Profile in Central Asia', *Comparative Strategy* 22: 2 (April 2003), pp. 139–57. C. Christine Fair, 'Indo-Iranian Relations: Prospects for Bilateral Cooperation Post 9-11', in *The 'Strategic Partnership' Between India and Iran*, Woodrow Wilson International Center for Scholars, Asia Program Special Report No. 120; A.K. Pasha, 'India, Iran and the GCC States: Common Political and Strategic Concerns', in *India, Iran and the GCC States: Political Strategy and Foreign Policy* (New Delhi: Manas Publication, 2000), pp. 227–28.

[10] This is consonant with India's past coordination with Tajikistan on shared regional goals: India worked with Tajikistan (along with Iran and Russia) to provide military assistance and training to the Northern Alliance during the days of the Taliban.

as one of the poles has been slow but steady'.[11] It proceeds to describe, in obtuse terms, benchmarks of this success including 'China's emergence during the year as a major importer and influencing factor in the volatile energy markets and as a country that is looking to part its excess capital in various projects across the globe, including in the US, [which] have made an initial impact, especially in the US'.[12]

Concomitant with this self-image and aspirations, India contends that its national endowments and capacities justify a permanent seat on the UN Security Council, which New Delhi views as tantamount to 'a full recognition of India as a great power, something that the Indian elite still craves'.[13] India hopes that the US will eventually support this position in full.

Thus far, the US has been very reticent and even evasive about this issue, notwithstanding the unprecedented expansion in US–India ties. During the visit by the Indian Foreign Minister Natwar Singh in April 2005, the Secretary of State Condoleeza Rice was explicitly pressed on this issue. Rice demurred and explained that while the US supports the positive and expanding global role for India, any reform of the UN Security Council would take place within the context of UN reform writ large.[14] For non-proliferation proponents, a UN Security Council seat would reward India for becoming a de facto nuclear power and would present a wrong incentive structure to aspirant proliferators. India's aspiration to the UN Security Council is somewhat problematic for the US because it has a number of allies who have a more robust history of supporting the US than has India. Despite these concerns, there are growing numbers of high-level proponents of bringing India onto the UN Security Council: the architect of the current US–India

---

[11] See Ministry of Defence, *Annual Report Year 2005–2006* (New Delhi: Government of India), pp. 6–8, at http://mod.nic.in/reports/(accessed on April 20, 2006).
[12] Ibid., pp. 2–3.
[13] Stephen Cohen, 'India and America: An Emerging Relationship', paper presented to the Conference on the Nation State System and Transnational Forces in South Asia, Kyoto Japan, December 8–10, 2000, p. 23.
[14] Secretary of State Condoleezza Rice, 'Remarks with Indian Minister of External Affairs Natwar Singh Following Meeting', Department of State, Washington DC, April 14, 2005, at www.state.gov/secretary/rm/2005/44662.htm (accessed on November 8, 2007).

relationship, Ashley Tellis, has argued clearly for India's inclusion on the UN Security Council.[15]

INDIA'S SECURITY PERCEPTIONS

Unlike the *National Security Strategy* that every American presidential administration is required to produce, India does not have a national security strategy document *per se*. For purposes of this inquiry, the most authoritative open-source document of India's security perceptions is the Ministry of Defence (MoD) *Annual Report*.[16] Recent annual reports identify several challenges that have remained constant over the last five years, with the intractable security competition with Pakistan figuring as the pre-eminent and enduring security challenge.[17] The *Report* also monitors developments elsewhere in the greater South Asian region, including the on-going efforts to stabilise and rehabilitate Afghanistan, the various developments in Nepal, the rise of 'Islamic [sic] fundamentalism' in Bangladesh and the attendant consequences for India's Northeast, and the stalled peace process in Sri Lanka between Tamil militants (the Liberation Tigers of Tamil Elam) and the Sri Lankan government and concomitant slippage back into all-out, if undeclared, war.[18]

The MoD annual reports consistently identify China as its long-term security challenge. India's strategy is diversified and it

---

[15] Tellis, *India as a New Global Power: An Action Agenda for the United States*, pp. 34–36.

[16] While this document is the most authoritative proxy for a national security strategy document, as India has increasingly sought to situate itself as an important arm's buyer, this document has increasingly become more of tool for potential arms sellers. A perusal of several years of this document also indicates an awareness that this document is being used by persons outside of India and there is a concomitant transformation in the way in which the document is written and issues presented. A strong argument can be made that this document has become part of India's communication strategy with the world's capitals to manage international perceptions about India's interests and intents. The evolution of the way in which India's energy interests have been characterised serve as a strong example of this change.

[17] Ministry of Defence, *Annual Report Year 2005–2006* (New Delhi: Government of India), pp. 6–8, at http://mod.nic.in/reports/ (accessed on April 20, 2006).

[18] Ibid., pp. 8–9. See also C. Christine Fair, 'Faltering Sri Lankan Peace Process: Sri Lanka's Drift Back into War', *Journal of International Peace Operations* 2:3 (November–December, 2006), at http://ipoaonline.org/journal/index.php?option=com_content&task=viewfid=274Itemid=28 (accessed on May 4, 2008).

includes the pursuit of enhanced political, military, diplomatic and economic ties with Beijing to pre-empt any significant confrontation while increasing its readiness in the event of some kind of confrontation manifesting in the future.[19] Despite New Delhi's efforts to secure ever-improved relations with Beijing, New Delhi remains committed to mitigating China's capabilities to restrict India's movement and presence in its extended neighbourhood, which encompasses Southwest, Central, South and Southeast Asia. New Delhi's desire to exert itself vis-à-vis China animates many of the bilateral relations cultivated by India in its extended strategic environment.[20]

To project its regional and extra-regional equities, India makes astute use of regional frameworks such as South Asian Association for Regional Cooperation (SAARC) and the Association of Southeast Asian States (ASEAN), among others. Recently, New Delhi has secured entry as an observer to the Shangai Cooperation Organisation and has taken a proactive role in the Bengal Initiative for Multi-Sectoral Technical and Economic Cooperation (BIMSTEC), which will serve as a regional bridge between South and Southeast Asia.[21]

The MoD annual defence report also details India's various internal security challenges. Insurgencies 'fanned by ethnic and tribal chauvinists' desire to achieve autonomy, left wing radicalism and extremism motivated by prevailing socio-economic deprivation and communal conflict encouraged by religious fundamentalism and caste conflict' are important security preoccupations.[22] These internal security challenges, as the MoD *Annual Report* notes, have forced the Indian army to remain engaged in high states of readiness throughout the country.[23]

The final security concern that merits discussion is India's energy security concerns, which have assumed prominence in recent years. While energy concerns have figured consistently in the MoD annual reports, the recent assessment departs from previous volumes in that it identifies energy supplies, in the guise of 'peaceful uses of nuclear energy', as a critical preoccupation for the Indian state. Rather than describing security aspects of energy supplies, the

---

[19] Ministry of Defence, *Annual Report Year 2005–2006*, pp. 9–10.
[20] Ibid., pp. 10–11.
[21] Ibid.
[22] Ibid., p. 11.
[23] Ibid., pp. 10–11.

2005 report explicitly calls attention to India's 'deliberate mission to enlarge the scope of use of nuclear energy for peaceful purposes, including for generation of power' and the dialogue it has pursued with the US and the Nuclear Suppliers Groups for 'unhindered access to nuclear technology'.[24]

WASHINGTON'S EVOLVING APPRECIATION OF INDIA'S THREAT ENVIRONMENT

Washington appreciates India's concerns regarding Pakistan's contributions to New Delhi's domestic woes and regional insecurity. However, Washington's relations with Pakistan remain principally focussed upon Islamabad's on-going 'collaboration' with the US in the Global War on Terrorism (GWOT). It can be argued that this concern supercedes other critical security matters such as nuclear proliferation, as evidenced by the relative US quiescence on on-going revelations about Pakistan's nuclear proliferation activities and the opacity surrounding Abdul Qadeer Khan's nuclear black market. Washington remains committed to the belief that there is no alternative to President Musharraf and has remained reluctant to push Musharraf harder on key issues such as cross-border insurgent activities in Indian-administered Kashmir and even in Afghanistan, where US and North Atlantic Treaty Organization (NATO) troops are vulnerable to Taliban attacks. Throughout 2007, as Musharraf's missteps galvanised nation-wide calls for democracy, Washington felt the pressure to increase its calls for democracy. While Musharraf's imposition of what was tantamount to martial law on November 3, 2007 raised hackles in Washington, the Bush administration largely stayed course while encouraging President Musharraf to hold free and fair elections as promised.

Given that US policy towards Musharraf has not *yet* moved beyond these parameters, Washington's public statements about Pakistan's support for militancy in Indian-administered Kashmir

---

[24] It is worth noting that no previous Annual Reports (since 1999) included this issue as a part of its regional threat assessment. Rather, previous Annual Reports (1999–2000, 2000–01, 2001–02, 2002–03, 2003–04, 2004–05) dilated upon the need to secure fossil fuels. In contrast, the most recent report made no mention of fossil fuels, which is odd given that 90 per cent of India's oil comes from offshore oil fields or is transported via sea transport. See Ministry of Defence, *Annual Report Year 2005–2006*, pp. 10–11.

and in India continue to countervail those preferred by New Delhi who is increasingly concerned about its ever-more unstable neighbour.[25] However, Washington's position has begun to turn due, at least in part, to on-going reports that Taliban forces, who enjoy various forms of sanctuary in Pakistan, and the failure of Pakistan's various deals with militants in South and North Waziristan. To Washington's ire, following the most recent deal inked in September 2006 between the government and local Taliban, insurgent attacks in Afghanistan increased three-fold.[26]

The cumulative effect of these developments has been that many observers fundamentally and openly question Pakistan's intentions in the border areas.[27] Many people in the US government have begun to ask whether Pakistan is doing too little to prevent these attacks or whether there may even be open cooperation from elements within the Pakistan state, even if few are willing to say publicly that this policy is approved by President Musharraf.[28] Thus, in the future, differences in the US and Indian positions towards Pakistan's role in the region may narrow.

---

[25] See C. Christine Fair and Peter Chalk, *Fortifying Pakistan: The Role US Internal Security Assistance* (Washington, DC: USIP Press, 2006). For a personal account of this pressured decision, see Pervez Musharraf, *In the Line of Fire: A Memoir* (New York: Free Press, 2006).

[26] The author has obtained a copy of the deal signed in September 2006 in Urdu. Copies will be provided upon request. According to this deal, the first party is the political agent representing the administration of the Northwest Frontier Province. The second party identified is a collective of parties that include the Utmanzai tribal elders, the local mujahadeen, the Taliban, the ulema and the Utmanzai tribe.

[27] See Seth Jones, 'Pakistan's Dangerous Game', *Survival* 49:1 (Spring 2007), pp. 15–32.

[28] This view has been expressed during author's meetings with US officials in Islamabad in August 2005, with members of US military personnel who served in Afghanistan in November 2006. There have also been a number of editorials expressing concern about the structure of the US–Pakistan relationship. See 'Some Ally: Pakistan Has Sold Out Afghan and US Interests by Signing an Agreement with Tribesmen that Aids the Taliban', *The Los Angeles Times*, November 6, 2006; Alan Cowell, Carlotta Gall, 'Pakistan is Accused of Terror Ties and Abuses', *The New York Times*, September 29, 2006; Somini Sengupta, Scott Shane and David Rohde, 'Pakistan's Help in Averting a Terror Attack is a Double-Edged Sword', *The New York Times*, August 12, 2006; David Rohde, 'The Afghanistan Triangle.' *The New York Times*, October 1, 2006; Rachel Morarjee, Farhan Bokhari and Jo Johnson, 'Pakistan "Not Involved" in Afghan Insurgency, *Financial Times*, September 7, 2006; Carlotta Gall, 'Musharraf Vows to Aid Afghanistan in Fighting Taliban', *The New York Times*, September 7, 2006; Syed Saleem Shahzad, 'Pakistan Reaches into Afghanistan', *The Asia Times*, October 3, 2006.

Nonetheless, Indian analysts have been restrained in criticising aspects of Washington's relations with Islamabad. Few Indian officials of any consequence have hectored Washington publicly for its on-going military alliance with Pakistan. This is in stark contrast to the past when Indian observers would loudly protest such ties. Instead, most Indian analysts and officials appreciate that the US is offering India an expansive strategic partnership that dwarfs the one available to Pakistan now or in the future.[29] Indian officials and commentators also understand that the US shares India's overall preference for Pakistan to become a peaceable democracy. However, there are many within the Indian establishment and, increasingly within the US government, who doubt the soundness of the US–Pakistan policy, which privileges the singular personality of Musharraf while being unprepared for the day when Musharraf is no longer relevant.

While the US and India disagree in some measure with respect to the optimal policy approaches to Pakistan, both have analogous visions for a rehabilitated Afghanistan—even if both states have a somewhat different set of preferred surrogates and partnerships to secure Afghanistan. New Delhi has made numerous contributions of its own to that effort, including more than $500 million for infrastructure projects, humanitarian assistance, and institutional and human resource development.[30] These investments have paid off: Afghanistan sees India as its most important ally in the region. In general, India's role in Afghanistan has been welcomed by Washington even if there are negative externalities for other US policies resulting from this assistance, as is discussed later in this essay.

With regards to India's other regional concerns (e.g., Bangladesh, Nepal and Sri Lanka), the US does not have a ready plan of engagement. Instead, it pursues various ad hoc measures depending upon the perceived salience of these regional issues at any given moment. For example, severe developments such as the 2005

---

[29] Again, see Tellis' comparison of the relationship offered to both states in Tellis, *India as a New Global Power*.
[30] See Ministry of External Affairs, *Rebuilding Afghanistan: India at Work* (New Delhi: Government of India, 2005).

tsunami galvanised US action, as did the revolution in Nepal, which kick-started a more coherent—albeit brief—policy focus on Katmandu. Similarly, the US' effort to more effectively monitor Islamism and Islamist violence in Bangladesh intensified in the wake of the August 2005 bombings, which included more than 500 small bombs being detonated in 63 of 64 districts over the course of roughly an hour. Increasingly, US officials have publicly stated that it turns to India for guidance on these regional concerns.[31]

Turning to the inevitable ascendance of China and the need to maintain regional balance of power, many officials and analysts within the US government seek to cultivate India as a variously construed counterweight to China, either as a part of a containment policy or as a partner in managing China's ascent. Whether one holds a preference for containment or managed ascent, India is critical to those who view China's rise throughout Southwest, Central, South and Southeast Asia as a threat to US interests in Asia. India, it is hoped, will disrupt the unchecked expansion of Chinese strategic influence in Asia simply by asserting its own equities with greater strategic, diplomatic, political, commercial and military presence.[32] US officials in recent years have become increasingly sensitive to the fact that India publicly eschews becoming part of any formal effort to limit or manage China's growth. While administration officials go to great lengths to deny any efforts to use India in this manner, at least in part to accommodate India's concerns,[33] India's

---

[31] See for example, the comments of Under Secretary of State for Political Affairs, R. Nicholas Burns at a talk called 'US–India Relations: The Global Partnership', attended by the author on Tuesday 16, 2006. Audiofile available at http://www.carnegieendowment.org/events/index.cfm?fa=eventDetail&id=884&&prog=zgp&proj=znpp,zsa,zusr (accessed on May 31, 2006).

[32] For a good discussion of the utility of India in the US efforts to 'preserve the future balance of power in Asia', again see Tellis, *India as a New Global Power*.

[33] A good example of this is given by the comments of Under Secretary of State for Political Affairs, R. Nicholas Burns at a talk called 'US–India Relations: The Global Partnership', attended by the author on Tuesday 16, 2006. Audiofile available at http://www.carnegieendowment.org/events/index.cfm?fa=eventDetail&id=884&&prog=zgp&proj=znpp,zsa,zusr (accessed on May 31, 2006). In this discussion, Burns made it clear that the US interest in India is not motivated by a desire to contain China.

utility to the US becomes increasingly contingent upon China's future trajectories.[34]

Finally, one of the most important long-standing areas of US–India engagement since 2000 is on counterterrorism and law enforcement. After President Clinton visited New Delhi in 2000, the US and India founded the US India Counterterrorism Joint Working Group. Both states point to their shared perceptions of the terrorist threat to explain the growing strategic consensus between India and the US, and both sides identify the importance of the working group in forging such consensus. While both partners define terrorism similarly in some areas such as sea-lanes of control, al Qaeda and the Taliban, there are notable issues about which New Delhi and Washington hold markedly different views of the threat and concomitant policy response. As noted, the US cannot yet take New Delhi's preferred approach to Pakistan—even if Washington agrees with New Delhi's fundamental assessment. Nor did India share the US contention that Iraq was a source of terrorism prior to onset of US military operations there, and India continues to resist US assertions about terrorism in Iran.

THE COSTS AND BENEFITS OF EXPANDED US–INDIA RELATIONS

While there is little doubt that India and the US expect tremendous benefits from their evolving partnership, there are distinct

---

[34] See Tellis, *India as a New Global Power*, where Tellis argues that 'if the United States is serious about advancing its geopolitical objectives in Asia [read China, among other things], it would almost by definition help New Delhi develop its strategic capabilities' (p. 41). Elsewhere on p. 42, he cites former US Ambassador to New Delhi, Robert Blackwill, who asked rhetorically 'why should the US want to check India's missile capability in ways that could lead to China's permanent nuclear dominance over democratic India'. For other accounts, see Francine R. Frankel and Harry Harding, eds, *The India–China Relationship: What the United States Needs to Know* (New York: Columbia University Press, 2004); Esther Pan, 'India, China, and the United States: A Delicate Balance', Council for Foreign Relations, *Backgrounder*, February 27, 2006, at http://www.cfr.org/publication/9962/ (accessed on October 11, 2006); Christopher Griffin, 'Containment with Chinese Characteristics: Beijing Hedges against the Rise of India', *Asian Outlook—AEI Online*, September 7, 2006, at http://www.aei.org/publications/pubID.24873/pub_detail.asp (accessed on October 11, 2006); Paul Richter, 'In Deal with India, Bush Has Eye on China', *The Los Angeles Times*, March 4, 2006; Michael T. Klare, 'Containing China: The US's Real Objective', *The Asia Times*, April 20, 2006.

costs—both direct and opportunity—that both states will endure as a consequence of the new terms of their engagement. Understanding the inputs into both sides' cost-benefit calculus yield some insights into the durability of this dyad. Thus, this section attempts to explicate these costs and benefits for both states, first from New Delhi's vantage point and then from that of Washington.

India's Cost-Benefit Calculus

One of the principal benefits for India is the US' acknowledgement of India's strategic significance within Asia and its recognition of New Delhi's growing importance globally. The second benefit that India has enjoyed in the post-9/11 world is that its perception on terrorism generally has been accepted. Many observers have come to recognise and accept New Delhi's mantra of 'cross-border terrorism'. This has enabled New Delhi to marginalise Pakistan politically even though Pakistan remains an importantally of the US in the GWOT. However, India remains frustrated that the US still considers the 'terrorism' in Jammu and Kashmir as distinct from the terrorism committed by al Qaeda[35] even if, as noted above, recent reports suggest that the US' views of Pakistan generally, and of President Pervez Musharraf in particular, may be changing.

Second, India has benefited from the fast pace of military-to-military ties with its heavy emphasis upon joint training. India's ambitions to become a blue-water navy are significantly advanced by the on-going military cooperation with the US. However, with respect to military hardware and India's planned extensive military modernisation, the role of US-supplied hardware remains undetermined at this point.[36] Given the late 2006 Congressional

---

[35] This view was expressed by people interviewed by the author in the Indian Ministry of External Affairs in September 2002. It was also expressed during conversations with a wide array of Indian officials interviewed in June 2004 and most recently during interviews with high-level officials in the Ministry of External Affairs and the Home Ministry in August 2006.
[36] See 'Modernization Plans of the Indian Army', in Lt. Gen. R.K. Jasbir Singh, ed, *Indian Defence Yearbook 2005* (New Delhi: Natraj, 2005), pp. 206–25; 'Modernization of the Indian Navy Gathers Pace', in Lt. Gen. R.K. Jasbir Singh, ed, *Indian Defence Yearbook 2005*, pp. 226–40; 'Modernization of the Indian Air Force on Course', in Lt. Gen. R.K. Jasbir Singh, ed, *Indian Defence Yearbook 2005*, pp. 241–64.

passage of the civilian nuclear deal, India's confidence in the US as a 'reliable supplier' may increase. This assessment is not diminished by Prime Minister Singh's October 2007 decision to slow negotiations on the nuclear deal to placate the concerns of his leftist coalition partners.

Many in India, recalling Pakistan's infamous F-16 experience and the Pressler Amendment Sanctions, remain reluctant to buy large weapons systems or other high-end platforms from the US because spare parts availability and supplier-provided maintenance will be subject to US policy decisions without a change in law. In addition, India has a number of other countries that are vying for this huge market, including among others, Israel, Russia, France, Britain and Sweden. All of these countries are generally more competitive than the US on price and contracting time lines. The primary advantage that the US has over these other competitors is 'quality' and the prestige that US technology and weapons systems confer. But it is far from clear whether or not India will find the increase in quality to be worth the marginal expense, longer and more complex contracting processes, and potential political 'strings attached'.[37]

Conditioned by its experience with Russia, where India can produce systems under licence and even co-develop systems, India strongly prefers—and indeed insists upon—joint development of weapons system and other high-end technologies (such as space cooperation) with the US. India seeks such arrangements with Washington to minimise its vulnerability to shifts in US policy. Co-development also satisfies India's desire to be seen as an equal—not junior partner—in the US–India relationship. The US has made great strides in accommodating India in this regard. One notable success is the founding of the High-Technology Cooperation Group to explore

---

[37] See section titled 'Global Military Cooperation', especially Chapter 17 ('India's Military Ties with Israel Reach New Heights', pp. 283–305); Chapter 18 ('Indo-US Strategic and Military Ties Enter New Phase', pp. 306–322), Chapter 19 ('India and Russia Strengthen Defence Cooperation, pp. 323–337); Chapter 20 ('Large Indo-French Defence Contracts in the Offing', pp. 334–337), Chapter 22 ('Indo-South African Deals Enhance Defence Cooperation, pp. 343–345); Chapter 23 ('Indo-Polish Defence Industry Partnership', pp. 346–349) in Lt. General R.K. Jasbir Singh, ed, *Indian Defence Yearbook 2005.*

opportunities for joint research and development. [38] (US officials remain dubious about the potential for this group given the yawning gap between Indian and US current capabilities and capacities—particularly in defence-related technologies.)[39]

Even if India ultimately demurs from making large-scale acquisitions from US defence suppliers, India will be in the coveted position of declining these offers. The current US disposition towards India contrasts starkly with the remote past when India was denied such technologies as the Cray Supercomputer or General Electric engines for its indigenous Light Combat Aircraft system. The new US willingness to explore these arrangements has done much to undo past acrimony over denied access to desired technologies.[40]

While the benefits are significant and compelling, there are several important costs that potentially confront India as a result of its on-going relationship with the US. Some of these costs are domestic and are salient for the current governing coalition rather than the Indian state. Prime Minister Manmohan Singh's government is a coalition of the Congress Party and leftist parties, including the Communist Party of India (Marxist). The leftist elements are vocal critics of the US and Indo-US relations. Prime Minister Singh needs to keep these oppositional elements within the fold of his government and this ostensibly imposes constraints upon his engagement with the US. This was evidenced by Prime Minister Singh's decision to slow the pace of negotiations on the US–India nuclear deal in the fall of 2007 as Singh was unable to forge a consensus on this contentious issue with elements that are reflexively inimical to a bettered US–India relations.[41]

---

[38] See 'Indo-US Strategic and Military Ties Enter New Phase', in Lt. General R.K. Jasbir Singh, ed, *Indian Defence Yearbook 2005*, pp. 306–22.
[39] Author conversations with persons in the United States Department of Defence in May and June 2006.
[40] For a discussion of this past antagonism over high-end items such as the Cray super computer, engines for the Light Combat Aircraft and so forth, see Limaye, *US-Indian Relations: The Pursuit of Accommodation*.
[41] Lisa Curtis, 'The Costs of a Failed US–India Civil Nuclear Deal', Heritage Foundation WebMemo 1688, November 2, 2007, at www.heritage.org/Research/AsiaandthePacific/wm1688.cfm (accessed on November 8, 2007).

This need to balance his foreign policies with the demands of these domestic constituents may explain Prime Minister Singh's other activities such as a high-profile meeting with Fidel Castro at the Non-Aligned Movement (NAM) summit in Havana in September 2006 and his endorsement of the summit's final communiqué.[42] Yet despite this potentially provocative visit, US officials and commentators generally refrained from making disparaging observations about the Cuban summit, which suggests a growing appreciation within Washington of India's independent foreign policy and the binding constraints of India's complex coalition democracy.[43] Washington's silence about the Singh–Castro engagement also suggests that both states have developed a sense of reciprocity in their efforts to avoid hectoring the other when there is difference of opinion about policies pursued.

New Delhi's relationship with Washington may impose some costs upon the often-proclaimed independence of India's foreign relations, notwithstanding vociferous statements to the contrary. One important example of such restraint was exhibited throughout 2006 during which time the US Congress was asked to pass legislation enabling the controversial US–India civilian nuclear deal. Since 2005, Iran's nuclear ambitions have become increasingly indisputable and compelled a series of actions within UN Security Council. New Delhi's leadership understood that its failure to vote with the US and international community to refer Tehran to the UN

---

[42] Prime Minister Singh's endorsement of the NAM summit's final communiqué, with its distinct anti-US elements, raised some questions in Washington about the expected benefits of its newfound relations with India. Indian analysts argued that Washington saw the benefits as India actively worked to make the communiqué less confrontational than it would have been otherwise. While President Musharraf traveled to the United States from Cuba, Prime Minister Manmohan Singh declined an offer to visit the United States and returned to India. Singh was one of only four leaders to meet with ailing Fidel Castro. See 'PM Recalls Memorable Meeting with Castro', *Times of India*, September 18, 2006, at http://timesofindia.indiatimes.com/articleshow/2001758.cms (accessed on October 9, 2006).

[43] For an alternative view, See Michael Krepon, 'India–US: partners of convenience', *Rediff.com*, September 25, 2006, at http://in.rediff.com/news/2006/sep/25mk.htm (accessed on October 9, 2006).

Security Council in September 2005 would imperil the deal, despite claims to the contrary by leadership on both sides.[44]

Another potential cost for India may be realised in its relationship with China. India's relevance to the US derives in part because of its utility in checking China's unchallenged rise in Asia. While the current US administration has adopted of a more conciliatory tone towards Beijing, future administrations may pursue a more aggressive posture that will challenge India to find ways of maintaining its own interests in China while retaining support from Washington.

India's challenge will be finding ways to fulfil some of the US' varied expectations and, more generally, making itself relevant to the US and its regional and extra-regional objectives—even if that requires making difficult decisions with repercussions on India's domestic and foreign policy-making.[45] The 2003 debate within India about sending troops to Iraq exemplifies such tough decision-making. Prime Minister Vajpayee's government seriously deliberated sending troops to Iraq, with the understanding that such a decision would be a 'crossing of the Rubicon' for US–India

---

[44] The US Ambassador to India, David Mulford, publicly warned that India's failure to vote to send Iran to the UN Security Council would have a devastating impact for the US–India nuclear deal as the US Congress would 'simply stop considering the matter' and the initiative will 'die.' US officials later claimed that these remarks were inappropriate and did not reflect the views of the administration. Indian officials chafed at what amounted to Washington dictating Indian policy. Needless to say, Indian officials understood that Mulford's admonition reflected more truth than not. See the discussion in C. Christine Fair, 'Indo–Iranian Ties: Thicker than Oil', Working Paper, Non-proliferation Policy Education Center, May 22, 2006, at http://www.npec-web.org/Essays/indo–iran_5_23_06.pdf (accessed on October 11, 2006). Also see Harsh V. Pant, 'The US–India Nuclear Deal: The End Game Begins', *Power and Interest News Report*, January 27, 2006, at http://www.pinr.com/report.php?ac=view_report&report_id=428&language_id=1 (accessed on October 11, 2006).

[45] Ashley Tellis also raises this issue and notes that while the United States has to determine how much resources it will devote to make India an important partner of the US, India will have to choose to make itself a relevant partner of Washington. See Ashley J. Tellis, 'South Asia: US Policy Choices', in Frank Carlucci, Robert Hunter, Zalmay Khalilzad, eds, *Taking Charge: A Bipartisan Report to the President-Elect on Foreign Policy and National Security—Discussion Papers* (Santa Monica: RAND, 2000), p. 88.

strategic relations. In the end, Vajpayee's electoral weakness and the need to satisfy the demands of a complex constituency—including some 150 million Muslims—ensured that India would not send a military contingent to Iraq. While Washington was disappointed, ultimately it understood New Delhi's concerns. Depending upon the nature and gravity of and motivation for future military contingencies, the US may not be as understanding of India's complex decision calculus. Indeed at some point in the future, US policy-makers may begin querying whether or when US investments in India will produce security dividends.

US Cost-Benefit Calculus

Washington's primary expected benefit from this alliance is that India can be a partner that will support—either tacitly or explicitly—many or even most US positions in multi-lateral fora, such as the UN. Washington hopes that India will break with its past pattern of sermonising and hectoring when it disagrees with Washington. Certainly, India holds a reciprocal expectation that the US will exercise restraint when disagreements arise and, as noted, there is ample evidence of such mutual discipline. Importantly, New Delhi need not actively support US initiatives in order for Washington to extract value from the relationship: the US will benefit from its new-found alliance if India simply demurs from taking high-profile contrary positions.

The second potential benefit that Washington highly prizes is India's stake in ensuring a balance of power in Asia, as described above. The US neither expects nor requires that India adopt a confrontational posture in Asia. Rather, Washington understands that simply by virtue of pursuing its own interests through the varied domains of Asia with increasing degrees of strategic presence and military capabilities, India could be a serious competitor to China and pre-empt China's singular rise in the region.

Third, the US expects India to be a robust and reliable military partner that will assume an increasingly prominent role in securing sea-lanes of control, engaging in counterpiracy and counterterrorism activities, search and rescue, humanitarian disaster relief and peace operations. With US forces stretched thin, this potential benefit cannot be overestimated. Some analysts and policy-makers expect India to eventually consider contributing forces to some ad hoc 'coalitions of the willing'. Another desired benefit is some degree of basing access for US aircraft and naval vessels as well as access to maintenance and refueling facilities for its ships and aircraft. In fact, the US Navy is already considering placing a ship repair unit in Kochi.[46]

Washington expects that the unprecedented expansion of military-to-military ties and other dimensions of the US–India relationship (e.g., the waylaid US–India nuclear and space deals) will increase commercial opportunities for US firms in India. Washington is hopeful about India's decision to retire its MiG-21, MiG-23 and MiG-25 fighter aircraft and commence the acquisition process for 126 multi-role fighters. Requests for information (RFIs) have been issued to France's Dassault Aviation for the Mirage 2000-9, SAAB of Sweden for the JAS-39C Gripen and the MiG Corporation of Russia for the MiG-29SMT MRCA. But, the US is optimistic that India will also consider Lockheed Martin's F-16C and F/A-18-E.[47]

Similarly, Secretary of State Rice, in her April 2006 testimony before the Senate Foreign Affairs Committee in support of the US–India civilian nuclear deal, argued that the deal will provide opportunities for US firms seeking to assist India in the construction of its planned slate of thermal power reactors. She also argued that participation in India's nuclear market will help make 'the American nuclear industry globally competitive, thereby benefiting our own domestic nuclear sector....This deal will permit US companies to

---

[46] See 'Indo-US Strategic and Military Ties Enter New Phase', in Lt. Gen. R.K. Jasbir Singh, ed, *Indian Defence Yearbook 2005*, pp. 306–22.

[47] See 'Modernization of the Indian Air Force on Course', in Lt. Gen. R.K. Jasbir Singh, ed, *Indian Defence Yearbook 2005*, pp. 241–64. Irrespective of which vendor is most competitive, given the varied Indian cost and quality constraints, all vendors will have to deal with the legacy of the Bofors scandal of the 1980s. As a consequence of this scandal, few Indian bureaucrats are willing to be bold in their acquisitions. One retired Indian ambassador explained to me that it is the highest accomplishment when a secretary of defence can defer large-scale acquisitions. Such officials fear that such deals will be viewed as opportunities for payoffs. Once they are out of office they will be scrutinized for ill-gotten gains. As a consequence, Indian analysts opine that modernization of the armed forces have been hampered by a crippled acquisition process and risk-averse bureaucracy. Also see Inder Malhotra, 'After the tehelka bombshell: NDA government already a lame duck', *The Tribune* (Chandigarh), March 22, 2001, at http://www.tribuneindia.com/2001/20010322/edit.htm (accessed on October 11, 2006); John Cherian, 'The Deals in Question: A Look at the Defence Deals on the Table that have Figured in the Latest Scandal', *Frontline Magazine* (Delhi) 18:7, April 12, 2001.

enter the lucrative and growing Indian market—something they are currently prohibited from doing'.[48] Critics of this argument counter that such sales are not likely to happen as US companies are not competitive on cost compared to other hopeful suppliers and such projects are likely to be crippled by difficulties obtaining insurance for nuclear projects in India due to, inter alia, security concerns.

While the potential benefits to Washington are important, there are some noteworthy costs that it will likely countenance while advancing better ties with New Delhi. First and foremost is the fact that, in truth, the US cannot pursue relations with India completely independent of Pakistan until the underlying causes of the Indo-Pakistan security competition are resolved. Second, India's prosecution of its own interests will have—and, indeed, have had—negative impacts for important US regional interests. For example, increased US–India military and strategic ties will have negative externalities vis-à-vis Pakistan's behaviour in the region as will implicit recognition of—and even encouragement of—India's expanded presence throughout Central Asia and beyond. It will doubtlessly foster greater insecurity in Pakistan and will in all likelihood encourage risk taking in the region through continued reliance upon proxy elements (militant groups) operating in India and Afghanistan.

India's involvement in Afghanistan exemplifies this necrotic dynamics. The US welcomes India's extensive and largely constructive presence in Afghanistan, including the employment of the Border Roads Organisation to rebuild some sensitive roads in Afghanistan, development of critical infrastructure and the maintenance of some eight consulates.[49] However, Pakistan views New Delhi's footprint on its border warily. Fearing a stable Afghanistan firmly allied with India, Pakistan pursues destabilising policies in the former to diminish the prospects of such an outcome, with loss of life for US and coalition forces as well as Indian

---

[48] See 'Remarks of Secretary of State Condoleeza Rice at the Senate Foreign Relations Committee on the US–India Civil Nuclear Cooperation Initiative, Wednesday April 5, 2006, pp. 10–11, at http://foreign.senate.gov/testimony/2006/RiceTestimony060405.pdf (accessed on April 20, 2006).

[49] For a comprehensive account of India's involvement in Afghanistan, see Ministry of External Affairs, *Rebuilding Afghanistan: India at Work*.

personnel working in Afghanistan.[50] Similarly, Pakistan will find ways of mitigating any presumed military advantages that India will extract from the US–India civilian nuclear deal. This may mean that Pakistan will seek a parallel nuclear deal with China as a counterweight to both the nuclear deal and larger Indo-US strategic alliance. Pakistan may also increasingly turn to Saudi Arabia—in concert with China—to develop a hedging strategy against the US–India relationship.

Third, as the US imagines ever-expanding vistas for India's involvement globally, Washington's already anemic interests in India's domestic policies will diminish further. Washington has not been interventionist with respect to New Delhi's mismanagement of the on-going dispute with the varied peoples of the Jammu & Kashmir region and the concomitant long-standing record of human rights violations there.[51] Washington has also been insouciant about the rise of Hindutva and the ever-evolving existential debates about the place of India's Muslims within the Indian national project. Washington remained quiet about the massacres of thousands of Muslims in Gujarat in 2002 and has remained so despite the numerous failures of the justice system to address those crimes.

This insouciance persists despite some limited mandate for the US to be more interventionist on these issues. For example, the US Commission on International Religious Freedom, created by the International Religious Freedom Act of 1998, is charged with monitoring the status of freedom of thought, conscious and religion as defined by the Universal Declaration of Human Rights and related international instruments, and to give independent policy recommendation to the president, secretary of state and the US Congress. Every year, the commission publishes a comprehensive

---

[50] See the discussion about India's role in Afghanistan and its impacts upon Pakistani thinking in Barnett R. Rubin, *Afghanistan's Uncertain Transition from Turmoil to Normalcy*, Council Special Report No. 12, 2006; Barnett R. Rubin and Abubakar Siddique, *Resolving the Pakistan–Afghanistan Stalemate*, United States Institute of Peace Special Report No. 176, 2006.
[51] Human Rights Watch, *'Everyone Lives in Fear': Patterns of Impunity in Jammu and Kashmir*, (New York and New Delhi: HRW, 2006), at http://hrw.org/reports/2006/india0906/(accessed on October 9, 2006). This report *also* details the abuses of the militant groups, which are in many cases backed and resourced by the Pakistan Army.

volume on all major countries, including India.⁵² (Unlike Pakistan and Bangladesh, India refuses to give permission to Commission delegates to even visit India.)⁵³

Second and more importantly, there are direct security implications for New Delhi's policies that impinge upon US interests. Notably, these decisions—as Indian analysts have opined—have likely fostered the increasing recruitment of Indian Muslims into groups such the Pakistan-based Lashkar-e-Taiba, as evidenced by the involvement of Indian Muslims in the Mumbai subway attack in July 2006.⁵⁴ Policies that radicalise the second-largest population of Muslims in the world and galvanise their participation in the globalised political–militant Islamist project are bound to have adverse consequences certainly for India but also for US regional and extra-regional counter-terrorism interests as well.

Third, the US–India nuclear deal (approved by both the US House of Representatives and the Senate in late 2006 but stalled in India) is seen as being a positive development for advancing US–India strategic relations. However, the deal may impose critical trade-offs on other US counter-proliferation and non-proliferation objectives, as Michael Krepon, Leonard Spector and Robert Einhorn, among others, have argued. Proponents of the deal have rubbished many—if not all—of these arguments.⁵⁵ Nonetheless, it remains one

---

[52] See the website of the US Commission for International Religious Freedom at http://www.uscirf.gov/home.html (accessed on October 24, 2006).

[53] Author discussions with officials at the Commission during the spring of 2006 and with a Senate staff member in the same period.

[54] See Praveen Swami, 'The Spreading Tentacles of Terror', *The Hindu*, August 31, 2003; Stavan Desai, 'On Our List, Gujarat Cops Who Didn't Act: Terror Suspect', *The Indian Express*, July 27, 2006; Praveen Swami. 2006. 'New Evidence on Mumbai Blasts Shows Up', *The Hindu*, August 1, 2006; Praveen Swami, 'The Road to Unimaginable Horror', *The Hindu*, July 13, 2006; Stavan Desai, Anuradha Nagaraj, Sagnik Chowdhury, 'Cops Follow Aurangabad Arms Haul Trail, Arrest Four and Look For Key Lashkar Man on the Run', *The Indian Express*, July 15, 2006.

[55] See, among other notable refutations of extant concerns about the nuclear proliferation implications of the deal, the following debate between Gary Milhollin against Dishaw Mistry and Sumit Ganguly. For Mistry and Ganguly's argument, see Dinshaw Mistry and Sumit Ganguly, 'The US–India Nuclear Pact: A Good Deal', *Current-History* 105 (November 2006), pp. 375–78. For a countering view, see Gary Milhollin, 'The US–India Nuclear Pact: Bad for Security', *Current History* (November 2006), pp. 371–73; Sumit Ganguly and Dinshaw Mistry, 'The case for the US–India Nuclear Agreement', *World Policy Journal* 23:2 (Summer 2006), pp. 11–19. Also, see Ashley Tellis, 'Atoms for War?: US-Indian Nuclear Cooperation and India's Nuclear Arsenal', Washington, DC, Carnegie Endowment, 2006.

of the most popular criticisms waged against the deal. Despite the persistence of the critics of the deal in the US, opponents of the deal in India seemed to have prevailed at least in the short term.[56]

US critics of the nuclear deal discount the future reliability of India in fulfilling its commitments by reminding observers that India 'chose to totally disregard its commitments to Canada and, in 1974, detonated a nuclear device using plutonium reprocessed from spent fuel from the CIRUS reactor'.[57] India had pledged to the US and to Canada that the reactor, heavy water and any plutonium produced through their use would be used only for peaceful purposes. David Albright testified that plutonium currently used in the nuclear arsenal was produced in CIRUS.[58] India, however, refuses to acknowledge this transgression, which vexes critics of the deal and legitimises their dubiety about India's future conduct. State Department officials have also sought to diminish the import of this concern in their own efforts to secure Congressional acquiescence to the Bush administration's preferred policy.[59] Critics continue to argue that nothing would preclude India from abandoning its current commitment to the US when it ceases being beneficial, as

---

[56] Lisa Curtis, 'The Costs of a Failed US–India Civil Nuclear Deal'.
[57] Canadian Department of Foreign Affairs and International Trade, http://www.dfait-maeci.gc.ca/nndi-agency/non-proliferation-en.asp (accessed on November 8, 2007), cited by Leonard S. Spector, 'US Nuclear Cooperation with India', testimony before the International Relations Committee of the House of Representatives, October 26, 2005, p. 4.
[58] Ibid., pp. 4–5.
[59] The State Department furnished responses to 82 questions posed by Richard Lugar, some of which addressed this issue. Senator Lugar asked about the 'status of India's violation of its peaceful use undertakings in the 1956 US heavy-water contract' and inquired whether these violations are 'on-going' or are they, as a result of the termination of US–Indian nuclear cooperation, no longer operative?' Under Secretary Joseph replied, 'The outcome was that a conclusive answer was not possible due to both the factual uncertainty as to whether US–supplied heavy water contributed to the production of the plutonium used for the device and the lack of a mutual understanding of scope of the 1956 contract language.' While Under Secretary Joseph expressed the administration's interest in focusing on the future, not the past, he did concede that to date India does not acknowledged to the U.S, 'that it considered that its use of US–supplied heavy water was a violation of the 1956 contract'. See 'Questions for the Record Submitted to Under Secretary Robert Joseph by Chairman Richard G. Lugar', Senate Foreign Relations Committee (#1a), November 2, 2005.

was done with previous commitments to Canada and the US.[60] For those analysts and policy-makers, who view India through a fundamentally transformed lens, such questions are seen as irrelevant, jejune and unsophisticated.

Proponents of the deal enumerated the benefits that may actually accrue for the non-proliferation regime by bringing several Indian facilities under the nuclear safeguards umbrella and by diminishing the possibility of horizontal proliferation from India. But even proponents of the deal must concede that the deal *is* inherently 'bomb friendly', in the words of Michael Krepon, in that it does not currently secure any restraint on India's nuclear weapons programme and in no way limits fissile material production for military purposes. This allows India to retain the option of re-optimising the size and structure of its arsenal as New Delhi sees fit.

Secretary Rice, in her congressional testimony, denied this characterisation although she conceded that the deal does *not* in any way seek to limit India's ability to process highly enriched fuel for its weapons programme. Rice flatly dismissed the concerns that this deal will allow India to expand its nuclear arsenal significantly by arguing,

> This is just not the case. The initiative does not cap Indian nuclear weapons production, but nothing under this initiative will directly enhance its military capability or add to its military stockpile. India could already build additional weapons within the limits of its capabilities if it is so desired, with or without this deal. But the Indian

---

[60] For a critique of the assumptions undergirding this deal, see George Perkovich, 'Faulty Promises: The US–India Nuclear Deal', Carnegie Endowment for International Peace Policy Outlook No. 21, September, 2005; Michael Krepon, 'Are the Basic Assumptions Behind the Bush Administration's Nuclear Deal with India Sound?', Henry L. Stimson Center, March 15, 2006, at http://www.stimson.org/pub.cfm?id=276 (accessed on April 20, 2006); See Michael Krepon, 'The US–India Nuclear Deal: Another Wrong Turn in the War on Terror', Henry L. Stimson Center, March 29, 2006, at http://www.stimson.org/pub.cfm?id=283 (accessed on April 20, 2006); Leonard S. Spector, 'US Nuclear Cooperation with India', testimony before the International Relations Committee of the House of Representatives, October 26, 2005; Robert J. Einhorn, 'The US–India Nuclear Deal', testimony before the International Relations Committee of the House of Representatives, October 26, 2005.

government has repeatedly confirmed in public that it intends to expand only its civil nuclear energy capability.[61]

Ashley Tellis also argued against the contention that India seeks to dramatically expand its military stockpile.[62] These arguments fail to mollify critics who believe that New Delhi's military intentions are belied by the details of this deal (the designation of the fast breeder reactor as a military asset) and who believe that there is no reason to assume that India's expanded interest in civilian nuclear activities preclude expanding military interests.

Perhaps the most persuasive potential cost of the deal derives from the requirement that the US must convince the international community to change the rules of the game and the Nuclear Suppliers Group to allow nuclear commerce for India. This task is not likely to be difficult given that the International Atomic Energy Agency chief Mohammad El Baradei has blessed the deal and given that several countries would be interested in selling nuclear technology and fissile material to India.[63] The challenge may come from the India-specific nature of these changes. Critics ask what would stop China from seeking a similar deal for its ally Pakistan. The Bush administration defends the India-specific nature of the policy rather than a criterion-based policy according to which such deals could be made with other deserving states. The Bush administration defines the sin of proliferation not by the deed, but the by the nature of the regime. But even solid proponents of the deal acknowledge that it raises questions of precedent and process in that Washington is simultaneously asking the international

---

[61] See 'Remarks of Secretary of State Condoleeza Rice at the Senate Foreign Relations Committee on the US–India Civil Nuclear Cooperation Initiative', Wednesday, April 5, 2006, p.13, at http://foreign.senate.gov/testimony/2006/RiceTestimony060405.pdf (accessed on April 20, 2006).
[62] Ashley Tellis, *Atoms for War?*
[63] See Sridhar Krishnaswami, 'Indo-US N-deal "Win–Win": IAEA Chief', *Rediff.com*, May 25, 2006, at http://ia.rediff.com/news/2006/may/25ndeal.htm (accessed on October 24, 2006).

community to take harsher measures against Iran and North Korea while encouraging leniency towards India.[64]

Concluding Thoughts: Potential Impediments

Recent years have witnessed a fundamental restructuring of US–India relations and hitherto unexpected progress has been made,[65] but there are a few areas of potential concern that merit some attention. Given the pace of Indo-US relations and the rhetoric on both sides about the nature and consequence of the relationship, both sides will have to manage or calibrate carefully their expectations of each other. For Washington's part, there is a belief that India will be the next 'Australia' or 'United Kingdom'. US officials have reached this conclusion in part because of India's vast assets: it's army is one of the world's largest and its personnel are competent, its navy and air force are also assessed to be high-quality and India has a solid track record in UN peace-keeping operations under Chapter VI (aka 'Blue Helmet' or 'peace-keeping') mandate.[66]

---

[64] Iran, for its part, has already argued the nuclear double standard implied by the US–India nuclear deal and US officials (e.g., Nicholas Burns) has strongly supported and defended this 'double standard' as appropriate. See comments by Under Secretary of State for Political Affairs, R. Nicholas Burns at a talk called 'US–India Relations: The Global Partnership', Tuesday 16, 2006, attended by the author, audiofile available at http://www.carnegieendowment.org/events/index.cfm?fa=eventDetail&id=884&&prog=zgp&proj=znpp,zsa,zusr (accessed on May 31, 2006).

[65] Fair, *The Counterterror Coalitions Cooperation with India and Pakistan*; and C. Christine Fair, 'US-Indian Army-to-Army Relations', *Asian Security*, 1:2 (2005); Ashley Tellis, *India as a New Global Power: An Action Agenda for the United States*; Stephen J. Blank, *Natural Allies: Regional Security in Asia and Prospects for Indo–American Strategic Cooperation* (Carlisle, PA: Strategic Studies Institute, 2005).

[66] John Lancaster, 'US Troops On Front Line Of Expanding India Ties', *The Washington Post*, January 25, 2006; comments of Under Secretary of State for Political Affairs, R. Nicholas Burns' at a talk called 'US–India Relations: The Global Partnership'. For a comprehensive discussion of expectations since 2000, see Fair, 'US-Indian Army-to-Army Relations'. Tellis, *India as a New Global Power*.

US officials, while appreciating these assets, need to keep in mind what India hopes to achieve with these assets and the complex electoral constraints that bind New Delhi's decision-making. With the possible exception of its hopes for a blue-water navy, India has not yet articulated a global force projection strategy. As one Indian official explained to this author in 2003, apart from 'sorting out a neighbour' Indian forces leave India only for Blue Helmet missions.[67] The US must calibrate its expectations for India's participation in any future ad hoc military coalition without a UN mandate, unless New Delhi's national security interests were at stake.[68] There is no reason to believe that India sees military coalitions as a fundamental element of strategic partnerships without an obvious and compelling threat to India's security interests.

Nor should the US presume that India's vision of its force posture will remain static. New Delhi's assessments of its optimal force projection is evolving, consonant with the role that it wants to establish for itself in Asia and beyond.[69] For example, it understands

---

[67] See Fair, *The Counterterror Coalitions Cooperation with India and Pakistan;* and Fair, 'US-Indian Army-to-Army Relations'.

[68] Indian operations in Sri Lanka in the late 1980s and early 1990s and Indian operations in the Maldives were not UN missions. In fact, the debacle of Sri Lanka (often compared to as India's 'Viet Nam') is pointed to as compelling reasons why India should not engage in such missions without a UN mandate. It must be understood clearly that decisions to participate in such coalitions of the willing is a policy decision that in the civilian institutions with little or no consideration of military interests or equities. In fact, military personnel interviewed by the author had hoped that the Indian decision making apparatus would decide to send troops to Iraq because they saw it as an opportunity to serve along side the world's pre-eminent army. Notably, the Indian armed forces are deliberately excluded from the apex decision-making bodies. While the previous (BJP-led) government under Vajpayee sought to bring the military into the corridors of power through the institutionalizing of the Chief of Defence Staff (CDS), the government was unable to do so for a variety of reasons. Manmohan Singh, a Congress Prime Minister allied in a leftist coalition, has not revisited this issue. Thus for the policy-relevant future, the military will not have a role to play in such decisions. See discussion of India's strategic culture in Fair, 'US-Indian Army-to-Army Relations'.

[69] The best sources to track this include the Ministry of Defence Annual Reports, the annual *Indian Defence Yearbook* which has been edited by Lt. Gen. R.K. Jasbir Singh and published by Natraj, as well as a the various journals and books from India's defence-related think-tanks such as the United Services Institution of India and Institute for Defence Studies and Analyses (IDSA).

that its rigid adherence to Chapter VI 'peace-keeping' operations and stringent avoidance of Chapter VII 'peace enforcement' operations may make India irrelevant in an area that it has extensive investment. Thus, the US needs to watch closely India's thinking in this area and adjust its expectations accordingly. The US of course has a role to play in helping India hone its strategic vision through the course of the varied US–India defence planning group meetings.

Finally, the US needs to rethink its expectations that India will be a large-scale purchaser of defence-related and nuclear-related equipment, raw materials and processes. The US contracting process, prices and perceived political contingencies of such purposes will likely be a big disincentive for such investments without serious changes in any or all of these dimensions.

For India's part, it needs to appreciate that while the Bush administration has made efforts to minimise the 'strings attached' to the US commitment to help India become a global power, there *are* expectations that India will find ways of being relevant to the US regional and global security agendas. It is encouraging that both India and the US have developed a more sophisticated comprehension of each other's complex bureaucracies. India has become increasingly cognisant of the fact that the US president is not the sole arbiter of US policy; rather, the US Departments of State and Defence as well as the US Congress have their own expectations of India as well as concerns about proposals to advance US–India relations.[70] India will need to remain aware of these multiple centres of policy-making and their particular equities, as exemplified by the US Congress' opposition to specific aspects of the deal that President Bush negotiated with Prime Minister Singh.

In the future, the US government may expect New Delhi to forge its foreign policies towards such countries as Iran with greater sensitivity to US interests. India's relationship with Iran will certainly become more significant as the conflict over Iran's nuclear programme continues to intensify. The US will look askance towards

---

[70] In the past, the Indian government did not appreciate that that the US government is not a coherent monolith. This lack in understanding of the US process was matched by that of the US government, which failed to understand the complexities of India's decision-making bodies. For a historical discussion, see Satu Limaye, *US-Indian Relations: The Pursuit of Accommodation* (Boulder, CO: Westview Press, 1993).

serious Indian investment in Iran, should sanctions go forward. Similarly, it would not welcome an Indian resistance to punitive measures against Iran, should this emerge as Washington's preferred approach. As the congressional row over India's naval exercise with Iran in March 2006 and the debates in Congress about India's expected votes at the IAEA in the Fall of 2005 demonstrate, this is a potentially combustible issue for the US Congress.

India needs to remain sensitive to the fact that while it wants joint-development of military technologies, there are large stakeholders in the US who hope that India will be a large-scale purchaser of technologies. India seems to understand this expectation in some measure as evidenced by its purchase of weapons-locating radar from the US in 2003. In fact, India cancelled a contract with Ukraine to buy the more expensive system as a confidence building measure towards Washington. After doing so, Indian officials complained to this author, that had they stayed with the Ukraine company, they would have had the system inducted much earlier because the US supply timeline was onerous and they would have paid much less.[71] With such experiences in mind, India may be reticent to make even larger investments with US technologies.

Finally, India will need to maintain its forbearance towards the US engagement with Pakistan. The US has historically pursued relations with Islamabad based upon a hierarchical set of priorities. In 1980s, it wanted to secure Pakistan's contribution to fight the Soviets in Afghanistan at the expense of Pakistan's pursuit of nuclear weapons and support of insurgency in India (e.g., Pakistan's support of Sikh insurgents throughout the 1980s). In the 1990s, it pursued non-proliferation concerns once the Soviets retreated from Afghanistan. Again, the US—at least for now—is singularly focussed on the Global War on Terrorism at the expense of nuclear proliferation or democratisation concerns. Since the onset of the war on terrorism, the US has put pressure on Pakistan to stop supporting the insurgency in India-administered Kashmir or terrorism within India *only* when militant acts have brought the two states to the brink of war (e.g., after the December 2001 attack on the Indian parliament and the May 2005 Kaluchak massacre).

---

[71] See discussion of this episode in Fair, 'US-Indian Army-to-Army Relations'.

In conclusion, none of these issues are 'deal breakers'. Both states have made remarkable strides in better calibrating the expectations of their partnership and they have come to develop ever more sophisticated appreciation for the multiple constraints that bind both countries' decision-making apparatus. Most important to the positive long term prognosis, this security dyad is the fact that the advancement of US–India relations is not dependent upon particular leadership personalities; rather, the commitment to the engagement has been nearly thoroughly institutionalised. Finally, in both states, constituents with vested interests in maintaining the relationship have taken firm root and they will serve as important ballast during times of strain and duress. In short, there is every reason to expect that the US–India alliance will not only endure but also continue its trajectory of expansion into new areas of collaboration and cooperation.

7

India and China: As China Rises, India Stirs

MOHAN MALIK*

At the beginning of the 21st century, India and China—the world's two oldest civilisation–states, once great powers and home to two-fifths of the world's population with the fastest-growing economies—are back as claimants to pre-eminence in Asia and the world. For the first time in more than half a millennium, both are simultaneously marching upward on their relative power trajectories. Both see Asia's rise on the world stage as bringing about the end of Western dominance. Both have similar, robust attributes of a strong power—massive manpower resources; scientific, technological and industrial base and formidable armed forces. Both are nuclear and space powers with growing ambitions. Historically too, both giants have demonstrated their will and capacity as hegemons who have dominated the security environment in the region. Both are engaging ever more deeply with the world economy. They also have a long history of bitter rivalry and an unresolved border dispute that erupted in war in 1962 and armed skirmishes in 1967 and 1987. Each has its weak point—regional conflicts, poverty and religious divisions for India; the contradiction within the 'Market-Leninist' system for China. Both are plagued by domestic linguistic, ethno-religious and politico-economic faultlines that could be their undoing if not managed properly.

This essay will examine the state of India–China relations by outlining the Chinese and Indian perspectives of each other and the historical, economic and strategic determinants of India's China policy. The last section of the essay focuses on the strategies and tools available to Indian policy-makers to cope with China's rise.

---

* The views expressed here are author's own and do not reflect the policy or position of the Asia–Pacific Center for Security Studies or the US Department of Defense.

It is argued that an increasingly confident India is unveiling a comprehensive strategy that moves the country away from 'non-alignment' to a multidimensional 'multialignment' with the world so as to meet the growing China challenge as well as facilitate its own rise as a great power.

Perceptions, Misperceptions, Expectations and Illusions

Despite growing interaction at the political, cultural and economic levels, the gulf between China and India—in terms of their perceptions, attitudes and expectations from each other—has widened over the last half a century. There exists in the Chinese mind a deep distrust of India—with the converse also holding true. There has been a lot of talk from both countries about partnership and mutual progress, but in reality each has sought to thwart the other. Publicly, diplomats from each capital point to declarations made on many occasions by both Prime Minister Wen Jiabao and Prime Minister Manmohan Singh that 'China's development and India's development are each other's opportunity rather than a threat'. Their actual policies and actions, however, demonstrate that in fact the opposite is true. Apparently, China and India continue to talk at, rather than talk to, each other.

Chinese Perspectives on India: 'Big Power Dreams'

Chinese leaders and diplomats often call upon India to 'change its attitude towards China'. While Indians constantly benchmark themselves against China, the Chinese, masters of self-projection, do not project their country as an Asian power but a global one that compares itself *only* with the US while making disparaging comments about India's 'unrealistic and unachievable "big power dreams" (*daguomeng*)'.[1] China, in fact, hates being spoken of in the same breath as India. Many Chinese find the growing global tendency to compare their country with India as 'offensive' and 'demeaning'.

---

[1] Andrew Scobell, '"Cult of Defense" and "Great Power Dreams": The Influence of Strategic Culture on China's Relationship with India', Chapter 13, in Malcolm R. Chambers, ed, *South Asia in 2020: Future Strategic Balances and Alliances* (PA: US Army War College, Strategic Studies Institute, November 2002), pp. 329–59.

As one letter to *Asia Times online* noted derisively: 'China is not competing with India[...]it is competing with the USA. Who wants to compete with India?' Traditionally, China has never looked at India as an equal, but merely as an upstart wannabe that likes to punch above its weight. Nor can Beijing comprehend the idea of India being China's equal in the future. China's leaders and strategic thinkers 'do not hold warm or positive views of India for China's future'. In particular, they remain dismissive of India's claims as 'the world's largest democracy'. Most are convinced that India's fractious polity will continue to limit its economic and military potential.

From the Chinese point of view, India is seen as an emerging South Asian 'regional power' (but one that can be easily contained) rather than a potential global player. Nearly 43 per cent of respondents in a Chinese opinion poll saw India as overly ambitious while 31 per cent saw their southern neighbour as unstable, hostile and aggressive.[2] More than 47 per cent see Beijing as following a policy of containing India, while 13 per cent thought it was a mix of containment and cooperation.[3] Beijing has been making significant inroads into India's backyard through cross-border economic and strategic penetration of Bangladesh, Burma, Nepal, Pakistan, Sri Lanka and the Maldives.[4] In the game of power competition, China has clearly surged far ahead of India by acquiring potent economic and military capabilities and the existing asymmetry in power and status serves Beijing's interests very well. Beijing's attitude towards the expansion of the UN Security Council and India's nuclear programme is an indication that China will not countenance the emergence of an Asian peer competitor.

However, over the last few years, China's India-watchers have started focussing on the strategic implications of India's high economic growth rates and New Delhi's efforts to forge strategic ties with the US, Japan and other 'China-wary' countries in Asia. Apparently, India's nuclear tests of 1998 did not cause as much

---

[2] Silvia Sartori, 'How China sees India and the World', *Heartland: Eurasian Review of Geopolitics* 3 (Hong Kong: Cassan Press, 2005), p. 57, at http://www.heartland.it/_lib/_docs/2005_03_chindia_the_21st_century_challenge.pdf (accessed on April 10, 2007).
[3] Sartori, 'How China sees India and the World', pp. 49–50.
[4] Mohan Malik, 'China's Strategy of Containing India', *Power and Interest News Report*, February 6, 2006, at http://www.pinr.com/report.php?ac=view_report&report_id=434 (accessed on May 25, 2007).

concern in Beijing as its success in sustaining a high economic growth rate of 8–9 per cent since 2004. Though India's 1 trillion dollar economy is still less than half the size of China's, if it keeps growing at 8–9 per cent per year and if Beijing cannot indefinitely sustain its current economic growth rate, the gap between India and China would narrow. A recent *Renmin Ribao* (*People's Daily*) commentary articulated this concern: 'Since India declared independence in 1947, it has always been determined to become a big power...*Although there are still people questioning the possibility, India did make "good achievement" in the following 60 years'*. The commentator accused New Delhi of seeking 'big power status with Washington's backing' and 'even stretch[ing] its tentacles outside Asia', and 'actively chas[ing] after strategic cooperation with some African countries'.[5]

The strategic consequences of India's economic resurgence coupled with the US Secretary of State Condeleeza Rice's offer in March 2005 to 'help make India a major world power in the 21st century' have bothered the Chinese. This offer and the long-term India–US defence cooperation framework and the July 2005 US-Indian nuclear energy deal that followed soon thereafter, have been compared by Chinese strategic analysts to 'the strategic tilt' towards China executed by former US President Richard Nixon in 1971 to contain the common Soviet threat.[6] Claiming that these developments have 'destabilising' and 'negative implications' for their country's future, China's India-watchers have started warning their government that Beijing 'should not take India lightly any longer'.[7] Apparently, Chinese leaders were led to believe that China's growing economic and military might would eventually enable Beijing to re-establish the Sino-centric hierarchy of Asia's past as the US saps its energies in fighting small wars in the Islamic world, Japan shrinks economically and demographically while India remains subdued by virtue of Beijing's 'special relationships'

---

[5] Commentary, 'Nuclear Agreement and Big Power's Dream', *People's Daily online*, August 30, 2007, at http://english.people.com.cn/90001/90780/91343/6251506.html (accessed on August 30, 2007). Italics mine.

[6] Praful Bidwai, 'Ties With China Sour as Alliance With US Grows', *Inter Press Service*, July 6, 2007, at http://www.ipsnews.net/news.asp?idnews=38444 (accessed on July 10, 2007).

[7] Discussions and conversations with China's South Asia specialists in Beijing, Shanghai, Honolulu, 2006–07. Bidwai, 'Ties With China Sour as Alliance with US Grows'.

with its South Asian neighbours. However, a number of 'negative developments', from Beijing's perspective, since early 2005—the Indian and Japanese bids for permanent seats on the UN Security Council, the formation of the East Asia Summit that includes India, Australia and New Zealand, the US–India nuclear deal, India's ability to sustain its high economic growth rate of 8–9 per cent and the strategic implications of India's 'Look East' policy—have upset the Chinese calculations.

Therefore, after a hiatus of a few years, Chinese media commentaries have resumed their criticism of Washington's 'hegemonic ideas' of drawing 'India in as a tool for its global strategic pattern', while accusing India of becoming a US monitoring station to collect intelligence on China. Some Chinese analysts express serious reservations about US efforts to draw 'India in as a tool for its global strategic pattern', arguing that 'India's DNA doesn't allow itself to become an ally subordinate to the US, like Japan or Britain'.[8] Nonetheless, most see India as a 'future strategic competitor' that would be an active member of an anti-China grouping due to the structural power shifts in the international system and advocate putting together a comprehensive 'contain India' strategy based on both economic tools (aid, trade, infrastructural development) and enhanced military cooperation with 'pro-China' countries. In response to a question on India's policy preferences, 47 per cent Chinese interviewees thought New Delhi would form an anti-China alliance with the US, while only 37 per cent believed India and China would join hands to form an anti-US alliance (the rest 16 per cent were unsure).[9]

More importantly, an internal study on India undertaken in mid-2005 (with inputs from China's South Asia watchers such as Cheng Ruisheng, Zhou Gang, Ma Jiali, Sun Shihai, Rong Ying, Shen Dingli, amongst others) at the behest of the Chinese leadership's 'Foreign Affairs Cell' recommended that Beijing take all measures to maintain its current strategic leverage (in terms of territory, membership of the exclusive Permanent Five and Nuclear Five clubs); diplomatic advantages (special relationships, membership of regional and international organisations); and economic lead

---

[8] *People's Daily online*, August 14, 2007; *China Daily*, June 7, 2007.
[9] Sartori, 'How China sees India and the World', pp. 54–55.

over India.[10] Although the evidence is inconclusive, the most plausible deduction is that this internal re-assessment of India lies behind the recent hardening of China's stance on the territorial dispute and a whole range of other issues in China–India relations.

The Chinese are concerned that the US–India nuclear deal and related agreements—if implemented—would bring about a major shift in the balance of power in South Asia that is currently tilted in China's favour. The recent strengthening of China's strategic presence in Pakistan, Sri Lanka, Bangladesh, Burma and its overtures to the Maldives should, therefore, be seen against this backdrop. Despite protestations to the contrary from India and the US that New Delhi is unwilling and unlikely to play the role of a closely aligned US surrogate as Japan or Britain, China's Asia strategy has come to be based upon the premise that maritime powers such as the US, Japan, Australia and India would eventually form an informal quadrilateral alliance to countervail continental China.[11] This assessment is substantiated by a survey of Chinese public opinion on the future of the US–China–India relationship and is shown in Table 7.1. This survey also identified issues that would negatively impinge upon the Sino-Indian relationship: the struggle for influence in East and Southeast Asia, energy and maritime security and a nuclear confrontation.

Table 7.1
Chinese Public Views on India–China Relations

	Yes	No	Other
1. Does China intend to contain India?	47%	40%	13%
2. Is an anti-Chinese US-Indian alliance likely?	49%	33%	18%
3. Is an anti-American Sino-Indian alliance possible?	23%	65%	12%

Source: Silvia Sartori, 'How China sees India and the World', in *Heartland Eurasian Review of Geopolitics* 3 (Hong Kong: Cassan Press, 2005), pp. 48–58, at http://www.heartland.it/_lib/_docs 2005_03_chindia_the_21st_century_challenge.pdf (accessed on April 10, 2007)

In their writings, Chinese analysts seem upset over their southern neighbour's all-consuming passion to become 'a big power' and see the nuclear deal as its key to unlocking the door leading to the big league in world politics. A *Renmin Ribao* commentary noted,

---

[10] Discussions and conversations with China's South Asia specialists, 2005–06.
[11] Rajat Pandit, 'China's Growing Military Clout Worries India, US', *Times of India*, April 10, 2007, p. 1.

The US-Indian nuclear agreement has strong symbolic significance for India in achieving its dream of a powerful nation…In recent years, it introduced and implemented a 'Look-East' policy and joined most regional organisations in the East Asian region…In fact, the purpose of the US to sign civilian nuclear energy cooperation agreement with India is to enclose India into its global partners' camp, so as to balance the forces of Asia [read, China]. This fits in exactly with India's wishes.[12]

Beijing believes that the implementation of the nuclear deal would end the nuclear symmetry between New Delhi and Islamabad (or, de-hyphenate the sub-continental rivals) and put India on par with nuclear China (re-hyphenate China with India). This, from Beijing's perspective, is quite disconcerting because a major objective of China's South Asia policy has been to perpetuate parity between India and Pakistan. Add to this India's military exercises with the US, Japan and Australia, support for the concept of 'concert of democracies' and attempts to establish strategic ties with countries that supposedly fall within China's sphere of influence (Mongolia, South Korea, Vietnam, the Philippines, Taiwan and Myanmar)—all of these 'new irritants' reinforce Beijing's fears about India's role in the US-led containment of China.[13] The Chinese have also made their strong displeasure over some Southeast Asian countries' attempts to draw India into the region (e.g., the East Asia Summit) known to regional capitals.[14] Beijing insists New Delhi abide by informal understandings (also known as 'Five Nos') that laid the basis for the Sino-Indian rapprochement in the 1990s:

- Do not peddle 'the China threat theory'.
- Do not support Tibet or Taiwan's independence.
- Do not counter the Sino-Pakistani 'all-weather relationship' or Sino-Burmese 'special relationship'.
- Do not align with the US and/or Japan to contain China.
- Do not see or project yourself as an equal of China or as a nuclear and economic counterweight to China in Asia.

---

[12] Commentary, 'Nuclear Agreement and Big Power's Dream'.
[13] For a review of Chinese media articles on India, see D. S. Rajan, 'China: Media Fears over India Becoming Part of Western Alliance', *Saag.org*, Paper No. 2350, August 29, 2007, at http://www.saag.org/papers24/paper2350.html (accessed on August 30, 2007).
[14] Seema Sirohi, 'ASEAN: Ah, Singhapuram...China Blocks India's Attempts to Join the Powerful ASEAN Plus', *Outlook.com*, December 3, 2007, at http://www.outlookindia.com/full.asp?fodname=20071203&fname=Asean+%28F%29&sid=1 (accessed on December 3, 2007).

As long as New Delhi subscribes to these 'Five Nos' (or, 'Five Principles'), both in words and deeds, Beijing is willing to develop its relations with India as part of its strategy to have good relations with all its neighbours.

Indian Perspectives on China: 'Rampant Dragon on the Prowl'

On the Indian side, a combination of emotions, illusions and attitudes shape its China policy. While emotions range from the euphoria of misperceived Sino-Indian brotherhood in the 1950s, to the bitterness of India's 1962 military defeat by China and back again to the illusion of imagined togetherness in the 21st century, policy attitudes that are mostly underpinned by the visions of an expansionist, rampant Chinese dragon on the prowl blocking the Indian elephant's path to glory. At one end of the spectrum are those who envision 'an India–China partnership that will produce an Asian Century' (very similar to former Prime Minister Jawaharlal Nehru's dream of joint Sino-Indian leadership of Asia, even though the Chinese show no enthusiasm for sharing leadership of Asia with anyone, least of all India). At the other end of the policy spectrum are those who retain anxieties about a resurgent and possibly revanchist, irredentist China.[15]

If the Chinese are increasingly disillusioned with their southern neighbour, India's complaints are many. First, there is an unresolved border dispute of Himalayan proportions linked intrinsically to Tibet, whose future evolution after the Dalai Lama remains uncertain, which has the potential to take China–India relations back to the 1950s. Apart from their territorial dispute over Tibetan lands, China's post-1962 'indirect strategy' of containing India through proxies—by arming Pakistan with conventional and nuclear weapons as part of the Sino-Pakistani 'all-weather' relationship—is the second most important driver in India–China competition. For India, Pakistan cannot be a threat without China's military support just as Taiwan cannot constitute a threat to China without US support. Beijing's indirect support to separatist movements is another

---

[15] For different schools of thought, see Mohan Malik, 'Eyeing the Dragon: India's China Debate', in Satu Limaye, ed, *Asia's China Debate* (Honolulu: Asia–Pacific Center for Security Studies Special Assessments, December 2003), p. 18, at http://www.apcss.org/Publications/APSSS/ChinaDebate/ChinaDebate_Malik.pdf (accessed on May 26, 2007).

major source of friction. All separatist insurgencies inside India are fought mostly with Chinese small arms. Nor do China's concerns about growing instability and terrorism from Pakistan dovetail with India's concerns. At Islamabad's behest, China recently blocked UN Security Council's move to declare *Jamat-ul Dawa* (formerly *Lashkar-e-Tayyeba*)—involved in numerous terrorist attacks in India—as an international terrorist organisation under UN Security Council Resolution 1373. As Prime Minister Manmohan Singh in his address to the Combined Commanders' Conference on October 20, 2005 observed,

> We cannot also ignore the strategic cooperation that Pakistan secured from China in many ways. We cannot rule out the desire of some countries [read, China] to keep us engaged in low-intensity conflict with some of our neighbours as a means of getting India bogged down in a low equilibrium.[16]

Indian military officials routinely express anxiety regarding China's efforts to modernise its military and supply arms to India's neighbouring countries. Delivering B. C. Joshi Memorial Lecture in November 2005, Air Chief Marshal S. P. Tyagi, Chief of Indian Air Force, remarked that 'China's strategic encirclement of India is already well under way…China is likely to view India as a regional economic threat and perhaps would be forced to attempt to stem its growth and influence in the region'.[17] Indian leaders routinely appeal to Beijing 'to show greater sensitivity to [India's] security concerns', and to ensure that 'each has sufficient strategic space in keeping with the principle of multipolarity'.[18] However, such appeals 'are often ignored in Beijing as the cry of despair by the weak'.[19]

Furthermore, Indian policy-makers bristle at China's description of their country as a 'regional player rather than a global player' entertaining 'big power dreams' and insist that 'India is not going

---

[16] Quoted in K. Subrahmanyam, 'Don't Get Fooled By China', *Times of India*, August 28, 2007.
[17] R. Swaminathan, 'India's Foreign Policy: Emerging Trends in the New Century', *Saag.org*, Paper No. 2194, April 5, 2007, at http://www.saag.org/%5Cpapers22%5Cpaper2194.html (accessed on April 10, 2007).
[18] Indian Foreign Minister Yashwant Sinha's speech at the Institute of Defence Studies & Analysis, New Delhi, November 22, 2003.
[19] Comment by an Indian China-watcher, New Delhi, July 2007.

to be defined by China but by itself'.[20] India has long seen itself as the only Asian country with the size, resources and all-round capabilities that can equal China. Claiming that derision and 'exclusion of India has long been a running thread in Chinese policy', Indians hold China responsible for blocking their country's membership in regional and international institutions.[21] Beijing's 'India allergy' has led it to create hurdles in India's membership in the ASEAN Regional Forum (ARF), Asia–Pacific Economic Cooperation (APEC), Asia–Europe Summit Meeting (ASEM), the Shanghai Cooperation Organisation (SCO), the UN Security Council and the Nuclear Suppliers' Group (NSG).[22]

Moreover, Indian observers point out that whilst forging all kinds of China-centred forums, dialogues and partnerships, Beijing loses no opportunity to criticise India for doing the same. A case in point is Beijing's unease over India-led regional cooperation forums such as the Mekong–Ganges Cooperation (MGC) and BIMSTEC (Bangladesh, India, Myanmar, Sri Lanka and Thailand Economic Cooperation). Indian policy-makers maintain that if the SCO member-states and the Russia–China–India triangle can hold high-level meetings to discuss issues of common concern and hold joint exercises, 'then why should India, the US and Japan shy away from holding discussions on issues of common interest?'[23] For its part, New Delhi sees the US–Japan–India triangular partnership as complementing the Russia–China–India triangular cooperation.

As regards to Chinese concerns about India's pro-US tilt, Indian officials draw attention to their long-standing preference for independence and strategic autonomy in policymaking. The Indian Navy's decision to hold joint exercise with the Chinese Navy in 2006

---

[20] Former ambassador to China, Salman Haider, quoted in D. Srivastava and P. Andley, *Great Power Dynamics: India, US and China* (Report of Panel Discussion, May 5, 2007, sponsored by Indian Army 15 Corps HQ, Srinagar and Institute of Peace and Conflict Studies, New Delhi), at http://www.ipcs.org/DiscussionReport_May07.pdf (accessed on May 10, 2007).

[21] Ibid.

[22] J. Mohan Malik, 'Security Council Reform: China Signals Its Veto', *World Policy Journal* XXII: 1, (Spring 2005), pp. 19–29; 'China Responds to the US–India Nuclear Deal', *China Brief* 6:7 (March 29, 2006), at http://www.jamestown.org/publications_details.php?volume_id=415&issue_id=3670&article_id=237096 (accessed on May 11, 2007).

[23] B. Raman, 'Tawang: Some Indian Plain-speaking At Last!' *Saag.org*, Paper no. 2273, June 22, 2007, at http://www.saag.org/papers23/paper2273.html (accessed on June 22, 2007).

India and China ▪ 173

soon after conducting trilateral US–Japan–India naval exercise in the Pacific Ocean and joint army exercises with China in December 2007 following the September 2007 quadrilateral naval exercises in the Bay of Bengal are cited as examples of India's engagement with all major powers. The Indians contend that 'just as China does not want India to object to Beijing's close strategic ties with India's neighbours, seeing them as part of "normal state-to-state relations", India hopes China would respect New Delhi's sovereign rights to build strategic partnerships and initiatives based on shared interests with like-minded countries in Asia and elsewhere'.[24]

The dramatic economic progress achieved by China in a quarter of a century evokes envy, admiration and a desire for emulation among Indians who lament that whether China practices communism (under Mao) or capitalism (post-Mao), it always does it better than India. However, many Indians see China as predatory in trade and look worryingly at China's robust growth rates, fearing that India will be left behind. The Chinese economy is about 2.5 times greater than India and China receives four times more foreign direct investment than India ($63.81 billion against India's $16 billion in 2007). India's poor transport network and frequent power shortages remain the Achilles' heel of India's fast-growing economy and they hinder its ability to compete with China. There is talk about partnering China's awesome manufacturing power with India's enviable IT and services sector which would make 'Chindia' the factory and back-office of the world. But the reality is that China wants to beat India in the services sector, too. As one *Beijing Review* commentary 'Hardnosed Software Battle' put it, in the IT software sector, '[a] fierce face-off with an old competitor—India—has [just] begun'.[25] Bilateral trade flows are rising rapidly (from a paltry $350 million in 1993 to nearly $30 billion in 2007 and it could cross $50 billion in 2010 and double again by 2015). But the bulk of Indian exports to China consist of iron ore and other raw materials, while India imports mostly manufactured goods from China—in confirmation of the classic 'dependency theory' school of international economic relations. On the positive side, unlike in

---

[24] Interview with an Indian diplomat, New Delhi, March 2007.
[25] Ding Wenlei, 'Hardnosed Software Battle: India and China Square Up in IT Ring', *Beijing Review*, 47:12 (March 25, 2004), pp. 36–39.

the past, growing economic ties provide a cushion in times of crisis over territorial, nuclear and military security issues in the future. A recent survey conducted by the Pew Global Attitudes Project found that while China's image is generally positive in Asia, it has grown somewhat more negative in India with 43 per cent expressing negative opinion about China compared to 20 per cent in 2002. China's recent hardening of its stance on the territorial disputes with India and Indian losses in its fierce global competition with China for energy resources worldwide may have contributed to this shift in public opinion. In contrast, every major survey has shown that Indians overwhelmingly support closer ties with the US. An increasing number of Indians also view China's growing military might negatively. Similarly, more of them see a growing Chinese economy as a bad thing than a good thing for their country (48 per cent versus 42 per cent).[26]

The fact of the matter is that China and India are locked in a classic security dilemma: one country sees its own actions as self-defensive, but the same actions appear aggressive to the other. Unwilling to play second fiddle to China, the rising India feels the need to take counter-balancing measures and launch certain initiatives, such as the 'Look East' policy, which are perceived as challenging and threatening China. Like China, India is actively seeking to reintegrate its periphery with the framework of regional economic cooperation. Like any other established status-quo great power, China wants to ensure that its position remains strong vis-à-vis the challenger—India—for strategic, economic and geopolitical reasons. On almost all counts, the two Asian giants clash or compete and remain vulnerable to any deterioration in relations.

KEY ISSUES IN INDIA–CHINA RELATIONS IN THE 21ST CENTURY

The India–China Territorial Dispute

Forty-five years after the 1962 War that erupted over their disputed border and after more than a quarter of a century of negotiations,

---

[26] Agencies, 'Growing Chinese Economy Bad, Say Indians', *The Times of India*, July 5, 2007, p. 1.

the 4,056 kilometre (2,520 miles) frontier between India and China, one of the longest interstate borders in the world, remains the only one of China's land borders not defined, let alone demarcated, on maps or delineated on the ground. While Indians doubt China's sincerity in border negotiations, Chinese question Indian leaders' will and capacity to settle the dispute in a 'give-and-take' spirit. Talks for a settlement have gone on since 1981—without producing any worthwhile result.

There was a great deal of optimism about a possible breakthrough until 2005. Evidence of this came during Prime Minister Vajpayee's China visit in June 2003, when New Delhi's readiness to address Chinese concerns on Tibet was matched by Beijing's willingness to resolve the Sikkim issue by recognising the trade route through the Nathu La pass on the China–Sikkim frontier with India and later showing Sikkim as part of India in its maps. For its part, New Delhi reiterated its stance on the Tibetan Autonomous Region as part of China. India indicated its willingness to settle for the territorial status quo by giving up claims to the Aksai Chin in Ladakh and hoped China would give up its claims to Arunachal Pradesh in the eastern sector and recognise the McMahon Line just as Beijing had accepted Xinjiang/Tibet's British-drawn colonial era boundaries with Afghanistan and Burma. In order to give a new thrust to the ongoing border negotiations, an 'Agreement on the Political Parameters and Guiding Principles for the Settlement of the Boundary Question' was signed during Chinese Prime Minister Wen Jiabao's visit to India in April 2005.

Since then, however, Beijing has upped the ante by demanding major territorial concessions in populated areas of Arunachal Pradesh on terms that many in New Delhi see as 'humiliating and non-negotiable'.[27] Tawang, in particular, has emerged as a sticking point since the Chinese claim it to be central to Tibetan Buddhism given that the sixth Dalai Lama was born there. Not surprisingly, China's increasing assertiveness over the disputed Arunachal Pradesh has led to a remarkable meltdown in the Sino-Indian border talks and a 'mini-cold war' has quietly taken hold at the diplomatic level in the past two years, despite public protestations

---

[27] India reportedly conveyed to China in June 2007 that 'it could not be pushed beyond a point on the boundary dispute'. See Rajeev Sharma, 'China Jams DD, AIR Signals in Border Area', *Tribune*, June 26, 2007.

of amity. Some observers argue that Hu Jintao's desire to control the choice of the next Dalai Lama has led to pressuring India to concede access to the Tawang Monastery which is crucial to this choice.[28] Others, however, do not see any sinister designs in western China's development. Instead, they attribute the recent downturn in Sino-Indian relations more to domestic power struggle within the CCP than to the Dalai Lama succession issue or to Chinese concerns about India's growing tilt towards the US.[29]

Tibet is the Key: Tibet remains the key to China's policymaking on the India–China boundary dispute. The Chinese still suspect that India prefers an independent Tibet and covertly supports Tibetan separatists.[30] Unless and until Tibet is totally pacified and completely Sinicized as Inner Mongolia has been, Beijing would not want to give up the 'bargaining chip' that an unsettled boundary vis-à-vis India provides it with. An unsettled border provides China the strategic leverage to keep India uncertain about its intentions and nervous about its capabilities, while exposing India's vulnerabilities and weaknesses and ensuring New Delhi's 'good behaviour' on issues of vital concern to China.[31]

Several recent commentaries in Chinese language sources confirm a shift towards a tougher Chinese stance on the territorial dispute with India.[32] Apparently, many Chinese strategic thinkers believe that China's comprehensive national power vis-à-vis India is likely to increase over time and that would enable Beijing to drive a better bargain on the boundary question in the future. Most Chinese analysts are convinced that the military balance has already shifted in their favour with the completion of the 1,118 kilometre

---

[28] Raman, 'Tawang: Some Indian Plain-Speaking At Last!'.
[29] Rajeev Sharma, 'India–China Border Row—No Headway Expected This Year', *Tribune*, June 8, 2007.
[30] Ma Jiali, cited in Scobell, '"Cult of Defense" and "Great Power Dreams"', p. 346.
[31] G. Parthasarathy, 'Disturbing Signs Flow from across the Himalayas', *Pioneer*, July 1, 2007.
[32] Liu Silu, 'Beijing Should Not Lose Patience in Chinese-Indian Border Talks', ['Zhongyin bianjie tanpan, Beijing bu neng ji'], *Wen Wei Po* (Hong Kong), June 1, 2007; Ramesh Ramachandran, 'Helping US May Derail Border Talks', *Asian Age*, July 25, 2007; 'Future Directions of the Sino-Indian Border Dispute', *International Strategic Studies* [*Guogji Zhanlue*], November 2006.

(695 miles) Qinghai–Tibet railway and other military infrastructure projects in Tibet and that negates the need for any territorial concession to India in the eastern sector. Besides, an unsettled boundary suits Chinese interests for the present because China's claims in the western sector are complicated by the Indo-Pakistan dispute over Kashmir, Pakistan's interests in the Sino-Indian territorial dispute and Beijing's interest in keeping India under strategic pressure on two fronts. These commentaries (a) advocate a 'constraining India' strategy, (b) foretell a long and torturous course of future border negotiations and (c) indicate an uncertain and unpredictable future for India's relations with China.

Chinese Foreign Minister Yang Jiechi's statement to his Indian counterpart Pranab Mukherjee made in June 2007 that the 'mere presence of populated areas in Arunachal Pradesh would not affect Chinese claims on the boundary' should be seen in this context.[33] Describing the Chinese move as 'a serious retrograde step', Mukherjee publicly rebuffed Beijing, saying that New Delhi would not part with populated portions of the state of Arunachal Pradesh: 'Any elected government of India is not permitted by the constitution to part with any part of our land that sends representatives to the Indian Parliament'.[34] Sending a clear signal against any Chinese designs over Arunachal Pradesh, India's foreign minister added,

> The days of Hitler are over. After the Second World War, no country captures land of another country in the present global context. That is why there is a civilised mechanism of discussions and dialogue to sort out border disputes. We sit around the table and discuss disputes to resolve them.[35]

The Indian government has also responded by unveiling plans for economic development and major infrastructure projects in the border areas along the undefined LAC. This would enable

---

[33] Indrani Bagchi & Saibal Dasgupta, 'India Red-faced as China Gets Tough', *The Times of India*, May 27, 2007; Seema Mustafa, 'New PRC Foreign Minister Hardens Border Dispute', *Asian Age*, August 4, 2007.
[34] Reuters, 'India Rebuffs Beijing on Disputed Border', *International Herald Tribune*, June 17, 2007.
[35] 'Pranab Says Can't Give Any Part of Arunachal', *The Indian Express*, June 17, 2007; Raman, 'Tawang: Some Indian Plain-speaking At Last'!

the Indian military to 'swiftly move forces into the region and sustain them logistically in the event of any untoward trouble or emergency'. Indian Defence Minister A. K. Antony told the Combined Commanders' Conference in July 2007 that 'China has been building a lot of infrastructure—railways, airports and roads [along the Indian border]. We are also doing the same thing.'[36] Although the probability of an all-out conflict is extremely low, the prospect that some of India's road building projects in disputed areas could lead to tensions, clashes and skirmishes with Chinese border patrols cannot be completely ruled out.

There is little or no sign of an early resolution to the conflicting claims, despite continuing negotiations and the recent upswing in diplomatic, political, commercial and even military ties between the world's two most populous countries. The border disputes have simmered in the background for more than 50 years, threatening to disrupt relations between Asia's two giants. With China insisting on the return of Tawang on religious, cultural and historical grounds, Indians have a more powerful case for the return of the sacred Mount Kailash–Mansarovar in Tibet, since it is a sacred religious place associated with the Hindu religion. Additionally, there is the contentious issue of the Shaksgam Valley that Pakistan handed over to China in 1963, which China's Foreign Ministry spokespersons now claim is a non-issue. Negotiating these issues will not be easy and will test diplomatic skills on both sides. Even if the territorial disputes were somehow resolved, India and China would still compete over energy resources, markets and for geostrategic reasons. A new potentially divisive issue for the future appears to be the ecological impact on the Indian subcontinent of Chinese plans to divert the rivers of Tibet for irrigation purposes in China.

Nuclear Competition

Major Western powers have, however grudgingly, acknowledged the reality of India's de facto nuclear status. But Beijing shows no sign of softening its demand that New Delhi initiate a complete roll-back of its nuclear weapons programme, and unconditionally sign the Comprehensive Test Ban Treaty (CTBT) and the Nuclear

---

[36] Rahul Bedi, 'India Develops Infrastructure on Chinese Border', *Jane's Defence Weekly*, July 18, 2007.

Non-Proliferation Treaty (NPT) as a non-nuclear weapon state, as per UN Security Council Resolution 1172 of June 6, 1998. Put it simply, China does not want India to get out of the nuclear doghouse to which it has been confined for nearly four decades. Not surprisingly, Beijing has been critical of the July 2005 US–India civilian nuclear energy deal. In the daily briefing on March 2, 2006, Chinese Foreign Ministry's Spokesperson Qin Gang said, 'India should sign the NPT and also dismantle its nuclear weapons... China hopes that concerned countries developing cooperation in peaceful nuclear uses will pay attention to these efforts. The cooperation should conform [to] the rules of international non-proliferation mechanisms'.[37]

Beijing is miffed at the nuclear deal not just because it will not only put India on par with China by conferring it with rights that are commensurate with China's in the nuclear domain—the right to have a nuclear arsenal as well as access to civilian nuclear technology—but will also provide access to advanced conventional weaponry and dual-use technologies from the West that are still denied to Beijing because of an arms embargo dating back to the Tiananmen massacre of 1989. A *People's Daily* commentary alluded to this concern: 'The US has explicitly proposed in the agreement that it would not hamper or intervene in the development of India's military nuclear plan, which will also help the country achieve its goals to be a nuclear power'.[38] Once the nuclear deal crosses all the 'big four hurdles' (opposition from pro-Chinese Communist parties in India, negotiations on IAEA safeguards, approval by the NSG and its passage by the US Congress), the balance of power between Beijing and New Delhi could shift in India's favour.[39] However, despite its strong disapproval of a pact that would narrow the power gap between India and China, Beijing would not want to take a stance that pushes India further into Washington's camp. Most likely, Beijing would use its NSG membership to further its own and its allies' interests by,

---

[37] Chinese Foreign Ministry's daily briefings, March 2, 2006, at http://www.china-embassy.org/eng/fyrth/t238267.html (accessed on April 28, 2007).
[38] Commentary, 'Nuclear Agreement and Big Power's Dream'.
[39] Bhaskar Roy, '123 Agreement and the People's Republic of China', *Saag.org*, Paper No. 2324, August 8, 2007, at http://www.saag.org/papers24/paper2324.html (accessed on August 8, 2007).

- Using the 'double standards' argument to question Washington's commitment to non-proliferation goals in the light of its decision to back India's nuclear industry while opposing the right to nuclear energy for Iran and Pakistan;[40]
- Insisting that any changes to the NSG guidelines to accommodate the deal must not be 'country [i.e., India]-specific' but 'universal criteria-based' so that 'all countries [read, Pakistan] can benefit from the peaceful use of atomic energy under the IAEA safeguards';[41]
- Using the deal to extract major concessions from Washington, including an end to the arms embargo and the lifting of bans on high-tech dual-use technology exports to China; and
- Seeking new assurances that US–India ties are not related to any 'contain China' strategy.

Energy Security Spawns Maritime Rivalry: Oil and Water Don't Mix

As their economies grow, China and India's search for energy and raw resources to satisfy their industrial needs becomes more intense. The two Asian giants are beginning to rub shoulders in different parts of Asia, Africa and Latin America. Their desires to establish strategic links with their overseas suppliers and consumers will invariably create some friction and tension. In the competition stakes, however, China currently has an overwhelming lead over India economically and diplomatically. China has been aggressively scouting for energy sources worldwide, as well as beating Indian firms in their own back yard—Kazakhstan, Iran, Bangladesh, Burma, Sri Lanka and Cambodia.[42] China's state-owned oil companies have outfoxed their Indian oil counterparts in securing oil deals in a number of countries because the former can draw on generous lines of credit from the Chinese government, which also offers military and diplomatic support to supplier states.[43] As noted earlier, China is also the only major power that

---

[40] Wang Peng, 'The US-Indian Nuclear Agreement: Cooperation or Threat?' *People's Daily*, August 11, 2007, p. 8.
[41] Chris Buckley, 'China likely to Swallow Anger Over Indo-US N-deal', *Reuters*, August 29, 2007.
[42] PTI, 'India Loses to China on Myanmar Gas', *Rediff.com*, August 23, 2007, at http://www.rediff.com/money/2007/aug/23gas.html (accessed on August 23, 2007).
[43] Sanjay Dutta, 'Government to Set Up Energy Security Panel to Counter China', *The Times of India*, March 7, 2007.

is lukewarm to India regaining access to the international nuclear energy market. Although the two countries concluded an energy cooperation pact in 2006, China shows willingness to cooperate with India in the energy sector only if the following three conditions are met:

- Indian oil companies are willing to play the role of junior partner to China's state-owned oil conglomerates.
- Energy resources do not lie in India's immediate neighbourhood (Burma, Bangladesh, Central Asia and Iran).
- Energy resources lie in countries or regions (Syria, Sudan, Iran, Venezuela, Columbia, Russia) where China–India cooperation would potentially cause a wedge between India and the US.

The traditional Sino-Indian geopolitical rivalry has thus acquired a maritime dimension. As a major trading nation and a world power, Beijing is laying the groundwork for a naval presence along maritime chokepoints in the South China Sea, the Malacca Straits, the Indian Ocean and the Strait of Hormuz in the Persian Gulf through acquisition of or access to naval bases in Cambodia, Burma, Bangladesh, Sri Lanka and Pakistan to protect its long-term economic security interests.

For its part, India has countered the Chinese efforts by promoting defence cooperation with Iran, Oman and Israel in the west while upgrading military ties with the Maldives, Madagascar and Burma in the Indian Ocean and with Singapore, Indonesia, Thailand, Vietnam, Taiwan, the Philippines, Australia, Japan and the US in the east. As part of its 'Look East' strategy, India has concluded over a dozen defence cooperation agreements over the last decade and the Indian Navy has been holding joint naval exercises with East and Southeast Asian countries to signal to the Chinese navy that its future presence will not go unchallenged.[44] As James Holmes notes, 'Any Chinese attempt to control events in India's geographic vicinity would doubtless meet with Indian countermeasures. The Chinese recognize that India's energy needs,

---

[44] Sudha Ramachandran, 'India Promotes "Goodwill" Naval Exercises', *Asia Times online*, August 14, 2007, at http://www.atimes.com/atimes/South_Asia/IH14Df01.html (accessed on August 14, 2007).

which resemble China's own, could impel New Delhi into zero-sum competition at sea'.[45] Perhaps sooner rather than later, China's military alliances and forward deployment of its naval assets in the Pakistani, Bangladeshi, Sri Lankan and Burmese ports would prompt India to respond in kind by seeking access to the Russian (Vladivostok), Vietnamese (Cam Ranh Bay), Taiwanese (Kaohsiung) and Japanese (Okinawa) ports for the forward deployment of Indian naval assets to protect India's East Asian shipping and Pacific Ocean trade routes and gain access to energy resources from the Russian Sakhalin province. In short, maritime competition is intensifying as Indian and Chinese navies show off the flag in the Pacific and Indian oceans with greater frequency.

BOUND TO BALANCE: FROM 'NON-ALIGNMENT' TO 'MULTI-ALIGNMENT'

Of all the countries on China's periphery, India is in a category of its own because it is the only Asian power that has long been committed to balancing China, especially since the late 1950s.[46] During the Cold War era, India relied mainly on the USSR and its leadership role in the Non-Aligned Movement (NAM) to counterbalance China. While the rest of the world started taking note of China's rise only in the 1990s, India has been warily watching China's rise since 1950 when the Chinese PLA marched into Tibet and converted the traditional Indo-Tibetan frontier into disputed India–China border that eventually culminated in the 1962 War. In other words, for New Delhi, China has been rising since the 1950s whereas the West took notice of China's rise only during the last decade of the 20th century. True, the US (and Japan) balanced China from 1949 to 1971, but then they allied with Beijing from 1971 to 1989 to contain the common Soviet threat. Much of China's spectacular progress is owed to the massive inflow of American

---

[45] James Holmes, 'China's Energy Consumption and Opportunities for US–China Cooperation', Testimony before the US–China Economic and Security Review Commission, June 14, 2007, at http://www.uscc.gov/hearings/2007hearings/written_testimonies/07_06_14_15wrts/07_06_14_holmes_statement.pdf, p. 2 (accessed on July 29, 2007).

[46] Many argue that India and China have been rival civilisations for millennia in the grand scheme of events. See Rajeev Srinivasan, 'A Millennia-old Tussle', *Rediff.com*, November 22, 2002, at http://www.rediff.com/news/2002/nov/23chin.html (accessed on August 4, 2007).

and Japanese capital and technology which contributed to China's rise as an economic and military power. In contrast, the strategic imperative to counterbalance China first drove 'non-aligned' India into the Soviet camp during the Cold War years, then made it gate crash the exclusive nuclear weapons club in the post-Cold War world and has now made it tilt towards the US in the early part of the 21st century. Since India was never part of the Sinic world order or tributary state system but a civilisation–empire in and of itself, it remains genetically ill-disposed to sliding into China's orbit without resistance.

Long preoccupied with balancing its northern neighbour, India has unveiled a comprehensive strategy to meet the growing China challenge as well as to facilitate its own rise as a great power. This strategy consists of internal balancing (increasing comprehensive national strength through economic development), external balancing (via strategic tilts, strategic partnerships with like-minded states), bilateral cooperation and engagement (with major power centres), regional economic integration (with Southeast and East Asia) and soft power diplomacy (via regional multilateral organisations). Since the 21st-century world is much more interdependent and strategically complex, an increasingly globalised India is moving away from 'non-alignment' to a 'multidimensional multialignment' with the world. It seeks to establish a web of diverse partnerships with major powers and multilateral forums to pursue a wide variety of interests so as to avail itself of multiple strategic options and enhance its strategic autonomy—the major Indian foreign policy objective. The premise underlying this strategy of forming a range of partnerships is to shape the strategic environment in ways that would induce China to evolve as a constructive, rather than revisionist or irredentist, power in Asia. In other words, since India is incapable of establishing the Asian power equilibrium on its own (despite being a rising power itself) because of its relatively weak economic base, fractious polity, preoccupation with internal security issues and seemingly unresolvable tensions in its immediate neighbourhood, it is on the lookout for credible, like-minded partners to help build a stable Asian security architecture.[47] This regional security structure would combine 'the "balancing"

---

[47] Brahma Chellaney, 'The Quad: Australia–India–Japan–US Strategic Cooperation', *Asian Age*, July 3, 2007.

and "integrative" processes to moderate a seemingly hegemonic China' (whose economic muscle, global reach and military power are being felt not only in the north, east, west and south of India but also increasingly reverberate within the country) and to maintain regional peace and security.[48] Thus, for historical, geopolitical, geoeconomic, cultural and civilisational reasons, India and other like-minded Asian countries (Mongolia, Japan, Vietnam and Indonesia) are strengthening their security ties with the US and with each other as part of their hedging and balancing strategy, even as they become increasingly dependent on the Chinese market for trade, prosperity and economic wellbeing.

Minding the Gap: Economic Strength

Having embarked upon economic liberalisation 13 years after China and lagging behind China on all economic indicators, India has a lot of catching up to do in the economic sphere. So India's topmost priority is to seek closer economic ties with the world's largest and second-largest economies—the US and Japan. From the US, India seeks synergy in the high-tech sector while Tokyo, as part of its 'China plus' strategy, has offered to invest strategically in Indian infrastructure and manufacturing industries. Once the US–India free trade agreement and Indo-Japanese comprehensive economic partnership agreement are concluded, India's economy is expected to narrow the gap between itself and China's. Sustained economic growth rate of 8–10 per cent is expected to impart greater sense of confidence and strength to pursue an independent, multi-aligned foreign policy—whether under Congress or BJP or a coalition government—without any fear of China's ability to undermine its vital interests. Robust economic growth in Asia's third-largest economy would also ensure that Asian security architecture is not tilted in favour of China.

Strategic Triangles, Tilts and Trilateral Equations

As China and India simultaneously march upwards on their relative power trajectories, geopolitical equations are undergoing significant realignments, permutations and formations. The SCO, the Russia–China–Iran and the Russia–China–India triangles are

---

[48] Rahul Bedi, 'India Eyes Major Player Status', *Jane's Defence Weekly*, July 18, 2007.

good examples. China's best-case scenario is that the US would over time willingly give up its insistence on maintaining the dominant strategic position in Asian and world affairs and reach an understanding with China just as Great Britain did with the US after the Second World War. However, the prospects of Sino-American accommodation, with the US pulling back strategically from Asia as China rises to regional leadership or a shared China–US hegemony or condominium seems remote for a variety of reasons. All the indications are that instead of walking away or reducing its footprint, Washington is going to practice power balancing as it has vital political, economic and strategic interests at stake in the Asia–Pacific region. This means that the US–China relations will be characterised by 'Cold Peace' (or, 'Cooperative Competition') for a long period of time.

Much like China, other powers are also working towards building new equations and partnerships in Asia and far from its shores. In the decades to come, the US–China–India and the US–Japan–India triangular relationships would be as important as was the US–Soviet–Chinese triangular relationship of the Cold War era. The US, Japanese and Indian interests lie in ensuring that Asia is not dominated by China and that the overall balance of power remains in favour of liberal democracies, not autocracies. The future of the Asian security environment will depend a great deal on how and in what way the US manages the rise of China and how and in what way China, in turn, manages the rise of India and accommodates India's interests. In fact, China's behaviour towards India is not much different from that of the US' behaviour towards China, for the simple reason that China is a status-quoist power with respect to India while the US is a status-quoist power with regards to China. Beijing's reluctance to adapt its policies to accommodate India's rise and the fact that both China and India value their ties with the US more than with each other provide Washington with enormous leverage vis-à-vis the two Asian giants. For its part, New Delhi sees some degree of US–China competition as in its interest because it makes India the object of courtship by both Washington and Beijing.

For the first time in decades, New Delhi is working to establish a multidimensional engagement with Washington. Concerned about a shift in the regional balance of power in view of Indo-US strategic engagement, Beijing is simultaneously coercing and wooing India so as to prevent Washington and New Delhi from coming too close for China's comfort. How India and China manage their differences on the border dispute, Pakistan, regional integration and the UN Security Council reforms will have significant implications on America's place in Asia. Other issues that will determine the nature of the India–China–US triangular dynamics include economic developments in India, nuclear proliferation, the War on Terrorism and the state of Sino-US ties. Strained US–China relations would make India the pivotal power ('the swing state') in the US–China–India triangle but tense India–China relations would put the US in a pivotal position. At the same time, India's historic quest for strategic autonomy, its self-identity as a great civilisation–empire that rivalled China and the great-power ambitions of its own mean that it will never be the kind of junior ally the US cultivated during the Cold War. Unlike Britain and Japan in the 1950s, India is a rising, not retiring, great power.

Just as India did not rely entirely on the USSR to balance China during the second half of the 20th century, India is surely not going to rely on the US alone to balance China in the 21st century. Much like India, Japan cannot be certain that the US and China will not reach an accommodation again in the future and deliver yet another 'Nixon shock' once, the Taiwan issue is settled between the two. Thus, India's drive for 'strategic autonomy' and Japan's fear of 'strategic abandonment' by Washington would bring the two closer to devise common strategies vis-à-vis China.

As China's power grows, the India–Japan relationship is becoming a key driving force in the construction of a new security architecture in Asia based on the protection of democratic values and market principles. By building strategic partnerships with two of China's biggest security concerns—the US and Japan—India hopes to acquire useful leverage in its dealings with China.[49] Privately, Indian officials say they are pleased that 'China is finally getting the message', and hope that the India–US strategic partnership will 'impel Beijing not to trample upon Indian interests'.[50]

---

[49] Seema Sirohi, 'Japan: The Sake is Warming', *Outlook*, August 27, 2007.
[50] Praful Bidwai, 'Five-Nation Naval Drill Presages "Asian NATO"?' *Inter-Press Service*, September 7, 2007, at http://www.ipsnews.net/news.asp?idnews=39175. (accessed on September 7, 2007).

Containment Begets Counter-Containment

India and China have long been involved in a zero-sum game in South Asia. Given their size and power, India in South Asia and China in Southeast and East Asia generate fear and suspicion ('big state versus small state syndrome') amongst their smaller neighbours and exploit it to each other's advantage. For example, India's entry into the EAS and ASEM was backed by China's East Asian neighbours despite Beijing's opposition for the same geostrategic reasons that India's South Asian neighbours backed China's admission into SAARC, despite New Delhi's opposition. China has long perfected the art of exploiting India's troubled relations with its South Asian neighhbours to expand its presence in the region. Nearly all of India's South Asian neighbours draw sustenance from the support they receive from China, bound as they are with Beijing in a string of defence and security agreements.

But containment begets counter-containment. Since the late 1990s, India has responded by fishing in the troubled waters in Central Asia, East and Southeast Asia, where countries have unresolved territorial and maritime disputes with China. As part of its 'Look East' strategy, New Delhi is forging economic and strategic partnerships with 'China-wary' countries (Tajikistan, Mongolia, Japan, Taiwan, Vietnam, Indonesia and Australia) to advance its security interests in Asia and beyond.

As Chinese and Indian power and ambitions grow, nearly all regions of the world bear the marks of their competitive economic and geostrategic outreach. However, India suffers from the disadvantage of being a latecomer and is still no match for China's economic clout and diplomatic influence in these regions. New Delhi's efforts to establish closer ties with Southeast and East Asian countries and to emerge as an independent power suggest future tension and friction between India and a China that aspires for regional and global dominance.

Soft Power Diplomacy

Both India and China are active participants in regional multilateral forums such as the ARF, ASEM, East Asia Summit (EAS), SCO, SAARC and the Group of Eight (G-8). In addition, China is also a key member of APEC and ASEAN Plus Three (ASEAN Plus China, South Korea, Japan). The China–India rivalry for one-upmanship is increasingly being played out in regional multilateral forums as well where each seeks advantage over the other. Both put forward proposals for multilateral cooperation that seek to marginalise or exclude the other. The MGC and the BIMSTEC frameworks promoted by India are cases in point. After obtaining observer status in SAARC, China vowed to 'dilute India's hold in the region as a major economic power'. For its part, India offers solace to those in Southeast and East Asia who remain wary of Beijing's ambitions to establish an 'East Asia Co-prosperity Sphere' under China's leadership.[51]

India and China are also engaged in a competition for soft power supremacy in Asia.[52] While China's soft power is state-driven and a function of its economic success, Indian soft power—its music and movie industries, other art forms, literature, print and electronic media—is mostly culture-driven. An important element of their competition for soft power supremacy is the attraction of their respective developmental models. Ever since the 1950s, India and China have been seen as crucibles in which different developmental models are being tried and tested. That still remains the case, albeit with one important difference. During the 1950s and 1970s, it was socialist democracy in India and Marxism–Maoism in China. However, both have long abandoned dogmatic, doctrinaire approaches and embraced pragmatism. Economically, both China and India have now moved closer to market-driven capitalist policies. But politically, they still remain on divergent paths—multiparty democracy (with capitalism) in India and one-party authoritarianism (with capitalism) in China.

The Chinese government is using the full panoply of foreign aid, trade concessions, investment, infrastructure development, educational and cultural exchanges, diplomatic charm offensive and peacekeeping to foster a more benign public image abroad of China's 'peaceful rise'. More importantly, the purportedly successful Chinese model of 'development-without-democracy' is being sold to the developing world as an alternative model for ending poverty. In a sense, this amounts to the revival of the old ideological debate over which political system—authoritarianism

---

[51] Bruce Loudon, 'India, China in Clash at Summit', *Australian*, April 4, 2007, p. 7.
[52] 'The Rising "Soft Power" of China and India', *Business World*, May 30, 2005, at http://www.ibef.org/artdisplay.aspx?cat_id=54&art_id=6275 (accessed on May 25, 2007).

or democracy—delivers more people from poverty and whether wealth or elections are a greater measure of freedom. This 'contest of ideas' opens the door for China to position itself to play the role of a balancer and enlarge its own sphere of influence.

In this newly revived 'battle of ideas', India plays an equally important role because it happens to be the world's fastest-growing free market democracy and thus offers a powerful alternative to China's authoritarian developmental model. To all those enamoured of the Chinese 'Market–Leninist' model of authoritarian capitalism, the success of the Indian development model shows that a giant, poor country of billion-plus population with its vibrant civil society can achieve economic development and poverty reduction, while remaining a liberal secular, multireligious democracy.

Conclusion

With the rise of Asian powers—China and India—reclaiming their historic place in the world economy, power transitions of historic magnitude are taking place at the beginning of the 21st century. India's relations with China remain volatile and friction-ridden because of past experience, war, territorial disputes, unparallel interests, conflicting world-views and divergent geopolitical interests. China has long figured in India's strategic calculus. As India gradually proceeds on its trajectory towards global-power status, it is beginning to figure prominently in China's strategic calculus, because India, just by being there as India—democratic, powerful, prosperous and successful—complicates Beijing's grand strategy and frustrates its attempts to re-establish a Sino-centric international order. Their disputes are many, but both share an interest in avoiding overt rivalry, confrontation and conflict, given their current focus on acquiring comprehensive national power. A degree of pragmatism informs their view of each other. Despite there being no breakthrough yet on finding a solution to the thorny boundary issue, trust between the two militaries is being established, especially through holding joint military exercises and confidence-building measures.

Optimists hope that as the relative weight of economic factors vis-à-vis military security concerns increases, the reality of the rapidly expanding bilateral engagement would provide a different template for addressing their disputes. Intensifying trade, tourism and commerce would, hopefully, eventually raise the stakes for China in its relationship with India and vice versa. While they are competitors for power and influence in Asia, China and India also share common interests in maintaining regional stability (for example, combating the growing Islamist fundamentalist menace, global warming, resource scarcity, terrorism, maintaining access to capital and markets and benefiting from globalisation). The normalisation of relations is thus based on a need to focus on social and political stability, strong economic growth and a sense of security, so that they can concentrate on realising their potential and avoid the perils of stagnation or decline.

Pessimists point to the territorial, strategic, economic and geopolitical roots of the India–China rivalry and paint a very different picture. They argue that India–China ties remain fragile and as vulnerable as ever to sudden deterioration as a result of misperceptions, unrealistic expectations, accidents and eruption of unresolved issues. The combination of internal issues of stability and external overlapping spheres of influence forestalls the chances of a genuine Sino-Indian rapprochement. Indeed, the issues that bind the two countries are also the issues that divide them and fuel their rivalry. Neither power is comfortable with the rise of the other. Each perceives the other as pursuing hegemony and entertaining imperial ambitions. Both are watching each other warily as they build up their respective militaries and jostle for power, influence and allegiance of small and medium-sized nations in Central, South and Southeast Asia, seek access to natural resources in remote parts of the world and compete for leadership positions in global and regional organisations. Significantly, the future of the India–China relationship is increasingly being influenced by 'the US factor'. India has unveiled a comprehensive 'multialignment' strategy to meet the growing China challenge as well as to facilitate its own rise as a great power.

Simmering tensions over territory, Tibet, energy resources and rival alliance relationships ensure that Indian Prime Minister Manmohan Singh's assertion that 'there is enough [geopolitical] space for the two countries to develop together' will remain more of a 'hope' than a conviction. The relationship between the two rising Asian giants will be characterised more by competition and rivalry than cooperation (or, 'competitive cooperation'). Indeed, the possibility of confrontation cannot be ruled out completely.

Improvement in China–India relations over the long term will depend upon Beijing's assessment of India's evolving political cohesion, economic growth and military potential. The existence of two economically powerful nations would create new tensions as they both strive to stamp their authority on the region. It is possible that economically prosperous and militarily confident China and India might eventually come to terms with each other as their mutual containment policies start yielding diminishing returns but this is unlikely to happen in the short and medium term (i.e., before 2030s).

8

India and Russia: Renewing the Relationship

DEEPA M. OLLAPALLY

Indo-Russian relations have had to be significantly refashioned since the end of the Cold War with the collapse of the Soviet Union and, along with it, the foundation of India's decades-old foreign policy.[1] The declining and uncertain relations of the 1990s have, however, given way to a more durable relationship under Vladimir Putin's leadership, spanning the regimes led by the Bharatiya Janata Party and Congress Party in India. This essay argues that a new equilibrium point has been reached, one that is propelled mostly by realist motivations, but buttressed by some shared ideational norms.

The essay shows how the convergence of Indian and Russian perceptions is evident at three critical levels: the global, bilateral and regional. It begins by considering how India and Russia have found common ground in adjusting to American predominance, which then turns to the bilateral arena where defence commerce is being taken to new heights. The critical regional stage is yet another area of convergent interests, one in which the rise of Chinese power has been an important, if unstated, catalyst for regional policy.

LIVING WITH UNIPOLARITY

In the aftermath of Soviet collapse in 1991 and a radical narrowing of Russia's strategic purview, India found itself cut adrift from its traditional foreign policy partner. Coming at a time when India

---

[1] This article is based on the author's 'Indo-Russian Strategic Relations: New Choices and Constraints', in Sumit Ganguly, ed, Special Issue on 'India as an Emerging Power', *The Journal of Strategic Studies* 25:4 (December 2002), pp. 135–56.

was facing one of the most serious economic crises in its history, the country was forced to craft an entirely new strategic framework with little confidence regarding Russia's reliability or a clear idea of its role vis-à-vis the subcontinent. Long accustomed to being defined by its superpower status on the global scene, Russia's search for a new identity initially went in different directions. From India's perspective, the central question was whether Russia would perceive itself first and foremost as a European power or a Eurasian one and what its new role would be in a global system that went from being bipolar to unipolar.

While Russia was 'collecting itself'[2] during the 1990s, India took several uncharacteristically bold steps in the changed global arena. These actions—weaponisation of its nuclear capability, deep economic reforms amounting to an overhaul of the Nehruvian paradigm and a diversification of its external ties such as Prime Minister Narasimha Rao's 'Look East' policy—were, however, consistent with India's long standing obsession to protect its strategic autonomy.[3] As the historic Russian transformation got underway, India found itself severely disadvantaged, having had intimate ties to the old Soviet Union and few friends among Russia's so-called new democrats who were swept into power with Boris Yeltsin. Within the Russian establishment, the Foreign Ministry under pro-western Andrei Kozyrev relegated India to a secondary position. Indeed, India's nuclear tests of May 1998 may be best explained by the loss of its most important strategic partner and the perceived greater need to 'go it alone' in the international system.

President Boris Yeltsin's clear tilt toward the western world and the search for a European identity (continuing the trend begun by his predecessor Mikhail Gorbachev) were interpreted as the President turning his back on Russia's Eurasian identity. Yeltsin's gamble failed to pay off as envisioned: the country had expected

---

[2] This is a historical reference to Russian Prince Aleksandr Gorchakov's comment, after the humiliating defeat in the Crimean war, that 'It is said that Russia sulks. Russia does not sulk. Russia is collecting itself'. Quoted in Celeste Bohlen, 'Putting the Power Broker', *New York Times*, August 26, 2001.

[3] For a discussion of India's strategic autonomy goal, see the author's 'India's Strategic Doctrine and Practice: The Impact of Nuclear Testing', in Raju G.C. Thomas and Amit Gupta, eds, *India's Nuclear Security* (Boulder, CO: Lynne Rienner Publishers, 2000), pp. 67–85.

rich dividends in the form of economic largesse and a nod for its great-power status by the US Instead, as Russia's economic health plunged, the leadership learned the hard way that little relief would be forthcoming on its huge debt, of which an astounding $100 billion was the inherited loans from the Soviet days. Domestic economics under the new market system did no better, with the resulting hybrid often described as 'criminal capitalism'. In addition, the first stage of North Atlantic Treaty Organization (NATO) expansion and the large scale military action against Yugoslavia in the spring of 1999 were a double shock for those Russians who had expected greater sensitivity to Russia's security concerns despite its loss of international stature.[4] The upshot of Russia's disillusionment with the West was the landslide victory of Vladimir Putin in March 2000. Putin was surrounded by former KGB/FSB (intelligence services) personnel who held the view, fairly widespread among Russia's elite, that the drive toward the European community and the US had failed to produce adequate results.

Russia's search for a European identity thus suffered a loss of credibility and it was to be replaced in part by more realist notions of international power and a willingness to let pragmatism dictate foreign policy. Putin made it clear at the outset that 'pragmatism' was second only to 'national interests' as a key principle of Russian foreign policy, both followed by 'economic efficiency'.[5] Putin's conceptions of Russia's power has tended to hark back to its past status as a great power and an independent power axis. Thus, rather than conforming to unipolarity as in the 1990s, Putin's regime sought to counter and even challenge, it at times. This reorientation under Putin included a more robust relationship with non-European regional powers, in particular India and Iran. The receptivity of India's leadership across political parties to Russia's renewed overtures, showed its own pragmatism. It also revealed a convergence of worldviews that chafed at unipolarity.

---

[4] See for example, Alexi Arbatov, 'Russia and NATO—Ten Years After', Paper prepared for the Conference on 'Russia—Ten Years After', Carnegie Endowment for International Peace, Washington, DC, June 7–9, 2001.

[5] Hari Vasudevan, 'Russia as a Neighbor: Indo-Russian Relations 1992–2001', Lecture at the Conference on 'Russia—Ten Years After', Carnegie Endowment for International Peace, Washington, DC, June 7–9, 2001.

FINDING THEIR BILATERAL FOOTING

During the Cold War years, many strategic analysts in India liked to point out a distinction they detected between the Soviet Union and American approaches to India: for the US, relations with India were a derivative from the superpower conflict, whereas the Soviets appreciated India for its own worth. Putin's trip to India in October 2000 with a 70-member delegation and his high profile stopover at the Bhabha Atomic Research Centre (BARC), India's premier nuclear research institution and the country's nuclear nerve centre, symbolically underscored Russia's independent attitude to India after the nuclear tests, to be distinguished from the US. The Russian president visited BARC with R. Chidambaram, then Chairman of the Atomic Energy Commission and Anil Kakodkar, Director BARC, both closely connected to the 1998 Pokhran tests. The two sides signed the Declaration of Strategic Partnership during Putin's trip, providing critical impetus to the relationship. Earlier in the year, President Bill Clinton had also visited India, signalling that major changes were afoot in global perceptions of India, not just by Russia.

India's foreign policy managers seem to have made a virtue out of necessity in response to Russia's prolonged indifference in the 1990s. For example, New Delhi attempted to redress the long neglect of the Asia–Pacific region by cultivating ties with Singapore, South Korea and, to a lesser extent, Japan. The most dramatic shift was the breakthrough achieved in Indo-US relations culminating in Bill Clinton's historic visit in 2000, despite India's nuclear tests two years earlier. Some termed this the beginning of an American 'India-first' policy (in contrast to a hyphenated Indo-Pakistan equation), bringing it closer to Russia's traditional view of India. As India's economic and military clout increased since the late 1990s, the urgency for a partnership with Russia receded in principle for India. That Indian policy-makers have not neglected relations with Russia suggests careful calculation about the role of Russia in India's foreign policy even as it moves closer to the US.

One area in which Indo-Russian ties have been nearly unbroken is arms transfers, although India faced a crunch in getting spare parts and equipment immediately after Soviet collapse. Even without the strategic and ideological dimensions of earlier ties, the two countries have maintained a solid relationship in this techno-commercial sector. The Indian leadership perceives defence deals with Russia as holding the advantage of price competitiveness, cutting-edge technology and the potential for technology transfers, as well as the Indian military's familiarity with Russian equipment. India's need to upgrade its Soviet-made conventional weapons arsenal and to step up the modernisation and expansion of its defence capabilities (especially after the 1999 conflict with Pakistan in Kargil), logically led it back to the Russians. Besides, because Russia is not in a position to finance production of weapons on a large scale, it has more incentive in conducting joint development and production of weapons systems, something that India welcomes given its own commitment to improving its defence industry.[6]

The stimulus for the arms trade since 1991 from the Russian side has been its pressing need to earn hard currency and safeguard its embattled defence industry. Russia's commercial imperatives in its defence sector are considerable: it inherited a huge military-industrial complex comprising of 1,600 defence enterprises with nearly two million personnel. The stark reality was that, without major outside markets, Russia's defence industry would languish. Large firms such as MiG MAPO were given the right to engage in arms transactions directly. Deputy Prime Minister Ilya Klebanov promised India that 'big contracts, joint work and joint production of arms are waiting for us [India and Russia] in the future'.[7] From India's point of view, this type of openness is extremely attractive given its persisting commitment to improve indigenous capability. The importance of India for the Russian defence industry may be gauged by the fact that Indians buy more military hardware from the Russian defence industry than Russia's own military forces.

Putin's visit to India in January 2007 (his fourth visit to India) was as India's chief guest at the Republic Day celebrations, an honour reserved for special friends. His predecessor Boris Yeltsin had visited India only once, in 1993. A great deal of the military equipment on display during the ceremonies was of Russian origin, a reminder of the strong bonds. The agreements forged

---

[6] Jyotsana Bakshi, 'India–Russia Defence Cooperation', *Strategic Analysis* 30:2 (April–June 2006), p. 459.

[7] Baidya Bikash Basu, 'Trends in Russian Arms Exports', *Strategic Analysis* 23:11 (February 2000), p. 1923.

during his trip have cemented the ties that his regime rejuvenated and demonstrated that Delhi's growing ties with the US has not negatively impinged on Indo-Russian relations. In a joint statement after the meeting between Prime Minister Manmohan Singh and President Putin, Russia offered to build four new nuclear power plants in India, in addition to the two reactors that are already under construction.[8] Coming on the heels of the historic US legislation allowing Washington to cooperate with India on its civilian nuclear power programme, the dialogue on nuclear reactor sales between India and Russia was noteworthy. As one Indian expert put it, 'It tells the Indian population that we are not on the US bandwagon'.[9] But its significance goes beyond atmospherics: Indian defence scientists and sections of the foreign policy establishment continue to repose greater confidence in Russia's long-term reliability as a supplier of critical nuclear related technology and equipment than the US. Thus, although it is the US policy shift that allowed in effect 'an India exception' to the non-proliferation regime and Nuclear Suppliers' Group guidelines, Russia is better poised to take advantage of this potential market (an estimated high of $100 billion), thanks to its track record and perceived lack of political constraints unlike the US.

India has a long memory and it will be difficult for the US to live down its past disruption of low enriched uranium for India's Tarapore power plant after 1974, despite the existence of an Indo-US agreement that had the force of an international treaty. In contrast, Russia supplied 50 tons of low enriched uranium for Tarapore under the safety exception clause in 2005, before the US-India civilian nuclear energy legislation was passed in December 2006. At the time, the US had expressed its reservations regarding Russia supplying nuclear fuel to India. Nicholas Burns, Undersecretary of State for Political Affairs, stated that,

> We think the proper sequencing would be that if India needs nuclear fuel for its reactors in Tarapur, that the proper way to do this would

---

[8] Amelia Gentleman, 'Russia Offers to Build Four New Nuclear Reactors for India', *International Herald Tribune*, January 25, 2007.
[9] Ashok Mehta quoted in Gentleman, 'Russia Offers to Build Four New Nuclear Reactors for India'.

be to have the US Congress act, hopefully change our laws, have the NSG act and change NSG practices, then countries would be free to engage at that point in civil nuclear trade with India.[10]

Russia's decision demonstrated a new assertiveness: in 1993, during the turbulent post-Soviet days, Moscow had been forced to rescind its agreement to provide India cryogenic engine technology for its space programme under US pressure.

Russia's broader importance for India in the critical energy sector has only grown as the Indian economy expands at an unprecedented rate. By 2030, India is expected to become the third-largest energy consumer, behind the US and China and ahead of Russia and Japan. At the 2007 summit, Prime Minister Singh declared that, 'Energy security is the most important of the emerging dimensions of our strategic partnership'. He went on to add that 'Russia remains indispensable to India's strategic interests'.[11] Russia's oil output has risen dramatically (after dropping nearly 50 per cent from the Soviet era peak), making it the world's second-largest producer, behind only Saudi Arabia. Russia is the world's largest producer of natural gas and has the biggest share of the world's gas reserves (32 per cent).[12] India's ONGC Videsh (the state-owned oil and gas company) is gaining an important foothold in Russia's oil and natural gas production, especially on Sakhalin Island. ONGC Videsh was allowed to acquire a 20 per cent stake in the Sakhalin I project totalling more than $2 billion, India's largest investment abroad. India is also slated to gain even greater access through Russia's planned Sakhalin 3 project—a much sought after prize. Coming at a time when Western companies are deliberately being shut out of Russia's hydrocarbon projects, this sends a strong message. Although Putin has been the key architect of this policy, his hand-picked successor Dmitry Medvedev (former head of Gazprom, Russia's gas monopoly) is expected to continue this line on energy despite being viewed as more moderate towards the West. But as the new Prime Minister, Putin will retain his influence.

---

[10] 'India and Russia in Energy Talks', BBC News, March 17, 2006, at http://news.bbc.co.uk/2/hi/sough_asia/4815588.stm (accessed on March 28, 2007).
[11] Quoted in Gentleman, 'Russia Offers to Build Four New Nuclear Reactors for India'.
[12] Vladimir Radyuhin, 'Russia Plays Energy Card', The Hindu, July 6, 2004.

Moscow has favoured India in defence production as well. India was selected by Moscow in 2007 to jointly develop the fifth generation fighter aircraft and a multi-purpose transport aircraft. As early as 2000, Putin had assured the Indian leadership that Russia was willing to share any cutting edge defence technologies that it had; this became evident in the subsequent joint development and production of weapons such as the Brahmos supersonic cruise missile, a highly advanced system.[13] India is fast becoming a very attractive target for arms exporters from the West, with the addition of US firms into the fray since 2005. India is the developing world's largest arms importer, reaching $5.4 billion in 2005. Although Russia remains the most important supplier at nearly 80 per cent, it faces an increasing competition in the Indian arms market and thus is trying to protect its market share. For example, in 2006, Russia set up a consignment warehouse and a service centre in India called Rosoboron Service, as part of a joint venture which is expected to meet India's significant demand for timely and uninterrupted supply of spare parts and repair and maintenance of Soviet and Russian equipment.[14] Estimates of India's arms demand calculated in 2007 for the next few years are above $30 billion, the most lucrative component being India's proposed purchase of 126 new fighter jets at approximately $11 billion.[15] After 10 years of negotiations, a $1.5 billion agreement was reached for the purchase of Russian aircraft carrier Admiral Gorshkov (INS Vikramaditya), retrofitted to Indian specifications, giving the navy a much sought after capability. Without another carrier, the Indian Navy's potential blue-water capability would be seriously in question. India is also holding out hopes for leasing nuclear powered submarines, on which Russia has been equivocating, apparently in response to US pressure. Still, as a senior Russian diplomat put it, '[t]he teeth of the Indian Navy will continue to be Russian'.[16]

Indo-Russian cooperation has extended into the space sector as well—considered by many Indian scientists and policy-makers as India's 'crown jewel' in high technology. An agreement for

---

[13] Radyuhin, 'Putin Visit: Chances for Course Correction', *The Hindu*, January 23, 2007.

[14] Jyotsna Bakshi, 'India–Russia Defence Cooperation', p. 454.

[15] Jan Cartwright, 'India and Russia: Old Friends, New Friends', South Asia Monitor, Center for Strategic and International Studies, Washington DC, No. 104, March 1, 2007.

[16] Quoted in John Cherian, 'The Defence Deals', *Frontline* 17:21 (October 14–27, 2000), p.1.

long-term collaboration in the joint development, operation and use of Russia's GLONASS global navigation system for peaceful purposes was signed during Putin's 2004 visit to India. This co operation envisions the launching of new Russian satellites from Indian launch pads with the assistance of Indian launch vehicles. Its effect will be to reduce India's dependence on the American Global Positioning System. There is an opinion that even foresees Indo-Russian use of GLONASS extending into the military sector.[17] Whatever the ultimate use, space cooperation is being taken to a higher level than ever before, thus bringing together the critical and strategic sectors in the two countries.

REGIONAL CONTEXT

In the regional arena, India's concerns impinge mostly on Pakistan, China and Iran. On all three, India has more convergence on policy and worldviews with Russia than with any other major power. While this convergence is not as robust as in the earlier Indo-Soviet period, it is surprisingly resilient.[18] On Pakistan, Moscow did make some gestures in 2000 that suggested a possible change in a strategy that had from the 1950s put all its eggs on the subcontinent in the Indian basket. Although Pakistan took the initiative to reach out to Russia, reports that Putin's special envoy, Sergei Yaztrzhemsy would visit Pakistan and perhaps even Putin himself, gave India a jolt. On the Pakistani side, the military leadership had been seeking ways to overcome the international isolation it faced before September 11, especially as it saw the US move steadily closer to India. Recognising Russia's vulnerability, Pakistani leader General Pervez Musharraf sent his Inter-Services Intelligence (ISI) chief Lt. General Mahmood Ahmed to Russia in August 2001, signalling that Pakistan might be ready to address Russia's concerns on terrorism and drug trafficking originating in Afghanistan.

Post-9/11, both India and Russia are in agreement on curtailing Pakistan's influence in Afghanistan and regaining their own favourable position in Afghanistan prior to 1979. Indeed, American overthrow of the pro-Pakistan Taliban has benefitted both Russia and India and they would like to ensure that the new environment

---

[17] Jyotsna Bakshi, 'Prime Minister's Moscow Visit: Commentary', *Strategic Analysis* 29:4 (October–December 2005), p. 736.

[18] For an early recognition of prospects for cooperation at the regional level, see Madhavan Palat, 'Jettison Past Baggage', *The Times of India*, October 3, 2000.

is not vitiated by Pakistan. Russia's short lived responsiveness to Pakistan in 2001 was stimulated no doubt by the upswing in Indo-US relations since 2000, leading to questions about a purely India-centric approach for Moscow. But Russia's relations with Pakistan never took off the ground and there has been no change in Moscow's long standing commitment of not selling arms to India's adversary. Russia has also taken into account Indian concern about China providing Pakistan with fighter aircraft made with Russian engines. Moscow invoked the end user provision in its agreement to stop China from supplying such aircraft.

India and Russia share an unspoken, but deep, concern about China's rapid rise and growing influence. In the past, both have had periods of significant antagonism with China. China remains the only regional power that can seriously challenge or potentially deny a dominant Russian role in Eurasia; likewise for India in Asia. Despite the enormous defence sales with China and soaring trade, the Russian elite are ambivalent regarding China's increasing power. The same could be said of Indian elite, almost across the board. India continues to be suspicious of China's intentions in its close relations with Pakistan. There is a strong sentiment in New Delhi that China seeks to hem in Indian power and restrict it to the subcontinent. The development of the Gwador port off the Baluchistan coast by China, China's growing ties with the military junta in Myanmar, its stepped-up role in development projects in Bangladesh and its ambition to be part of the South Asian Association for Regional Cooperation (SAARC), are all viewed with concern by New Delhi.

In Russia, there has been increasing debate about Moscow's military-technical cooperation (MTC) which includes Russian arms transfers to China and license and technology transfers.[19] The main rationale for Russia's arms sales is economic and it has been defended on the grounds that assistance is restricted to defensive capabilities and does not pose a threat to Russia itself. Russian analysts also tend to see China's security orientation as geared towards Taiwan and the South China Sea, rather than towards Russia and Central Asia. At the same time, these experts have urged greater caution. Indeed, some have argued that Russia's overall interests

---

[19] See for a good discussion, Paradorn Rangsimaporn, 'Russia's Debate on Military-Technical Cooperation with China', *Asian Survey* XLVI:3 (May/June 2006), pp. 477–95.

are better protected through arms sales to India rather than China.[20] The prospects of a Chinese threat via Russia's own arms is not lost on the Russian establishment. China, which has serious gaps in its military arsenal, lags behind Russia by 15 or more years, hence it could continue to absorb substantial amounts of Russian weaponry without shifting the balance. Meanwhile, India seems to be counting on Russia's own self-interest to ensure that China is not provided unchecked military equipment. Russia's choice of India over China to jointly produce the fifth generation aircraft suggests as much. Indo-Russian defence cooperation is deepening beyond a techno-commercial relationship: in May 2003, the two countries held joint naval exercises in the Arabian Sea, their first since the breakup of the Soviet Union in 1991. In an attempt to consolidate their relationship, annual summits between the Russian president and the Indian prime minister have been held without fail since 2000, providing an excellent opportunity to talks at the highest levels.

There are however emerging concerns and common worldviews that are bringing India, Russia and China closer together—almost all of them relating to America's unrivalled predominance. From concrete institutions like the Shanghai Cooperation Organisation (SCO) to renewed rhetoric on multipolarity, their dissatisfaction with US unilateralism is hard to miss. The informal growth of a trilateral dialogue between Russia, India and China since 2005 stands in some contrast to the failed attempt by Russia to counter US hegemony and regain its lost ground with the 'Primakov Plan in the late 1990s'.[21] Russian Prime Minister Yevgeny Primakov's trial balloon had aimed to form a 'strategic triangle' comprising of China, India and Russia, a grouping that could be an antidote to American hyper-power. Although some experts have argued that the notion of triangular cooperation is unlikely to emerge due to the realities of the international balance of power or 'structural realism', a conclusion that most analysts would still agree with, it is all the more notable that cooperation has come as far as it has.[22]

Ironically, it seems that apart from the underlying mutual distaste for America's unilateralism, each of the three is also concerned

---

[20] Ibid, p. 482.
[21] See for example, Sunanda K. Datta-Ray, 'Suppose Russia, India and China Could Really Could Get Together', *International Herald Tribune*, January 5, 1999.
[22] See for example, Harsh V. Pant, 'The Moscow–Beijing–Delhi "Strategic Triangle": An Idea Whose Time may Never Come', *Security Dialogue* 35:3 (September 2004), pp. 311–28.

about the others' cultivation of ties with America itself. This is especially true of China, which cannot but notice the sea change in Indo-US relations since 2000, most recently the unprecedented nuclear deal designed by the Bush administration that amounts to 'an Indian exception' to the nuclear non-proliferation regime. More pointedly, the underlying motivation for stepped-up Indo-US ties and the increasing importance attached to India by US defence planners reflect a mutual concern with China, with the most extreme viewpoints in New Delhi and Washington seeing the need to 'contain' China. Thus, China may be seen as following a dual policy with its growing receptivity to India's inclusion in institutions and dialogues beyond South Asia and dramatically improving ties on the one hand and, on the other hand, continuing to forge close ties with Pakistan to try and check Indian ambitions.[23] In the past, China had resisted being drawn into equations that elevated India's standing, such as including it in any non-South Asia nuclear dialogues in the 1990s. China was also extremely wary of engaging in talks of any nature that gave the appearance of India being on par with it. Thus the reference to civil nuclear energy cooperation for the first time in the joint declaration after Hu Jintao's visit to India in 2006 may be seen as a watershed.[24] China's has also shown greater openness to Indian participation in regional organisations that Beijing no doubt hopes to wield significant influence. India's admittance into the SCO as an observer (along with Pakistan and Iran) in 2005 signalled that the group was on its way to potentially becoming a key Eurasian actor economically and strategically. Having begun as a Russian-Chinese creation in 1996 to demilitarise their borders, its agenda has clearly expanded. Indeed, in July 2005, the group grabbed international attention when it issued a timeline for US forces to pull out of Uzbekistan, a move that led some to conclude that it had already become a potent anti-US bulwark.[25]

The incipient Russian-Chinese-Indian trilateralism is being displayed more openly than ever and, by all accounts, Russian President Putin has been the most instrumental broker. Putin

---

[23] China has been instrumental in building up Pakistan's civil nuclear sector. It built the 300 MW Chashma reactor and is building a second one.
[24] Siddharth Varadarajan, 'New Delhi, Beijing Talk Nuclear for the First Time', *The Hindu*, November 22, 2006.
[25] Lionel Beehner, 'The Rise of the Shanghai Cooperation Organization', Council of Foreign Relations, June 12, 2006, p. 2.

can take much credit for institutionalising the emerging trilateral dialogue among Russia, India and China, despite initial scepticism, especially in Beijing. Russia's consistent view of India (with the exception of the 1990s interlude) has not been lost on observers. As K. Subrahmanyam, a leading Indian strategic analyst, put it, 'Russia has seen India as a key to Asian stability for the past 50 years, some four decades before George W. Bush's administration reached that conclusion'.[26] It was on Russian soil that the foreign ministers of the three countries met together for the first time in May 2005, separate from any international forum. In July 2006, a three-way summit took place on the sidelines of the G-8 meeting in St. Petersburg, fuelling the notion that trilateralism was gaining ground.[27] In February 2007, India took the lead and hosted its first high-level meeting of the three powers. The joint communiqué released on February 14 referred to the 'trilateral' nature of the meeting of the three foreign ministers and noted that they discussed 'the political, security and economic aspects of the current global system'. A centrepiece of their agenda was the need to build 'a more democratic multipolar world', not so obliquely challenging the US dominated world order.[28] The fact that this declaration came only four days after President Putin stunned Western leaders by denouncing American foreign policy during a security conference in Munich added to its significance.

Although Putin's Russia has been in the forefront of challenging US dominance, both China and India share the aversion to American interventionism and the Bush administration's activism. In 2003, at the height of delicate Indo-US bilateral efforts to strengthen their cooperation, India turned down America's request for troop support in Iraq. The Pentagon, which had hoped that India would deploy a division—15,000–20,000 soldiers—was apparently caught by surprise.[29] But this was entirely in keeping with long-held Indian

---

[26] K. Subrahmanyam, 'The Lessons from Putin's Visit', rediff.com, January 29, 2007 (accessed on March 23, 2007).
[27] Vladimir Radyuhin, 'Putin Visit'.
[28] Jeremy Page, 'Giants Meet to Counter US Power', The Times (London), February 15, 2007.
[29] See the author's 'US–India Relations: Ties That Bind?', The Sigur Center Asia Papers, No. 22, The Elliott School of International Affairs, The George Washington University, Washington, DC, 2005, pp. 3–5.

preferences against external intervention, a position shared by Russia and China. Indeed, despite India's own prolonged fight against extremism and terrorism and the US post 9/11 'war on terror', the strong belief in New Delhi is that American action in Iraq has been a boost to Islamic radicalism. As one well-known commentator put it, 'We will pay for US mistakes in Iraq'.[30] Moreover, all three are opposed to outside interference in separatist conflicts, something on which they are all vulnerable—from Chechnya, Xinjiang and Kashmir.

Finally, the three countries also hold similar views on how to handle one of America's newest and stickiest challenges: Iran's nuclear programme. On the one hand, it is notable that China, Russia and India have not openly challenged the US in its campaign to isolate Iran, despite all three countries having strong energy interests in Iran. (India has had the most difficult balancing act on Iran, given the concurrent deliberation of the civil nuclear deal in the US Congress since 2005). There is clear convergence between the three against any military option by the US against Iran. Their preference is for a negotiated settlement via the International Atomic Energy Agency. The standoff between the US and Iran has however forced India, Russia and China to clarify their own position on Iran and nuclear weapons, but their preferences are ambivalent. While it is becoming evident that none of the three are entirely comfortable in accommodating nuclear weapons for Iran, they are not in favour of militarily foreclosing this option for Iran. Meanwhile, at this stage, their energy interests dominate any concern over Iran's nuclearisation.

India has resisted US efforts to divert it from the highly politicised proposed India–Pakistan–Iran gas pipeline.[31] The US aim is to isolate and economically punish Iran as part of its broader strategy to put pressure on Iran on the nuclear front. The pipeline is seen as rewarding Iran. Rhetorically at least, India is keeping the project alive, moving ahead for example on negotiation over the price of gas with Iran. Russian-Indian energy cooperation is extending to

---

[30] Swaminathan S. Anklesaria Aiyar, 'Kush vs. Berry', *The Times of India*, October 10, 2004.
[31] Iranian President Mahmoud Ahmadinejad's meeting with Prime Minister Singh in April 2008 and their references to the pipeline suggests that India has not shifted its positiion as much as the US would like. See *The Hindu*, April 30, 2008.

this regional project as well. Gasprom, Russia's gas monopoly, has expressed its interest in taking part in the gas pipeline which has a price tag of $7 billion. It has indicated a willingness to be involved as a contractor to do feasibility studies and as an investor. In an oblique reference to this controversial project during his 2007 visit, President Putin pointed to vast opportunities for cooperation 'in building facilities for gas production and transportation in India and the adjacent region'. Deputy Prime Minister Sergei Ivanov openly stated that they 'are pegging big hopes on Gasprom–GAIL strategic partnership, including joint efforts in building the Iran–Pakistan–India gas pipeline'.[32]

Assessing the Drivers of Indo-Russian Relationship

Whether we consider the bilateral, regional or global levels, current Indo-Russian orientations reveal an enormous degree of consensus. What are the major drivers of this convergence? As the above discussion shows, strategic as well as ideational factors draw the two states together. In pure power terms, Russia's resurgence and greater consolidation is a favourable international outcome for New Delhi. Globally, India has a strong and abiding preference for a multipolar world, an objective which a weak and chaotic Russia could not contribute to. Russia's unwillingness to bend to US pressure and its drive to protect its position as an 'independent pole' in the international system fit in well with long held Indian views. The Yukos standoff between Russia and the US was one of the most dramatic instances of Russia standing up to American pressure and a sign of its new found assertiveness.[33] Despite the qualitatively improved ties between India and the US, India's discomfort with American unipolarity is clear. At the January 2007 meeting, Prime Minister Singh and President Putin once again

---

[32] Quoted in Igor Tomberg, 'Russia–India Energy Dialogue: Traditions and Prospects', *Energy Daily*, February 7, 2007, at http://www.energy-daily.com (accessed on March 23, 2007).

[33] This affair between 2004 and 2006 involved British and American oil companies trying to gain a controlling share in Russia's biggest oil company, Yukos, only to be thwarted by Putin's extreme measure of arresting the head of the company on charges of fraud and tax evasion.

made direct references to their commitment to a multipolar world. Shortly thereafter, at a trilateral meeting between the foreign ministers of India, Russia and China, there were calls for a more multipolar world. Thus normatively, Indo-Russian preferences on the global world order show a clear convergence.

But Russia's renewed global power is viewed by many in India as facilitating India's pursuit of its own national interests, in a realist framework as well.[34] Bilaterally and regionally, a strengthened Russia is in a better position to play a useful role, from joint defence production to promoting India in the SCO. India accepts a large international role for Russia. Conversely, Russia has continuously recognised India's dominance in South Asia and is in favour of India emerging as a strong power in Asia and on the world stage. Indian leaders do not want the cementing of relations with the US to come at a cost to the country's long protected strategic autonomy. Russia's independence on the global stage offers India greater maneuvering space. Russia clearly does not want to be relegated to the position of the weakest of the Western powers as it was in the 1990s. Putin's more overt nationalism and his perceived autocratic style have led observers in the West to question Russia's commitment to democratic and cosmopolitan norms. From Moscow's point of view, a robust relationship with a democratic and plural India, whose global influence is rising, is symbolically attractive.

As in the previous Soviet period, ties are strongest in the defence field, with the economic sector nearly stagnant. The volume of bilateral trade has increased only minimally, from $1.5 billion in 1996 to $2.7 billion in 2006. In comparison, India's trade with China has rapidly grown from $1 billion to $18 billion. Russia's trade with China was over $36 billion in 2006 and it is rising at more than 30 per cent annually.[35] This gap in the economic realm is not likely to improve quickly, but the other dimensions of their relations appear strong enough to compensate. For example, Russia's energy resources will be critical for sustaining India's rapid economic growth. For India, the relationship with Russia is consistent with both its

---

[34] See for example, M.K. Bhadrakumar, 'Putin Comes to India Riding on Russia's Resurgence', *rediff.com*, January 25, 2007 (accessed on March 23, 2007).
[35] Vladimir Radyuhin, 'Putin Visit'.

normative and realist conceptions of India's global role—there are few voices of dissent in India on stronger ties with Russia while the same cannot be said for Indo-US or Sino-Indian relations. Still India cannot take Russia for granted: as US–India ties reached new heights in 2007 with 'quadrilateral' naval exercises between India, US, Japan and Australia, some observers detected a sudden chill from Russia. If Moscow takes an increasingly nationalistic stand against the US, India will be hard-pressed to find a balance between two of its most imporant friends.

Conclusion

Indo-Russian relations have recovered from the doldrums following the collapse of the Soviet Union and have become surprisingly robust once again. Indeed, it is difficult to identify any issue on which their interests significantly diverge. Developments at the regional arena are particularly important to both Russia and India but are likely to be the most unpredictable. In this regard, China and Iran are key variables.

In the new global system, it has become necessary to diversify a country's ties: economic globalisation and the breakdown of power blocs have given rise to cross cutting and transnational issues. Thus partnerships and coalitions have to be more tactical in nature, often made on a case by case basis. In this environment, India and Russia (and others like China) are learning to hedge their bets by not cultivating any exclusive ties. In Indo-Russian relations, the logic of today's international system is reinforced by their own enduring proclivities and interests, driving them closer together than ever imagined after the Soviet Union's demise. This essay has shown how such a convergence is occurring at the bilateral, regional and global levels, thus providing the basis for a well balanced relationship in the 21st century.

9

India and the EU: A Long Road Ahead

FRASER CAMERON

This essay considers the rapidly changing and deepening relationship between India and the European Union (EU), evidenced by the launch of the EU–India strategic partnership in November 2004 at the fifth India–EU Summit in Hague.[1] At the EU–India summit in New Delhi in September 2005, British Prime Minister Tony Blair, the then chair of the EU, and President José Manuel Barroso of the European Commission praised India's impressive development and stressed the need for the EU and India to engage more with each other. The EU leaders noted that the EU's relationship with India was far behind those with Japan and China, its other strategic partners in Asia. India and the EU also agreed on a joint action plan at the New Delhi summit covering cooperation in several areas.[2] At the summit in Helsinki on October 13, 2006, the two sides welcomed progress in the implementation of the action plan, especially the new security dialogue, and agreed to further deepen their relations by opening negotiations that could pave the way to a bilateral free trade agreement (FTA). Speaking after the summit, both President Barroso and Prime Minister Manmohan Singh agreed that relations between the EU and India 'were developing in a satisfactory manner'. The joint summit statement covered several areas of cooperation and mutual

---

[1] For official EU on India documentation, see http://ec.europa.eu/comm/external_relations/india/intro/index.htm (accessed on January 5, 2008).

[2] The new EU–India consultation mechanisms that were put into place include, among others, a Security Dialogue, a Dialogue on Migration Issues and Visa Policy, Sectoral Working Groups on Pharmaceuticals and Biotechnology, Agriculture and Marine Products, Food Processing, Technical Barriers to Trade, Sanitary and Phytosanitary Issues and an informal Joint Action Plan Implementation Steering Committee. A High Level Trade Group was also constituted to study and explore ways and means to deepen and widen the bilateral trade and investment relationship.

interest, including the Middle East, Iran, North Korea, Afghanistan, Nepal, Myanmar and Sri Lanka.³ Progress in the FTA negotiations and climate change were the main subjects for the latest summit held on November 30, 2007, in New Delhi.

India's relationship with Europe is not a recent development. India was amongst the first countries to establish diplomatic relations with the European Community (EC) in the early 1960s. Colonial ties with individual member states are of course much older, with late 15th-century colonies maintained by France, Portugal, Holland and Britain, amongst others. India is an interesting partner for the EU for many reasons. At 1.2 billion, India is the second-most populous state and the largest democracy in the world, it has a large and growing pool of intellectual talent and it ranks among the top ten of the world's industrialising nations.⁴ If India is extremely promising in economic terms, its political voice too, as heard at the G-20 and WTO negations as a leader of developing and less developed countries, makes it an increasingly important international player. In recent years all eyes have been on China but India has started to emerge from its Asian neighbour's shadow and was the number one theme at the 2006 Davos meeting as well as merited a cover edition of *Foreign Affairs* in July/August 2006. India has been growing at a remarkable 8 per cent a year and on current projections it will be the third economic power in the world—after the US and China—by the middle of the century. This remarkable economic growth has helped raise India's profile as a regional and global political actor and forced the EU to pay more attention to New Delhi.

Although there is some scepticism about the EU in official circles,⁵ India has also become more interested in the EU as a result of the steady development of the EU as an international actor, fuelled by internal developments such as the creation of the Single

---

[3] The statement also welcomed the EU's admission to observer status of SAARC and India's admission to ASEM. The documentation surrounding the summit can be found on the web pages of the European Commission, DG External Relations, at http://ec.europa.en/external relations/India/summit1006/euindia joint statement.pdf (accessed on January 5, 2008).

[4] Economic Intelligence Unit Country Reports, India: Country Strategy Paper 2002–06, European Commission, DG External Relations at http://ec.europa.en/external/relations/India/summit1006/euindia joint statement.pdf (accessed on January 5, 2008).

[5] See Karine Lisbonne-de Vergeron, *Contemporary Indian Views of Europe*, Chatham House Briefing, September 22, 2006.

Market and the euro, and external policies such as enlargement and its leadership role in trade, environment and other issues. The member states, especially the UK, continue to figure higher than the EU on the Indian radar screen (there are 1.5 million Indians living in the UK) but gradually there is more appreciation of the EU as an actor. It ranks way behind the US and China as a strategic actor. Indians feel that the EU has not yet made its mark in terms of a real military actor, that the divisions within it are still considerable and that the EU is more interested in soft than hard power.[6] It is viewed more as an inspiration for regional cooperation in the world and is not perceived as a model for social, economic or cultural issues. Despite these alleged shortcomings, there has been a considerable upsurge in the number of Indian academics studying the EU. In 2006–07 alone the Radiant publishers put out no less than five volumes covering different aspects of India–EU relations.[7]

Both sides are now seeking to develop a strategic partnership that would broaden the relationship to cover issues from global politics and security (including the role of the UN and other multilateral organisations, cooperation in counterterrorism, energy security, global environmental questions, and global and regional development) to a wider economic dialogue (managing and responding to globalisation, communications technology, space exploration, as well as the Doha development agenda), to discussion and joint projects about, and with, civil society (from encouraging interaction among think-tanks, business and NGOs, to the different but related challenges both India and the EU face on diversity, multiculturalism, regional disparities, issues of nationalism and religious fundamentalism).

The EU is already India's largest trading partner with two-way trade amounting to 40 billion last year—a significant figure but just a fifth of EU–China trade. India resents the EU's textile quotas and there are continuing disagreements on how to bring Doha to a successful conclusion. The Indian press has also been critical of what they see as a scarcely veiled racist European reactions to an Indian tycoon's bid for the Arcelor steel company. But despite, or perhaps because of, the emphasis on trade and aid, there is very little appreciation of the EU as a political or security actor. Unlike with

---

[6] India receives most of its development assistance (27%) from the EU with few strings attached.
[7] See also C. Raja Mohan, *Crossing the Rubicon: The Shaping of India's New Foreign Policy* (London: Penguin, 2005).

China, the EU has found it difficult to engage India in a serious dialogue on strategic issues or even non-proliferation. The question must be asked, therefore, regarding what instigated this recent and significant economic and political commitment to a future as strategic partners. What does the partnership hope to achieve? What are the opportunities and what are the likely constraints? First, it is important to consider the background to India–EU relations.

EU–INDIA RELATIONS: BACKGROUND

EU–India relations are based on the 1994 cooperation agreement that extended the relationship beyond trade and economic cooperation. A joint political statement that provided for annual ministerial and official meetings was agreed at the time. The agreement provided for an EC–India joint commission as the central body to oversee the entire range of cooperation activities between India and the EC. Three separate sub-commissions—on trade, economic cooperation and development cooperation—were set up to cover a more detailed agenda and they report directly to the joint commission.[8]

A 1996 Commission communication calling for an *EU–India Enhanced Partnership* was endorsed by the Council and European Parliament but did not lead to any major forward development in the relationship.[9] More important was the 2004 Commission communication *Towards an EU–India Strategic Partnership* that set out concrete proposals to upgrade the relationship. The commission paper was wide-ranging in nature and started from the premise that the EU and India already enjoy a close relationship, based on shared values and mutual respect.[10] In October 2004, the Council endorsed the commission paper, recalling the ambition of the European Security Strategy (ESS) to move towards a strategic partnership with India.[11] It also endorsed the priorities for the relationship:

---

[8] COM (2004) 432 16.06.94, at http://ec.europa.en/external relations/india/news/2007 com.pdf (acessed on January 5, 2008).
[9] See http://ec.europa.eu/external relations/india/intro/com 96275.pdf (accessed on January 5, 2008).
[10] COM (96) 275 26.06.96, at http://ec.europa.en/external relations/india/news/2004 comm.pdf (accessed on January 5, 2008).
[11] The ESS can be found on the Council website (Solana's pages), at http://www.consilium.europa.eu (accessed on January 5, 2008).

- strengthening the economic partnership and boosting trade and investment, through better market access and continued economic reform;
- working towards more effective EU–India cooperation in the UN and other multilateral fora, including on conflict prevention and post-conflict reconstruction;
- increasing cooperation on non-proliferation of weapons of mass destruction and their means of delivery, and on the fight against terrorism and organised crime;
- pursuing the dialogue on democracy and human rights in a mutually respectful and constructive manner;
- deepening the cultural relations, based on expanding people-to-people contacts;
- promoting sustainable development and the good management of globalisation;
- supporting India's path towards the achievement of the Millennium Development Goals through a more focussed development cooperation; and
- reinforcing the dialogue on all aspects of international migration.

The Council also drew attention to the importance of regional cooperation in South Asia, called on the Indian government to pursue economic reform with vigour and heralded the prospect of enhanced EU–India collaboration in science and technology as well as on climate change and energy efficiency. The Council did, however, acknowledge that— notwithstanding the dynamic evolution of the EU–India relations—'the EU faces the challenge of raising its profile in India and deepening the understanding of the EU's role and nature'.

India's Response

In December 2004 the Indian government published a detailed response to the EU's communication.[12] It praised the EU in glowing terms stating that

> India accords highest importance to its relations with the EU which has emerged as a major geo-political and economic force in the new

---

[12] See http://www.indembassy.be/home.asp (accessed on January 5, 2008).

world order. We are in total accord with the EU's desire to develop a strategic relationship which we see as a relationship of sovereign equality, based on comparative advantage and a mutuality of interests and benefits, intended to promote the prosperity and well being of the peoples of the EU and of India.

After praising the introduction of the euro, the historic enlargement process and the EU's technological base, the paper continued: 'The EU has become, perhaps, the most politically influential, economically powerful and demographically diverse regional entity in the world.' It had become 'one of the most important poles of a multi-polar world' and its commitment to multilateralism makes it a 'natural partner' for India.

The paper then turned to a number of areas where it wanted to see closer cooperation with the EU. These included a formal dialogue on UN matters; the Middle East, including Iraq and Afghanistan ('areas of vital interest to India'); crisis management; terrorism and proliferation. It proposed a dialogue between the new European Defence Agency and the Indian Ministry of Defence and suggested that India's growing ties with other Asian countries could be a fruitful dimension for discussions with the EU. But the paper warned the EU of interfering in Kashmir as this problem was 'a bilateral matter'. On other sectors the paper defended Indian positions (e.g., on Doha) or took up problem areas that it wished to see resolved (e.g., better treatment for Indian workers in the EU). It provided a comprehensive overview of what New Delhi wanted to see in areas ranging from transport, energy and biotechnology to trade and investment. The paper concluded that that 'notwithstanding the tremendous changes that the Indian economy and society have undergone in the past two decades, the country's image in the Western mind has undergone little change'. This echoed the point in the EU's own paper about the dismal lack of knowledge about the EU in India.[13]

EU AND INDIA—RHETORIC AND REALITY

The above papers demonstrated the willingness of both sides to heap praise on the other. But there is a sizeable gap between the

---

[13] For further Indian views on how to develop the relationship see the Annex.

rhetoric and the reality of the relationship. The EU–India 2004 declaration commits both sides to a comprehensive dialogue on issues ranging from terrorism and non-proliferation to human rights and environment. The action plan notes 35 areas for deepening cooperation including strengthening the multilateral system, satellite navigation (Galileo), scientific research, environmental issues and educational exchange. But so far the nascent dialogue has exposed as many differences as areas of agreement between the two sides.

Security policy is a good example. The continuing emphasis on hard security by India's political and military elite is explained as being due to India's problems with its neighbours, notably Pakistan, China, Myanmar and Sri Lanka. New Delhi planners agree that, in light of such a troubled neighbourhood and the continuing insurgency in Kashmir, India must continue to maintain a strong military. The legacy of the Cold War still lingers on in the corridors of power in New Delhi with a mix of fascination and suspicion for both the US and Russia. India is happy to be courted by Washington as a potential ally against a resurgent China and far more Indians (over 60 per cent) have a favourable view of US foreign policy compared to Europe. This relationship was given a fillip by the visit of President Bush to India in March 2006 and the resultant deal on nuclear technology (explored elsewhere in this volume) which later produced a backlash in Indian political circles. The nuclear deal did not receive any official EU comment as the member states were divided. While the two nuclear member states, Britain and France, were broadly supportive of the Indian-US deal, the others were either neutral or opposed.

Given the predominance of the realist approach in Indian foreign and security policy, what are the chances of the EU and India pursuing their aim of 'effective multilateralism'? In terms of the UN, India has pushed hard for a permanent seat on the UNSC but, given EU divisions on that subject, it has not been able to support India. Nor (unlike the US) has the EU been able to agree that India should join the Nuclear Suppliers Group. Unlike the US, some EU member states have not forgiven India for going nuclear. With some misgivings India signed up for the 'responsibility to protect' principle and the new human rights council at the UN. But India will always put its national interests first. For example, it needs the cooperation of the military junta in Rangoon to deal with the smuggling of small arms and drugs across the 3000 km border it shares with Myanmar. Contrary to the EU, New Delhi believes that it can best influence the authorities in Rangoon through a policy of engagement rather than isolation. It was reluctant to condemn the government crackdown on demonstrators in Myanmar in October 2007.

India is suspicious of the EU's crusade to promote democracy and human rights around the world and resents Members of the European Parliament (MEPs) poking their noses into Kashmir. India is content that it is a democracy but sees no reason to push democracy on unwilling neighbours. Unlike the EU, it has little interest in human security, humanitarian aid or climate change. India has noted increasing EU activity with its neighbours in South Asia and would like to be consulted as a privileged partner before the EU takes any new initiatives. India would also like to be consulted by the EU on the Middle East and Central Asia. It considers that it has some lessons to offer the EU on how to run a peaceful, multicultural society. Migration, visas, terrorism and energy are the other themes at the top of India's wish list. Indian planners regret the absence in the action plan of any military dialogue (unlike China). The EU and India already hold regular exchanges on human rights, yet there is scope for broadening the dialogue to include issues such as the role of the International Criminal Court (ICC), the abolition of the death penalty, the strengthening of the convention against torture, gender discrimination, child labour and labour rights, corporate social responsibility and religious freedom. These are all sensitive issues but the mark of a real partnership is the ability to conduct frank and open discussions on all subjects. For India and the EU there is still some way to go before they achieve that.

INDIA, THE EU AND OTHER MAJOR POWERS

Both the EU and India are seeking to upgrade their relations with the US, China, Japan, Russia and other major players. For the EU, the relationship with the US is by far the most important political and economic relationship in the world. But the transatlantic relationship has changed with the end of the Cold War and the overwhelming emphasis of the US on the 'war on terrorism'. The dispute over Iraq was the worst phase in transatlantic history and the wounds have still not entirely healed. The Iraq war and the war on terror, however, has led to a greater appreciation in Washington of the role of the EU. As leading US officials have commented, there is no other global actor that has so many tools and instruments to help the US achieve its aims than the EU.[14]

US–India relations have also had their troubles, notably over different views on India's regional and global ambitions. Washington was opposed to India (and Pakistan) joining the nuclear club and has been lukewarm in supporting Indian ambitions for a permanent seat on the UN Security Council. The largely uncritical US support for Pakistan (an ally in the war on terrorism) has also been an irritant in the relationship. Sales of US F-16 jetfighters to Islamabad were perceived as destabilising for the region and confirmed to New Delhi that the US administration is prepared to develop US-Pakistani military relations to the disadvantage of regional stability and conflict-free US–India relations. However, in January 2004, the US and India signed an agreement on trade for dual-use technology, technology with civilian and military applications. This coincided with a reappraisal in Washington of the importance of supporting India as a counter to growing Chinese influence. The Bush visit and the reciprocal visit of Mr Singh to the US have led to a further upgrading of relations between the two countries. Despite latent anti-Americanism, it would appear that there is a wide consensus within the Indian political and security elite that India should develop a new and deep strategic partnership with the US. This development could lead to some tensions with the EU over arms sales (as well as Boeing versus Airbus sales). Rising energy demands could also see India (and China) compete with the EU for scarce resources.

While India accepts that the US is the predominant world power and is prepared to seek deals with Washington in certain areas, it has no desire to be drawn into any US dominated anti-Chinese alliance. India will act in its own interests and in some areas such as nuclear matters and terrorism it will tilt towards the US and in other areas such as the UN and Doha more towards Europe. Unlike the bilateral discussions between the EU and the US which cover Asia (mainly China), there are no discussions about the EU during US–Indian bilateral meetings.

---

[14] Fraser Cameron, *US Foreign Policy after the Cold War* (London: Routledge, 2005).

Relations between India and China have improved significantly following the April 2006 visit of Chinese Premier Wen Jiabao to India. Both sides agreed to form a strategic partnership that reflects a major shift in relations between the two Asian giants, whose ties have long been defined by mutual suspicion. The talks revealed a shared desire to forget some of the past mistakes and historical legacies and move the new relationship forward. A minority of Indian scholars and policy-makers, on the other hand, still point to China as a 'potential military threat', claiming that not only Pakistan's nuclear ambitions but also China's nuclear arsenal 'forced' India to go nuclear in 1998. Both China and India buy significant shares of their crude oil supplies from the Middle East (above all from Iran) and they could become competitors for natural resources and energy in the future. Others, however, talk of the shared interests and complementary economic relationship between China and India, leading to the coining of the 'Chindia' phenomenon.

The EU is also seeking to develop a strategic partnership with China which has become its second-largest trading partner. There has been an increasing number of political and official contacts and preparations are in hand for a complete upgrading of the relationship. But there are problems, notably criticism by some EU member states of the lack of democracy and disrespect for human rights in China. This has prevented the EU from lifting the arms embargo imposed after the Tiananmen Square massacre of 1989.[15] Many Indians resent the EU's apparent fixation on China as witnessed by the numerous high-level visits to Beijing as opposed to New Delhi.

Closer Indo-Japanese relations and more regular high-level exchanges over recent years between the two countries have partly been motivated by the perception of China as a regional and global economic and political challenge and/or threat. But India's relations with Japan are second to those with China. Although a minority in both countries perceive China as a 'threat' (rather than 'just' a challenge), they are clearly aware of China's rapidly growing economic, political and military influence in the region and

---

[15] The US is strongly opposed to the lifting of the arms embargo lest it leads to increased sale of high-tech weaponry to China.

have recently decided to intensify their dialogue on political and security issues. Japan, however, is aware that it needs to maintain a balance in its diplomatic relations with China and with India to maintain a leading position in Asia and secure the best possible political and economic relations with them. This is a task that has become increasingly challenging in view of tense Sino-Japanese relations. The new Japanese Prime Minister, Mr Abe, seemed to realise the importance of reducing these tensions and started his term in office with a diplomatic success by visiting China and South Korea. India and Japan have both been seeking a permanent seat on the UN Security Council and (together with Brazil and Germany) decided to support each other's candidacies. India sought to secure China's support for Japan while Japan sought to persuade Pakistan to support India's bid. Neither effort met with success.

The EU also has a 'strategic partnership' with Japan and a corresponding action plan. But little has been achieved in moving the relationship beyond traditional economic and trade issues. There were high hopes in Brussels that Japan would support the EU's efforts to strengthen the multilateral system and much disappointment at former Prime Minister's Koizumi's obvious preference for close ties with Washington and uncritical support for US foreign policy. Japan does not really have an impact on the EU-India relationship.

Russia was traditionally one of India's main partners and remains an important supplier of energy and arms. The EU is also struggling to define a new relationship with Russia as the ten-year partnership and cooperation agreement expires in 2007. EU member states are divided on how to deal with Russia. Nearly all have signed bilateral energy deals but some would like a tougher policy on human rights. Russia's use of energy for political purposes and its relations with its neighbours, including Central Asia, are two obvious points for discussion in EU–India relations. A new EU–Russia strategic partnership would also have an impact on Indian perceptions of the EU.

India and ASEAN maintain close economic and business relations and are looking to intensify relations in view of rapid economic growth in both India and ASEAN. In 1992, India became a sectoral dialogue partner of ASEAN and a full dialogue partner in 1996, including in the ASEAN Regional Forum (ARF). India is an active member of the ARF, but tense India–Pakistan relations dominate India's security agenda leaving only limited capacities for India's involvement in Asian security issues. Although since the inclusion of Burma/Myanmar into ASEAN, India and ASEAN share a land boundary of 1,600 km, it is unlikely that India will play a more active role in East Asian security (getting more involved in regional security issues such as the nuclear crisis on the Korean peninsular and Taiwan Straits tensions) through the ARF. Pakistan's admission to the ARF in July 2004 was welcomed by India although Indo-Pakistani issues are not being discussed in the forum. In fact, the ARF members agreed on Pakistan's membership on the condition that Islamabad would not use the forum to address Indo-Pakistani issues. The EU also has formal links with ASEAN, including the ARF, but these are under-developed and there is little interaction between India and the EU regarding ASEAN affairs.

ECONOMIC AND TRADE RELATIONS

The dramatic economic growth in India during the past decade has been perhaps the biggest factor pushing Europe to take more interest in the world's biggest democracy. The crucial economic reforms of 1991 effectively set the stage for the Indian economy as it exists today: more than 80 per cent of India's draconian Licence Raj was dismantled, current account convertibility was introduced, many of the stifling restrictions on Indian businesses were abolished, and by 1995 tariffs were reduced to 65 per cent from the prevailing 300 per cent.[16] The success of the Singh reforms is manifest in the sustained growth of the economy after 1991, the fact that the country has successfully transformed itself from an entirely inward-looking closed economy to an important player in the high-tech global market, with significant innovative and research capabilities and a diversified industrial and technology base. Despite its recent economic success, India remains an economy of sharp contrasts: it is a labour intensive economy, with 65 per cent of the population engaged in agriculture and 70 per cent living in rural areas, but with pockets of highly skilled intellectual capital. India has the third-largest pool of engineering and science talent in the world, but 37 per cent of the populace remains illiterate.

---

[16] For details on the process of economic liberalisation in India and its consequences, see Gurcharan Das, *India Unbound: The Social and Economic Revolution for Independence to the Global information Revolution* (New York: Alfred A. Knopf, 2001).

These contrasts give India a unique mix of comparative advantages, including both abundant low-skilled, low-cost and high-skilled low-cost labour.

Although India acknowledges the EU as an economic superpower, most businessmen still think about doing business with individual member states. They talk of the British or German market rather than the European market. There is also a widespread feeling that the EU is over-protectionist tinged with racism (viz, Mittal/Arcelor). The decision of the UK to allow an Indian takeover of its entire steel industry may help mitigate this image.[17] Many Indians also think that Europe is too small, divided and backward-looking to be more than a niche player providing luxury goods and services in the future. The US is regarded more as the benchmark for economic performance. It will perhaps change attitudes if the EU were able to meet its own Lisbon agenda targets to make it the most competitive economy in the world by 2010. Most Indians choose to go to the US for postgraduate studies, though for undergraduate studies the UK is the favourite destination.

Despite rising trade between the EU and India, there appear to be several areas of untapped trade potential for both economies. For instance, there is a tremendous opportunity to widen the scope of trade, currently dominated by textiles and clothing. Crucially, there is a stark imbalance between relative levels of trade: where the EU accounts for roughly 21 per cent of India's two-way trade, India's share in EU trade is less than 1 per cent; where the EU is India's key trading partner, India ranks 14th in the EU's comparable list.[18] At the same time, while there has been an increase in Foreign Direct Investment (FDI) into India from the EU, India still receives only 0.2 per cent of the EU's FDI flows.[19]

It is against this background that the 2006 summit gave the green light for negotiations on a broad new agreement on trade

---

[17] It is interesting to note that Indian restaurants contribute more to the UK's GDP than the steel industry.
[18] Speech by Kamal Nath, 'India–EU Strategic Partnership: Steps Ahead', 14th January 2005, at http://commerce.nic.in/publications/india wto newletter. asp?link=newsletter jan feb 2005. htm4id=%3C%25=request.querystring (accessed January 5, 2008); Jayashree Sengupta, *EU–India Strategic Partnership*, Observer Research Foundation, at www. observerindia.com/strategic/st041108.htm (accessed on January 5, 2008).
[19] Sengupta, *EU–India Strategic Partnership*.

and investment. The words FTA were not mentioned in the final text as the idea of a FTA is opposed by the liberal reformist Indian government's coalition partner, the Communist party. Both India and the EU are well aware of the dangerous symbolism of opening bilateral free trade talks as both are founder members of the GATT and WTO. Neither wishes their move to be interpreted as undermining the multilateral trade system in which they both strongly believe. But both are concerned at the US' aggressive approach to FTAs and do not want to be left out of the picture.

If the trading potential is to be realised, however, the EU insists that India must continue and speed up economic reforms. Numerous barriers to investment, including the lack of IPR protection and poor infrastructure, remain. There are a number of key areas that need to be addressed by both the parties in order to reap the full economic benefits of a strategic partnership: the removal of tariff and non-tariff barriers to trade, a successful conclusion to the Doha round and measures to encourage FDI into the Indian economy. While India speaks of a 'fortress Europe' that is increasingly difficult to penetrate and in urgent need of harmonisation,[20] India's average tariffs remain amongst the highest in the world. Where the EU argues India's formal barriers to trade are the main reason behind discouraging EU trade figures, India argues that it is the EU's informal barriers that create a protected and impenetrable market for India's exports.

India and the EU have worked closely on the Doha round and both played a pivotal role in the formulation and adoption of the framework agreement adopted in Geneva in July 2005. While both parties share a desire to protect their agricultural sectors,[21] their essential areas diverge in other areas such as market access for industrial goods, services, trade facilitation and anti-dumping. India is also sometimes suspicious of the EU's perceived neo-liberal views on economic policy. Within the EU there is often a significant difference between the institutions that are keen to move forward with the partnership and conservative member states who are afraid

---

[20] See the Indian prime minister's speech at the India–EU Business Summit, September 7, 2005, at http://pmindia.nic.in/1 speech.asp?id=189 (accessed on January 5, 2008).

[21] See Walden Bello and Aileen Kwa, *G20 Leaders Succumb to Divide and Rule Tactics*, August 10, 2004, at http://www.globalexchange.org/campaigns/wto/2946.html (accessed on January 5, 2008).

to give institutions too much room to negotiate analogously.[22] In India, the foreign ministry often lacks adequate leverage to exert pressure on national and state governments. The result is two difficult bureaucracies trying to arrive at a consensus while they often do not know what that consensus should be.

THE IMAGE PROBLEM

One of the key problems in the EU-Indian relationship is the lack of knowledge in India about the EU. Europe is still viewed primarily through the prism of its largest member states, especially the UK. Many of the Indian elite were educated in the UK and the BBC is still the preferred source of foreign news. At the September 2005 summit with Blair and Barroso, newspaper readers could be forgiven for thinking it had been an Anglo-Indian affair. The visits of most European leaders to India raise little interest. Indians respond that the EU does not appear on their radar screens as a political and security actor. They acknowledge that it helped broker a peace deal in Aceh, Indonesia, but they point to disarray within the EU Security Council over Iraq and reform of the UN as examples of Europe's failure to get its act together. There are no quick-fixes on this front. The member states have a crucial role to play in performing as a team, but with no single telephone number in Brussels to contact them it is an uphill struggle. More visits by Commissioners might help. In 2005 fifteen Commissioners visited China and only two made it to India.

Many officials involved in EU–India relations complain about the lack of awareness and understanding of one another's economies and the resultant policy positions as *the* major predicament in the development of the EU–India relationship. Some consider that this is complicated by the fact that the European end of the strategic partnership is driven by very small circles in Brussels, with an inadequate number of 'experts'. India, for its part, seems sceptical of a hidden European protectionist agenda and uncertain about how to engage with the EU. The various ministries in New Delhi have also struggled to deal with the range of new issues that have emerged onto the EU–India agenda. According to one

---

[22] There is an additional problem in the EU where decisions such as migration need to be taken by member states through the Shengen Treaty rather than by the institutions.

senior Indian official, there is a serious lack of trained personnel in New Delhi who understand the EU.[23]

Conclusion

Given that the current unipolar world is unsustainable in the long run, there is a compelling case for India and the EU to develop a genuine strategic partnership based on shared values and interests. The two entities also share many common problems, including the development of a multicultural society and popular acceptance of governance structures. In the same vein, while the EU and India share a common objective of economic growth, each faces different internal concerns that often lead their external policies in different directions, making a partnership more difficult to manage.

The EU–India strategic partnership is in certain aspects a natural progression from the 1994 cooperation agreement and associated annual summits. However, there are a number of factors that suggest that the partnership may be more than a mere strengthening of current relations between the EU and India. India and the EU share common commitments to democracy, international law, multilateralism, human rights, stable institutions, economic liberalisation and development (this is not the case with all of the EU's other strategic partners, particularly Russia and China). They also share similar long-term objectives: the EU is determined to implement the Lisbon strategy to make it the most competitive economy and India is striving to stimulate growth, investment and employment to meet its Millennium objectives. Each is confronted by similar problems of democratic deficits, competing claims of federalism and regional autonomy and the demands of presiding over multiple cultures, religions and languages within a secular framework. Thus, the EU–India partnership, built on reasonably strong foundations, comes at a time when both are emerging as more significant global players—India through its nascent economic prowess, size, its leading role in South Asia and the G-20 and nuclear power status; and the EU by building on its already significant trade role, enlargement and its increasingly important role in multilateral fora.

At the same time, both India and the EU are looking towards the US and China. The Bush revolution is drawing to an end without any agreement on the future course of US foreign policy. Much will

---

[23] Personal communication.

depend on the fall-out of the Iraq war and its impact on American domestic opinion and politics. But with the US moving towards embracing India as a 'strategic partner', the EU will have to redouble its efforts in engaging India. As India and the US come closer, there will be greater opportunities for the EU to come to terms with a rising India than before, though the EU will have to work harder in presenting itself as an attractive option when compared to the US. It is therefore imperative for the EU to expand its ties with India faster and more meaningfully than it has done so far. India's role as a strategic balancer in the Asia–Pacific is going to be crucial in the coming years and if the EU decides to ignore it now, it will lose out vis-à-vis the US in gaining sufficient diplomatic leverage in the region.

The EU and India are committed to chasing China whose 'claws' are encircling India. China's phenomenal growth and the business and political links it has built up are pulling into its orbit a group of countries—Korea, Japan, Taiwan, Australia, Vietnam, Myanmar and even Pakistan. If democratic India remains poor and if its growth stalls, its influence in Asia will diminish as authoritarian China's grows. Today it is not just higher energy prices that India and the EU will have to cope with as they chase China. Higher inflation, higher interest rates, slower American growth and intensifying protectionist pressures are all going to make their task harder. In these circumstances a closer partnership between India and the EU makes eminent sense. But a strategic partnership depends not only on common values and interests. It should be for the long-term, be able to withstand ups and downs in the relationship, and it also implies some coordination before major decisions and a high level of interaction. Given these criteria, the EU–India relationship has a long way to go before it can properly be termed strategic.

ANNEX

INSTITUTIONAL ARCHITECTURE
Existing Structures and New Proposals

I. Existing Fora

India–EU Summit

Political
1. Ministerial Level Troika Meeting
2. Senior Officials Meeting Troika

3. Joint Working Group on Consular Matters
4. Joint Working Group on Anti-terrorism (scope to be expanded to include all issues relating to security; to be renamed JWG on Security Cooperation)
5. India-EU Round Table Conference meetings
6. Brainstorming Sessions

Economic

I. **Joint Commission**
a) High level dialogue on WTO
b) Working Group on Environment
c) Steering Group on Science & Technology
d) Sub-Commission on Economic Cooperation
e) Sub-Commission on Development Cooperation
f) Sub-Commission on Trade
   i) Working Group on Textiles and Clothings
   ii) Working Group on Telecommunication & Information Technology
   iii) Working Group on Agriculture & Marine Products
   iv) Expert Level Group on Trade Defence

II. **New fora/Agreements recommended**

Political

1. JWG on Security Cooperation—proposed by India.
    Sub Group on Narco-terrorism
    Sub Group on Money-laundering
    Sub Group on Cyber-terrorism
    Sub Group on Document security
    Sub Group on Institutional Cooperation with Europol/Office of EU Anti-terrorist Coordinator
2. High Level Coordination Dialogue on UN matters—proposed by India.
3. Joint Discussion Groups on:—proposed by India.
    - Middle East
    - Political and economic reconstruction of Iraq
    - Political and economic reconstruction of Afghanistan
4. Dialogue between Indian Integrated Defence Staff and European Defence Agency—proposed by India.
5. Expert level dialogue on Nuclear non-proliferation—proposed by India/EU
6. India—EU Civilisational Dialogue—proposed by India.
7. MOU/Cooperation Agreement between Indian Multi Agency Task Force and Europol—proposed by India.

8. Establishment of Institute of Indian Studies at Brussels—proposed by India.
9. Interaction between the Parliamentary Committees of India and the EU and Formation of an 'India Delegation' in European Parliament—proposed by India.

Economic
1. High level dialogue between RBI and European Central Bank(ECB) on Economic and Monetary Matters leading up to the Troika level meeting of the Finance/Economic Ministers—proposed by EU/India
2. India–EU structured dialogue on trade impact of enlargement—proposed by India
3. India–EU JWG on research, development, collaboration for future cooperation in identified areas of biotechnology—proposed by EU/India
4. India–EU Panel on energy to guide JWGs proposed to be formed for dealing with fossil fuels, hydro energy, renewable and nuclear energy, energy management—proposed by EU/India
5. India–EU Civil Aviation Agreement—proposed by EU
6. India–EU Agreement on Investment, Promotion and Protection—proposed by India
7. India–EU investment promotion bureau—proposed by India
8. India–EU MOU/Agreement on Mutual Legal Assistance in civil, commercial and criminal matters—proposed by India
9. India–EU joint study of skill sets including outsourcing and identifying areas where EU would need outside professionals—proposed by India
10. India–EU JWG on Technical Standards and SPS measures—proposed by EU/India
11. India–EU Sectoral Dialogue on pharmaceutical, drugs and traditional medicines—proposed by India
12. India–EU Business Round Table meetings—proposed by EU
13. Joint Research in 'Fusion Energy'—proposed by EU/India

PART III
India's Regional Policy

10

India and South Asia: Towards a Benign Hegemony

STEPHEN F. BURGESS

For much of the past sixty years, India's relations with South Asia have been largely unilateralist and hegemonic in nature. In 1971, India supported a democratic resistance in East Pakistan against pogroms conducted by the Pakistan army and then invaded the territory, reducing by half its principal adversary in South Asia. In 1961, India annexed the Portuguese colony of Goa and, in 1974, the independent principality of Sikkim. In the 1980s, India proclaimed a doctrine against foreign intervention in South Asian affairs, while covertly supporting Tamil rebels in their conflict with the Sri Lankan government. In 1987, India mounted a peace support operation to Sri Lanka and attempted to forcibly impose peace, while insisting that other powers not interfere. In 2002, India placed 700,000 troops along its border with Pakistan, applying pressure that complemented diplomatic efforts to convince Pakistan to control cross-border terrorism in Jammu and Kashmir. Clearly, India used hard-power and exercised hegemony in South Asia in order to consolidate its territorial sovereignty, oppose regional and global adversaries and ensure access to water and other resources for a very large and expanding population.

While using hard-power in South Asia, India has established a reputation for the use of soft-power and multilateral leadership, especially at the UN and in the Non-Aligned Movement. After the economic reforms in 1991 and the loosening of Cold War constraints, India developed its economy, became a beneficiary of globalisation and became less defensive and more outgoing in the subcontinent.[1] India stepped up its engagement in the South Asian

---

[1] C. Raja Mohan, *Crossing the Rubicon: The Shaping of India's New Foreign Policy*, (New Delhi: Penguin/Viking, 2003). The US opposed Indian leadership in South Asia during the Cold War but now encourages that leadership.

Association for Regional Cooperation (SAARC). Until recently, India, as the world's largest democracy, has chosen to promote non-alignment, rather than democratisation, though it occasionally enforced rules that opposed the abuse of power in South Asia (e.g., in East Pakistan in 1971 and Sri Lanka in the 1980s).[2] Since 2001, India became actively engaged in fostering democracy in Nepal and Sri Lanka. At the same time, India has not put pressure on the Burmese military dictatorship as it suppressed mass demonstrations for democracy in 2007. Thus, it appears that India has been moving from a predominantly unilateral and hard-power approach towards the subcontinent to a more multilateral and soft-power approach. At issue is the extent to which Indian behaviour will continue to shift.

India dwarfs its South Asian neighbours in terms of population and gross domestic product. India has more than one billion people (1.13 billion) followed by Pakistan with 165 million and Bangladesh with 150 million. Smaller states include Afghanistan with 32 million, Nepal with 29 million and Sri Lanka with 21 million; and the micro-states are Bhutan with 672,000 and the Maldives with less than 400,000. Therefore, India has been in a position, on paper at least, to dominate its South Asian neighbours as well as to economically attract them.

A hegemon is a power that has more capability than any other state or coalition of states in an international system and dictates and enforces international rules, partly through the exercise of hard (mainly military) power, in order to maximise its interests and maintain its dominance.[3] A contemporary example of a power exercising hegemony is the US, when it acted without UN Security Council

---

[2] C. Raja Mohan, 'Balancing Interests and Values: India's Struggle with Democracy Promotion', *Washington Quarterly* 30:3 (July 2007), pp. 99–115.

[3] Joshua S. Goldstein, *Long Cycles: Prosperity and War in the Modern Age* (New Haven, Conn.: Yale University Press, 1988), p. 281; Joseph Nye, *Bound to Lead: The Changing Nature of American Power* (New York: Basic Books, 1990), pp. 37–48; A.F.K. Organski and Jacek Kugler, *The War Ledger* (Chicago: Chicago University Press, 1980), Chapter 1. According to Organski and Kugler, hegemons are one of two or three great powers that are able to set the international rules. Over the past three hundred years, the UK and the US have been liberal hegemons, setting rules upholding free trade and other freedoms. The power transition between the US and the UK from the 1870s to the 1940s did not result in conflict, because the two great powers were both liberal hegemons with shared interests.

approval and used hard power in invading Iraq, ostensibly to create a new (democratic and anti-Islamist) order in the Middle East.[4]

A benign hegemon is a power that has more capability (military, economic and diplomatic) than any other state and dictates the rules, enforces rules through the exercise of both hard and soft power, and fosters cooperation. However, more than one state benefits. Often, benign hegemons exercise non-reciprocity, allowing other states to benefit, while demanding little in return.[5] In the 1990s, the US acted primarily as a benign liberal superpower, multilateral leader, and skilled user of 'soft-power'.[6] A 'leader' is a state with as many capabilities as any other state in a system, that builds consensus through the use of soft-power in favour of international rules and practices non-reciprocity where other states benefit from the status quo.[7]

Historically, authoritarian great powers have tended to seek classic hegemony, while democratic great powers have been more

---

[4] Joseph Nye, *The Paradox of American Power: Why the World's Only Superpower Can't Afford to Go It Alone* (Oxford: Oxford University Press, 2002) p. 15; Benjamin R. Barber, *Fear's Empire: War, Terrorism, and Democracy* (New York: Norton, 2003) pp. 35–41. Historically, empires were the most common hegemons. In recent years, the US acted as a hegemon, when it bypassed the UN Security Council and exercised 'hard power' in its invasion of Iraq. Afterwards, US leaders and policy-makers began wrestling with the issue of how they should respond to rising levels of discontent against what was perceived as America's path of hegemonic unilateralism.

[5] Robert Gilpin, *War and Change in World Politics* (Cambridge: Cambridge University Press, 1981), p. 144; Nye, *The Paradox of American Power*, pp. 10–12; Charles A. Kupchan, 'After Pax Americana: Benign Power, Regional Integration, and the Sources of a Stable Multipolarity', *International Security* 23:2 (Fall 1998), pp. 40–79; Nye, *Bound to Lead*, 49–68. See, also, Peter M. Dawson, *Liberal Hegemony, Democratic Peace, and United States Policy* (Newport, RI: Naval War College, 1996). Some scholars have categorised the UK during the 'Pax Britannica' of the 19th century and the US since 1945 as benign hegemons. Robert Keohane has characterised the period from 1945 to the early 1970s, in which the US established and directed a new world economic order, as one of 'hegemonic leadership', which fostered 'hegemonic cooperation'.

[6] Nye, *The Paradox of American Power*, p. 16. Occasionally, the US resorted to hard power, as in the wars with Iraq (1991) and Serbia (1995 and 1999) but always with multilateral approval. Before 2003, France, Germany and other allies in the community of democracy accepted benign, multilateral US leadership and exercise of power.

[7] Nye, *Bound to Lead*, pp. 258–59. Nye is reluctant to use the term hegemon to characterise the US for most of the period since 1945, because it implies domination and prefers to use the term 'leader'.

likely to be benign hegemons or multilateral leaders. Democracies are constrained by legislatures, public opinion and the media from using hard-power, unless there is a compelling national security reason to employ force. Given the constraints on the use of hard-power and the widespread use of persuasion and bargaining in the domestic arena, democratic powers tend to use soft-power more often and more skillfully than authoritarian powers and tend to engage in multilateral leadership.[8]

Given the preceding definitions, India has tended to act as a regional hegemon which translated its preponderance of power into a proven ability to use hard-power in order to set and enforce rules governing a regional system. Recently, India has worked to become a regional leader, where it is using soft-power and striving to develop trust with the neighbouring states and build consensus in favour of international rules, including democratisation, that benefit most states in the region.

Opposition to hegemony comes from states that have interests that are different from those of the actual or aspiring hegemon and that have the power to resist. Within a region, one or two discontented states can hamper or stymie regional powers from dictating and enforcing rules or building consensus and integrating their respective regions.[9] In South Asia, Pakistan has been India's main opponent, but Bangladesh, Sri Lanka and Nepal banded together in the 1980s to form the SAARC in order to provide an alternative to Indian unilateralism and hegemony. Finally, regional powers that attempt to exert hegemony must contend with opposition from global powers in the regional rule-setting process. The US came to oppose India's hegemonic behaviour in South Asia during the Cold War, which caused India to become more defensive.

The purpose of this essay is to examine India–South Asia relations and predict where they are headed, based upon past and present trends. Of particular interest is the issue of whether or not India continues to act primarily as a hegemon or is transitioning to greater multilateral leadership using soft-power. The focus is first

---

[8] Nye, *The Paradox of American Power*, p. 11.
[9] Nye, *The Paradox of American Power*, 16–17, 132–33. In the case of US, opposition to unilateralism and hegemonic behaviour comes from both inside and outside the US. While opponents or discontents can pose an annoyance to a global hegemon, one or two can stymie regional powers from exercising leadership or hegemony.

on India's relations with the South Asian subcontinent as a whole, including the rivalry with Pakistan that dominates the region, and then on India's bilateral relations with South Asian states.

The Development of Indian Regional Hegemony

With a long history of states, civilisations and empires, and with the British Empire controlling and tying together the South Asian subcontinent, the main successor state—India—was well-situated to be a regional leader after the Second World War and the Independence in 1947. The new country had the potential to use hard-power, with a large army that was battle-tested in two world wars. India also had soft-power potential, with a large economy, rich culture and a sizeable bureaucracy and diplomatic corps. However, the British partition of India left the country weakened and faced with an instant enemy in the new state of Pakistan, which inherited a substantial part of the Indian army and which tried to forcibly annex the princely state of Jammu and Kashmir. Thus, India was faced with a struggle to keep its territory together.

In pursuing economic development, the new Indian government adopted self-reliant economic policies which prevented it from trading extensively with other economies in the region. Furthermore, Indian economic growth was slow and plagued by agricultural backwardness, a huge impoverished population and excessive red tape. Thus, Indian trade with its neighbours was negligible. India found it difficult to establish leadership of the subcontinent and preferred to act unilaterally in relations with each of its neighbours.

From 1954 onwards, India found the US in a Cold War partnership with Pakistan, which impeded Indian efforts to assert its interests in the subcontinent. Also, India confronted China in a border dispute and struggle for influence over Tibet, which culminated in defeat in the 1962 Sino-Indian war. Subsequently, India asserted its power in the South Asian subcontinent as a counter to Pakistan, China and the US. India moved towards the USSR which began to supply warplanes and other military hardware and helped build Indian defence capabilities in both conventional and nuclear areas. In the wake of China's 1964 nuclear test, India developed its own nuclear weapons programme.[10] In August 1971, India signed a twenty-year Treaty of Peace, Friendship and Cooperation with the USSR. In December 1971, India's invasion of East Pakistan demonstrated its hegemonic tendencies, coming in the face of opposition from the US and China and led to the creation of Bangladesh, which became a client state for several years. India and Pakistan subsequently negotiated the 1972 Simla Agreement that stabilised relations until the mid-1980s.[11]

In 1974, India conducted a 'peaceful' nuclear test of a crude fission device. The nuclear test, the victory over Pakistan and the creation of Bangladesh began to change India's reputation from that of a weak state to that of a regional power and hegemon. In the 1970s and 1980s, India continued its nuclear and conventional military build-ups. During this period, evidence emerged that Pakistan was developing a nuclear weapons programme, which touched off a South Asian arms race. In 1983, India began a ballistic missile programme which led to an India–Pakistan missile race in the late 1980s. In 1987, Prime Minister Rajiv Gandhi decided to forge ahead with a thermonuclear weapons programme. In 1989, the launching of a Pakistan-supported insurgency in Jammu and Kashmir led to the worsening of relations. In 1987 and 1990, Indian and Pakistani military exercises appeared to be the precursor to conflict and risked the possibility of nuclear war.[12]

The 'Indira' and 'Rajiv' Doctrines and Hegemony

In 1983, late in the tenure of Prime Minister Indira Gandhi, the Indian government proclaimed India's equivalent to the US Monroe Doctrine in the Americas. Subsequently, India demonstrated hegemonic tendencies, particularly in Sri Lanka where it favoured the Tamil minority in its rebellion with the government. Under the so-called called 'Indira Doctrine', India insisted that problems in the subcontinent be resolved bilaterally and that the US, China and other external powers should have no role in the region. Indira Gandhi declared that any South Asian country needing military

---

[10] Baldev Raj Nayar and T.V. Paul, *India in the World Order: Searching for Major Power Status* (Cambridge: Cambridge University Press, 2003), 172–73. See, also, George Perkovich, *India's Nuclear Bomb: The Impact on Global Proliferation* (Berkeley: University of California Press, 1999).

[11] J.N. Dixit, *India–Pakistan in War and Peace* (London: Routledge, 2002), pp. 225–29.

[12] Perkovich, *India's Nuclear Bomb*, pp. 300–02.

assistance should first approach India and only if it refused should that country seek help elsewhere. South Asian countries were also expected to ask for India's approval for conducting peace talks to settle internal conflicts. Peace talks were to be conducted in a manner that India approved and the final settlement should be acceptable to India.[13]

In October 1984, Indira Gandhi was assassinated and her son, Rajiv Gandhi, succeeded her. Under the 'Rajiv' Doctrine, which replaced the 'Indira' Doctrine, India sought to resolve the conflict in Sri Lanka on its own terms and excluded other states.[14] In 1987, Prime Minister Rajiv Gandhi committed troops to Sri Lanka to impose a peace settlement between the Tamil Tigers and the Sri Lankan government. In exchange, the Sri Lankan government agreed that (1) military bases would not be offered to any other country; (2) foreign naval vessels (especially US Navy ships) would not be allowed to dock in Sri Lanka's Tricomalee harbour in a manner prejudicial to India's interests; and (3) Voice of America broadcasting facilities would not be expanded in Sri Lanka.[15]

By the beginning of 1990, it was clear that the Indian peacemaking, and the peacekeeping mission in Sri Lanka, had failed. Indian troops withdrew. India's failures demonstrated that it had not been able to shape and control a country in the South Asian region by political or military means and that the 'Indira' and 'Rajiv' doctrines had not been sufficiently underwritten by Indian power. Subsequently, Indian unilateralism and hegemony receded in the 1990s. The exception was the Indian efforts to dominate and deter Pakistan.

---

[13] K.M. de Silva, *Regional Powers and Small State Security: India and Sri Lanka, 1977–90* (Baltimore: Johns Hopkins University Press, 1995), pp. 123–43; Mahnaz Ispahani, 'India's Role in Sri Lanka's Ethnic Conflict', in Ariel E. Levite, Bruce W. Jentleson and Larry Berman, eds, *Foreign Military Intervention: The Dynamics of Protracted Conflict* (New York: Columbia University Press, 1992), pp. 213–16; Alan J. Bullion, *India, Sri Lanka and the Tamil Crisis, 1976–1994: An International Perspective* (London: Pinter, 1995), pp. 41–42; Sumantra Bose, *Sri Lanka, India and the Tamil Elam Movement* (Thousand Oaks, Calif.: Sage Publications, 1994), pp. 134–35; S.D. Muni, *Pangs of Proximity: India and Sri Lanka's Ethnic Crisis* (Oslo, Norway: PRIO, 1993), pp. 52–58. See, also, Martha Crenshaw, *India and the Sri Lanka Dilemma*, Case Study, Department of Government, Wesleyan University, November 2001.
[14] Bullion, *India, Sri Lanka and the Tamil Crisis*, pp. 42–43.
[15] Ibid., 106–07.

While India sought to keep foreign powers out of the South Asian subcontinent through the proclamation of the 'Indira' and 'Rajiv' doctrines, discontent rose in the early 1980s in Bangladesh, Sri Lanka and Nepal against India's hegemonic tendencies and the harmful effects of the India–Pakistan conflict. The three states launched a multilateral initiative and persuaded India and Pakistan to participate, along with Maldives and Bhutan. This initiative led to the founding of the SAARC and the signing of the SAARC Charter at the first summit in December 1985. In the late 1980s, SAARC's agenda was dominated by bilateral disputes between India and Pakistan, Sri Lanka, Bangladesh and Nepal. During this period, SAARC became a platform for confidence-building measures among heads of government.[16]

THE END OF THE COLD WAR AND RISE OF INDIAN MULTILATERALISM

The end of the Cold War and the withdrawal of the two superpowers from South Asian affairs created the opportunity for India to shift from defensive unilateralism and hegemony to forward-looking, multilateral leadership in South Asia. The liberalisation of India's economy in 1991 created the opportunity to engage in greater trade with its neighbours and economic interests in South Asia became more important in India's foreign policy towards the region.[17] India promoted the development of free trade within SAARC. In December 1991, SAARC approved the establishment of an Inter-Governmental Group (IGG) to formulate an agreement to establish a SAARC Preferential Trading Arrangement (SAPTA). Given the consensus within SAARC, the framework agreement on SAPTA was finalised in 1993 and it formally came into operation in December 1995. SAPTA was the first step towards the transition to a South Asian Free Trade Area (SAFTA), leading perhaps towards a customs union and, eventually, a common market and economic union. The SAFTA treaty was negotiated and signed in January 2004 at the SAARC summit in Islamabad.

---

[16] Christian Wagner, 'From Hardpower to Softpower: Ideas, Interactions, Institutions, and Images in India's South Asian Policy', Heidelberg Papers in South Asian and Comparitive Politics, Working Paper No. 26, March 2005, p. 11, at http://archiv.ub.uni-heidelberg.de/voltextserver/voltexte/2005/5436/pdf/hpsacp26.pdf (accessed on April 24, 2008).
[17] Ibid., p. 13.

In recent years, India's rapidly growing economy and efforts to increase economic cooperation with its neighbours have created new challenges for SAARC. India reached bilateral trade agreements with Sri Lanka and Nepal. Bangladesh signalled its willingness to enter into similar negotiations. Nonetheless, Indian exports to South Asian neighbours have increased slowly since India opened up its economy in 1991.

In 1996, Prime Minister I.K. Gujral promulgated a new doctrine for Indian policy in South Asia, which emphasised the principle of 'non-reciprocity'.[18] Thus, India, as the biggest country in SAARC, indicated its willingness to give more than it would achieve in bargaining with its smaller neighbours. Indian non-reciprocity made it possible to solve disputes with Nepal and Bangladesh. Furthermore, as a result of the changes in Indian diplomacy and economic relations, at the 1996 SAARC summit, India was prepared to assert a leadership role within the organisation.

India's growing interest in regional cooperation was not confined to SAARC. India has engaged in efforts to strengthen sub-regional cooperation with Bangladesh, Bhutan and Nepal in the northeast of the subcontinent. India intensified other regional cooperation projects, including the creation of the Bangladesh, India, Myanmar, Sri Lanka, Thailand–Economic Cooperation (BIMST-EC) in 1998 and the Indian Ocean Rim Association for Regional Cooperation (IORARC) in 1997. India also strengthened its collaboration with the Association of Southeast Asian Nations (ASEAN), including new Indo-ASEAN institutions and a common summit, as well as intensified trade and investment.[19]

In the 1990s, India offered to broaden dialogue and open cooperation with Pakistan, including within the SAARC framework. However, Pakistan refused, insisting that the status of Jammu and Kashmir be resolved first before talks and cooperation could begin. India's desire to intensify economic relations with Pakistan through the grant of Most Favoured Nation (MFN) trading status was rebuffed, because hardliners in Pakistan feared that any economic engagement would weaken the country and its resolve. The Indian and Pakistani nuclear tests of May–June 1998, the Kargil War of

---

[18] Ibid., p. 13.
[19] Ibid., p. 3.

May–June 1999 and General Pervez Musharraf's coup of October 1999 further dampened the hopes for dialogue and cooperation. In spite of the setbacks, India used bilateral talks during the SAARC summits to continue to engage Pakistan. At the January 2004 SAARC summit in Islamabad, Indian Prime Minister Vajpayee reached out to Pakistan, which led to a new era of détente and to a four-fold increase in India's trade with Pakistan.

To sum up, India's emergence as a strategic and economic power in the 1990s enabled it to assume regional leadership and promote economic cooperation as well as dispute resolution. India came to use SAARC as a mechanism for confidence-building and free trade in a region where mutual trust is in the process of gradual development.

Indian Leadership in Riverine Cooperation

Over the decades, India has played a leading role in multilateral and bilateral efforts to deal with the rivers and water resources in South Asia—especially the three major rivers: the Indus, Brahmaputra and Ganges. India worked with the World Bank and other South Asian riverine states (i.e., Pakistan, Nepal and Bangladesh) to promulgate treaties, agreements and arrangements, which cover the largest irrigated area of any one river system in the world and provide a mechanism for consultation and conflict resolution through inspections, exchange of data and visits. The most notable treaties were the 1960 India–Pakistan Indus Waters Treaty and the 1996 Indo-Bangladesh Waters Treaty.[20]

In 1996, India and Bangladesh reached a 30-year agreement over the sharing of the waters from the Ganges because of the work, done behind the scenes, by water specialists, politicians and scholars on both sides, particularly at the non-governmental level. Bangladesh, being in the downstream and delta portion of the huge watershed, has been most vulnerable to the water quality and quantity that flows from upstream. In the 1960s, India had built

---

[20] Stephen Brichieri-Colombi and Robert W. Bradnock, 'Geopolitics, Water and Development in South Asia: Cooperative Development in the Ganges–Brahmaputra Delta', *The Geographical Journal*, 169:1 (March 2003), pp. 43–64; Sanjoy Hazarika, 'South Asia: Sharing the Giants—Water Sharing of the Indus, Ganges and Brahmaputra Rivers', *UNESCO Courier* 54:10 (October 2001), pp. 32–33.

the Faraka Barrage which blocked the natural flow of water into the country during the dry season, causing severe water shortages. It also led to sudden water releases in the rainy seasons, causing floods and extensive damage, including the loss of property and lives. The principal objective of the 30-year treaty was to determine the amount of water released by India to Bangladesh at the Faraka Barrage. The water-sharing arrangements, primarily for the dry season, were established in regard to the river's flow in any particular year. The treaty aimed to achieve 'optimum utilisation' of the waters of the region and relies on the principles of 'equity, fair play and no harm to either party', with a clause for the sharing arrangements to be reviewed every five years.[21]

At the same time, India resolved a dispute with Nepal over the Mahakali River and several barrages. The Treaty of Mahakali settled Nepal's entitlement to water flows and electricity from the Indian side, improving on a 1992 agreement.[22] The treaty was opposed by various Nepalese groups who claimed that it was unfair.

A dispute has occurred over China's failure to disclose information on the Brahmaputra River. In 2000, a landslide in Tibet caused a dam to collapse, unleashing a huge wall of water that destroyed every bridge on the river in the Indian border state of Arunachal Pradesh. The water rushed through the Indian state of Assam and devastated parts of Bangladesh causing extensive damage. An effective early-warning flood system could have prevented the disaster. According to Indian officials, China had not shared any information on the build-up of water pressure and the heavy rains in the upstream catchment area of the river. Another concern has centred on Chinese plans to divert the waters of the Brahmaputra and construct a dam to tap its hydroenergy potential.[23] Given the concerns over climate change and the prospects of even greater water shortages in the future, riverine and water disputes will continue to occur, which India must seek to resolve on both multilateral and bilateral levels.

---

[21] Hazarika, 'South Asia: Sharing the Giants', pp. 32–33.
[22] 'The Treaty of Mahakali', February 12, 1996, at http://www.nepaldemocracy.org/documents/treaties_agreements/indo-nepal_treaty_mahakali.htm (accessed on November 12, 2007).
[23] Hazarika, 'South Asia: Sharing the Giants', pp. 32–33.

INDIA–US PARTNERSHIP IN SOUTH ASIA SINCE SEPTEMBER 11, 2001

Bush administration's overtures and India's growing self-assurance led it to join the US coalition against terrorism after the September 11, 2001 attacks, provide US forces with over-flight and port rights and offer basing rights in the struggle against the Taliban and Al-Qaeda. India offered cooperation partly because the US was fighting many of India's adversaries in Operation Enduring Freedom. However, Pakistan President Musharraf pre-empted India by offering the US over-flight and basing rights. US entry into the region led to the end of the Taliban regime that was hostile to India and put pressure on Pakistan to diminish its support for anti-Indian terrorism in Jammu and Kashmir. On November 9, 2001 in Washington, DC, Prime Minister Vajpayee spoke of the US and India as 'natural allies' and reiterated his support for Bush's 'Global War on Terror'. In deference to the US and its need to placate Pakistan, India restrained itself from fully coming to the assistance of the Karzai government in Afghanistan.

After the terrorist attack on the Indian Parliament on December 13, 2001 and the mobilisation and posting of 700,000 troops on the Line of Control and Pakistan border, India threatened but did not launch offensive operations and even refrained from 'limited conventional war' actions.[24] During 2002, the US exerted considerable pressure to forestall an Indian punitive attack against Pakistani forces and terrorist camps. US war-gaming analysis indicated that any Indian limited conventional warfare action would spiral into nuclear war.[25]

The Indian government was uncertain of the threshold that would set off a Pakistan nuclear strike. India also did not possess the capabilities (especially, attack helicopters) to undertake low-risk 'limited conventional warfare actions', such as raiding terrorist

---

[24] Gaurav Kampani, 'India's Compellence Strategy: Calling Pakistan's Nuclear Bluff over Kashmir', Center for Nonproliferation Studies, June 10, 2002, at http://cns.miis.edu/pubs/week/020610.htm (accessed on November 12, 2007).
[25] Subhash Kapila, *United States War-Gaming on South Asia Nuclear Conflict: An Analysis*, South Asia Analysis Group, Paper no. 476, June 14, 2002.

bases and quickly returning to India.[26] As an alternative, India maintained an attrition military strategy, hoping that Pakistan would be unable to sustain a large military presence along the Line of Control.

US efforts to resolve the 2002 crisis and its support of India's position against terrorism in Jammu and Kashmir helped pave the way for increased Indo-US cooperation. In 2002, India began to engage in a regional security dialogue with the US and fostered an understanding of India's concerns. These included India's policy towards the ongoing conflict in Sri Lanka between the Tamil Tigers and government forces, in which India favoured the devolution of some powers to the Tamils.[27]

India's pressure on Nepal to democratise marked a shift in foreign policy and a new interest in democracy promotion. From 2001 to 2006, India—working with the US and the EU—persuaded and cajoled the Nepalese monarchy to end its monopoly of power in the face of a growing Maoist insurgency and mass discontent. In 2006, these efforts helped lead to the transfer of power from the monarchy to an elected parliament, the inclusion of rebels in the political process and the establishment of a democratic republic.[28]

US–India cooperation in the war on terror and on regional issues helped pave the way for the 2004 'Next Steps in the Strategic Partnership' and the US–India nuclear agreement.[29] Evidently, Indian and US interests have converged in South Asia, while the US remains focussed on fighting the war on terror in Afghanistan and Pakistan's ungoverned areas.[30] The US has recognised the significance of the partnership with India, South Asia as India's sphere of influence and India's regional leadership, democracy and

---

[26] Anthony S. Cordesman, *The India–Pakistan Military Balance* (Washington, DC: Center for Strategic and International Studies, May 2002). India lacked attack helicopters and other airborne assault capabilities.
[27] Mohan, 'Balancing Interests and Values', p. 111.
[28] Ibid., p. 110.
[29] C. Raja Mohan, *Impossible Allies: Nuclear India, United States and the Global Order* (New Delhi: India Research Press, 2006); Henry Sokolski, 'Negotiating the Obstacles to US-Indian Strategic Cooperation', in Henry Sokolski, ed, *Gauging US-Indian Strategic Cooperation* (Carlisle, Penna.: Strategic Studies Institute, March 2007), pp. 1–11.
[30] Zalmay Khalizad, et al., *The United States and Asia: Toward a New US Strategy and Force Posture* (Santa Monica, Calif.: Rand, 2001), pp. 24–31.

dynamic economy as positive forces. The US–India partnership and India's economic growth have paved the way for India to assert its leadership over a region that is becoming less known for disputes and increasingly credited with economic growth and democratisation.

INDIA'S RELATIONS WITH ITS NEIGHBOURS

Nepal

India has traditionally counted on the Himalayan barrier of northern Nepal as its natural defence against China. However, Nepal drew closer to China following India's defeat in the 1962 border war and rejected India's offers of a defence pact. In 1989, India imposed a trade embargo on Nepal and closed most transit routes because of the expiration of treaties that had provided for preferential reciprocal trade terms and transit rights.[31] In the past decade, the rise of a Maoist insurgency in Nepal led to Indian concerns that extremist groups could use Nepal as a base of operations.

Since 2000, the Maoist insurgency and Nepalese democratic forces have been putting considerable pressure on the monarchy. In early 2005, King Gyanendra assumed direct and absolute power, dismissing the parliament. While China, Pakistan and Russia viewed the king's coup as a purely domestic Nepalese issue, India reacted negatively and chose not to participate in a regional summit with the king. India—Nepal's main weapons supplier—temporarily suspended military supplies to protest the coup. The Indian stance shifted quickly when Prime Minister Manmohan Singh met with the king at the Afro-Asian summit in Jakarta in April 2005. India resumed military aid such as jeeps, bullet-proof jackets and mine-proof vehicles. This action led to protests by democratic forces who believed that India was strengthening the hand of monarchy.[32]

The defeat of the king by democratic forces and the decision to establish a democratic republic, instead of a democratic monarchy, enhanced India's role as a promoter of democracy in Nepal. In turn, India redefined its political, economic, diplomatic and cultural relations with Nepal to account for the new democratic reality.

---

[31] Prakash Chandra Jha, 'India Needs to Redefine its Relations with Nepal', *India Post*, June 11, 2007, at http://indiapost.com/article/perspective/498/ (accessed on November 12, 2007).
[32] Ibid.

Prime Minister Girija Prasad Koirala's visit to India in June 2006 led to Prime Minister Singh's offer of considerable assistance in order to help meet Nepal's high expectations of its new democracy. The two prime ministers agreed to enhance the India–Nepal development partnership for expanding rural and economic infrastructure, developing education and healthcare facilities and building human resources. India extended a free trade area with generous concessions to Nepal, especially given the country's least developed status.[33]

Bhutan

India–Bhutan relations have been similar in character to India–Nepal relations. Bhutan is a monarchy, has served as a buffer between India and China and has been the home to anti-Indian insurgent groups. However, Bhutan is well behind Nepal in terms of opening to the outside world and democratisation. The 1949 friendship treaty defined Indian relations with Bhutan in terms of India's non-interference in Bhutan's isolated status, while India managed the kingdom's defence and foreign affairs. However, in the past decade, anti-Indian insurgents operating from Bhutan led India to apply pressure and, in 2003, insurgent camps were cleared.

In 2007, the Bhutanese government, led by its 27-year old monarch—King Jigme Khesar—and India negotiated and signed a new friendship treaty under which Bhutan would conduct its own foreign and defence policy. The king saw the treaty as part of India helping to guide Bhutan's modernisation and democratisation. In 2008, he announced plans to usher in major internal changes that would lead to democratisation and economic development. The 2007 friendship treaty committed both countries to cooperate on issues relating to their national interests and not allow the use of territories for activities harmful to the national security interest of the other. Also, the treaty included fresh provisions for expanding economic relations and cooperation in the fields of culture, education, health, sports, science and technology, as well as the hydroelectric sector.[34]

---

[33] Ibid.
[34] Iwasbir Hussain, 'India and the Upcoming Druk Democracy', *Himal South Asian*, May 2007, at http://www.himalmag.com/2007/may/analysis_india_bhutan_relation.htm (accessed on November 12, 2007).

Bangladesh

India has become increasingly concerned about Bangladesh, its declining stability and state capacity, and the rising Islamist forces there over the past decade or more. China has been gaining influence in the country. India–Bangladesh relations have stagnated due to border problems as well as the feeling on the Indian side that security-related issues—including arms trafficking, movement of people, transit and a gas pipeline—have not been given the importance they deserve in Dhaka.[35]

For Bangladesh, the issues have been the sharing of the waters of the Ganges, Brahmaputra and other rivers, the controversial Indian 'river-linking' project (that could threaten the flow of water to Bangladesh) as well as trade and a variety of border-related concerns, including smuggling. Already, nearly $2 billion worth of Indian goods are smuggled into Bangladesh annually, in addition to the $1.5 billion worth of goods that enter the country legally. The Bangladesh market is flooded with Indian goods, many of which are smuggled across the border.[36]

The growing Indian private sector has been making contributions towards reviving bilateral relations. The Tata Group has been progressing towards a $2.5 billion investment in Bangladesh in steel, fertiliser and power plants. Exploratory talks have also been underway on a coal mining concession. The Essar, Reliance, Mittal and Birla groups have shown their interest. A state-of-the-art hospital has been opened in Dhaka, in collaboration with India's Apollo Group. Sun Pharmaceuticals has begun its operations in Bangladesh. Many Indian companies are already involved in the information technology and readymade garment sectors. A number of major buying houses in Bangladesh are owned and operated by Indians, as are some leading readymade garment manufacturers and exporters.[37]

Bangladesh is considering an Indian proposal for a free trade agreement (FTA). The FTA between Bangladesh and India could be

---

[35] Harsh V. Pant, 'India and Bangladesh: Will the Twain Ever Meet', *Asian Survey* 47:2 (March/April 2007), pp. 231–49.
[36] Farooq Sobhan, 'Estranged Neighbours', *India Seminar* 557 (January 2006), at http://www.india-seminar.com/2006/557/557%20farooq%20sobhan.htm (accessed on November 12, 2007).
[37] Ibid.

based on the Indo-Sri Lankan FTA. However, given Bangladesh's least-developed country (LDC) status, India could very well extend more concessions to Bangladesh, similar to those given to Nepal. The FTA could have a major impact in expanding exports into India and increasing Indian investments. A bilateral FTA with India would mean that Bangladeshi firms would be given immediate duty-free access to Indian market for all goods, including ready-made garments. On the other hand, Indian goods would be given duty-free access to the Bangladeshi market over a period of time, possibly eight or more years.[38] A World Bank report has warned that Indian subsidies to wheat, rice and sugar producers could hurt the Bangladeshi economy.[39]

India has been encouraging Bangladesh to build east-west highways and rail links to connect India with Burma and Southeast Asia. India has offered to develop Chittagong port, which has the potential to serve as a regional port for Bangladesh, Nepal, Bhutan and Northeast India. However, Bangladesh has been reluctant to admit Indian companies to Chittagong. In order for India–Bangladesh relations to progress, considerable trust needs to be built. China may be able to build trust more quickly and comprehensively.

Sri Lanka

India–Sri Lanka relations have grown closer, even though the conflict between the government and Tamil Tigers has resumed. Trade and investment have increased, infrastructure links are being improved and defence collaboration has grown. India's position on the resumed civil war has been to continue to favour a politically negotiated settlement acceptable to all sections of Sri Lankan society (specifically the minority Tamils and majority Sinhalese), within the framework of an undivided Sri Lanka and consistent with democracy, pluralism and respect for human rights. India continues to support the Norwegian facilitation in the peace process. It continues to impress upon the government

---

[38] Ranabir Ray Choudhury, 'India–Bangladesh FTA Prospects', *The Hindu Business Line*, April 16, 2007, at http://www.blonnet.com/2007/04/16/stories/2007041601450800.htm (accessed on November 12, 2007).

[39] A. Z. M. Anas, 'Bangladesh to Gain Little from FTA with India: WB Report', *Financial Express*, December 6, 2006. http://www.bilaterals.org/article.php3?id_article=6610 (accessed on November 12, 2007).

of Sri Lanka that war is not an option, that the 'ceasefire' is not sustainable without political dialogue and that there is a need for the government of Sri Lanka to put forward a credible devolution package. India has offered to share its own federalist constitutional experience in finally resolving the conflict.

The Indo-Sri Lankan Free Trade Area (FTA) has been a success since becoming operational in 2000. Empirical data indicates that the FTA has had an impact in expanding Sri Lanka's exports into India and has also resulted in a sizeable increase in Indian investments in Sri Lanka.[40] As part of the FTA, the India–Sri Lanka Open Skies Agreement has brought significant increases in the air traffic between the two countries.[41]

Indian defence cooperation with Sri Lanka continues to expand. A major part of the training of the Sri Lankan Armed Forces is carried out in India. There has been a significant increase in the number of training slots offered to Sri Lankan personnel in recent years. There is continued cooperation in terms of exchange of visits and cooperation between navies. India was the first country to respond to Sri Lanka's request for assistance after the tsunami in December 2004. India assisted in the clean-up of a major oil spill in February 2006 and the evacuation of Sri Lankan nationals from Lebanon in July 2006.[42]

Afghanistan

India established close ties with Afghanistan after the Taliban was routed in December 2001 and especially with the presidency of Hamid Karzai, who had spent many years in India. However, in deference to the US and its alliance with Pakistan, India chose not to send troops to Afghanistan, instead opting to provide stabilisation, reconstruction and development assistance.[43] However, in recent

---

[40] Nagesh Kumar, 'An Agenda for Safta's Dhaka Summit', *Financial Express*, November 8, 2005, at http://fecolumnists.expressindia.com/full_column.php?content_id=107951 (accessed on November 12, 2007).

[41] N. Manoharan, 'Consolidating Bilateral Ties: Rajapakse's India Visit', Institute of Peace and Conflict Studies, Article No. 1920, January 6, 2006, at http://www.ipcs.org/South_Asia_articles2.jsp?action=showView&kValue=1933&country=1016&status=article&mod=a (accessed on November 12, 2007).

[42] 'Brief on India–Sri Lanka Relations', The High Commission of India, Colombo, August 2006, at http://www.hcicolombo.org/Ind_sl_bilateral.shtml (accessed on November 12, 2007).

[43] Mohan, *Crossing the Rubicon*, pp. 217–80. See, also, Mohammed Ayoob, 'South-West Asia after the Taliban', *Survival* 44:1 (Spring 2002), pp. 51–68.

years, members of the North Atlantic Treaty Organization or NATO-led coalition in Afghanistan have sought to get India more directly involved in fighting the Taliban in the country, especially given the shortfall of European forces.

Recently, India pledged $450 million in aid to the Karzai government, including a highway (the Zaranj–Delaram) that would connect Kandahar—Afghanistan's major city in the volatile south of the country—with the Iranian border.[44] The highway is the most high profile of several Indian projects in Afghanistan and Indian engineers working on the project have been the target of frequent attacks. In order to protect Indian nationals in 'Taliban country', India has sent several hundred highly trained commandos of the Indo-Tibetan Border Police (ITBP) force, which specialises in high-altitude operations in the Himalayas. Previously, ITBP units had been guarding the Indian embassy in Kabul and consulates in Kandahar and Jalalabad.

The new deployment entailed that almost 400 commandos would be in the area to combat Taliban attempts to halt the construction of the highway. The move suggests that India is prepared to take on a more significant role in security operations against the Taliban within Afghanistan, something for which the leading members of the NATO-led coalition in Afghanistan have been urging for some time. The boost to the troop numbers in the region has caused protests in Pakistan, which regards Afghanistan as its own rear area and is suspicious of any signs of Indian encirclement.

Conclusion

India's relations with South Asia have been unilateral in nature from the 1940s until the mid-1990s when India began working more on a multilateral basis, including on the platform of SAARC. The conflict with Pakistan and the suspicion of other states have kept India—the world's largest free market democracy—from realising its potential as a regional democratic power and a promoter of free market democracy. Until recently, India remained content to let its free market democracy provide a demonstration effect.

Before the 1990s, India attempted to impose its will on its neighbours, culminating in the hegemonic 'Indira' and 'Rajiv' doctrines and its intervention in Sri Lanka. Opposition to India's

---

[44] Bruce Loudon, 'Indian Troops to Fight the Taliban', *The Australian,* June 12, 2007, at http://www.theaustralian.news.com.au/story/0,20867,21890061-31477,00.html (accessed on November 12, 2007).

hegemonic tendencies helped to influence Indian leaders to move away from a unilateral approach. The SAARC initiative, led by Sri Lanka, Nepal and Bangladesh, helped to forestall Indian hegemony. By the mid-1990s, India had changed its course, participated in SAARC and began to practise non-reciprocity with member states.

In the past decade, India has moved towards the exercise of multilateral leadership. India has managed a difficult transition period and is now better able to cope with the era of globalisation, especially since it has a dynamic free market economy and democratic system. Thus, India has advantages when compared with less democratic regional powers, such as China. India's behaviour is increasingly similar to that of recent Western democratic leaders or benign hegemons, specifically the US and the UK. Regional democratic powers are more likely to exercise multilateral leadership and India is proving this hypothesis in helping to bring democracy to Nepal and peace and protection of minority rights in Sri Lanka.

The increasing prosperity of India will continue to attract the surrounding states. The process of ending disputes in South Asia and the growth of regional cooperation have led to an expansion of India's conception of its South Asian neighbourhood. India's interests feature an increasing need to protect trade routes, as trade continues to grow and guarantee access to supplies of oil and gas as the economy and population expand.[45] In order to defend these and other interests, India will most likely continue to forge a partnership with the US.[46] As India's international expansion and cooperation with the US continues, the opposing Pakistan–China partnership becomes less able to resist the growing Indian leadership in the South Asian subcontinent.

---

[45] Mohan, *Crossing the Rubicon*, pp. 221–24, 234–36. India will be receiving increasing amounts of oil and gas from Central Asia and will have to maintain its partnership with Russia, and it may form alliances with Russia, Kazakhstan and other states in order to protect energy flows. India will most likely participate in the protection of the Gulf, the Red Sea and the South China Sea. Eventually, India and China could clash over the South China Sea, the Straits of Malacca or the Indian Ocean.

[46] Sumit Ganguly, 'India's Alliances 2020', in Michael R. Chambers, ed, *South Asia in 2020: Future Strategic Balances and Alliances* (Carlisle, Penna: US Army War College Strategic Studies Institute, November 2002), 363–84. See, also, Gary K. Bertsch, Seema Gahlaut and Anupam Srivastava, eds, *Engaging India: US Strategic Relations with the World's Largest Democracy* (New York: Routledge, 1999) and Kanti Bajpai and Amitabh Mattoo, eds, *Engaged Democracies: India–US Relations in the 21st Century* (New Delhi: Har-Anand Publications, 2000).

11

India and the Middle East: A Re-Assessment of Priorities?

Harsh V. Pant

There has been a remarkable reorientation of the Indian foreign policy in the Middle East since the end of the Cold War. At a time when the Middle Eastern region is passing through a phase of unparalleled political, economic and social churning, India is being called upon by the international community to play a larger role in Middle Eastern affairs. This is evident in the pressure on India to adopt a more visible role in Iraq and to use its leverage on Iran to curtail Iran's pursuit of nuclear weapons. In a first of its kind, India was invited by the US to participate in the West Asian peace conference at Annapolis in November 2007 as a recognition of India's growing stature in the international system. A stable and prosperous Middle East is as important for India as it is for the rest of the world and India is increasingly being asked to step up to the plate. It is, therefore, important to understand the factors driving India's foreign policy in the Middle East in the contemporary global order. This essay will argue that while domestic constraints played the defining role in shaping Indian foreign policy towards the Middle East during the Cold War, it is the structural changes after the Cold War that have made it possible for India to bring about some remarkable shifts in its foreign policy in the region. Its definition of its own interests in the Middle East is becoming more clear-eyed and it is more aggressively pursuing these interests.

The extent to which Indian foreign policy towards the Middle East has changed in the last few years is evident from the fact that a review of Indian foreign policy in Middle East that covered the time period from 1947 to 1986 argued that Indian policy towards the region had been too ideological and had paid insufficient attention to its national interests by focussing on India's subdued ties with Iran, Saudi Arabia and Israel.[1] Today, it is precisely these

---

[1] P.R. Mudiam, *India and the Middle East* (London: British Academic Press, 1994).

three states around which India's new policy towards Middle East is taking shape. While many contradictions remain and domestic constraints still continue to exert considerable influence, it is clear that India is charting a new course in Middle East. This essay will first examine its ties with Iran, Saudi Arabia and Israel so as to draw attention to its changing priorities in the region and then will go on to delineate main factors that are shaping India's contemporary relations in Middle East.

INDIA AND IRAN: A TANGLED WEB

India's relations with Iran have come under intense scrutiny in recent times. A few years back, the RAND Corporation termed this relationship as 'the Tehran–New Delhi axis' and, in its opinion, it was one of the ten international security developments that were apparently not getting appropriate attention. It went on to argue that closer ties between India and Iran might have an impact on the regional political dynamics of Southwest Asia and Middle East in ways which might not necessarily help the US interests in these regions.[2]

India, as part of the Indus Valley civilisation and Iran have been interacting since prehistoric times as neighbouring civilisations. With the advent of British supremacy on the Indian subcontinent in the 18th century, Indo-Iranian interactions started to dwindle; they revived only after India's Independence in 1947. Despite sharing civilisational affinities to an exceptional degree, the vagaries of international politics made it difficult for India and Iran to share a close bilateral relationship during the Cold War. But a number of factors have led to the convergence in Indo-Iranian interests in the post-Cold War period, such as the unipolar nature of the current international system, India's need to counter Pakistan's influence in the Islamic world, the increasing geopolitical importance of Central Asia and the need to strengthen economic and commercial ties.[3]

---

[2] A brief analysis of this 'India–Iran Axis' by a RAND Corporation's analyst can be found in 'Headlines Over the Horizon', *The Atlantic Monthly* 292: 1 (July–August 2003), p. 87.

[3] For details on the factors that have brought India and Iran closer in recent years, see Harsh V. Pant, 'India and Iran: An "Axis" in the Making', *Asian Survey* 44:3 (May/June 2004), pp. 372–77.

The absolute US dominance of the post-Cold War international order has created unease among the major second-tier states like Russia, China and India. Although they are in no position to challenge the US predominance in any significant measure, they have made attempts to upgrade their bilateral relations. Iran, however, faces a different set of problems as its relationship with the US remains difficult to manage. While the relationships of states like Russia, China and India with the US have improved dramatically in recent times,[4] the US posture towards Iran remains hostile, despite a growing pro-democracy movement in Iran.

Though India has also made enormous efforts in recent years to improve its ties with the US, it has refused to let this dictate its foreign policy priorities. India has its own apprehensions about the US foreign policy which it sometimes views as highly unilateral and insensitive to vital concerns of other states. This correspondence between Iran's desire to end its international isolation by cultivating its relationship with other states and India's desire to impact a degree of autonomy to its foreign policy has brought India and Iran close to each other in recent years.[5]

During the visit of the then Iranian President, Mohammed Khatami, to India in January 2003, both India and Iran were categorical in their rejection of the US stand on Iraq, arguing that the sovereignty and integrity of a nation should not be violated.[6] The very fact that Iran's president was visiting India at a time when the US was positioning itself to attack Iraq, resulting in turmoil in West Asia, demonstrated India's rather subtle attempt to distance itself from the US foreign policy vis-à-vis West Asia.

---

[4] On recent changes in the US ties with Russia, China and India, see Harsh V. Pant, 'Feasibility of the Russia–China–India "Strategic Triangle": Assessment of Theoretical and Empirical Issues', *International Studies* 43:1 (January–March 2006), pp. 65–69.

[5] For a concise explication of the significance of an 'autonomous' strain in the Indian foreign policy and its impact on India's attempt to forge alliances in future, see Sumit Ganguly, 'India's Alliances 2020', in Michael Chambers, ed, *South Asia in 2020: Future Strategic Balances and Alliances* (Carlisle, PA: Strategic Studies Institute, 2002), pp. 363–79.

[6] 'Iran, India show Solidarity with Iraq', *The Times of India*, New Delhi, January 28, 2003. Also, see the text of the 'New Delhi Declaration' signed by the Indian prime minister and the president of Iran on January 25, 2003. The full text is at www.meadev.nic.in (accessed on December 20, 2007).

India also views Iran as an influential Islamic state that can effectively counter Pakistan's anti-India propaganda in the Islamic world. Given Iran's strained relations with the West, India is seen by Iran as an important partner and a possible conduit to the West. In recent years, Tehran has shown some willingness to rehabilitate itself with Europe, despite its anti-West rhetoric. Iran views India as a nation that can be helpful in fostering a 'dialogue between civilisations', which some of the Iranian leaders have been aggressively promoting for the last few years, in response to the 'clash of civilisation' thesis emanating from the West.[7] India also has the largest number of Shia Muslims in the world after Iran and both states are concerned about the festering Shia-Sunni strife in Pakistan. Though Pakistan is not seen as an adversary of Iran even now, the Sunni fundamentalism of jihadi variety considers the 20 per cent Shia population of Pakistan as apostates. This is the same variant of Islamic fundamentalism that supports and sends jihadi terrorists to India.

There was also a perception shared by India and Iran that Pakistan's control of Afghanistan via the fundamentalist Taliban regime was not in the strategic interests of either state and was a threat to the regional stability of the entire region. As opposed to Pakistan that promptly recognised the Taliban regime,[8] India and Iran did not establish diplomatic contacts with the Taliban.[9] India and Iran, together with Russia, were the main supporters of the anti-Taliban Northern Alliance that routed the hardline Islamic regime in Afghanistan with the US help in November 2001.

Military-to-military contacts between India and Iran have also gained momentum as a consequence of improving bilateral ties between the two states. While India is seen by Iran as a major source of conventional military assistance, Iran is perceived as a major

---

[7] For the seminal argument about an impending 'clash of civilizations', see Samuel P. Huntington, *The Clash of Civilizations and the Remaking of World Order* (New York: Simon and Schuster, 1996). On a detailed explication of 'Dialogue Among Civilizations' in the context of Indo-Iranian relationship, see Mushirul Hasan, 'Dialogue Among Civilizations', *The Hindu*, New Delhi, January 29, 2003.

[8] For Pakistan's reasons in supporting Taliban and its impact on Pakistan's foreign policy, see Kenneth Weisbrode, 'Central Eurasia: Prize or Quicksand?', *Adelphi Paper 338* (London: International Institute for Strategic Studies, 2001), pp. 68–71.

[9] For a background of Iran's relations with Taliban, see Amin Saikal, 'Iran's Turbulent Neighbor: The Challenge of the Taliban', *Global Dialogue*, 3:2/3 (Spring/Summer 2001), pp. 93–103.

potential buyer of its military hardware by India. Iranian military is in desperate need of modernisation and India can become its principle source of modern arms and spare parts. Moreover, India can provide crucial technical assistance and training opportunities to the Iranian armed forces. Defence ties between India and Iran have also evolved in the last few years, especially after the signing of a Memorandum of Understanding on defence cooperation by these two countries in 2001. Even as the US was conducting its war games in the Persian Gulf in March 2007, its largest show of force in the region since the 2003 invasion of Iraq involving *USS Eisenhower* and *USS Stennis*, the Iranian Naval Chief was visiting India, a reflection of the importance that Iran attaches to its growing defence ties with India. This visit has reportedly resulted in the establishment of a joint defence working group that would look into Tehran's request that India train its military personnel.[10]

India and Iran also share a long-term economic complementarity that has strengthened their bilateral ties. This is particularly true in the energy sector where India's search for energy security has made it imperative for it to seek a partnership with Iran. India also shares with Iran an interest in a stable political and economic order in Central Asia. After the disintegration of the Soviet empire, Central Asia has emerged as an important region where many countries, including the US and China, have evinced a keen interest, especially since it has emerged as a major oil-producing region.[11] India and Iran are equally threatened by the menace of drug trafficking, smuggling in small arms and organised crime, emanating largely from Central Asia.[12]

India's relations with Iran have also been shaped significantly by Iran's solidarity with the Indian Muslim population. India has

---

[10] Vivek Raghuvanshi, 'India, Iran to Deepen Defence Relationship', *Defence News*, March 18, 2007, at http://defencenews.com/story.php?F=2620792&C=asiapac (accessed on December 20, 2007).

[11] For a theoretical exposition of the importance of Central Eurasia to global politics, see Zbigniew Brzezinski, *The Grand Chessboard: American Primacy and Its Geostrategic Imperatives* (New York: Basic Books, 1997). On the energy potential of this region and the resulting geopolitical maneuvering, see Dan Morgan and David Ottaway, 'Pipe Dreams: The Struggle for Caspian Oil', *The Washington Post*, Washington, DC, October 4–6, 1998. p. A1

[12] For a background on Iran's relations with its Central Asian neighbours, see Edmund Herzig, *Iran and the Former Soviet South* (London: Royal Institute of International Affairs, 1995).

the second largest Shia Muslim population in the world. This has produced a cultural and religious involvement that animates Iran's policy towards India. While this provides Indian and Iran one more area of convergence of interests, it has also been and continues to be a major source of irritation in their bilateral relationship. As of now, Iran seems to have made a strategic choice in favour of downplaying its Muslim identity in its relation's vis-à-vis India. But for India, Iran's pronounced Islamic identity is a matter of fact that cannot and should not be underestimated. As a consequence, India's domestic policy and its treatment of its Muslim population will go a long way in determining the long-term strength of the Indo-Iranian relationship. If the Hindu nationalists in India decide to take their anti-Muslim stance to an extreme, Indo-Iran bilateral ties could come under severe strain. Even otherwise, the volatile situation in Kashmir and the resulting uncertainty will remain a major hurdle in the Indo-Iranian ties in the foreseeable future.

After establishing full diplomatic relations with Israel in 1992, India has moved considerably closer to Israel, so much so that India and Israel now share a growing defence partnership. It will be difficult for India to maintain strategic partnerships with both Israel and Iran for a long time, given the peculiar nature of relations among the West Asian countries. Iran's policy towards the Palestine issue can become a major stumbling block in Indo-Iranian relations as Iran supports not only the Palestine cause and the right of its people to reclaim the occupied lands as their homeland but also non-recognition of Israel. As has been pointed out by some analysts, this basically means the elimination of the Israeli state.[13] This anti-Israel posture of Iran has got worse under the present administration of Mahmoud Ahmadinejad, further muddying the waters for Indian diplomacy.

INDIA AND SAUDI ARABIA: NEW-FOUND CONVERGENCE

In January 2006, Saudi King Abdullah bin Abdul-Aziz Al Saud visited India where he was a guest of honour at its national Republic Day celebrations. It was the first visit of a Saudi monarch to India

---

[13] See, for example, Shahram Chubin, 'Whither Iran?: Reform, Domestic Politics and National Security', *Adelphi Paper 342* (London: International Institute for Strategic Studies, 2002), pp. 98–103.

since King Saud's brief visit to the subcontinent in 1955. Relations subsequently froze as Riyadh sided with Washington during the Cold War, and New Delhi drifted closer to Moscow. Saudi-Indian ties strained further after the Indian government failed to condemn the 1979 Soviet invasion of Afghanistan while the Saudi government helped bankroll the opposition Afghan mujahideen.[14] However, with the end of the Cold War, such impediments to Saudi-Indian relations evaporated.

The two countries have significant interests beyond oil. While India is not a Muslim-majority country, it still hosts the second-largest Muslim population in the world,[15] a constituency that remains interested in Saudi Arabia as the site of the holy shrines at Mecca and Medina. There is already significant cultural interchange. The approximately 1.5 million Indian workers constitute the largest expatriate community in the kingdom.[16]

Riyadh, for its part, has agreed to support New Delhi's petition for observer status in the Organisation of Islamic Conference. It has also been supportive of Indian moves to reduce tension in Kashmir and has tried to move beyond its traditional approach of looking at India through a Pakistani prism.

New Delhi has also cultivated Riyadh for strategic reasons. To Indian strategists, any ally that can act as a counterweight to Pakistan in the Islamic world is significant. Initially, New Delhi sought to cultivate Tehran, but such efforts stumbled in recent years as the Islamic Republic has adopted an increasingly aggressive anti-Western posture.[17] Saudi Arabia now fills that gap. Indeed, Iranian nuclear ambitions have helped draw New Delhi and Riyadh closer.

The Saudi government has its own reasons for cultivating Indian ties. Saudi Arabia and Iran have long competed for power and influence in the Persian Gulf.[18] The 1979 Islamic Revolution in Iran added a new edge to the rivalry, as Iranian ayatollahs sought

---

[14] Mudiam, *India and the Middle East*, pp. 85–97.
[15] Detailed statistics can be found at Government of India, Ministry of Home Affairs, 'Census of India', at http://www.censusindia.net/religiondata/Religiondata_2001.xls (accessed on December 20, 2007).
[16] Divya Pakkiasamy, 'Saudi Arabia's Plan for Changing Its Workforce', Migration Information Service, at http://www.migrationinformation.org/Feature/display.cfm?id=264 (accessed on December 20, 2007).
[17] See Pant, 'India and Iran', pp. 369–83.
[18] R.K. Ramazani, *Revolutionary Iran: Challenge and Response in the Middle East* (Baltimore: Johns Hopkins University Press, 1986), pp. 8–11.

increasingly to challenge the Saudi officials on religious matters, such as the rules and regulations surrounding the hajj or pilgrimage to Mecca. The fact that about 40 per cent of Saudi Arabia's oil-producing eastern province is Shiite and resents Wahhabi rule worries Riyadh.[19] The anxiety is mutual. In 1994, the Iranian intelligence ministry designated Salafi terrorism as the primary threat to Iranian national security.[20] Tehran's nuclear drive, Iranian interference in neighbouring Iraq and Iranian president Mahmoud Ahmadinejad's aggressive rhetoric further raise Saudi anxiety of a resurgent Iran and these were subjects of discussion during the king's meeting with the Indian prime minister.[21]

Still, the relationship is not all rosy. The Indian military has been fighting separatist groups in its northern state of Kashmir for several years now. Thousands of lives have been lost because of Islamist terrorism or the associated crackdown. Saudi financiers bankroll many of the Pakistani and Kashmiri groups that conduct the terrorism.[22] The Indian government would like its Saudi counterparts to manage the funds transferred to India better, a substantial portion of which ends in Islamist pockets. The Indian prime minister and Saudi king used their New Delhi meeting to sign a memorandum of understanding dealing with terrorism, transnational crime and underworld operations.[23] Both governments agreed to cooperate towards the conclusion of a comprehensive convention on international terrorism before the UN General Assembly and to establish an international counterterrorism centre as called for by the International Conference on Counterterrorism held in Riyadh in February 2005.[24]

While the Indian government would like political reforms to take hold in Saudi Arabia to mitigate the Islamist threat,[25] energy is

---

[19] Anthony H. Cordesman, *Saudi Arabia Enters the Twenty-First Century: The Political, Foreign Policy and Energy Dimensions* (London: Praeger, 2003), p. 206.

[20] Mahan Abedin, 'The Iranian Intelligence Services and the War on Terror', *Terrorism Monitor*, 2:10, Jamestown Foundation, May 20, 2004.

[21] C. Raja Mohan, 'Iran, Iraq to figure in PM–Saudi King Talks', *The Indian Express* (New Delhi), January 24, 2006.

[22] Husain Haqqani, 'The Ideologies of South Asian Jihadi Groups', *Current Trends in Islamist Ideology*, 1:1 (April 2005), pp. 23–4; J. Millard Burr and Robert O. Collins, *Alms for Jihad* (Cambridge: Cambridge University Press, 2006), pp. 26–50.

[23] *The Hindu* (Chennai, Madras), January 26, 2006.

[24] 'Final Report of the *Counter-Terrorism International Conference*', Riyadh, February 5–8, 2005.

[25] *The Indian Express* (New Delhi), January 24, 2006.

now the driving force in Saudi-Indian relations. Riyadh is the chief supplier of oil to India's booming economy and India is now the fourth-largest recipient of Saudi oil after China, the US, and Japan.[26] As with Saudi Arabia and China, energy infrastructure investment is a major component in the development of Saudi-Indian relations. During the state visit, King Abdullah and Indian Prime Minister Manmohan Singh signed an Indo-Saudi 'Delhi Declaration' calling for a wide-ranging strategic partnership, putting energy and economic cooperation on overdrive and committing to cooperate against terrorism.[27] According to some reports, the king waived off Saudi bureaucratic concerns about precedents that the declaration might create by calling India a 'special case'.[28]

Riyadh's close relationship to Islamabad will also constrain its relations with India. Pakistan not only receives oil from Saudi Arabia at discounted rates, but there remains speculation that Saudi interests underwrote Pakistan's nuclear programme and missile purchases,[29] presumably to allow Saudi Arabia ready access to nuclear and ballistic missile technology if the need arose. Pressure has increased on Saudi Arabia to open its nuclear facilities as the IAEA suspects that Pakistani nuclear cooperation has advanced Saudi Arabia's programme to a level warranting international safeguards.[30] Washington also wants Riyadh to provide unhindered access to its nuclear facilities. The Saudis argue that they would do so only if other states—Israel—do the same.

Saudi authorities may also be uncomfortable with improvements in Indian relations with Israel.[31] New Delhi may not accept Saudi pressure to downgrade their relationship to Jerusalem.

---

[26] 'More Crude Imports from Saudi Arabia Soon: Aiyar', *The Hindu Business Line* (Chennai), March 29, 2005.
[27] *Delhi Declaration*, Joint Declarations & Statements, Ministry of External Affairs, New Delhi, India, January 27, 2006.
[28] 'Saudi King Took Initiative on "Delhi Declaration"', *The Tribune* (New Delhi), January 27, 2006.
[29] Thomas Woodrow, 'The Sino-Saudi Connection', *China Brief*, Jamestown Foundation, October 24, 2002.
[30] Paul Kerr, 'IAEA Board Seeks Strengthened Safeguards', *Arms Control Today*, (July/August 2005).
[31] On Sino-Israeli ties, see P.R. Kumaraswamy, 'At What Cost Israel–China Ties?', *Middle East Quarterly* 13:2 (Spring 2006), pp. 37–44; Dan Blumenthal, 'Providing Arms: China and the Middle East', *Middle East Quarterly* 12:2 (Spring 2005), pp. 11–19. On India–Israel ties, see Harsh V. Pant, 'India–Israel Partnership: Convergence and Constraints', *Middle East Review of International Affairs* 8:4 (Dec. 2004), pp. 60–73.

Unwillingness to compromise on their antagonism towards the Jewish state may pose a quandary for hard-line Saudi officials. Nor will Riyadh enjoy a monopoly over outreach to India. Despite recent tension in Indo-Iranian relations, Indian officials insist that the 1,625-mile, $4.16-billion pipeline project to transport gas from Iran through Pakistan to India remains on track.[32]

INDIA AND ISRAEL: A DIFFICULT PARTNERSHIP

There has been a steady strengthening of India's relationship with Israel ever since India established full diplomatic relations with Israel in 1992, despite Indian attempts to keep this flourishing bilateral relationship out of public view. This bilateral relationship assumed an altogether new dynamics and came under full public scrutiny with the visit of Ariel Sharon to India in September 2003—the first ever by a ruling Israeli prime minister. The excitement surrounding this visit and the future prospects of Indo-Israeli relationship signalled the sea change in relations between the two states. In sharp contrast to the back-channel security ties that existed even before the normalisation of bilateral relations, India now seems more willing to openly carve out a mutually beneficial bilateral relationship with Israel, including deepening military ties and countering the threat posed by terrorism to the two societies. However, notwithstanding the convergence of interests on a range of issues between India and Israel, this bilateral relationship will have to be carefully managed because of a host of constraints which circumscribe this relationship.

India recognised the state of Israel in 1950, two years after its establishment in 1948. However, diplomatic relations were not established until 1992.[33] After the end of the Cold War and the collapse of the Soviet Union, India was forced to reorient its foreign policy to accommodate the changing international milieu. India also embarked on a path of economic liberalisation, forcing it to open its markets to other nations. It was in 1992 that it granted full diplomatic recognition to Israel, leading the two countries to

---

[32] ' India, Iran Pledge Commitment to Build Gas Pipeline', *Associated Foreign Press*, February 24, 2006.
[33] A detailed examination of the Indo-Israeli relations in a historical context can be found in P.R. Kumaraswamy, 'India and Israel: Emerging Partnership', *Journal of Strategic Studies* 25:4 (December 2002), pp. 193–200.

establish embassies in each other's country. Since then, the Indo-Israeli bilateral relationship has attained a new dynamics with a significant upward trend. However, while the exchanges in diverse fields have intensified, the overall connection deliberately remained low profile. Such an approach was thought to be necessary in order to insulate India's other interests in the Middle East from being affected by the Arab animosity towards Israel. In this context, Ariel Sharon's visit to India in September 2003 was an important benchmark in that it made clear to the world that India was no longer shy about its burgeoning relationship with Israel.

There was some concern that the change of government in India, from the Hindu nationalist Bhartiya Janata Party (BJP)-led National Democratic Alliance to the Congress Party-led United Progressive Alliance (UPA) in 2004, might be inimical to Indo-Israeli ties. But so far they seem to be on track, with the UPA government seemingly determined to continue on the path of strengthening its relations with Israel. Fighting terrorism is a major issue and challenge for both India and Israel. Both are democratic, pluralistic states with large domestic Muslim minorities and both face the scourge of Islamist terrorism, which is sponsored by their neighbours. This shared dilemma has led to a better understanding of each other's concerns.[34]

India has found it increasingly beneficial to learn from Israel's experience in dealing with terrorism since Israel has also long suffered cross-border terrorism. And the terrorism that both India and Israel face comes not only from disaffected groups within their territories but it is also aided and abetted by the neighbouring states, mostly under non-democratic regimes, increasingly capable of transferring weapons of mass destruction to the terrorist organisations. States such as Pakistan in South Asia and Iran and Syria in Middle East have long used terror as an instrument of their foreign policies. There are, thus, distinct structural similarities in the kind of threat that India and Israel face from terrorism. It is also important to note that when the extremist mullahs call upon their followers to take up arms in support of an Islamic jihad,

---

[34] For a discussion of overlapping Indian and Israeli interests in the area of counterterrorism, see Ilan Berman, 'Israel, India and Turkey: Triple Entente?', *Middle East Quarterly* 9:4 (Fall 2002), pp. 37–38.

their topmost exhortations have always been the 'liberation' of all of mandatory Palestine and Kashmir and the annihilation of the US. Israel also sees major benefits in coming closer to a country with a big Muslim population, the second-largest in the world, hoping that it might help dilute the importance of the religious component in the Arab-Israeli conflict. Both states are also islands of stability in an otherwise largely chaotic region stretching from North Africa to the Himalayas, which some have argued should be seen as a single strategic region.[35] The search for strength in each other's inner reserves is natural for India and Israel in their quest for security and the fight against terror.

As a result, a basic understanding has emerged between India and Israel that despite the fact that circumstances surrounding the nature of terrorism they face are different, there can be no compromise with terror. India sees Israel as a source providing training for its personnel and materiel in its fight against terrorism and Israel is more than willing to offer India both material and moral support in this regard.[36]

The ballast for Indo-Israeli bilateral ties is provided by the defence cooperation between the two states with India emerging as Israel's largest arms market, displacing Turkey and with Israel becoming India's biggest arms supplier. With the end of the Cold War, the lure of the Russian arms market for India has diminished due to a high degree of obsolescence. Moreover, with Israel specialising in upgrading Russian equipment, it has emerged as an alternative source of hi-tech defence procurement as India has decided to diversify its defence purchasing.

On the other hand, for Israel, empowering the Indian military has meant becoming a major exporter to that large, financially rewarding arms market. More than the harm to the general Israeli economy caused by the conflict with the Palestinians, Israel's defence industry has always been dependent on exports to reach a point where it could produce enough to remain financially solvent. In fact, in its vigorous search for new markets for its defence products, Israel has emerged in 2006 as the fifth-largest arms-exporter

---

[35] See, for example, Jim Hoagland, 'A Test of True Allies', *Washington Post*, November 8, 2001, p. A31.
[36] Saurabh Shukla, 'India, Israel Tie Up to Combat Terrorism', *Hindustan Times*, September 11, 2003.

in the world.[37] In this context, Israel's growing defence relationship with India goes a long way towards sustaining its own local defence industry and this in turn is also a significant boost to Israel's economy as a whole. As a consequence, the Indo-Israel defence partnership has reached a critical mass in recent years.[38]

With huge investments in research and development, Israeli weapon systems are considered the cutting edge in various areas of the international arms market, even compared to American and European products. This is primarily because a high technology defence industry is a matter of vital national security for Israel. The extent of Israel's defence industry reflects its precarious geopolitical situation of a nation of about six million surrounded by a largely adversarial Arab world many times its size. Despite enjoying a close relationship with the US, self-reliance in defence is a mantra that Israel has followed almost to perfection. Israel has also adopted a pragmatic attitude with respect to weapon sales to India, as opposed to other developed states that have looked at weapons sales to India from the perspective of balance of power in South Asia. Israel was willing to continue and even step up its arms sales to India after other major states curbed their technological exports to India following India's nuclear tests in May 1998. From anti-missile systems to hi-tech radars, from sky drones to night-vision equipment, Indo-Israeli defence cooperation has known no bounds in recent times.[39]

Though cooperation in the realm of defence and anti-terrorism has driven India and Israel closer, the two states are also making concerted attempts to diversify this relationship. The emergence of India and Israel as industrialised and technologically-advanced states makes their cooperation on a range of fields meaningful and mutually beneficial. There has been a six-fold increase in India's trade with Israel in the last decade, with India becoming Israel's second-largest trading partner in Asia in non-military goods and services.

---

[37] Alon Ben-David, 'Israel Establishes Itself as fifth-largest Arms Exporter', *Jane's Defence Weekly* 44:2 (January 10, 2007), p. 17.
[38] Paul Watson, 'Arms at the Heart of India–Israel Embrace', *Los Angeles Times*, September 9, 2003.
[39] Saikat Datta, 'Indo-Israeli Defence Deals Get a Big Push', *Indian Express*, September 11, 2003.

Despite a significant convergence of interests between India and Israel on a host of issues, there remain a number of constraints within which the two states will have to chart out their bilateral relationship. The most significant of these constraints, perhaps, emerges from the Indian domestic political milieu. India cannot ignore the sentiments of its substantial Muslim populace of about 140 million that are overwhelmingly against Israel's policy regarding the Palestinians. Fear of alienating its Muslim population has been a major factor that prevented India from normalising its relations with Israel for decades. India has also been a strong supporter of Palestinian self-determination.

Even as the Indian government was welcoming Ariel Sharon in 2003, it made it clear that India would neither dilute its traditional support for the Palestinian cause nor abandon Yasser Arafat as the leader of the Palestinians. Until his death, India saw Arafat as a symbol of Palestinian nationalism and as such central to any peace process in the Middle East, a view in complete contrast to that of the Sharon government, which was in favour of expelling Arafat and allowing for the emergence of an alternative Palestinian leadership.[40] This disagreement over Arafat's role is not to say that a subtle re-evaluation of India's Middle East policy is not underway. Before 1992, India had made the normalisation of relations with Israel contingent upon the resolution of the Palestinian issue. In 1992, India decided to delink the two, making it clear that it was not prepared to make an independent Palestinian state a precondition for improving its relations with Israel. This was in tune with the policy already followed by much of the world.

Over the years, the Indian government has also toned down its reactions to Israel's treatment of the Palestinians. Israel's policy towards the Palestinians has evoked little more than mild disapproval from the Indian government in recent years. India has also begun denouncing Palestinian suicide bombings and other terrorist acts in Israel, something that was seen earlier as rather justified in light of the harsh policies of Israel against the Palestinians.

Despite India's tilt towards Israel in the 1990s, it will be forced to operate its bilateral relationship with Israel within the constraints

---

[40] Pramit Pal Chaudhuri, 'It's Time to Look Beyond Arafat: Israel to India', *Hindustan Times*, September 8, 2003. Also see Pranay Sharma, 'Terror & Truce Mix for Sharon', *The Telegraph*, September 9, 2003.

imposed by its domestic politics and its interests in the Middle East. It will have to be careful not to let its relationship with Israel be projected as a Jewish-Hindu axis against Islam. Israel's handling of the Palestine issue will also be a major factor as it would be difficult for India to justify its continuing support for Israel in case Israel's policies become blatantly harsh. Also, despite India's disillusionment with the Arab world, about three million Indians work in the Persian Gulf and are valuable foreign exchange earners. India also gets about one-fourth of its oil supplies from the Middle East. In sum, India will have to balance its growing relationship with Israel without sacrificing its core interests in the rest of the region. India needs Israel as a political and military partner but without being pushed into any new confrontation with the Islamic world. While Israel has long faced enmity from much of the Islamic world, India's national interests and its large Muslim population make it especially careful to avoid such a fate.

Another constraint on India's enhanced engagement with Israel is India's flourishing relations with Iran. While the US overthrow of Saddam Hussein may have removed one of Israel's enemies, it also seems to have created new opportunities for Iran to increase its influence in Israel's immediate neighbourhood.

In this respect, Israel is concerned about India's growing ties with Iran.[41] It is especially worried about India sharing with Iran some of the military technology that it receives from Israel. Israel would like India to acknowledge the threat posed by a nuclear-armed Iran and would like India to make efforts to help in the stabilisation of the volatile security situation in West Asia. While India and Israel need not make their bilateral relationship a function of each other's relationship with any third country, both will have to manage it carefully in light of India's relations with other countries in Middle East and with Iran in particular.

DRIVERS OF INDIAN FOREIGN POLICY IN THE MIDDLE EAST

After a review of the above three bilateral relations that have come to dominate the Indian foreign policy towards the Middle East in

---

[41] 'Tel Aviv Worried about New Delhi's Ties with Iran', *Times of India*, September 11, 2003.

recent times, certain broader trends can be delineated. First, the loosening of the structural constraints imposed by the Cold War has given India greater flexibility in carving its foreign policy in the Middle East. The most notable change has been India's attempts to enhance its ties with Israel on the one hand and with its traditional antagonists such as Iran and Saudi Arabia on the other, India is no longer coy about proclaiming its gradually strengthening ties with Israel, despite apprehensions in some quarters that the Arab world will not take very kindly to these developments. On the contrary, it seems that the Arab world has reacted cautiously so far and has deepened its engagement with India for fear of losing it wholly to Israel. But the biggest test of this balancing act will be how India manages its relations with Iran who remains the most openly hostile neighbour of Israel.

There is also a realisation in India that its largely pro-Arab stance in the Middle East has not been adequately rewarded by the Arab world. India has received no worthwhile backing from the Arab countries in the resolution of the problems it faces in its neighbourhood, especially Kashmir. There have been no serious attempts by the Arab world to put pressure on Pakistan to reign in the cross-border insurgency in Kashmir. On the contrary, the Arab world has firmly stood by Pakistan using the Organisation of Islamic Conference to build support for Islamabad and the Jihadi groups in Kashmir.[42] There is a growing perception in India that if Arab nations, such as Jordan, have been able to keep their traditional ties with Palestine intact, while building a new relationship with Israel, there is no reason for India not to take a similar route which might give it more room for diplomatic maneuvering.

Second, domestic constraints imposed by the large Muslim community in India have traditionally been a significant factor in shaping India's Middle East policy. While this remains a potent variable, there are signs that Indian foreign policy has had some success in recent times in overcoming this constraint. Again, India's relations with Israel are a case in point. India has developed these ties despite a significant opposition from the left parties. More recently, India has chosen to side with the West, on a few occasions,

---

[42] For a trenchant critique of the Arab world's policies towards India, see Abdullah Al Madani, 'Indo-Israeli Ties: Arabs have None but Themselves to Blame', *Gulf News*, September 14, 2003.

on the issue of the Iranian nuclear programme, keeping aside domestic political considerations. However, they would remain a major constraint especially as the Congress party, who has not been a favourite of the Indian Muslim community in the last few years, decides to woo the Muslim community. It is possible that it might have an impact on how India orients its foreign policy in the Middle East.

India's response to the hanging of Saddam Hussein and the passing of the UN Security Council resolution against Iran underscores the continuing salience of domestic political imperatives in shaping its foreign policy. When the death sentence against Saddam Hussein was announced India denounced it as 'victor's justice' and when he was hanged, India declared it an 'unfortunate event'.[43] Both these reactions were aimed at assuaging the Indian Muslim community that has been agitated over the Indian government's perceived dalliance with the US. The Left parties and some of the regional parties were not satisfied with India's official reaction and denounced the government as a stooge of the US. Similarly, When the UN Security Council unanimously passed a resolution in late December 2006 banning the import and export of materials and technology used in uranium enrichment, reprocessing and ballistic missiles with the intent of curbing Iran's nuclear programme, India found it very difficult to come up with a credible and coherent response. While India reiterated that Iran has undertaken certain obligations as a member of the NPT, it also added that Iran does have the right to pursue its nuclear programme for peaceful civilian use.[44] Unlike the rest of the members of the Security Council, including Russia and China, India did not explicitly ask Iran to abide by legal commitments under the NPT.

Some have suggested that the confused Indian reaction to the Security Council resolution in December 2006 was driven in large measure by the impending elections in the crucial north Indian state of Uttar Pradesh where the Shia Muslim community plays a significant role in electoral calculations.[45] While this may or may not be true, domestic political considerations continue to play

---

[43] 'Some Tears for Saddam, Left and Center', *The Indian Express*, December 31, 2006.
[44] 'India Says Iran has Right to Pursue Nuke Plan for Civilian Use', *The Indian Express*, December 25, 2006.
[45] Raja Mohan, 'It's Not About Uttar Pradesh', *The Indian Express*, December 26, 2006.

a significant role in the foreign policy calculations in India. The Indian Left parties and some regional parties in the recent past have attacked India's Iran policy with an eye on their domestic political constituencies. After India voted against Iran at the IAEA in September 2005 and February 2006, many parties brought the issue to the streets, demonstrating against the position of the government. Many in the Congress Party, the leader of the coalition currently running the government, also expressed their apprehensions about their party losing the crucial Muslim votes in the future. This led to a change in India's policy to an extent that it found it difficult to unambiguously support a Security Council resolution imposing sanctions on Iran backed even by Russia and China. Domestic political constraints were also responsible for the Indian Parliament's lopsided view of the conflict in Lebanon last summer, when it criticised Israeli attack against Lebanon and its civilian population but remained silent on the actions of Hezbollah against Israel.

Another factor that is increasingly shaping not only India's approach towards Middle East but also broader Indian foreign policy priorities is India's burgeoning demand for energy. With an economy that is projected to grow at a rate of 7–8 per cent over the next two decades, meeting its rapidly increasing demand for energy is one of the biggest challenges facing India. Burgeoning population, coupled with rapid economic growth and industrialisation, has propelled India into becoming the sixth-largest energy consumer in the world, with the prospect of emerging as the fourth-largest consumer in the next 4–5 years.[46] India is also rated as one of the highest energy-intensive economies in the world (energy intensity being a measure of energy required by an economy to produce one unit of GDP growth). India's greatest challenge as of now is to ensure successful diversification of sources for oil procurement to minimise possibilities of disruption in supplies. It is towards this end that India has devoted its diplomatic energies in recent times.

Not surprisingly, perhaps, the focal point of India's energy diplomacy has been Middle East as around 65 per cent of its energy requirements are met by this region. It is in this context that India's relationship with Iran has come under global scrutiny in

---

[46] Ashish Vachhani, 'India's Energy Security Dilemma', *The Hindu Business Line*, April 26, 2005.

recent years.⁴⁷ India's large and growing energy demand and Iran's pool of energy resources make the two nations natural economic partners. India's search for energy security in a rather volatile energy market makes Iran, with its fourth-largest reservoir of oil and second-largest reserves of natural gas, highly attractive. In fact, when Iran's former President, Mohammed Khatami, visited India in 2003, he described India as one of Iran's best customers and even offered to supply more crude oil to India in case of a disruption caused by an American military attack against Iraq.⁴⁸

This energy relationship between India and Iran is at the heart of a strong bilateral partnership between the two countries, despite the fact that Indo-Iranian relations have significantly diversified across various sectors in recent years. The proposal to build a gas pipeline between India and Iran has consumed a lot of diplomatic energy in recent years.⁴⁹ Various options such as offshore and overland routes have been under consideration for quite some time now. Both these options have their problems, especially the problem of relying on Pakistan for the security of these pipelines. Despite concerns expressed by the US, India officially continues to insist that the 1,625 mile-long, $4.16 billion pipeline project, intended to carry gas from Iran through Pakistan to energy-starved India, remains firmly on track.⁵⁰ India has enjoyed traditional ties with Iran and Iraq for long, partly to meet its energy requirements. However, with Tehran adopting an aggressive anti-Western posture and pursuing an independent nuclear programme in defiance of its obligations under the NPT and the ongoing instability in Iraq, India has been looking to expand its influence beyond the Persian Gulf to the Saudi peninsula.⁵¹

India has now emerged as Saudi Arabia's fourth-largest destination for oil exports, with Riyadh being the largest supplier of

---

⁴⁷ Pant, 'India and Iran'.
⁴⁸ 'Iran Offers More Crude to India', *The Hindustan Times*, New Delhi, January 27, 2003.
⁴⁹ R.K. Pachauri, 'The Pipeline of Peace', *The Indian Express*, New Delhi, January 21, 2003.
⁵⁰ 'India, Iran Pledge Commitment to Build Gas Pipeline', *Associated Foreign Press*, February 24, 2006.
⁵¹ On recent developments in India–Saudi Arabia relations, see Harsh V. Pant, 'Saudi Arabia Woos China and India', *Middle East Quarterly* 13:4 (Fall 2006), pp. 45–52.

oil to India. India's crude oil imports from the Saudi kingdom are projected to double in the next twenty years. India, like China, is reshaping its diplomacy to serve energy needs as its booming economy also needs new supplies of oil to ensure its continued growth. During his visit to India earlier this year, the Saudi King emphasised his country's commitment to uninterrupted supplies to a friendly country such as India irrespective of global price trends.[52]

Reliance, a private Indian energy firm, has decided to invest in a refinery and petrochemicals project in Saudi Arabia and India's state-owned energy firm, Oil and Energy Gas Corporation (ONGC), is also planning to engage Saudi Arabia as its equity partner for a refinery project in the Indian state of Andhra Pradesh. The recent upheavals in India's relationship with Iran and Iran's decision to renege on some of its oil supply commitments in the aftermath of India's vote against Iran at the IAEA have also alerted India to the importance of having a diversified set of suppliers in the Middle East. India is also attracted to Iraq's oil assets. The Iraqi government has invited India to step in and help in Iraq's reconstruction with its technology and management expertise. Iraq is slated to be world's biggest oil supplier by 2015 and Indian companies are looking forward to operating there. Iraqi businesses are also exploring opportunities for joint ventures with their Indian counterparts in the field of cement, petrochemicals, hotels, oil and gas upstream and downstream projects.[53]

India's foreign policy towards the Middle East will also be increasingly influenced by the rise of Islamic extremism and its growing wariness about the impact of global Islamic extremist networks on its domestic Muslim population. A major impediment in India's ties with Saudi Arabia is the proliferation of Saudi-funded religious schools in the country. The Salafi movement has taken advantage of India's liberal environment and Muslim unease with resurgent Hindu nationalism to preach radicalism to India's 130 million-strong Muslim populace.

Madrasa (Islamic school) education has long been a part of life for many Muslim children in India. Madrasas in India number

---

[52] The details of the 'Delhi Declaration' signed by Saudi Arabia's king and the Indian prime minister can be found at http://meaindia.nic.in (accessed on December 20, 2007).

[53] Vikas Dhoot, 'Iraqi Trade Delegation in Town, Indian Businesses Line Up', *The Indian Express*, March 28, 2007.

between 8,000 and 40,000.[54] But concerns have been rising in India about the dated and, with Saudi financing, increasingly radical curricula. In 2001, a report of the Group of Ministers on 'Reforming the National Security System' recommended the need to modernise madrasa education.[55]

Saudi financial assistance has gone to a range of Indian-Islamic organisations resulting in the establishment of mosques, madrasas and publishing houses inculcating the Saudi worldview.[56] Riyadh also provides scholarships to Indian students to study religion in its universities. These Saudi-educated imams often return and preach Salafi ideology to unemployed and susceptible Indian Muslims. Some of the returning Indians also transfer funds to local Islamic institutions, often through the hawala system in which no records of individual transactions are produced.[57]

Terrorism might brake Saudi relations with India. New Delhi and Riyadh differ over the definition of terrorism. Most Arab states, including Saudi Arabia, argue in the context of the Israeli-Palestinian conflict that liberation struggles justify acts of terror, while the Indian government categorically opposes terrorist attacks on civilians. The two states had intended to sign a mutual legal assistance treaty on criminal matters during the king's visit. Such a treaty usually serves as a precursor to an extradition treaty. But, unable to break the impasse, the two sides' diplomats could only agree to a watered-down memorandum of understanding on combating crime.[58] New Delhi is especially sensitive given Saudi links to jihadi groups such as Lashkar-e-Taiba, which have staged attacks within India.[59] The group has tried to recruit Indian Muslims—so far with only limited success—for its radical causes from the Indian diaspora

---

[54] Amir Ullah Khan, Mohammad Sadiq and Zafar H. Anjum, 'To Kill the Mockingbird', India China Economic and Cultural Centre, New Delhi, accessed on June 28, 2006.
[55] 'Reforming the National Security System—Recommendations of the Group of Ministers', February 19, 2001, at http://mod.nic.in/newadditions/rcontents.htm.
[56] Yoginder Sikand, 'Intra-Muslim Rivalries in India and the Saudi Connection', Jamia Hamdard University, accessed June 28, 2006.
[57] Haqqani, 'The Ideologies of South Asian Jihadi Groups'.
[58] 'What's Terror? India, Saudi Differ', *Hindustan Times*, January 27, 2006.
[59] G. Parthasarthy, 'Saudi-Pakistani Nexus on Terrorism', *The Tribune*, September 25, 2003; Husain Haqqani, 'India's Islamist Groups', *Current Trends in Islamist Ideology* 1:1 (April 2005), pp. 10–23.

in Saudi Arabia and other states in the Persian Gulf. It has been claimed that, despite the best efforts of Lashkar, it has not been very successful in wooing Muslim youth within India.[60]

China is becoming a major player in global politics and its influence in the Middle East is on the rise. Though India's relations with China have improved considerably in the last few years, this relationship remains by and large competitive, if not outrightly conflictual.[61] This is particularly true with regard to the two giants trying to compete for global energy resources. Moreover, India's aspirations to emerge as a major global power may also lead it to counter China's growing influence around the globe. China's ties with major Middle Eastern nations are on an upswing and this would be a major factor in determining how India shapes its Middle East policies in the long term. The relationship between India and Iran can also suffer from Iran's close defence relationship with China. Chinese firms are key suppliers of ballistic and cruise missile related technologies to Iran.[62] China is also helping Iran in pursuing the development of a nuclear fuel cycle for civil and nuclear-weapon purposes, despite Beijing's 1997 bilateral commitment to the US to forgo any new nuclear cooperation with Iran.

While Iran's development of nuclear-weapons and ballistic missiles will change the strategic landscape of India's neighbourhood, China's growing leverage over Iran can also shape Iran's attitudes towards India in the coming years. China has so far been very successful in hemming India in from all sides and if Iran decides to follow China's lead, it might make India geopolitically handicapped. It is, therefore, extremely important for India to make sure that Iranian stakes in good relations with India increase dramatically over the next few years.

While Riyadh might welcome its upgraded relations with both Beijing and New Delhi, constraints might limit future expansion of their ties. Sino-Indian energy competition may force an unpalatable

---

[60] B. Raman, 'Al-Qaeda, the IIF and Indian Muslims', South Asia Analysis Group, paper no. 1743, March 20, 2006.
[61] Harsh V. Pant, 'India's China Policy: Devoid of a Strategic Framework', *South Asian Survey* 12:2 (July–December 2005), pp. 209–22.
[62] 'The Worldwide Threat: Evolving Dangers in a Complex World', Testimony of the Director of Central Intelligence, George J. Tenet, before the Senate Select Committee on Intelligence, February 11, 2003, at http://www.cia.gov/cia/public_affairs/speeches/dci_speech_02112003.html (accessed on December 20, 2007).

choice upon Saudi officials. And once Washington is thrown into the mix, the picture becomes more complicated. With the US viewing China as its greatest future challenge[63] and Washington working actively to bolster US-Indian ties,[64] joint pressures upon Riyadh will only build. US officials are already concerned that Beijing's outreach to the Middle East has undercut non-proliferation efforts and challenged US standing.[65]

India would also be concerned about Israel forging a close defence relationship with China or even with Pakistan in the future, which would have adverse strategic consequences for India. Israel is apparently keen on reviving its bilateral relations with China after they suffered a major setback when Israel cancelled the Phalcon spy plane deal with China under US pressure. Counterterror cooperation and defence trade seem to be driving Sino-Israel relations just as in the case of Indo-Israel relations.[66] Israel sees China not only as another huge market for its defence products, but also as a significant global player that can play a constructive role in favour of Israel in multilateral forums like the UN. Though Israel's relations with China will indubitably be conducted under the watchful eyes of the US, India will have to be concerned about the ramifications of close defence cooperation between Israel and China, especially in light of China's close defence ties with Pakistan.

Finally, the US remains the predominant player in the Middle East despite the visible failure of its policy in Iraq. India's ties with the US have dramatically expanded in the last few years and this has already emerged as a significant factor in shaping Indian foreign policy towards Middle East. The most visible manifestation of this has been its attempt to recalibrate its ties with Iran. The shadow of the US will loom large over Indian foreign policy in the years to come especially as the conflict between the US and Iran gets intensified. India is trying hard to project itself as a responsible nuclear power, especially after the signing of the

---

[63] *Quadrennial Defence Review Report 2006*, US Department of Defence, February 6, 2006, pp. 29–30; Richard R. Russell, 'Oil for Missiles', *The Wall Street Journal*, January 25, 2006.
[64] Harsh V. Pant, 'The Indo-US Nuclear Deal: Much More Than Meets the Eye', *Royal United Services Institute Journal*, 151:2 (April 2006), pp. 60–63.
[65] Blumenthal, 'Providing Arms: China and the Middle East'.
[66] Barbara Opall-Rome, 'Israel, China to Revive Ties', *Defence News*, December 15, 2003.

civilian nuclear cooperation agreement with the US. It will be very reluctant to challenge US non-proliferation priorities in the Middle East that views Iranian nuclear programme as a major challenge. Moreover, it is in India's interest now that nuclear proliferation in its neighbourhood is contained.

The main constraint in the Indo-Iranian bilateral relationship might potentially be the role of the US in the foreign policy calculus of the two countries. India has made a serious attempt in recent times to align itself with the US on major international issues, ranging from the tackling of transnational terrorism to the US pursuit of National Missile Defence. There are many in India and the US who see both countries as natural partners because of their converging interests and vibrant democratic institutions. On the other hand, the US remains hostile to Iran. Iran has been isolated from the mainstream international community since the 1979 Revolution, primarily because of the persistent hostility of the US leadership towards the dispensation in Iran.[67] After September 11, 2001, the US relations with Iran have further deteriorated as it views Iran as one of the major countries sponsoring and supporting terrorist networks like the Lebanese Hizbollah, Hamas and the Palestine Islamic Jihad. Many in the US considered Iran, supporting various terrorist networks and on its way to acquire weapons of mass destruction, as a greater threat than Iraq even before the US-led invasion of Iraq.[68] The declaration by Iran that it would reprocess spent nuclear fuel and mine uranium to meet a growing demand for electricity has also not made matters easier for US–Iran relationship. The US strongly believes that Iran's announced plans are a pretext to develop nuclear-weapons as an ambitious nuclear programme for electricity does not make sense for a country with huge oil and gas reserves and limited uranium supplies. The US has been at the forefront of putting pressure on Iran to come clean about its nuclear programme and has demanded strong action by

---

[67] For an authoritative account of the US–Iran relations since the Islamic Revolution of 1979, see Gary Sick, 'The Clouded Mirror: The United States and Iran, 1979–99', in Esposito and Ramazani, eds, *Iran at the Crossroads* (New York: Palgrave, 2001), pp. 93–122.

[68] A detailed account of Iran's financing and orchestrating of international terrorism can also be found in Matthew Levitt, *Targeting Terror: US Policy Towards Middle Eastern State Sponsored Terrorist Organizations, Post-September 11* (Washington, DC: The Washington Institute for Near East Policy, 2002), pp. 62–71.

the international community against Iran's clandestine nuclear activities. As a consequence, while India seems to be getting closer to the US, Iran is moving further apart. As the US–Iran tensions rise, India will be forced to make some foreign policy choices that it would rather not make.

India's ties with Israel will also be constrained by how far the US wants this engagement to go. Though the US has welcomed the growing ties between India and Israel, it has a significant veto over Israel's defence exports. This is not to deny, however, that the growing security relationship between India and Israel has, to a large extent, been nurtured with the help of the US. Many see a larger design behind the US desire to make the two states work closely with each other and the US, mainly to counter-balance a rising China, which may become America's main competitor in the coming years. Also, since to a large extent defence cooperation is driving the Indo-Israeli relationship, there is a real danger that any decline in such cooperation may seriously undermine the bilateral relationship. It is a distinct possibility that once the US arms market becomes more fully open to India, the Israeli market would lose its relative attraction.

Conclusion

The importance of the Middle East for the Indian foreign policy can be discerned from a statement of former Indian Foreign Minister Jaswant Singh: 'For a long time, India has not been seen in its true dimensions...When we [India] talk about Indonesia or Central Asia or Gulf, it is because of our [India's] interest and our [India's] sphere of influence.'[69] This statement highlights the growing Indian ambitions. Since the end of the Cold War, there has been a gradual expansion in India's assessment of its interests in the Middle East, resulting in a more aggressive pursuit of those interests compared to the past.

While this essay largely focuses on India's ties with three major actors in the Middle East—Iran, Saudi Arabia and Israel—the region encompasses a number of other states. However, compared to a few years back when these states were largely on the periphery of

---

[69] 'Singing Bush's Praise', *The Times of India*, April 13, 2001.

India's Middle East policy, today these states are the pivot around which Indian foreign policy towards the region seems to be shaping up. In August 2007, the Indian Navy undertook a series of naval exercises with a number of Persian Gulf states thereby lending its hand to Indian diplomacy in expanding India's reach in the Middle East. It made port calls and conducted exercises with the navies of Kuwait, Oman, Bahrain, Saudi Arabia, Qatar, United Arab Emirates and Djibouti, when it embarked on a 48-day tour of the Persian Gulf region. It also used the opportunity to engage with the navies of other major powers in the region such as the US, the UK and France. This was yet another sign of India's growing foreign policy interest in the Middle East, something that has been palpable for quite some time now. Just in the last three years, there have been about a dozen odd high profile visits to India from the Gulf States including the King of Saudi Arabia, the King of Jordan and the Emir of Kuwait and Qatar. Domestic constraints, though still important, are no longer as salient as before and the Indian foreign policy has become more flexible and less dogmatic in its pursuit of its interests. There is a realisation that India can no longer rely on its past approach to the region, that has become not only outdated but is thoroughly inadequate to meet the complex challenges of the future. As a consequence, India is now focusing on a pragmatic engagement with all sides and has tried to shed its covertly ideological approach towards the region. Most countries in the region are also now seeking comprehensive partnerships with India based on a recognition and appreciation of its role in shaping the emerging regional and global order. As India has tried to re-define its interests in the Middle East, its diplomacy has also become more oriented on the outcome. From energy security to defence ties, from countering China to courting the US, India now has an array of interests in the Middle East and there is a growing realisation that these interests can be best served by a greater degree of realism in foreign policy.

But several contradictions and constraints remain. How India navigates these will, to a large extent, determine whether it is successful in emerging as a major player in the Middle Eastern region in the coming years.

12

India and Central Asia: Part of the New Great Game

Stephen Blank*

The most striking development in recent Indian foreign policy is the Indo-American nuclear deal. It was announced in 2005, fully formulated in 2006 and then ratified by the Congress. Although this deal has provoked much commentary for and against it and about its nuclear details and has been stalled before the Indian Parliament, its overriding geopolitical significance has been overlooked. This aspect of the deal represents Washington's acceptance and acknowledgement of India's ambitions to be a great power in Asia, its willingness to assist in that process and accept the consequences thereof.[1] And key observers like Senator Richard Lugar (R-Indiana) acknowledge that this agreement is the Bush administration's 'most important strategic diplomatic initiative'.[2] Indeed, Indian planners believe that a profound strategic realignment is underway in Asia and that India is fated to be a major actor in that drama.[3]

The US acknowledgment of India's importance and weight had earlier been stated openly by Secretary of State Condoleeza Rice who stated, in March 2005, that it was US policy 'to help make India become a major world power in the twenty-first century'. Moreover, in this selfsame statement, senior officials underscored that they fully understood what such a commitment meant, because

---

* The views expressed here do not represent that of the US Army, the Defence Department or the US government.
[1] US Department of State, 'Background Briefing by Administration Officials on US–South Asia Relations', March 25, 2005, at http:// www.state.gov/r/pa/prs/prs/ps/2005/438553.htm (accessed on March 26, 2005).
[2] Krishnadev Calamur, 'Indo-US Nuclear Deal Blasts Ahead', *Asia Times Online*, July 1, 2006, at www.atimes.com (accessed on July 1, 2006).
[3] Brigadier Arun Sahgal (Retd.) and Parama Sinha Palit, 'The "Singh Doctrine"', *Armed Forces Journal*, May 2006, p. 21; Martin Walker, 'India's Path to Greatness', *Wilson Quarterly* XXVIII: 2 (Summer 2006), p. 26.

they also talked about American support for Indian requests for 'transformative systems in such areas as command and control, early warning and missile defences'.[4] Furthermore, it is clear that Indo-American discussions now include, as a matter of course, a review of all the outstanding security issues in South and Central Asia, if not Southeast Asia, China and the Gulf.[5] The revelation of such discussions has already led Pakistani analysts to claim that the US has recognised India's 'sphere of influence' in Asia.[6] And senior American officials like Under-Secretary of State R. Nicholas Burns write that, 'As India is both a rising power and a democracy, we in Washington view its growing influence in the world as broadly congruent with US interests.'[7]

Whether or not the new partnership goes that far, US certainly does accept the self-evident fact that India is, and will be, the primary power on the subcontinent and that, therefore, it requires intimate bilateral strategic–military, political and economic coordination across a range of issues with India and not just in South Asia. Most importantly, India's legitimate, substantial and growing interests and capabilities in regard to Central Asia are fully accepted as normal by all the major powers that are active there. Moreover, they are all competing with each other for influencing New Delhi whose strategic leverage is enhanced by its ability to engage in non-binding partnerships with the US, Russia and China.[8]

---

[4] US Department of State, 'Background Briefing by Administration Officials on US–South Asia Relations'.

[5] Ibid.

[6] Musahid Hussain, 'Pakistan's Quest for Security and the Indo-US Nuclear Deal', *Korean Journal of Defense Analysis* XVIII:2 (Summer 2006), pp. 128–31, citing K.P. Nayar, 'The US Recognises South Asia as India's Sphere of Influence', *The Telegraph*, (Calcutta), April 5, 2006, at www.telgraphindia.com/1060405/asp/opinion/story_6056145.asp (accessed on September 17, 2006).

[7] R. Nicholas Burns, 'America's Strategic Opportunity with India', *Foreign Affairs* LXXXVI:6 (November–December 2007), p. 139.

[8] Vladimir Skosyrev, 'India and Pakistan on Verge of Détente. But Situation Could be Complicated by US Arms Deliveries' (in Russian), Moscow, *Nezavisimaya Gazeta*, August 10, 2005, *Foreign Broadcast Information Service Centred Enrasia* (FBIS SOV), August 10, 2005; Alexei Andreyev and Yevgeny Verlin, 'Geometry of Asian Security: Vajpayee Seeks to Improve Relations with Beijing, and Musharraf with Washington' (in russian), Moscow, *Nezavisimaya Gazeta*, June 25, 2003, *FBIS SOV*, June 25, 2003; Abanti Bhattacharya, 'China's Foreign Policy Challenges and Evolving Strategy', *Strategic Analysis* XXX:1 (January–March 2006), pp. 186, 198–200.

And Burns' observations, along with continuing Russo-Chinese-Indian discussions, suggest that New Delhi has been able to maintain that congruence with all the major powers until now.

In Central Asia, both the US and India want India to become, and be seen as, a magnet for the development of Central Asian states. It is important for Washington that Central Asia does not fall under exclusive Russian and/or Chinese influence. Since the thrust of the new US policy is to give local governments other alternatives—e.g., in energy cooperation and foreign investment—the growth of India's presence in Central Asia and its ability to influence key economic and political decisions there are decidedly in the US interest. Obviously, the same strategic reasoning of providing alternatives to Moscow and Beijing holds true for India, perhaps with more emphasis on China. Indeed, already in 1997, Russia's press reported that in private Indo-Russian diplomatic conversations, 'Russian and Indian diplomats willingly open the cards: both Moscow and New Delhi see a threat in the excessive strengthening of China and the Islamic extremists'.[9] Indian experts saw the Russian weakness in Central Asia in the 1990s as opening the way to a Chinese-orchestrated encirclement of its interests there and regarded such a trend negatively.[10]

Therefore, it is hardly surprising that in 2006 the US government launched a major diplomatic effort with India to tie South Asia and Central Asia together, in order to give the states of Central Asia precisely those alternatives to Russian energy domination

---

[9] Jyotsna Bakshi, 'Russia's Post-Pokhran Dilemma', *Strategic Analysis* XXII:5 (August 1998), p. 721, quoted in Jerome M. Conley, 'Indo-Russian Military and Nuclear Cooperation: Implications for the United States', INSS Occasional Paper No. 31, Proliferation Series, USAF Institute for National Security Studies, USAF Academy, Colorado Springs, Colorado, 2000, pp. 24–25.

[10] S. Enders Wimbush, 'India's Perspective', *Russia in the International System: A Conference Report*, Central Intelligency Agency, June 1, 2001, at www.cia.gov/nic/pubs/conference_reports/russia_conf.html, p. 31 (accessed on January 29, 2004). See, also Sumit Ganguly, 'India's Alliances 2020', in Michael R. Chambers, ed, *South Asia in 2020: Future Strategic Balances and Alliances* (Carlisle Barracks, PA: Strategic Studies Institute, US Army War College, 2002), pp. 370–76.

over them.[11] This initiative encompasses a reorganisation of the State Department to place the Central Asian states in a newly restructured Department of South Asian and Central Asian Affairs with its own assistant secretary of state, giving this area a much needed injection of bureaucratic power. But beyond this and a stepped-up programme of high-level visits to South and Central Asia, starting with President Bush's visit in March 2006, there is also a major US initiative to stimulate infrastructural and electrical power connection and investments throughout Central Asia. This would allow India to play more effectively in this region as a source of, and market for, trade, investment and energy. One benefit for India from this initiative is that it would also substantially help India satisfy its enormous energy needs.[12] Moreover, American pressure upon Iran and support for the idea of a gas pipeline linking Turkmenistan, Afghanistan, Pakistan and India (the so-called TAP line) is a major consideration in India's developing energy policy because the US pressure on Iran impedes the realisation of an alternative pipeline (also supported by Moscow) from Iran to Pakistan and then India (IPI).[13]

But, at the same time, there is also no doubt that India sees itself as a major independent economic player with a leading role to play, not only in South Asia but also in Central Asia. M. K. Narayanan, India's National Security Advisor, told the annual Wehrkunde conference in Munich in 2006 that,

---

[11] Assistant Secretary of State Richard A. Boucher, 'The US–India Friendship: Where We Were and Where We're Going', Remarks at the Confederation of Indian Industries, New Delhi, April 7, 2006, at www.state.gov/p/sca/rls/rm/2006/4320. htm; Assistant Secretary of State Richard A. Boucher, 'Remarks at Electricity Beyond Borders: A Central Asia Power Sector Forum', Istanbul, Turkey, June 13, 2006, at http://www.state.gov/p/sca/rls/rm/2006/67838.htm (accessed on June 15, 2006); 'Electricity Relights Washington's Central Asian Policy', *Jane's Foreign Report*, June 29, 2006, at http://www4.janes.com/subscribe/frp/doc_view.jsp?K2DocKey=/content1/janesdata/mags/frp/history/frp2006/frp70038.htm@current&Prod_Name=FREP&QueryText=(accessed on June 29, 2006); Joshua Kuchera, 'USAID Official Outlines Plan to Build Central-South Asian Electricity Links', *Eurasia Insight*, May 4, 2006, at www.eurasianet.org (accessed on May 4, 2006).
[12] Ibid.
[13] Stephen Blank, 'India's Energy Options in Central Asia', Paper Presented at the Conference on Eurasian Pipelines, Columbia University, New York, November 12–13, 2007.

In South Asia, for example, those of our neighbors who were farseeing enough to understand the benefits of linking their economies to the Indian economic motor have been rewarded handsomely. Whether they are addressing demands of services, energy, or goods, their rising living standards tell their own story. In fact, as the full potential of the emerging socio-economic processes begin to be appreciated, new options could well emerge even for historically intractable problems. It is with this optimism of new opportunities and broader horizons that India now approaches its neighbors and the rest of Asia. ... India's location, straddling as it does all the major sub-regions of Asia, provides it with a unique vantage point. ... If the basis for a stable and prosperous Asia lies in both political and economic integration—cutting across cultures, historical divisions, ideologies and barriers (both physical and ideological—then India is eminently suited to play a leading role.[14]

This is very clearly not an individual view but the considered view of the government in New Delhi. In a 2005 speech in Washington, Foreign Secretary Shyam Saran stated that,

> Countries across the globe are beginning to see India as an indispensable economic partner and seeking mutually rewarding economic and commercial ties with our expanding economy, ... Should not our neighbors also seek to share in the prospects for mutual prosperity India offers to them? Do countries in our neighborhood envisage their own security and development in cooperation with India or in hostility to India by seeking to isolate themselves from India against the logic of our geography?[15]

But beyond this vision, for Americans, equally striking is what he told a Shanghai audience in January 2006 about India's vision for Asia. Saran here announced that,

> We regard the concept of neighborhood as one of widening concentric circles, around a central axis of historical and cultural commonalities. In this, we see India's destiny interlinked with that of Asia. From this point of view, developing relations with Asian countries is one of our priorities, while pursuing a cooperative architecture of pan-Asian regionalism is a key area of focus in our foreign policy. Geography imparts a unique position to India in the geopolitics of the Asian

---

[14] M.K. Narayanan, 'Asia's Global Foreign Policy and Security Interests', *Hampton Roads International Security Quarterly* 2 (2006), p. 51.
[15] K.P. Nayar, 'The US Recognizes South Asia as India's Sphere of Influence', *The Telegraph* (Kolkata), April 5, 2006, at www.telegraphindia.com/1060405/asp/opinion/story_6056145.asp (accessed on April 5, 2006).

282 ▪ Stephen Blank

> continent, with our footprint extending well beyond South Asia and our interests straddling across different sub-categories of Asia—be it East Asia, West Asia, Central Asia, South Asia, or Southeast Asia. To those who harbor any skepticism about this fact, it would suffice to remind that we share one of the longest land borders in the world with China, that Central Asia verges on our northern frontiers, that we have land and maritime borders with three South East Asian countries, that our Andaman and Nicobar Islands are just over a hundred kilometers from Indonesia, and that our exclusive economic zone spans waters form the Persian Gulf to the Straits of Malacca. It is this geopolitical reality and our conviction that enhanced regional cooperation is mutually advantageous, which sustain our enthusiasm to participate in endeavors for regional integration, ranging from [the] South Asian Association of Regional Cooperation to [the] East Asia Summit and [the] Shanghai Cooperation Organisation.[16]

Clearly, Shyam Saran here laid down a marker, not only for his audience but also to all other observers who watch Indian activities in Central Asia, if not throughout the Asian landmass.

Similarly, Defence Minister Pranab Mukherjee linked India's economics and security with its expansive vision of itself as a potential stabiliser in Central Asia, in a 2005 speech at the Carnegie Endowment for International Peace in Washington.

> The restoration of traditional links with Central Asia is not important only for the sake of trade and economy. Traditionally, Central Asia has been at the crossroads of trade and culture, a major hub in the Silk Route. This is the region through which Buddhism spread as far as Mongolia and Korea. It is also the region through which Islam enriched India. Today, it is a theater in the battle between fundamentalism and tolerance, extremism and moderation in Islam with fundamentalist outfits actively trying to destabilise the secular governments of the region. India has a secular polity that shares with liberal democracies, values of democracy, fundamental, and religious freedoms. It is, by virtue of its inherited historical character, composition, size, population, economy and military strength and experience, a natural bulwark against fundamentalist extremism and a factor for peace and stability in Asia. By nature, India is not inclined to export ideologies, even ideologies it believes in and follows. India would rather promote

---

[16] 'Present Dimensions of the Indian Foreign Policy', address by Foreign Secretary Mr Shyam Saran at the Shanghai Institute of International Studies, *Ministry of External Affairs Internet Version*, New Delhi, January 12, 2006, FBIS SOV, January 12, 2006.

democracy in the region by precept and example. Freer traffic between India and Central Asia would be a factor in favor of moderation and democracy there.[17]

Thus India's achievements now have forced the great powers—Russia, China and the US—to acknowledge the legitimacy of its security and energy interests in Central Asia and to seek to harness Indian policy to support their goals or at least to make them parallel in Central Asia, if not beyond. In other words, they need Indian friendship as much as, if not more than, India needs their friendship. For example, Russia supports India's full membership in the Shanghai Cooperation Organisation (SCO).[18] Russian and Indian diplomats also began discussions in February 2006 on the possibility of enlarging the Collective Security Treaty Organisation (CSTO), Russia's military alliance in Central Asia, and on whether India might participate in its forums.[19] The reasons for these consultations appear to ratify Russia's and India's appreciation of potential challenges there and the contribution that India could make in overcoming them.

While this factor continues the Indian tradition of relying, in practice, upon a major ally—historically the USSR, to advance its Asiatic interests, this new trend breaks new ground because it also comprises India's growing sense of itself as an independent major power. Clearly, India will pursue an independent course. However, it may align with any one or two powers at any given time. For example, it appears that the most tangible Indian interest in the aforementioned strategic triangle with Russia and China is to secure reliable energy supplies and trade from Russia and Central Asia through the generation of infrastructural development projects in the field of energy and transportation.[20] India certainly is not

---

[17] Address by Defense Minister Pranab Mukherjee at the Carnegie Endowment for International Peace, Washington, DC, June 27, 2005.
[18] Vinay Shukla, 'India Pitches for Full Membership of Shanghai Cooperation Organization', *Press Trust of India* (New Delhi) October 26, 2005, *FBIS SOV*, October 26, 2005; Ranesh Ramachandran, 'Russian Wants India in Shanghai Pact', *The Asian Age* (New Delhi), January 3, 2006, at *FBIS SOV*, January 3, 2006, at www.opensource. gov (accessed on January 3, 2006).
[19] Ilyas Sarsembaev, 'Russia: No Strategic Partnership With China in View', *China Perspectives* 65, (May–June 2006), p. 30.
[20] 'Statement by Indian External Affairs Minister K. Natwar Singh at SCO Council Heads of Government Meeting in Moscow, October 26, 2005', New Delhi, Ministry of External Affairs Website, at http://meaindia.nic.in. (accessed on October 27, 2005), *FBIS SOV*, October 27, 2005.

much moved by the anti-Americanism that drives Moscow and Beijing. Indeed, in 2002, Foreign Minister Jaswant Singh said that America could not now give up its bases there and should even maintain its military presence in Pakistan indefinitely to sustain stability there as well. Moreover, the government then stated that it had no opposition to the further presence of US forces there as part of the war on terrorism.[21]

So, even if India becomes a full member of the SCO, it is unlikely to be a party to anti-American intrigues there. This particular fact should remind us that even as it rises to major-power or even great-power status, India, like the other great powers, has its own interests and agenda in Central Asia. And those interests pertain first of all to physical security, energy access and overall commercial ties including energy.

INDIA'S INTERESTS IN CENTRAL ASIA

India's interests and objectives in Central Asia can be stated simply although pursuing them and achieving them even in part are anything but simple.

> India's primary instinct, to put it another way, is self-preservation. ... India wants to see the Central Asian Republics (CARs) evolve into progressive, secular democracies, neutral in disposition and independent in fact. ... [T]he inherent weakness of some of the CAR's makes them extremely vulnerable to hostile forces and destabilisation. To prevent this India needs to be proactive on various fronts. Russia's influence in the region is receding at a remarkable pace and the resultant space is being filled by various conflicting forces. If there is any consensus by the major powers on Central Asia, it is on the need to check the inroads by militant Islamic forces. But state and non-state forces from Pakistan, the Middle East, and some other countries are continuing to erode the region's secular character. Economic and military competition, if not outright rivalry among the big powers, is also, inadvertently in some cases, adding to regional contradictions. Within the republics, a volatile mix of ethnic and religious groups is pulling in different directions.

---

[21] *The Indian Express* (New Delhi), July 8, 2002, at www.opensource.gov (accessed on July 8, 2002), *FBIS NES*, July 8, 2002; Jim Hoagland, 'Staying On in Central Asia', *Washington Post*, January 20, 2002, p. B7.

The democratic urge is battling autocratic tradition. Abruptly dispossessed economic classes are railing against the affluent. In short, Central Asia is caught in an age of turbulence.²²

Given this turbulence, India must strive to moderate it lest it reach India's own territory, to ensure that its voice is heard above the regional cacophony and to assure itself that it has access to vital commercial and energy linkages as has historically been the case. Indeed, at present India faces what one writer called 'a wall of instability' along virtually all of its peripheries, a view shared by military leaders as well.²³ But, beyond that, it must forestall the efforts of antagonistic great powers like China or lesser powers like Pakistan to form a bloc in Central Asia that would further cut India off from the area and impose either a Chinese form of strategic encirclement upon India or a successful Pakistani attempt to dominate its so called 'strategic hinterland'.²⁴ Insofar as the effort to form such blocs is now in full bloom with the formation of Russia's Collective Security Treaty Organisation (CSTO) and the SCO, it is obvious that India will strive not just for observer status in the latter but also for full membership there.²⁵

By the same token, the Indian determination to project its overall power and influence in Central Asia and not necessarily military power alone, dictates to New Delhi that it strive to uphold the Karzai government in Afghanistan and render it considerable assistance against its enemies.²⁶ In doing so, India not only extends its influence into Central Asia, but also exacerbates its rivalry

---

²² Indranil Bannerjee, *India and Central Asia* (Northolt, Middlesex: Brunel Academic Publishers Ltd., 2004), p. xii.
²³ Chietigj Bajpaee, 'India Held Back by Wall of Instability', *Asia Times Online*, June 1, 2006, at www.atimes.com (accessed on June 1, 2006); 'India's Strategic Environment and the Role of Military Power', Carnegie Endowment for International peace, August 22, 2006, at www.ceip.org (accessed on August 22, 2006).
²⁴ Stephen Blank, *Energy, Economics, and Security in Central Asia: Russia and Its Rivals* (Carlisle Barracks, PA: Strategic Studies Institute, US Army War College, 1995), pp. 23–26; Stephen Philip Cohen, *The Idea of Pakistan* (Washington, DC: Brookings Institution Press, 2006), pp. 87–88, 97.
²⁵ *FBIS SOV*, October 26, 2005.
²⁶ 'Kabul Hopes for Strategic Ties With New Delhi', *Radio Free Europe Radio Liberty Newsline*, August 18, 2006; 'PM Offers Helping Hand to Kabul, Karzai A Bridge To Entire Region', *The Indian Express*, August 29, 2005.

with Pakistan. Pakistan has looked upon Afghanistan as its 'strategic hinterland' which it must influence, if not control, so that it has a secure strategic rear against India. It also has sought over the years to ensure that any government in Kabul will recognise the British drawn Durand line as the boundary between Afghanistan and Pakistan and not try to unite the Pushtuns, Afghanistan's dominant ethnic group, on both sides of that line in a single state which would undermine Pakistan's integrity. In this context,

> Pakistan views this ongoing contest for influence in Afghanistan as an essential issue in its national security. According to diplomats, it also views US forces in Afghanistan as providing security for Pakistan in its strategic depth, which role cannot be minimised. Pakistan also considers that India, Iran, China and Russia will not consider it in their own interests for Pakistan to have a final, completely safe border with Afghanistan. This Pakistani view, whether correct or not, is the perception by which Islamabad views its national security interests in Central Asia.[27]

Thus the rivalries and conflicts in South Asia are inextricably bound up with the rivalries and conflicts of Central Asia. In the 1990s Pakistan's quest for influence also took on a more stringently religious Islamic aspect, leading it to look for support among the terrorists operating against Kashmir in India and for the Taliban. Since 9/11 Pakistan has been constrained to accept formally the fall of the Taliban. Nevertheless, there is considerable evidence that it is assisting the Taliban to regroup in and around the Pakistan–Afghanistan border areas.[28] Moreover, in 2006 it signed a peace agreement with the tribes in Waziristan and other regions that border Afghanistan, suggesting its inability or unwillingness (if not both) to deal firmly with the terrorist enclaves there. And the results were predictable: a further decline in Pakistan's ability to control its borderland. As one assessment of this accord observes, it probably formalises a situation of continuing cross-border destabilisation from Pakistan to Afghanistan.

---

[27] LTC Kurt H. Meppen 'Central Asia and the Competition of National Interests: A Study of Colliding Interests', Unpublished Paper, US Institute of Peace, June, 2006, p. 27.
[28] Marvin G. Weinbaum, 'Afghanistan and its Neighbors: An Ever Dangerous Neighborhood', US Institute of Peace, Special report, No. 162, 2006, pp. 8–11.

As part of this agreement, the Pakistani military will cease its unpopular military campaign in the semi-autonomous North Waziristani region. In exchange, the local Taliban militants will halt their attacks on Pakistani forces and stop crossing into nearby eastern Afghanistan to attack Western and Afghan forces hunting Al-Qaeda and Taliban militants. For Pakistan, this was an acceptance of the ground reality that its military would never be able to defeat tribal militants in a region where Pakistan's writ has never extended. For the critics, however, the deal amounts to giving an effective amnesty to the insurgents, allowing them even more freedom to cross into Afghanistan and pursue their militant agenda. While Pakistani officials claim that foreign militants can stay in the region only if they obey Pakistan's laws and stay away from militancy, it is unclear how this can be enforced in a region that has become even more out of bounds for the Pakistani government after this agreement.[29]

Undoubtedly, Islamabad's fear about rising Indian influence there and in Central Asia is not the least of its motives for assisting forces trying to destabilise Afghanistan.[30] India's endeavours are hardly altruistic but reflect enduring geopolitical interests. Therefore it is hardly surprising that former US intelligence analyst Michael Scheuer observed that,

> India, having invested $750 million, has deployed what appears to be half of its diplomatic corps and moved in commandos to protect its nationals. India clearly envisions an Afghanistan that is pro-New Delhi, is perceived by Islamabad as an Indian vassal and provides a platform for Indian intelligence operations into Pakistan.[31]

Neither is India uniquely cynical in this regard given the extent of continuing Pakistani support for the Taliban and the large-scale intervention by all of Afghanistan's neighbours in its affairs.[32]

India's interests in Afghanistan comprise of both security and access to energy either through Turkmenistan and Afghanistan or

---

[29] Harsh V. Pant, 'The Resurgence of the Taliban in Afghanistan', *Power and Interest News Report*, September 25, 2006, at www.pinr.com (accessed on September 25, 2006).
[30] Weinbaum, 'Afghanistan and Its Neighbors', p. 16.
[31] Michael Scheuer, 'Clueless into Kabul', *The American Interest* 1:4 (Fall 2006), p. 116.
[32] Ibid.

through Iran and Afghanistan. A recent study by the US Institute of Peace illustrates the scope of Indian efforts in Afghanistan and the linkages between energy and security.

India has worked hard to win the confidence of the Post-Taliban government in Kabul. New Delhi has contributed $565 million toward Afghan reconstruction—the sixth largest contributor—divided among infrastructure repair, humanitarian assistance and institutional and human resource development. A wide spectrum of programmes includes highway repair, communications, energy, health care and capacity building in contributors to secondary education and the training of diplomats and bureaucrats. India will finance the construction of a new parliament building at a cost of $50 million. Indian-donated Tata buses are a key part of Kabul's public transportation. *Assistance to Afghanistan's reconstruction advertises India's claims to be a regional economic power, ready to assume regional responsibilities* (italics mine). Indian activities in Afghanistan regularly draw complaints from Pakistan. Few actions rankled the Pakistanis more than the opening of Indian consulates in several Afghan cities, where they seem designed mostly as listening posts to monitor Pakistani influences and activities. But Pakistan sees more sinister motives than simple intelligence gathering, accusing the Indians through its consulates in Kandahar and Jalalabad of fostering an insurgency inside Pakistan's Balochistan. Pakistan takes this especially seriously because the Chinese built port at Gwadar stands at the southern boundary of the province. The port is central to Pakistan's plans to create a new international route for sea traffic that cold serve China, but also Afghanistan and Central Asia. Meanwhile India is building an $80 million road linking Afghanistan's Kandahar province with the Iranian port at Chahbahar and providing a 300 man paramilitary force to ensure the security of Indian workers.[33]

Interestingly enough, the heightened pace of Indian support for the Karzai regime is now to the liking of the US government which apparently is encouraging India to do all it can to support that government, including security cooperation.[34]

Afghanistan underscores the linkage between security against terrorism, projection of India's role as a major regional power through

---

[33] Weinbaum, 'Afghanistan and Its Neighbors', p. 16; Ashraf Khan, 'Tribal Warlords Step Up Attacks on Chinese Projects: US and India accused of Backing Militants in Province', *South China Morning Post*, March 16, 2006.
[34] Burns, 'America's Strategic Opportunity with India', p. 138; Nayar; 'Threat of Taliban Revival Brings Kabul, Delhi Closer', *Indian Express*, August 28, 2005.

the use of both hard and soft power instruments and the importance to India and Pakistan of reliable access to energy and even of economic stability in India's peripheries. It is very much in India's interests that stable democracies exist throughout South Asia and not just that there is reliable energy access.[35] Indeed, the second key Indian interest, which ties directly to the first one of the security of Central Asia, is the provision of reliable energy supplies from the region. There can be no disputing the importance of this for, as Prime Minister Manmohan Singh has said, 'energy security is second only in our scheme of things to food security'.[36]

Thus, India's dependence upon secure oil and gas supplies from the Gulf and Central Asia, as well as its energy firms' quest for equity holdings in Russian, Angolan, Sudanese, Venezuelan and, most of all, Iranian energy fields or for major deals with states like Iran is of vital national interest. But since India is physically cut off from Central Asia it becomes all the more urgent that Central Asia, including Afghanistan, be secured against internal shocks or externally generated upheavals, not to mention the combination of the two.

In other words, there is a seamless logical web from the objective of ensuring Central Asian stability and India's voice there to the conclusion that India must also ensure reliable energy access to oil and gas sources originating in Central Asia. Because India's rapid economic growth is strengthening the saliency of economic objectives as a factor in its overall security policy and since the new threats India faces involve threats to its economic interests as much, if not more than, to classical political interests, India will have to forget geographical boundaries and prepare to protect its interests beyond its borders, including the securing of a reliable energy access. In other words, India will have to develop, and maybe actually use, its expanding capabilities for power projection abroad.[37]

---

[35] 'India's Strategic Environment and the Role of Military Power', Carnegie Endowment for International Peace.
[36] Edward Luce and Quentin Peel, 'FT Interview Manmohan Singh', *The Financial Times*, November 8, 2004, p. 5; Quentin Peel, 'India's Terms of Engagement', *The Financial Times*, November 11, 2004, p. 15.
[37] 'India's Strategic Environment and the Role of Military Power'.

Therefore, the requirements of energy security also postulate, first, a continuing positive relationship with Moscow, even had the past fifty years not been one of unbroken friendship and, second, friendly ties to all the Central Asian states. Third, India must create firm ties among the energy exporting states of Central Asia, particularly Kazakhstan, Uzbekistan and, if possible, Turkmenistan. Fourth, given Iran's historically good relations with India, it is essential for India to preserve those ties to avail itself of the possibility of securing large-scale Iranian cooperation with India in energy issues. In fact, Indo-Iranian relations exemplify the pattern whereby economic and energy security become inextricable parts of a web of greater security and defence interests.

But even so, since Iran and India are also not contiguous to each other, there is an argument to be made that an amelioration of relations with Pakistan is desirable, not only for the sake of peace and reduced vulnerability either to war or continuing terrorism, but also because that way energy can become a shared resource and a possible point of unity or at least common interest. Specifically, if India wants to get Central Asian or Iranian and Russian energy directly through land-based pipelines, it must do so through Pakistan and that logically entails that Afghanistan and the supplying countries cannot be permanently unstable places. It also probably means that Iran will not be a reliable partner for India until its problems with Washington are overcome. This is as much due to US pressure as it is due to Iran's policies. Even though India could conceivably satisfy its need for energy through maritime and internal means, the vagaries of Gulf and Middle Eastern politics suggest to India the importance of having a third card to rely upon—in this case Central Asia. Moreover, the important goal of Central Asian and Afghan stability would greatly be enhanced by the materialisation of such prospects.

Therefore, India, to play the role it now wants and feels it needs to play in Central Asia, is pulled in two directions. One is to develop all the instruments of power at its disposal and use them wherever feasible in Central Asia. But by doing so it runs the risk of further alarming and inflaming Pakistani fears and ambitions, which could foment lasting instability in Afghanistan and Central Asia, if not India itself and the larger region of the South Asian subcontinent. The continuing assistance, by elements within the

Pakistani government, for the Taliban and Kashmiri terrorists exemplifies that aspect of the Indo-Pakistani relationship as it applies to Central Asia.[38] Indeed, it appears that American mediation between Pakistan and Afghanistan was needed to bring about an agreement between them in August–September 2006 for collaboration against terrorists, though only time will tell if this cooperation is for real.[39]

But, on the other hand, if India wishes to truly stabilise the entire Central Asian 'theatre' and ensure its access to Central Asian energy, it must find a way to participate in joint energy ventures with Pakistan in order to justify the cost of building pipelines south from Central Asia or east from Iran, all the way to its territory. And, at the same time, it must retain strong ties to all the major actors who are interested in Central Asia and find ways of cooperating with them. Only in this way can it leverage its growing economic power in Central Asia. Indeed, for example, Defence Minister Mukherjee, in a Washington speech of 2005, stated that, despite the biggest challenge to India's strategic task of making up the historical strategic deficit of neglecting the immediate and extended neighbourhood, particularly Central Asia and beyond, it is precisely this vision of an integrated region based upon the Indian market and Indian economic power that gives New Delhi a vested interest in peace with Pakistan.[40] At the same time, he overtly

---

[38] 'Pakistan's Musharraf Says Relations with Afghanistan Are Tense', *Bloomberg*, March 6, 2006; Farkhan Bokhari, 'Musharraf Urges US To Intervene in Afghan Dispute', *The Financial Times*, March 7, 2006; Pamela Constable, 'Pakistan's Awkward Balancing Act on Islamic Militant Groups', *Washington Post*, August 26, 2006, p. 10; Naveed Ahmad, 'The London Terror Plans: Pakistani-Afghan Connection', *Eurasia Insight*, August 23, 2006; 'Karzai Tells Neighbors to Stop Meddling', *Washington Times*, February 19, 2006, p. 9; Ahmed Rashid, 'Afghan President Confronts Pakistani Counterpart Over Suicide Bombers', *Eurasia Insight*, February 21, 2006; Alyssa Ayrees, 'Regional Terror Goes Global', *Wall Street Journal*, August 18, 2006, p. 14; Ron Synovitz, 'Afghanistan: US Reports "Breakthrough" on Afghan-Pakistan Security Cooperation', *Radio Fee Europe Radio Liberty Features*, August 25, 2006; Intikhab Amir, 'The Waiting Game', *The Indian Express* (North American Edition), September 1, 2006, pp. 12–13.
[39] Ibid.
[40] 'Address by the Defense Minister Pranab Mukherjee at the Carnegie Endowment for International Peace', Washington, DC, June 27, 2005. (Henceforth Mukherjee Address)

linked the realisation of this economic vision to the triumph of forces of moderation and democratisation over those who espouse terrorism.[41]

Thus, India's strategy for Central Asia has been to draw simultaneously closer to all the main players: Moscow, Beijing and Washington, as well as to all the local regimes. While this can mean clashes with any of them over specific issues—e.g., over Iran's nuclear programme where Iran demands support and Washington opposition and India must navigate between both of them—it also shows India's self-confidence and patience over the last decade. In this sense, its ability to move forward on major energy negotiations—like the possibility of a pipeline from Iran through Pakistan (IPI) or a pipeline starting in Turkmenistan and shipping gas from there through Afghanistan and Pakistan to it (TAP)—was already foreshadowed in the 1990s.[42]

Finally, in this connection, India may well have to make a choice whether it wants to rival Pakistan or find ways of cooperation with it. The fragility of Pakistan as a state may well be increasing as it confronts intensifying pressures from without to hunt down terrorists whom it has tolerated and supported, increasing pressures from within from those elements who support those forces in Pakistan and from disaffected minorities as in Balochistan. These internal issues are of utmost concern to New Delhi or at least they should be. This is because a destabilised or Islamic radical government in Pakistan, a nuclear state, could be the ultimate nightmare for New Delhi as well as the world. Of less frightening quality, though still vital to India, is the prospect of a destabilised Pakistan for that would effectively foreclose any of the main options for gas and oil from Central Asia, either from Turkmenistan and/or Afghanistan or from Iran. This is because continuing outbreaks of unrest in Balochistan threaten both pipeline schemes and the construction of Pakistan's future main port at Gwadar. An unstable

---

[41] Ibid; Robert McMahon, 'Central Asia: Defence Minister Touts India's Potential Moderating Influence in Region', *Radio Free Europe Radio Liberty Features*, June 28, 2005.

[42] C. Raja Mohan, *Crossing the Rubicon: the Shaping of India's New Foreign Policy*, (New York: Palgrave Macmillan, 2004), p. 223.

Pakistan not only creates potential military and political threats for India, it also puts India's energy security at risk.

INDIAN DEFENCE AND SECURITY POLICY IN CENTRAL ASIA

There is no doubt that India's hard security interests in Central Asia do not end at the Afghan border. In late 2003, to signify its sense of itself as a rising Asian power, Prime Minister Atal Bihari Vajpayee's government opted for a twenty-year programme to become a world power whose influence is felt across the Indian Ocean, the Arabian Gulf and all of Asia.[43] Vajpayee directed planners to craft defence strategies that extend beyond South Asia and transcend past sub-regional mindsets. He claimed that India's expanded security perspectives require fresh thinking about projecting power and influence, as well as security in all these directions. India will seek more defence cooperation with states in the Gulf, Southeast and Central Asia, presumably going beyond intelligence sharing about terrorist activities. This cooperation will proceed to more bilateral exchanges and exercises and greater sharing of defence advice with friendly nations. In this context, strategic partnership with Washington is essential because Russia's ties with India are tempered by Moscow's dependence on the West, particularly America. In the absence of a partnership with Washington, this situation would severely constrain Indian options since it could no longer hide behind Russia if it clashed with America.[44]

While India formally eschews offensive military projections that intervene unilaterally in other countries, it announced its air base in Ayni, Tajikistan that had been operational since 2002 and it hopes to undertake the following military programmes through 2013:

- Improve military logistics in Iran, Tajikistan, Kazakhstan and Uzbekistan.
- Increase military interaction with Malaysia, Indonesia, Singapore, Thailand, Laos and Vietnam.

---

[43] Vivek Raghuvanshi, 'India Aims To Project Power Across Asia', *Defense News*, November 10, 2003, p. 10.
[44] Ibid.

- Increase naval interaction with South Africa, other African states, Iran, Oman, the UAE and other Gulf nations.
- Extend infrastructure, logistic and material support to Myanmar to contain Chinese activities there.[45]

Beyond those policies, all the Indian military services are undertaking a major military build-up of conventional weapons, ways of delivering nuclear weapons and defences against nuclear missiles by improving communication and surveillance systems. This ongoing build-up obviously intends to project Indian power and influence, not just to Central Asia, but also throughout Asia and represents what analysts are calling 'strategic assertion'.[46] More recently it has become clear that India is reshaping its procurement and training plans to enhance its capacity for power projection and insertion of forces behind enemy lines.[47] This is clearly a programme that embraces all arms of the Indian armed forces.[48] For example, the Indian Air Force wants to evolve into an expeditionary force with a strategic reach beyond its borders because it believes that in the future it may well have to project power anywhere from the Persian Gulf to the Straits of Malacca and Central Asia and to be ready for an enormous range of potential contingencies.[49]

Since 2002, if not before, India has been projecting its military power and influence into Central Asia. Retired Brigadier General V.K. Nair, a leading strategist, spoke for the entire Indian establishment when he told the US National Defence University in 2001 that,

> India needs to evolve a broad based strategy that would not only ensure the security of its vital interests but also provide policy options

---

[45] Ibid.
[46] Rahul Bedi, 'India—Regional Focus: Power Play' *Jane's Defense Weekly*, July 13, 2005, at www4.janes.com/K2/doc.jsp?t (accessed on July 13, 2005).
[47] Vivek Raghuvanshi, 'India Plans Weapons, Training to Project Power', *DefenseNews.com*, February 20, 2006 (accessed on February 20, 2006).
[48] Donald L. Berlin, 'India in the Indian Ocean', *Naval War College Review* 59 (Spring 2006), pp. 58–89; Raghuvanshi, 'India Aims to Project Power Across Asia', *Defense News*, November 10, 2003, p. 10; Vivek Raghuvanshi, 'India Embraces New War Doctrine', *Defense News*, November 8, 2004, p. 14; 'India's Strategic Environment and the Role of Military Power'.
[49] Rajat Pandit, 'IAF may Follow US Air Force', *The Times of India* (Mumbai), October 28, 2005, at www.opensource.gov (accessed on October 28, 2005), *FBIS SOV*, October 28, 2005.

for effectively responding to developing situations in the area. India's geostrategic location dictates that the primary focus of its security policies must be its relationship with the neighboring countries and the countries that form part of its 'extended security horizon' which in one official publication is defined as 'regions with economic, social, cultural and environmental linkages [that] result in overlapping security interests'.[50]

Central Asia is explicitly and widely cited as part of this 'horizon' and this interpretation of that term was publicly conveyed to Central Asian audiences at a Tashkent conference in 2003 by Foreign Minister Yashwant Sinha.[51] And the strategic goals of projecting economic and military influence and power abroad are clearly tied to this determination to cut a major figure in Asian politics.

India's policies also reflect the rising importance of military factors and instruments in its overall national security policy. While its conventional power projection capabilities have always been primarily intended for use against Pakistan, they are fungible and usable wherever applicable—e.g., against terrorist activities on the high seas or for aerial reconnaissance over Central Asia or Pakistan's interior through Airborne Warning and Control System (AWACS) or satellite technology. These examples show what capabilities India is developing, improving or seeking to acquire from its suppliers.[52] Simultaneously, India also projects military power into Central Asia in other forms.

First, responding to Pakistan's closing of its air space, India negotiated base rights with Tajikistan in 2002. While little is known about this air base, it is reportedly at an operational level and could therefore be used for operations against either

---

[50] Brigadier Vijai K. Nair VSM PhD, 'Challenges for the Years Ahead: An Indian Perspective', Paper Presented to the Annual National Defense University Asian–Pacific Symposium, Honolulu, March, 2001, at www.ndu.edu/inss/symposia/pacific2001/nairpaper.htm. (accessed on October 29, 2002).
[51] Bagila Bukharbayeva, 'India seeks Increased Engagement in Central Asia', *Associated Press*, November 6, 2003.
[52] Stephen Blank, 'Central Asia, South Asia, and Asian Security', *Eurasian Studies* II:3 (June 1995), pp. 19–22; John W. Garver, 'The Future of the Sino-Pakistani *Entente Cordiale*', in Michael R. Chambers, ed, *South Asia 2020: Future Strategic Balances and Alliances* (Carlisle, PA: Strategic Studies Institute, 2002), pp. 397–401, 429–436.

Central Asian insurgents in support of a friendly government or Pakistan.[53] Today this base at Ayni is also collocated with a Russian air base at Farkhor, Tajikistan.[54] However, this base may not be India's last one or remain small. Indeed, it could become the spearhead of a deepening Indian involvement in Central Asian defence. Thus, the ties with Tajikistan led in 2003 to joint Tajik-Indian military exercises involving the air, airborne and ground forces of both sides.[55] Tajikistan has since then appealed to India to deepen existing military ties and provide 'military–technical cooperation', i.e., arms sales, since its forces lack modern, effective weapons and equipment.[56]

It was clear by 2003 that India was emerging as a major military player in the area. As one Indian analysis oberved then,

> Joint military exercises have been held with both Tajikistan and Uzbekistan and, in November 2003, Indian Defence Minister George Fernandes announced plans to enhance anti-terrorism cooperation with both countries. Kazakhstan's leader, Nursultan Nazarbayev, has proposed that India go a step further and join Central Asia's regional security alliance, the Shanghai Cooperation Organisation—a suggestion welcomed by Russia, but opposed by China. Also in the works: six Ilyushin mid-air refueler planes on order from Uzbekistan

---

[53] Rahul Bedi, 'Indian Base in Tajikistan "Quietly Operational"', *Irish Times*, August 22, 2002; Shaikh Azizur Rahman, 'India Strikes for Oil and Gas with Military Base in Tajikistan', *Washington Times*, September 2, 2002; John Hassell, 'An Update on the Great Game: Power Plays in the Graveyard of Empire', *San Diego Union-Tribune*, September 1, 2002, p. G-5; 'India has Acknowledged Establishing an Air Base in Tajikistan', *Aviation Week & Space Technology*, August 26, 2002, p. 19; 'High-Level Tajikistan Defence Delegation Meets Fernandes', *The Press Trust of India*, December 2, 2002; Stephen Blank, 'India's Rising Profile in Central Asia', *Comparative Strategy* XXII:3 (2003) pp. 150–51; Kumar Amitav Chaliha, 'India Moves on Central Asia', *Asia Times Online*, October 16, 2003, at www.atimes.com (accessed on October 16, 2003); 'India Planning to Join Shanghai Cooperative Organization', *ITAR-TASS News Agency*, Moscow, October 29, 2002.
[54] 'Russia, India may Jointly Use Tajik Military Airfield—Russian Defense Minister', *ITAR-TASS*, December 5, 2005; 'India Rebuilding Air Base in Tajikistan: Diplomat', *www.DefnseNews.com*, April 25, 2006, taken from Agence France-Presse.
[55] Dushanbe, *Tajik Television First Channel* (in Russian), August 5, 2003, *FBIS SOV*, August 5, 2003; Elizabeth Wishnick, 'India Walks Central Asian Tightrope', at www.isn.ethz.ch.ch/news/sw details.cfm?ID=7245, (accessed on August 28, 2006).
[56] Roger N. McDermott, 'Tajikistan Diversifies Its Security Assistance', *Eurasia Daily Monitor*, September 22, 2004.

and a pledge of financial support for a navy to defend Kazakhstan's Caspian Sea oil routes.[57]

Since then India has also built a burgeoning security relationship with Uzbekistan based on a common antipathy to Islamic terrorism. Indian scholars believe these two states to be natural allies who confront the same threats: terrorism, insurgency, separatism, drugs, etc. Uzbekistan has steadily widened its security discussions with India to include intelligence sharing, military and paramilitary training and joint working groups against terrorism as India has done with Washington and Moscow.[58] And more recently, in spite of the Andijan massacre, Uzbek soldiers have undergone counterterrorism training in India.[59]

India's increased ability and willingness to sell weapons to Central Asian countries and to buy from them earlier Soviet models parallel Pakistan's capability as both are entering the international arms market to find new export markets and keep defence plants open.[60] Indian spokesmen frankly admit the drive to find export markets among former 'pariah' states like Israel and South Africa to achieve economies of scale for their domestic defence industry. They hope that capturing those markets will then reduce Indian dependence upon foreign suppliers, especially as India can increasingly compel them to transfer technology and know-how as part of their sales.[61] Probably India will provide training and assistance to Central Asian militaries as do Turkey, Russia, China and the US, and also find in them willing buyers of its weapons, especially those made jointly with Russia.

But India has even broader objectives. Because it competes with China in the small arms market and also seeks to penetrate

---

[57] Ibrahim Alibekov, 'India Set to Expand Presence in Central Asia', *Eurasia Insight*, December 3, 2003.
[58] McDermott, 'Tajikistan Diversifies Its Security Assistance'.
[59] Tashkent, *Uzreport.com*, January 3, 2006, *FBIS SOV*, January 3, 2006.
[60] *Jane's Intelligence Digest*, December 13, 2002, at www4.janes.com/search97cgi/s97_cgi (accessed on December 13, 2002); Douglas Frantz, 'Around the World, Hints of Afghanistans to Come', *New York Times*, May 26, 2002.
[61] Vivek Raghuvanshi, 'India Eyes Markets Abroad', *Defense News*, May 20–26, 2002, p. 36; Vivek Raghuvanshi, 'Indian Munitions Plants Fear Sales Losses, Seek Exports', *Defense News*, January 14–20, 2002, p. 10; Nadeem Iqbal, 'Pakistan's Arms Industry Aims High', *Asia Times Online*, October 4, 2002 (aceessed on October 4, 2002); Anil Sharma, 'Indian Drive to Increase Arms Exports', *Asia Times Online*, November 6, 2002 (accessed on November 6, 2002).

into Southeast Asia and Central Asia, where China seeks to expand its influence, India must compete with China on price and quality in the same categories of weapons. India sells small arms, ammunition, patrol ships, light field guns, trucks, trucks and aircraft parts to Southeast Asia at reduced price and with better equipment.[62] Furthermore,

> Over the next decade, India intends to produce weapons systems China cannot, including an indigenously designed air defence ship—basically a small aircraft carrier. Through subsidies, loans and higher technology, New Delhi hopes to supplant China as a major regional arms supplier. It also can take advantage of underlying concerns about China within Southeast Asia, touting Indian weapons systems as free from the risks of being swallowed by an aggressive China in the future.[63]

All this also applies to Central Asia which is already the target of an Indian arms sales offensive. India has sold Kazakstan and Tajikistan Ilyushin-76 transports and helicopters respectively.[64] And to ensure that it has a capacity for projecting power abroad as intended, India also bought six Il-78 mid-air refuelers from Uzbekistan in 2004.[65]

Here again New Delhi emulates Moscow, Washington, Ankara and Beijing. More importantly it has only begun to display its military instruments of power locally. As long as security threats remain and Pakistan seeks to obstruct India or to use this area as a 'strategic hinterland' against it, India's projection of all forms of military power is likely to grow. Indeed, the threat of terrorism against India and its measures to fight that threat have evidently received sympathetic hearing in Kazakhstan and Kyrgyzstan and have

---

[62] Ibid; 'Defense Industry Globalization: A Compendium of Papers Presented at a Conference on Defense Industry Globalization', Washington, DC, November 16, 2001, Atlantic Council of the United States, 2002; Raghuvanshi, 'India Opens Arms Factories to Foreign Investors', p. 4; 'India Furthers Strategic Goals by Reaching out to Arms Markets', *stratfor.com*, October 29, 2002, at www.stratfor.com (accessed on October 29, 2002).
[63] Ibid.
[64] Ibid.
[65] Amit Mukherjee, 'IAF to Get 5th IL-78 Refueler Soon', *The Times of India* (Mumbai), internet version, September 29, 2004 (accessed on September 29, 2004), *FBIS SOV*, September 29, 2004; Moscow, *Agentstvo Voyennykh Novostey*, December 23, 2004 (accessed on December 23, 2004), *FBIS SOV*, December 23, 2004.

allowed India to build enduring security and intelligence cooperation with those states.[66] Indian analysts have also called for heightened cooperation with Central Asian governments on issues like border management.[67] Thus India fully intends to play an independent role as a security provider in Central Asia and to offer assistance to local governments even as it cultivates mutually beneficial partnerships with Washington and Moscow and to a lesser degree (given the continuing level of rivalry and suspicion, in spite of partnership) with Beijing.

India's Energy Policies in Central Asia

Although India's overriding concerns in this region may be security concerns, those concerns have a pronounced instrumental quality as stability and security are essential for India to obtain the energy it needs. And apart from the possibilities of energy trade with Central Asia,

> India also sees Central Asia as an enormous consumer market for Indian products as well as its human capital and manpower. Indian commodities have already established a foothold in the various Central Asian markets such as tea, pharmaceuticals and chemicals, but India wants to increase the number and kinds of products it exports to Central Asia. India also hopes to secure important contracts for infrastructure projects such as ports, airports, roads and railways and India sees important opportunities in providing banking and insurance services, information technology and other such services. Indian infrastructure projects will also enable Indian goods to move from India through Central Asia to Russia and even to Europe via the 'North–South Transport Corridor built by Russia, Iran and India'.[68]

For example, illustrating the centrality of economic motives in India's membership in the SCO, Foreign Minister Singh's address of October 2005 at the SCO Council Heads of Government meeting

---

[66] Juli A. MacDonald, 'Rethinking India and Pakistan's Regional Intent', *NBR Analysis*, XIV:4 (November 2003), p. 20.
[67] P. Stobdan, 'Central Asia and India's Security', *Strategic Analysis*, January–March 2004, p. 79.
[68] C. Christine Fair, 'Indo-Iranian Ties: Thicker Than Oil', Paper written for the Non-proliferation Education Policy Center, 2006, pp. 8–9.

focussed on opening up trade and transportation routes to India from Central Asia.[69] This particular approach is closely tied to a coordinated effort launched in 2003 to increase India's overall trade with Central Asian and CIS countries through exchanges of business and governmental elites, assistance to exporters and chambers of commerce, trade fairs in both sets of states and help in promoting various market promotional activities. There is no doubt that these programmes have led to a substantial increase in trade between India and the Central Asian states and this growth suggests that there are still enormous vistas for further expansion of this trade.[70]

One should not think that access to energy means only oil and gas. As noted above the recent US initiative to tie India to Central Asia through the provision and transmission of electricity is no less important to both India and the Central Asian and South Asian states along the route of projected power lines. Nor should we think that the issue of access to all forms of energy—oil, gas, electricity and nuclear power—has been solved by the new agreement with the US which will increase India's capacity for obtaining and using nuclear energy peacefully, or that its oil and gas concerns are merely short-term. As a recent study of Iran's relations with its neighbours, including India, observes,

> While India faces energy shortfalls today, its primary concerns is that greater production shortages in the future will prevent it from maintaining strong growth rates. In this context, India does not view the civilian nuclear deal with the US as a replacement for the Iran pipeline project. While this may be the case in the short term, India has a far longer time horizon and it will remain an attractive market for Iranian gas. Furthermore, neither the deal with the US nor the Iran pipeline is by any means finalised. Indeed, in early April [2006] Condoleeza Rice admitted that even if Congress passed the nuclear deal, there were no guarantees that the Iran–India pipeline would not go ahead.[71]

---

[69] New Delhi, Ministry of External Affairs Website, October 28, 2005, at http://meaindia.nic.in/(accessed on October 28, 2005), *FBIS SOV*, October 28, 2005.
[70] Ibrokhim Mavlanov, 'India's Economic Diplomacy in Central Asia', *Sapra India Bulletin*, March 2006, pp. 7–14.
[71] Robert Lowe and Claire Spencer, *Iran, Its Neighbors, and the Regional Crises* (London: Royal Institute of International Affairs, 2006), p. 47.

Similarly, the electricity programme connecting India to the US and Central Asian and South Asian power lines is hardly risk-free to India. At the Sochi meeting of the Eurasian Economic Community—Russia's project for binding Central Asian economies to it—in August 2006, the members confidentially discussed the potentially explosive issue of a hydropower consortium, an issue that is crucial for Central Asia but fraught with complexities and risks for local governments. As a recent commentary on that summit observes, this discussion revolved around a Russian proposal for a hydropower consortium, financed by the Eurasian Bank of Russia and Kazakhstan, that could be the first step toward creating 'a technologically and economically powerful system for addressing the interconnected problems of water distribution and the development of hydropower infrastructure for the region'.[72]

Moscow's proposal clearly is a riposte to the US programme for connecting South and Central Asian power lines in which Washington counts on support from New Delhi and Kabul as key players in the area and which would help get Washington back in the game in Central Asia. Certainly, this programme is based on India's desire for secure access to energy from Central Asia and its immense desire to play a major role there. For example, the recent visit of Tajikistan's President Ermomali Rakhmonov to India included a discussion of hydropower initiatives in the agenda.[73] But if the EEC programme goes through, it will undermine the US proposal—which is the intention behind Moscow's proposal—and put considerable stress upon Indian relations with Moscow, Central Asia and Beijing.[74]

Therefore, there are no risk-free options for India here, but a sure maximiser of risk would be a policy that inclines too far toward or against any major provider of energy. Consequently, Indian energy policies must aim, as noted above, not just at a prior stabilisation of the Central Asian region, but also at maintaining India's influence and friendship with all the major players. And under conditions

---

[72] M.K. Bhadrakumar, 'Moscow Making Central Asia Its Own', *Asia Times Online*, August 24, 2006 (accessed on August 24, 2006).
[73] Ibid.
[74] Ibid.

of great-power rivalry in Central Asia and the intensifying crisis around Iranian nuclearisation, this means walking a very stressed tightrope. Nevertheless, India has conducted a wide-ranging and often innovative effort to ensure reliable access to Central Asian and Azeri energy sources and trade. By 2005, India was seeking energy from all the major Central Asian producers and had launched formal initiatives to bring them together with China and states like Uzbekistan in some form of joint collaboration to restrain the Indo-Chinese bidding war for access to new fields all over the world and to discuss the building of a pan-Asian gas grid to end 'the wretched Western dominance'.[75] Such ideas of collaboration with China were the brainchild of then Energy Minister, Mani Shankar Aiyar and they reflected his ambition to tie India into Asian energy networks as a whole, in the form of a new Silk Road, and not just Central Asia.[76]

As part of this programme, India formed working groups on hydrocarbons with Kazakhstan which have since led to agreements by KazMunaiGaz to give India access to lucrative energy blocks on Kazakhstan's energy shore.[77] Aiyar also sought to arrange energy deals with Azerbaijan.[78] Indeed, he contended that the TAP line, supposed to originate in Turkmenistan, could actually begin in Azerbaijan and include Uzbekistan as well, necessitating pipeline construction from the Caspian Sea through Central Asia to India![79] While Aiyar has since been replaced—not necessarily for his Central Asian policies and vision—it is clear that so grandiose

---

[75] Siddarth Srivastava, 'The Foundations of an Asian Oil and Gas Grid', *Asia Times Online*, December 1, 2005, at www.atimes.com (accessed on December 1, 2005); 'India Eyes Alliance With China and Uzbekistan for Oil Assets', *Alexander's Gas & Oil Connection* X:23 (December 8, 2005).

[76] Srivastava, 'Aiyar Calls for Reviving "Silk Route" for Il Supplies to India from Caspian Sea', *Hindustan Times*, June 9, 2005.

[77] Almaty, *Interfax-Kazakhstan I* (in Russian), February 17, 2005, *FBIS SOV*, February 17, 2005; New Delhi, Government of India Press Information Bureau Website, February 19, 2005, at http://pib.nic.in/(accessed on February 19, 2005), *FBIS SOV*, February 19, 2005; 'Astana to Meet Indian Energy Requirements', *SAPRA India Bulletin*, August 2005, p. 26.

[78] Baku, *Turan* (in Russian), June 10, 2005, *FBIS SOV*, June 10, 2005.

[79] 'Uzbekistan, Azerbaijan can join Pipeline Project: India', *The Hindu*, November 28, 2005.

a vision will face enormous obstacles in the path of realisation. Many of these are inherent in the nature of the energy business where multinational pipelines are always a nightmare to negotiate and coordinate, even where relations among all the actors are amicable.

Nevertheless, it is clear that India as of 2007 is firmly ensconced in Central Asian energy agendas. This goes beyond the US-backed plan to include it in the transmission of electricity or its success in dealing with Kazakhstan. Certainly, as Burns' article suggests, the convergence or strategic partnership with Washington continues, not least as regards other 'theatres' in Asia. For, as Burns writes, 'we share an abundance of plitical, economic and military interests with India today'.[80] In April 2006 India signed a memorandum of understanding with Uzbekistan allowing Indian firms to explore for oil and gas in Uzbekistan and all profits will be split on a parity basis.[81] In May India announced that it would join the TAP gas line.[82] And during the summer of 2006 it became clear that plans for Indo-Chinese collaboration and even possible joint bids on pipelines in Kazakhstan and elsewhere had been launched.[83]

While major projects like the TAP line or the Iran–Pakistan–India pipeline have to overcome the obstacles with regard to security, prices and tariffs before they can become a reality, the main point is clear. India is now a full-fledged player in the Central Asian energy sweepstakes and will proceed aggressively with respect to all producers to ensure reliable energy supplies and will therefore become even more enmeshed in the region's security agenda. Its economic growth, domestic security and standing as great power are all implicated in this trend and are inextricable from it.

CONCLUSIONS

India now enjoys an unprecedented window of opportunity, given the good relations it has and is continuing to develop with all the

---

[80] Burns, p. 131.
[81] *Radio Free Europe Radio Liberty Newsline*, April 27, 2006.
[82] 'India to Join TAP Gas Pipeline', *Alexander's Gas & Oil Connection*, XI:11 (June 8, 2006).
[83] 'China, India for Joint Kazakh Oil Bid', *Gulf Times*, June 11, 2006; 'India, China May Jointly Bid for Energy Assets', *The Financial Express*, July 8, 2006.

major players and actors in Central Asia and its new partnership with the US. Its rising capacities and expanding interests also drive it to assume a greater role as security provider and partner in and around Central Asia. These trends also appear to be set for a long time to come. India's quest to realise its great-power ambition could lead it in the future into unforeseen complications, but it is also true that India cannot escape the consequences of its geographical location or enhanced capabilities in an age of globalisation. Central Asia will not let India be aloof from its own regional development, whether it is peaceful or turbulent. And neither can a growing India remain aloof from what has historically been its 'near abroad'. How that interaction will play out in the future cannot be determined given the speed, and multilateral and multilevel character of developments in world politics generally and in this region in particular. But there can be no doubting that India is, and will continue to be, a vigorous player of what again is a new great game.

13

India and East Asia: A Region 'Rediscovered'

MANISH DABHADE

India's 'Look East' policy is now blossoming and showing results on the ground. I consider our participation in the India–ASEAN Summit and East Asia Summit to be essential pillars of this policy, and vital for the *qualitatively enhanced engagement* which India seeks with the region.[1]

Indian engagement of East Asia in the post-Cold War era has, indeed, assumed significant proportions and remains a top foreign policy priority for the Indian leadership. India is now a full dialogue partner of the Association of South East Asian Nations (ASEAN) since 1995, a member of the ASEAN Regional Forum (ARF), the regional security forum since 1996 and a founder member of the East Asian Summit launched in December 2005. India is also a summit partner of ASEAN on par with China, Japan and South Korea since 2002. Over the years, India has also come to have extensive economic and trade linkages with various countries in the region. For instance, trade with ASEAN has galloped to US$ 30 billion in 2007 from a paltry US$ 2.4 billion in 1990. Similarly, India's trade with China has increased from US$ 265 million in 1991 to an all time high of US$ 13.6 billion in 2004. India is also currently negotiating a region-wide ASEAN Free Trade Area (AFTA), expected to be clinched soon. In the security arena, in September 2007, India conducted large scale joint naval exercises off the coast of the Bay of Bengal with the navies of the US, Japan, Australia and Singapore. India, also very recently began joint military counterterrorism exercises with China, termed historic as it is first of its kind after the 1962 Sino-Indian border war.

---

[1] Indian Prime Minister Manmohan Singh, on the eve of his departure to attend the sixth India–ASEAN Summit and the third East Asia Summit held in Singapore on November 21, 2007, Ministry of External Affairs, 2007, emphasis mine.

India has, indeed, emerged from the margins, at the end of the 1980s, to become one of the key pillars and players in East Asia at the beginning of the 21st century. In fact, a leading Indian strategic analyst pointed, as early as 1998, that India's growing links with this region 'seems to be pushing India in the direction of an East Asian Identity'.[2] This ever-increasing multidimensional Indian engagement, since 1991, raises fundamental questions about Indian motivations in the region. What sets of variables/drivers largely explain this profound transformation in Indian thinking and behaviour in East Asia? Is it sheer geographical proximity or domestic economic imperatives in this era of globalisation, or civilisational-historical factors or systemic variables at play in contemporary international politics? I argue that systemic changes induced by the end of the Cold War have resulted in an entirely new set of challenges and opportunities for India that are largely driving its foreign policy in East Asia in recent years.

East Asia today displays a range of trends on issues of geopolitics and geo-economics. Geographically, and for analytical purposes, East Asia is divided into two distinct areas: the Northeast Asia which includes China, Japan and the two Koreas; and the Southeast Asia which contains the ASEAN member states of Brunei, Cambodia, Indonesia, Laos, Malaysia, Myanmar, the Philippines, Singapore, Thailand and Vietnam. The region is a classic current example of geopolitical rivalry being played out by the US, the only 'extra-territorial', 'residential' status-quoist great power exercising tremendous influence in East Asia, and China, the rising great power in East Asia, increasingly expanding and asserting its economic, political and strategic power and influence. In addition, the responses (balancing and/or bandwagoning) of the secondary states like Japan and South Korea, and Indonesia, the Philippines, Singapore and Malaysia to the rise of China are also of considerable interest to analysts worldwide.[3] The region also hosts many economic powerhouses, the so-called Asian tiger economies relying

---

[2] Kanti Bajpai, 'Enhancing Ties between India and Southeast Asia: An Indian View', in Satu P. Limaye and Ahmed Mukarram, eds, *India, Southeast Asia and the United States: New Opportunities and Prospects for Cooperation* (Singapore: Institute of Southeast Asian Studies,1998), p. 111.

[3] Robert Ross, 'Balance of Power Politics and the Rise of China: Accommodation and Balancing in East Asia', *Security Studies* 15:3 (July–September 2006), p. 357.

heavily on foreign trade and investments. In 1992 itself, the combined economies of East Asia (Japan, China, South Korea, Taiwan, Hong Kong and Singapore, along with the states of the ASEAN, nearly matched those of either North America or Western Europe, each of the three accounting for about 30 per cent of world GDP.[4] In spite of the 1997–98 Asian financial crisis, the East Asian economies are growing rapidly. In September 2003, Japan ($604.8 billion) and China ($364.7 billion) together accounted for well over 50 per cent of the total global foreign exchange reserves, a sign of the increasing economic clout of the region as a whole.[5]

India, by its sheer location in the Asian subcontinent, has come to share a high geographic proximity with the East Asian region. Most significantly, India shares a 4,056 km long boundary with China, its northern neighbour. It also shares an over 1,600 km long eastern land boundary with Myanmar, maritime boundaries with Myanmar, Thailand and Indonesia, and is separated from Indonesia by just about 90 miles.

Though the Indian engagement with East Asia in the post-Cold War era has been the focus of a number of studies, there has been a lacuna on two counts: first, most studies have narrowly dealt with the Indian policies in the Southeast region either bilaterally or multilaterally or vis-à-vis China, Japan and South Korea, and not the entire East Asian region in a holistic manner; and, second, scholars have differed on the motivations driving India's policies in East Asia. Many scholars have looked at the Indian engagement of the region from an economic perspective—as a function of India's economic diplomacy pursued in the wake of the economic reforms initiated in 1991. Thus, New Delhi's Look East policy was 'largely dictated by economic considerations'.[6] According to one former Indian diplomat, 'India–South East Asia relations today are primarily driven by internal factors, rather than external ... it is primarily the economic impulse arising internally which will

---

[4] Peter Katzenstein, 'Introduction: Asian Regionalism in Comparative Perspective', in Peter J. Katzenstein and Takashi Shiraishi, eds, *Network Power: Japan and Asia* (Ithaca and London: Cornell University Press, 1997), p. 12.
[5] 'Sustainable Development in a Dynamic World', *World Development Report* (Washington, DC: World Bank, 2003), pp. 234–35.
[6] Arabinda Acharya, 'India and Southeast Asia in the Age of Terror: Building Partnerships for Peace', *Contemporary Southeast Asia* 28:2 (August 2006), p. 304.

impact on the relationship'.[7] Adding the historical and cultural drivers, the then External Affairs Minister Yashwant Sinha, in his 2003 speech at Harvard University, surmised that,

> In the past, India's engagement with much of Asia, including South East and East Asia, was built on an idealistic conception of Asian brotherhood, based on shared experiences of colonialism and of cultural ties. The rhythm of the region today is determined, however, as much by trade, investment and production as by history and culture. This is what motivates our decades old 'Look East' policy.[8]

Even the present Indian Prime Minister Manmohan Singh, reiterating India's Look East policy, said: 'The "Look East" policy is more than a slogan, or a foreign policy orientation. It has a strong economic rationale and commercial content.'[9] Similarly, an observer of India's engagement in East Asia has stated that 'India's Look East policy in recent years has assumed a greater economic dimension than a parallel political, strategic or even cultural one'.[10] Some scholars have indicated that 'geographic proximity' was driving India's relations with East Asia. India, sharing its land boundaries with China and Myanmar and maritime boundaries with some ASEAN states has heavily impinged on India's thinking on relations with East Asia. For others, it is strong civilisational bonds, cultural affinities and feelings of pan-Asianism shared by India and East Asia driving India's policies. Some scholars have indicated that the East Asian norm of 'cooperative security' has moulded India's behaviour in East Asia. The approach to cooperative security delineates that security management of all issues should be handled through consensual and cooperative means at national, sub-regional or regional levels. It reflects a

---

[7] Sudhir Devare, *India and Southeast Asia: Towards Security Convergence* (Singapore: Institute of Southeast Asian Studies, 2006), p. 210.
[8] Dong Zhang, 'India Looks East: Strategies and Impacts', AUSAID Working Paper (September 2006), pp.1–37.
[9] Manmohan Singh, Speech Delivered at the Third India–ASEAN Business Summit, New Delhi, October 21, 2004, quoted in Sudhir Devare, *India and Southeast Asia: Towards Security Convergence*, p. 28.
[10] Baladas Ghoshal, 'Some New Thoughts on India's Look East Policy', *Institute of Peace and Conflict Studies*, Issue Brief No.54, October 2007, p.1.

de-emphasis in three key areas: ideology; military spending arising from ideological, political or military threats; and superpower rivalry.[11] However, an increasing number of scholars are now focussing on the systemic factors driving India's policies in East Asia, necessitated by the recent burgeoning of strategic relations between India and the region as a whole. This chapter attempts to further elaborate, identify and analyse the systemic drivers motivating India's foreign policy in East Asia.

INDIA'S 'REDISCOVERY' OF EAST ASIA: SYSTEMIC DRIVERS

The Indian 'rediscovery' of East Asia in the post-Cold War era is a result of two sets of significant systemic factors: first, India's own long-held ambitions to emerge as a great power and, second and most important, the structural changes that occurred in international politics with the end of the Cold War, giving India the much needed multidimensional space to re-engage East Asia.

India, since its Independence in 1947, has always believed in its 'manifest destiny' as a great power in Asia and the world at large. India's centuries-old civilisational existence, its geography, and its vast human and material resources, according to its elites, place it in a unique position to play this role. This idea of India has heavily impinged on fashioning India's approach to the external world in the post-Second World War era, till this date. Indian statesmen and leaders, starting from Jawaharlal Nehru to the current Prime Minister Manmohan Singh, have repeatedly pronounced India as trying to seek a rightful place in the comity of nations and have seen India at the core of the emerging international order. Writing on India's emerging central position in the evolving international relations, India's first Prime Minister Jawaharlal Nehru wrote as early as 1944, in his book *The Discovery of India* (1946),

> The Pacific is likely to take the place of the Atlantic in the future as the nerve centre of the world. Though not directly a Pacific state, India will inevitably exercise an important influence there. India will also develop as the centre of economic and political activity in the Indian Ocean area,

---
[11] K. S. Nathan, ed, *India and ASEAN: The Growing Partnership for the 21st Century*, (Kuala Lumpur: Institute of Diplomacy and Foreign Relations, 2000), pp. 2–3.

in Southeast Asia, right up to the Middle East. Her position gives an economic and strategic importance in a part of the world which is going to develop in the future.[12]

This vision for India in international politics was reinforced by recalling the powerful and pivotal role British India had played in the regions surrounding it. Here, Lord Curzon, former Viceroy of India and British Foreign Secretary, remains a source of strategic inspiration for those clamouring for increasing India's power and influence in Asia and beyond. Writing at the peak of the British imperial presence in the subcontinent, Curzon emphasised India's uniquely core status in Asia and the world at large. In his 1909 essay 'The Place of India in the Empire', Curzon laid out the essence of his understanding of India's pivotal role:

> It is obvious, indeed, that the master of India, must, under modern conditions, be the greatest power in the Asiatic Continent, and therefore, it may be added, in the world. The central position of India, its magnificent resources, its teeming multitude of men, its great trading harbours, its reserve of military strength, supplying an army always in a high state of efficiency and capable of being hurled at a moment's notice upon any point either of Asia or Africa—all these are assets of precious value. On the west, India must exercise a predominant influence over the destinies of Persia and Afghanistan; on the north, it can veto any rival in Tibet; on the north-east and east it can exert great pressure upon China, and it is one of the guardians of the autonomous existence of Siam. On the high seas it commands the routes to Australia and to the China Seas.[13]

India, after Independence, strove to achieve the vision envisaged but singularly failed to do so by the dominant Cold War international system, India's non-alignment and, later, close ties with the USSR, its preoccupations with China and Pakistan and autarchic economic policies pursued till the end of the 1980s.[14]

It was, however, the end of the Cold War in 1990–91 that really brought East Asia back to the forefront of India's foreign

---

[12] Quoted in Bajpai, 'Enhancing Ties between India and Southeast Asia: An Indian View', p. 112.
[13] C. Raja Mohan, *Crossing the Rubicon: The Shaping of India's New Foreign Policy* (New Delhi: Viking, 2003), pp. 204–05.
[14] Ibid., pp. 205–06.

policy horizons. The disintegration of the USSR radically transformed the structure of the then prevailing international system and brought to the fore new challenges and opportunities for countries like India. India was forced to reorient its approach towards international affairs in general and East Asia in particular. Analysing India's new focus on East Asia, former Indian Prime Minister A. B. Vajpayee was right when he stated that 'the Cold War moulds have been broken and this has enabled us to strengthen our links without ideological barrier'.[15]

The most significant outcome of the structural change that occurred with the end of the Cold war, from the Indian point of view, has been the rise of China. China's rapid economic modernisation since the late 1970s, followed by ongoing military modernisation, has seen its emergence as a major power in Asia, with some serious political, security, diplomatic and economic implications for India. India's non-alignment, which had achieved for itself a leadership role in Asia, also lost its relevance in the post-Cold War era. The Non-Aligned Movement (NAM) struggled and continues to struggle in finding a role for itself in the changed international environs. India, thus, lost a very significant tool to pursue its interests in international affairs.

India's own ambitions to play a key role in international affairs and the structural changes brought about in the international system by the end of the Cold War largely influenced India's initiation of re-engagement with East Asia. Now that the Cold War was over and India was free from the constraints imposed therein, India 'rediscovered' East Asia by pursuing a new approach towards the region. Thus, the Indian foreign policy establishment 'decided to place greater emphasis on domestic economic development, the augmentation of India's already substantial military capabilities, and the pursuit of greater power status within the international system'.[16]

In the light of the above discussion on identifying the systemic drivers motivating India's foreign policy in East Asia, the following section analyses the policies adopted vis-à-vis East Asia that reflect these systemic variables.

---

[15] Faizal Yahya, 'India and Southeast Asia: Revisited', *Contemporary Southeast Asia* 25:1 (April 2003), pp. 79–80.
[16] Sumit Ganguly, 'India's Foreign Policy Grows Up', *World Policy Journal* XX:4 (Winter 2003/04), at www.worldpolicy.org/journal/articles/wpj03-4/ganguly.html (accessed on October 30, 2007).

India's Foreign Policy in East Asia: Quest for Power and Influence

With the weakening of the structural constraints after the end of the Cold War, India focussed its energies on re-engaging East Asia by pursuing a new foreign policy. This new foreign policy was aimed at establishing India a major power in the region. Thus, Indian policy-makers, in the post-Cold War era, 'decided to place greater emphasis on domestic economic development, the augmentation of India's already substantial military capabilities, and *the pursuit of greater power status within the international system*'.[17] In fact, with the dampening of the US–USSR competition in the late 1980s, India had already begun to re-engage the region. The then Indian Prime Minister Rajiv Gandhi's visits to Myanmar and Indonesia point to the changes already taking place in India's thinking on the region.[18] The most significant policy change, however, was his visit to China in 1988, which began a rapprochement between the two after the 1962 war.

India's new foreign policy toward East Asia, that displayed the systemic implications of the end of the Cold War, involved the following five core components: 'congage' China;[19] robust political engagement, maximal economic integration and interdependence, strong security linkages, and active promotion and participation in regional and multilateral initiatives.

'Congage' China

The rise of China in Asia in the 1990s, and its security, political, economic and diplomatic implications, have emerged as the main pivot around which India has formulated its foreign policy vis-à-vis the East Asian region, and, thus, they call for detailed explication. However, since India's ties with China have been dealt with elsewhere in this volume, I will just point out that India has responded to an increase in China's power and influence in East Asia by resorting to a policy that involves a simultaneous *covert* containment and *overt* engagement of China.

---

[17] Ibid., emphasis mine.
[18] Devare, *India and Southeast Asia: Towards Security Convergence*, p.1.
[19] The term 'congage' is borrowed from the work of Mohan Malik.

Indian political and diplomatic energies, in all the contacts mentioned above, have been concentrated on resolving the border dispute with China and seeking a Chinese understanding of Indian sensitivities in its interactions in South Asia—principally, in China's relationship with Pakistan. But, as the border issue remains unresolved till date, coupled with the dramatic expansion of China's power and influence in South Asia and East Asia, and India's own ambitions to emerge as a great power, India has also adopted a policy of balancing China. India has resorted to two common mechanisms for doing so: internal balancing and external balancing. Internal balancing typically involves enhancing one's own strategic capabilities to counter the perceived threats. External balancing involves building alliances and relationships aimed at countering the perceived threats. Herein, India has sought to cultivate strong relationships with China's regional rivals in East Asia, including, most significantly, the US, Japan and Vietnam.

Robust Political Engagement

As part of its strategy to emerge as a key player in East Asia, India has sought to build and strengthen its political relationship with key states in the region. This was deemed important to understand and address each other's concerns and policies, as the lack of contacts and exchanges amongst some states had led to a series of misperceptions and lack of sensitivity towards their varied concerns during the Cold War. Accordingly, Indian political leadership, starting from the highest levels, has regularly engaged the leadership of various states in the region by visiting respective state capitals and hosting them in India on various occasions. India has also interacted with such states on the sidelines of various multilateral fora as well. Since 1991, the intensity and frequency of these exchanges at the political levels have increased leading to a much better appreciation of each other.

India's relations with Japan, after the acrimony of the 1998 nuclear tests, also entered a new phase of high political cooperation after Japanese Prime Minister Mori's visit to India in August 2000.[20] It resulted in establishing a 'Global Partnership Agreement in the

---

[20] S. Jaishankar, 'India–Japan Relations after Pokhran II', *Seminar*, Special Issue no. 427, 2000, at www.seminar.com (accessed on October 30, 2007).

21st Century' between the two. This process of increased political interaction got further strengthened with a state visit, after the gap of nearly a decade, by the Indian Prime Minister Vajpayee to Japan in December 2001, followed by his counterpart Koizumi's visit to India in April 2005. During Prime Minister Manmohan Singh's visit to Japan in mid-December 2006, India sought Japan's cooperation in removing Nuclear Suppliers Group (NSG) restrictions on nuclear cooperation. Mr Singh also addressed the Diet, a sign of close political relationship. Similarly, India has sought close political links with several key states in the region, including South Korea, Thailand, Singapore, Vietnam, Philippines and Indonesia.

To prove its credentials as a strong stakeholder and supporter of regionalism, and peace and security in East Asia, and to earn political trust and confidence, India signed the Treaty of Amity and Cooperation at the ASEAN–India Bali Summit in October 2003. India also signed the ASEAN–India Partnership of Peace, Progress and Shared Prosperity at the third ASEAN–India Summit held in Vientiane in November 2004.[21]

Maximal Economic Integration and Interdependence

The economic reforms programme initiated in 1991, which led to gradual economic integration with external economies, was seen by India's policy-makers as a new golden opportunity and a primary vehicle to re-engage the world in the post-Cold War era. Growing trade and interdependence came to be seen as part of India's grand strategy to seek power and influence in such states. India's post-1991 economic diplomacy was to be the launching pad to reach out to countries and regions wherein India had lost out due to its insular economy. India initiated the 'look east' policy in 1991, aimed at expanding its economic ties with East Asia.

Beginning with a paltry trade of US$ 2.4 billion in 1990, India's trade with ASEAN grew to a high of US$ 30 billion in 2007. Encouraged by this overall trend, India and ASEAN agreed, in their December 2007 Summit, to set an ambitious, yet attainable, target of US$ 50 billion by 2010. In 2003, at the Bali summit, India signed a

---
[21] Devare, *India and Southeast Asia: Towards Security Convergence*, p. 214.

Framework Agreement on Comprehensive Economic Cooperation. India is also currently negotiating a regional free trade area with ASEAN, to be finalised by 2008.

India also opened its economy to its rival China, leading to its emergence as India's second-largest trading partner by 2006. The total bilateral trade between the two has galloped from US$ 265 million in 1991 to an all-time high of US$ 13.6 billion in 2004, with both sides aiming at about US$ 25–30 billion in the next five years.[22] Similarly, India has sought to galvanise its economic ties with other countries in the region. A recent example of that was Manmohan Singh's visit to Japan in 2006 with economic relations as the centrepiece of the visit. In his address to the Diet, he said: 'Economic ties must be the bedrock of our relationship and a strong push is required in this area. Our trade and investment ties are well below potential.'[23] At the conclusion of the Summit, India announced the launching of negotiations towards a Comprehensive Economic Partnership between the two countries. India has also signed a similar Comprehensive Economic Cooperation Agreement (CECA) agreement with Singapore in June 2005, and recently announced the operationalisation of the Free Trade Agreement (FTA) with Singapore. Similarly, India remains involved in negotiating a FTA with Thailand.

These rapidly growing economic linkages with various countries in East Asia are viewed by Indian analysts as making these countries a stakeholder in India's economic prosperity, and providing India a key mechanism for exercising political, diplomatic and strategic influence.

Strong Security Linkages

Creating strong defence linkages with significant states in the region constituted another important part of India's grand strategy in the region. India's desire to seek strong defence linkages were drastically constrained as India was on the other side of the Iron Curtain, in the Soviet camp. With the Cold War coming to an end,

---

[22] 'India–China Bilateral Trade Touches $13.6 Billion', *Press Trust of India*, March 5, 2005.
[23] Manmohan Singh, 'PM's Address to the Joint Session of the Diet', December 14, 2006, at http://pmindia.nic.in/visits/contentasp?id=142 (accessed on December 30, 2007).

India renewed its efforts at cultivating defence ties to enhance its power and influence in East Asia and constantly looked for opportunities to do so.

In the 1990s, India undertook a number of confidence building measures (CBMs) to allay the Cold War fears of certain Southeast Asian states regarding India's growing naval capabilities in the Indian Ocean region. Besides periodic naval exercises and the bi-annual get-together of regional navies in the Bay of Bengal, called the Milan, at Port Blair in the Andamans, India has entered into bilateral defence cooperation agreements with Malaysia, Vietnam, Singapore, Laos and Indonesia. With ever increasing political an economic contacts, India's incremental extension and projection of its military capabilities were found to be less objectionable by the Southeast Asian states.[24] India has also been actively involved in assisting the armed forces of Myanmar and Thailand. For instance, Singapore has not only made use of India's missile testing range to test its guns and missiles, but also used Indian facilities to train its naval personnel—the first ever instance of India providing such a facility to a foreign country. Similarly, Thai pilots are being trained in India to operate the aircraft carrier, and the Myanmarese get anti-insurgency training. India and Indonesia frequently conduct joint patrolling along their maritime boundary close to the critical straits of Southeast Asia, ensuring security of sea lanes of communication. India's naval diplomacy in the region is aimed at furthering two core objectives: first, to balance China's influence in EA an second, to familiarise the Indian navy with a potential theatre of operations—the South China Sea—that would probably be important in any contingency involving conflict with China. India's naval presence in the region also is likely to be intended to stymie the apparent flow of arms across the Bay of Bengal to insurgents in India's northeast and to the Tamil Tigers in Sri Lanka. Finally, the deployment would also demonstrate the navy's ability to operate far from home.

In its attempt to further consolidate defence ties after 9/11, India signed a Joint Declaration with ASEAN in October 2003 at the Bali Summit for Cooperation to Combat International Terrorism.

---

[24] Prasun K. Sengupta, 'Globalization of Security and its Regional Implications', *Asian Defence Yearbook, Asian Defence Journal* (Kuala Lumpur), 2001, p. 8; and 'India's ASEAN Strategy', *Jane's Intelligence Digest*, October 17, 2003, at www.janes.com/subscribe.jic/doc (accessed on October 30, 2007).

The Declaration clearly 'rejects any attempt to associate terrorism with any religion, race or nationality' and regards 'acts of terrorism in all its forms and manifestations committed wherever, whenever and by whomsoever'.[25] Further, India and the Philippines agreed on an Extradition Treaty in March 2004.[26]

India also signed a Treaty on Mutual Legal Assistance in Criminal Matters with Thailand in 2004. During Singapore Prime Minister Lee Asein Loong's visit to India in June 2005, the Treaty on Mutual Legal Assistance was signed. India is simultaneously enlarging this policy of defence cooperation with the countries of Northeast Asia as well. India and Japan have started an Annual Comprehensive Security Dialogue. Interaction between the navies has gone up significantly. In addition to the regular visits by the military chiefs and frequent port calls by the naval ships, the coastguards of the two countries have conducted five bilateral anti-piracy and sea lane safety exercises so far. Significantly, for the first time, visits by the defence ministers have begun to take place since 2000. During Koizumi's visit to India in 2005, a Joint Statement entitled 'India–Japan Partnership in a New Asian Era: Strategic Orientation of the India–Japan Global Partnership' was supplemented by an 'Eight-fold Initiative for Strengthening India–Japan Global Partnership'. Enhanced security dialogue and cooperation, and cooperation, in responding to global challenges and opportunities were included in these eight initiatives.

India has also injected defence linkages in its relations with China. Besides the exchange of visits by military personnel, starting at the highest levels, holding of a bilateral naval exercise between India and China in 2004, though militarily insignificant, was a historic moment. India has also established a security dialogue with China starting in 2000. As pointed earlier, India and China began their first ever joint military counterterrorism exercises in late December 2007, touted as a historic CBM, since their border war in 1962. Similarly, India has established a strategic dialogue with South Korea.

China's increasing strategic profile in Asia and beyond has also spurred attempts, though informal, non-threatening and low-key,

---

[25] 'ASEAN–India Joint Declaration for Cooperation to Combat International Terrorism, 2003', text available in Devare, *India and Southeast Asia: Towards Security Convergence*, pp. 229–31.

[26] 'India and the Philippines Sign Extradition treaty', *The Hindu*, March 14, 2004.

to create an axis of powerful Asian democracies to counter the highly possible threat of China. Known as 'the Democratic Quad', it comprises the key powers in East Asia, viz., the US, India, Japan and Australia. This recent initiative aims to engage in a strategic dialogue at the highest levels, in a bid to pre-empt China from exercising hegem-ony in Asia.[27] It needs to be pointed here that these democracies had, in fact, come together to create a Core Group to provide immediate disaster relief by their respective militaries after the Tsunami had struck the region in late December 2005.

Active Promotion and Participation in Regional and Multilateral Initiatives

India has actively engaged itself in a number of regional institutions and promoted multilateral initiatives in a bid to maximise its power in East Asia. India became a sectoral dialogue partner of the ASEAN in 1992 and acquired full dialogue partner status in 1995. India joined the ARF in 1996. India also turned into a full summit partner in 2002 and joined the East Asian Summit in 2005.[28]

Indian participation in these for a serves Indian interests in a number of ways. It gives India an opportunity to shape their agendas to its benefit. Also, most significantly, India has looked upon for a like the ARF as a the mechanism to create greater confidence and transparency in security matters in the region and also as a vehicle to strengthen its own credibility.

India has also initiated and actively promoted a number of multilateral initiatives like the BIMSTEC and the Ganga–Mekong Cooperation Group. Such multilateral initiatives under its leadership provide increased avenues to further strengthen its relationship with important states in the region.

INDIA AND THE US IN EAST ASIA: MANAGING CONVERGENCE AND DIVERGENCE

East Asia has come to assume significance for the US grand strategy due to a number of reasons: strategic, economic and political. In fact,

---

[27] Harsh V. Pant, 'The Emerging Balance of Power in the Asia–Pacific', *The RUSI Journal* 152:3 (2007), p. 50.
[28] Vibhanshu Shekhar, 'India–ASEAN Relations: An Overview', *IPCS Special Report* No. 39 (March 2007), pp. 1–6.

according to Adm. Michael McDevitt, a strategist and historian, 'the primary motivation behind US statecraft in all of its manifestations of the past 200 odd years has been to be included in—or perhaps more aptly, not to be excluded from—East Asia. America's policy prescriptions for Asia—in other words, its strategic choices—have revolved around that simple objective'.[29] That logic continues to animate US policy even today in the post-Cold War era. A 2001 study by the RAND Corporation concluded that,

> The United States must begin to formulate a strategy aimed at a pivotal long-term objective: preventing the worsening of the security situation in Asia. Central to this objective is the need to preclude the rise of a regional or continental hegemon. This is important for two main reasons: to prevent the US from being denied economic, political, and military access to an important part of the globe; and to prevent a concentration of resources that could support a global challenge to the United States on the order of that posed by the former Soviet Union.[30]

It is only in the East Asian theatre that the US finds a serious contender, a rising great power in the form of China, possessing the capabilities, actual and potential, to rival US interests and ambitions. China has been using its rapidly increasing economic prowess to expand its power and influence in the region. China is also dramatically modernising its strategic capabilities, for e.g., the Anti-Satellite (ASAT) missile test, to complicate US efforts to defend Taiwan, its renegade province. China's growing profile has also raised anxieties in the whole region, making the states look at the US to guarantee peace and security. US have, thus, forged strong alliances with Japan, South Korea and Taiwan in the northeast of the region, and Thailand, the Philippines, and Singapore in southeastern part of the region. The US has stationed thousands of troops in Japan and South Korea, and deployed significant maritime capabilities in the region to protect its friends and allies. Nuclear proliferation concerns in the region have also come to the fore and assumed a priority with the incremental acquisition of nuclear capabilities by North Korea. After the 9/11 terrorist attacks

---

[29] Paul D. Taylor, ed, *Asia and the Pacific: US Strategic Traditions and Regional Realities* (Newport: Naval War College Press, 2001), p. 101.
[30] Zalmay Khalizad, etal, *The United States and Asia: Toward a New US Strategy and Force Posture* (Santa Monica, California: RAND, 2001), p. 43.

on the US soil, Southeast Asia has also re-emerged as the focus of more US attention. In fact, Southeast Asia has been described as the second front in the global war on terror.[31]

East Asia also assumes significance for the US from an economic point of view. Two-way trade with the economies of East Asia and the Pacific totaled US$ 607 billion in 2003, and accounted for 31 per cent of total US international trade. Four of America's top ten trading partners were in East Asia and the Pacific region—Japan, China, South Korea and Taiwan.[32] This has further increased US' stakes in the region.

Indian perceptions and foreign policy in East Asia since 1991, as discussed earlier, clearly reveal a growing convergence of priorities and policies between the US and India. To begin with, the dramatic rise of Chinese power and influence in East Asia and beyond, in the post-Cold War era, in all aspects—political, economic, military and strategic—constitutes a serious foreign and security policy challenge for both states. Maritime security represents another issue area where the interests of India and US converge. Both India and the US and its allies in East Asia remain critically dependent for energy supplies that flow from West Asia to East Asia via the Indian Ocean. The increasing menace of piracy and Chinese desire to increase its naval presence, exemplified by its acquisition of naval bases in Pakistan and Myanmar, constitute another area of increasing convergence between the two. Finally, the threat of transnational terrorism after 9/11, to both Indian and US interests, represents another significant area where the security interests of the two converge. Being open, democratic and free market economies, both India and the US share a common interest in promoting these values in East Asia.

The rise of China and the global war on terror caused India and the US to forge strong linkages at all levels of interaction between the two. In June 2005, India and the US signed a landmark 'New Framework for Defense Relations', a 10-year agreement that paves the way for increased joint military exercises and aims for more

---

[31] John Gershman, 'Is Southeast Asia the Second Front?', *Foreign Affairs* 79:4 (July/August 2002), pp. 60–74.
[32] Brad Glosserman, '*US Perspectives on East Asian Security*', in N. S. Sisodia and G. V. C. Naidu, eds, *Changing Security Dynamic in Eastern Asia: Focus on Japan* (New Delhi: Institute for Defence Studies and Analyses, 2005), p. 47.

'opportunities for technology transfer, collaboration, co-production, research and development' and expanded collaboration on missile defence.[33] On July 18, 2005, India and the US signed the most significant deal, the so-called nuclear deal, which implicitly recognised India as a nuclear-weapon state, and its security concerns vis-à-vis China. Over a few years, especially after the advent of the Bush Administration since 2001, these intensive, multidimensional bilateral interactions between India and the US have led to complementary, though not always identical, perspectives and strategies to deal with the emerging strategic challenges in East Asia and beyond. Recent events bear testimony to this increasing strategic convergence. India and the US recently conducted joint naval exercises off the coast of Bay of Bengal with the navies of Japan, Australia and Singapore. As pointed out earlier, India and the US have sought to forge the 'Quad', an axis of powerful Asian democracies comprising Japan and Australia as well to counter the future possible threat of a rising China.

This growing convergence between the two states has not been free from differences on crucial issues of concern to both. Despite growing strategic convergence and partnership with the US in Asia, Indian policy-makers strongly desire to retain 'strategic autonomy' to pursue its vital interests throughout its 'extended strategic neighborhood', that is Asia from the Middle East to the Strait of Malacca. India has also been loath to signify its current bonhomie with the US as aiming to form an explicit military alliance against China. India has also differed on strategies to deal with issues of terrorism in East Asia. India, being home to the second-largest Muslim population after Indonesia, does not share the US characterisation of the current war on terror to be against Islamic terrorism. Besides, India strongly believes in responding to terrorist threats in a comprehensive manner and not focussing on military means alone.

Conclusions

In an anarchic, self-help international system, survival remains the primary motivation of state behaviour in the international arena.

---

[33] New Framework for US–India Defence Relationship', June 28, 2005, at http://www.indianembassy.org/pressrelease/2005/June/31.htm (accessed on October 30, 2007).

Therefore, states constantly search for opportunities to ensure their survival by preserving and maximising their relative power and influence. The end of the Cold War provided such an opportunity for states like India to reconfigure their foreign policy priorities and, in the light of the systemic changes, use the newly created space to attempt to maximise their power and influence in the international system.

The disintegration of the USSR, leading to the consequent heralding of the US-led unipolar world, coupled with the rise of China as a major power in East Asia, forced India to 'rediscover' East Asia. India's own great-power ambitions could be pursued with greater vigour as the structural limitations imposed by the bipolar international system had vanished.

India has, accordingly, pursued a more assertive foreign policy in East Asia. It involves a policy of 'congaging' China; robust political relations; maximal economic integration and interdependence; incremental security cooperation; and, finally, proactive regionalism and multilateralism. As India accumulates greater power and influence in East Asia and emerges as a major actor in the region, it will correspondingly desire more space to achieve its strategic objectives. In pursuance of this strategy, India also has sought to engage the US, the sole superpower today, and harmonise its interests—political, security, economic and diplomatic—with it in East Asia. India's consistent and forceful engagement with East Asia in the post-Cold War era is leading to its emergence as a key player in the region, with serious implications for the evolving security dynamics in East Asia.

Afterword

HARSH V. PANT

India seems to have travelled a long distance from 2009, when the first edition of this volume was published, to 2012, when I am writing this Afterword. This has been a tough time for the country underscoring the fragility of its rise over the last decade. In fact, there is an all-pervading sense of gloom as the economy has stalled, politics has stagnated and the social tensions have escalated. Economically, the ruling Congress party has found it difficult to proceed with the second generation of reforms programme. In June 2012 the global credit rating agency, Standard and Poor's (S&P) cautioned that India may become the first 'BRIC' (Brazil, Russia, India and China) country to lose its investment grade rating.[1] It warned that slowing growth and political roadblocks in policy-making could lead to Indian paper being relegated to junk bond status.

Socially, the stench of corruption is now too odious to bear. The old image of India as a nation entrenched in corruption has once again come back haunting. First it was the telecommunications sector and then it was coal — one by one the crony capitalism that has come to pervade the Indian liberalisation story has been revealed for what it is.[2]

Politically, the party in power has lost all the capital it had earned in the 2009 elections. There is no coherence in the government with all departments working as if there are no national imperatives, only departmental interests. Most damagingly, the collapse of the governing authority has been as remarkable as it has been swift. All major institutions of governance have been struggling to retain their legitimacy.

The Indian political leadership has become a subject of ridicule not only in India but increasingly around the world. The *Time* magazine has described the Indian Prime Minister, Manmohan Singh, as an 'underachiever'[3] while the *Washington Post* has labelled

---

[1] Joydeep Mukherji and Takahira Ogawa, 'Will India be the First BRIC Fallen Angel?', Standard and Poor's, June 8, 2012, see http://www.standardandpoors.com/spf/upload/Ratings_US/IndiaFirstBRICFallenAngel080612.pdf (accessed on December 3, 2012).

[2] Vikas Bajaj and Jim Yardley, 'Scandal Poses a Riddle: Will India Ever be Able to Tackle Corruption?', *New York Times*, September 15, 2012.

[3] Krista Mahr, 'A Man in Shadow', *Time*, July 16, 2012.

him as a 'tragic figure'.[4] The Prime Minister and the top leadership of the Congress party, including Sonia and Rahul Gandhi, do not like engaging with the public. Neither do they explain their decisions, or talk to the people of the nation directly, nor do they seem to believe that there is any need to connect with ordinary Indians. The Prime Minister and his government have made no real effort to create and mould public opinion to help in governance and in support of government's policies.

That this should be happening at this juncture in India's economic transition is a real tragedy. The Western world remains mired in an unprecedented economic crisis. The eurozone crisis has made it impossible for most European economies to grow, and this will remain the case for a number of years. The United States (US) is also finding it difficult to get out of the economic morass it has sunk into. As a consequence, the developed world is looking inwards as a vacuum is felt in global leadership. More significantly, China's economic growth — the engine of global economy — has also weakened.

This should have been India's moment to lead the way. But the Indian story seems to be over even before it really took off. The Indian Rupee remains Asia's worst performing currency, there is a growing deficit, investors are refusing to invest in India due to policy uncertainty, and the common man is facing the spectre of an everrising inflation. Domestically, there is a persistent sense of chaos with the government unable to take major policy decisions and having the force of will to implement them. The government's allies and the opposition have sensed this weakness and are making sure that this government, which will be in office till 2014, becomes a lame duck entity. Though some initiatives have been announced to get the growth momentum back, it is not readily evident if the government will be able to do enough to get out the crisis of confidence.

For the outside world, especially for India's friends and allies, this has been a disappointing period. The US, which has invested significantly in a strategic partnership with India, finds the relationship struggling to regain the past glory. India's allies in East and Southeast Asia, who had hoped New Delhi would emerge as

---

[4] Simon Denyer, 'India's "Silent" Prime Minister Becomes a Tragic Figure', *Washington* Post, September 4, 2012.

a critical balancer vis-à-vis China, are looking elsewhere. India's friends in Afghanistan are shifting their loyalties fearing Pakistan's resurgence after the North Atlantic Treaty Organization (NATO) forces withdraw in 2014.

An opinion poll conducted by the Pew Research Center in September 2012 suggested that more and more Indians are pessimistic about their country — especially when it comes to its economic performance.[5] This does not augur well for a nation that wants to emerge as a major power in the global hierarchy.

Yet despite the domestic travails in India, the structural imperative continues to shape the trajectory of Indian foreign policy. As was highlighted in the first edition, the changing international balance of power, the rapidly evolving global nuclear architecture, the worldwide struggle against terrorism, and a search for energy security continue to frame Indian foreign policy choices, as New Delhi struggles with domestic political constraints in meeting its national security objectives.

The United States–China–India Triangle

After trying to create a strategic partnership with China soon after assuming office, the Obama administration has started taking a realistic approach in dealing with the emerging superpower. The US–China ties have been undergoing a transformation of their own as Washington, has become geopolitically active in the Indo-Pacific, trying to assuage the concerns of its partners that it is there to stay in the region.

Despite attempts by the Association of Southeast Asian Nations (ASEAN) member states to turn a non-binding 2002 political declaration into a legally binding 'code of conduct' to discourage aggression, China continues to reject arrangements that would force it to negotiate with a bloc of nations over the disputes, instead preferring one-to-one talks with individual claimants. This makes America central to the strategic calculus of the smaller regional states.

---

[5] 'Deepening Economic Doubts in India', Pew Research Center, Global Attitudes Project, September 10, 2012, available at http://www.pewglobal.org/files/2012/09/Pew-Global-Attitudes-Project-India-Report-FINAL-September-10-2012.pdf (accessed on December 3, 2012).

It is against this backdrop that New Delhi and Washington are recalibrating their bilateral ties. But these are not the best of times for US–India partnership. Troubles are mounting on several fronts. India's economic dynamism, the most potent of factors in transforming the US–India relationship over the last two decades, is under threat primarily because of policy paralysis plaguing New Delhi. Some of the expectations from the New Delhi–Washington entente have clearly been unrealistic, but most of the responsibility for a seeming backsliding in the tone and tenor of this very important relationship lies in the corridors of power in New Delhi. The Obama administration's tightening of restrictions on the entry of highly educated Indian professionals in the information technology sector has created a climate suspicion with some even warning about an impending 'trade war'.

On Iran, New Delhi is making a concerted attempt to reduce its dependence on Tehran, but Washington would like India to do much more. Despite public pronouncements of defiance, India had been cutting down its oil imports from Iran since the year ending on March 31, 2012, witnessing a decrease of more than 20 per cent from the previous year.[6] Washington is also pushing for a revival of the nuclear pact and is now seeking a higher profile for India in Afghanistan.

But it is China that is exercising the diplomatic energies of both Washington and New Delhi as differences mount between China and the US and the region struggles to come to terms with a rising China. Confident of its economic prowess, Beijing views the US as a declining power. The US has started working proactively to challenge that perception and a strong US–India partnership will do a long way in managing power transition in Asia.

With Sino-India friction growing and the probability for conflict remaining high, the challenge to India is formidable. India is increasingly bracketed with China as a rising or emerging power — or even a global superpower — though it has yet to achieve the economic and political profile that China enjoys regionally and globally. India's main security concern today is not the increasingly decrepit state of Pakistan but rather an ever more assertive China, whose ambitions are likely to reshape the contours of the regional

---

[6] Rakesh Sharma and Santanu Choudhury, 'India Cuts Back on Iran Oil Imports', *Wall Street Journal*, May 2, 2012.

and global balances of power with deleterious consequences for Indian interests.

India's ties with China are gradually becoming competitive, with a sentiment gaining ground among Indian policy elites that China is not sensitive to India's core security interests and does not acknowledge its status as a global player.[7] India is rather belatedly gearing up to respond to China's rise with a mix of internal consolidation and external partnerships. The most important element in this matrix is India's emerging strategic partnership with the US. New Delhi has looked to Washington for support as both Sino-India and Sino-US competition has come into sharper relief in recent years. As Sino-India ties pass through a phase of turmoil, Washington will have to play the critical role of a balancer with even greater finesse than before. The US has a key stake in the trajectory of Sino-India ties in view of the changing balance of power in Asia and China's growing assertiveness. As a new balance of power takes shape, India will be an indispensable element in that architecture, even as the US remains a key player in managing the Sino-India dynamic. New Delhi will not be part of an explicit alliance framework with the US against China but instead will look to the former to manage the power transition in Asia and its attendant consequences.

The dichotomy between China and India's global convergence and their growing bilateral divergence has allowed India to collude with China as a power bloc against Western positions at the global-level, even as at the bilateral-level New Delhi is not averse to leveraging its relationship with Washington in order to constrain China. India's burgeoning relationship with the US gives New Delhi some crucial strategic room to manoeuvre. China's rapid global ascent will bring the US and India even closer, but India's traditional desire to retain strategic autonomy will preclude the emergence of any formal structure defining this bilateral relationship. India is beginning to receive attention from Washington as a rising power at par with China. This process is likely to continue with US policy-makers viewing Asia as a single region whose future will to a large extent be shaped by the trajectory of Sino-India ties. The US faces the prospect of an emerging power

---

[7] On recent trends in Sino-India relations, see Harsh V. Pant, *The China Syndrome: Grappling with an Uneasy Relationship* (New Delhi: HarperCollins, 2010).

transition in Asia, and its robust partnership with India will go a long way in stabilising the strategic landscape in the region.

Although it is clearly in the interest of both China and India to stabilise their relationship by seeking out convergent issue areas, a troubled history, coupled with the structural uncertainties engendered by their simultaneous rise, it is propelling the two Asian giants on a trajectory that they might find rather difficult to navigate in the coming years. Pursuing mutually desirable interests does not inevitably produce satisfactory solutions to strategic problems. Sino-India ties have entered turbulent times, and they are likely to remain there for the foreseeable future.

INDIA'S 'MULTIVECTOR' FOREIGN POLICY: RUSSIA AND THE EUROPEAN UNION

The rise of China is also becoming an important factor in the re-shaping of India's ties with Russia in the coming years. There are few examples of a relationship between countries that has been as stable as the one between India and Russia. Despite the momentous changes in the international environment after the end of the Cold War, there remains a continued convergence of interests that makes it advantageous for both India and Russia to maintain close ties. Barring a fleeting hiccup during Boris Yeltsin's term as Russia's president, New Delhi and Moscow have been extraordinarily successful in nurturing a friction-free relationship that harks back to the Soviet era.

India–Russia is a unique bilateral relationship in the Indian foreign policy matrix that refuses to become an insignificant one and was only marginally affected by the unprecedented structural changes ushered in by the end of the Cold War in the early 1990s. Though there was a brief period of neglect in the 1990s, a convergence of regional and global interests soon brought the two together again. Despite striking changes in Indian foreign policy since the end of the Cold War, the country's ties with Russia have remained by and large stable. The Indian Prime Minister has admitted that 'although there has been a sea-change in international situation during the last decade, Russia remains indispensable to the cause of India's foreign policy interests'.[8] The India–Russia

---

[8] Vladimir Isachenkov, 'Russia, India Eye Deal on Nuclear Reactors', *Associated Press*, January 26, 2007.

relationship enjoys consensual support in both the countries and has managed to withstand the test of time. If India and Russia managed to have a strong bilateral partnership during the Cold War years and are coming closer again, it is based on a commonality of interests. India remains determined to preserve and strengthen its special relationship with Russia. Much like the Cold War period, the contemporary state of Indo-Russian ties is also being shaped by a new convergence across a whole range of factors that are fundamental to the security interests of both states.

India's relations with the European Union (EU) have become serious but the economic crisis in the eurozone has made it difficult for the EU to focus on foreign policy. Though India was among the first countries to establish diplomatic relations with the European Economic Community, it was only in 2004 that the EU formalised its ties with India into a 'strategic partnership'. This was a very significant gesture, given the EU has strategic partnerships with only five other countries: the US, Canada, Russia, Japan, and China. Bilateral ties have grown considerably since 2004 and the aim is to have a much stronger and intensive relationship over the entire gamut of exchanges, be they political or multilateral, economic or academic, to name a few.

It is a natural partnership, at least in theory. As the largest open societies in the world, the EU and India share a commitment to participatory democracy, human rights and the rule of law. Both share concerns about China's rising economic power. India is seen as a more trusted partner, and also as a balancing power to Beijing. While China is not fully integrated into the international system, India, a liberal democracy, is considered as almost a fellow traveller.

The partnership works best in the economic sphere. India has been a major beneficiary of the EU's Generalized System of Preferences scheme that provides duty reductions and duty- and quota-free access to products from developing and least-developed countries. The EU is India's largest trading partner and one of its main sources of Foreign Direct Investment (FDI). In coming years India and the EU might explore the possibility of starting joint research projects on climate change.

Yet significant constraints limit these ties from reaching their full potential. For a start, some EU policy-makers still view India as a regional South Asian power or, more damagingly, equate it with Pakistan. This latter tendency pushes Brussels to find a fine balance between New Delhi and Islamabad. For a long time this led the EU to ignore Indian security concerns arising from Islamist extremism and terrorism being used by Pakistan as instruments of state policy against India, even as India was pilloried for its human-rights violations in Kashmir. Unlike Washington, which has for some years now viewed India as a 'major pole' in an emerging multi-polar global order and a balancer in the Asia–Pacific strategic landscape, Brussels has been unable to articulate what role it sees for India in the emerging security architecture. These aspects continue to circumscribe India's ties with the EU though both have begun to recognise the importance of each other in their foreign policy calculus.

INDIA'S SOUTH ASIA CONUNDRUM

For long, the dominant narrative with regards to South Asia has been how the India–Pakistan rivalry constrains Indian foreign policy options in the region. That is now rapidly losing its salience with China's growing dominance of the South Asian landscape. The country's rising profile in South Asia is no news. What is astonishing is the diminishing role of India and the rapidity with which New Delhi is ceding strategic space to Beijing in the subcontinent. China is becoming the largest trade partner of most states in South Asia, including India. It entered the South Asian Association for Regional Cooperation (SAARC) as an observer in 2005, supported by most member states. India could do little about it and so acquiesced. Now, much to India's consternation, Pakistan, Bangladesh and Nepal are supporting China's full membership in the SAARC.

Pakistan's 'all-weather' friendship with China is well-known, but the reach of China in other South Asian states has been extraordinary. Bangladesh and Sri Lanka view India as more interested in creating barriers against their exports than in spurring regional economic integration. India's protectionist tendencies have allowed China to don the mantle of regional economic leader. Instead of India emerging as facilitator of socio-economic development in Sri Lanka, Nepal and Bhutan, it is China's developmental assistance that is having a larger impact.

India's attempts to keep China out of the subcontinent have clearly not worked, and it is time to re-evaluate its South Asia policy.

The country's strategy towards South Asia is premised on encircling India and confining her within the geographical coordinates of the region. This approach of using proxies started with Pakistan and has gradually evolved to include other states in the region, including Bangladesh, Sri Lanka and Nepal. It is entering markets in South Asia more aggressively through both trade and investment, and improving linkages with South Asian states through treaties and bilateral cooperation. Following this up by building a ring of road and port connections in India's neighbourhood and deepening military engagements with states on India's periphery, China has firmly entrenched itself in India's backyard.

This quiet assertion of China has allowed various smaller countries of South Asia to play the country off against India. Most states in the region now use the China card to balance against the predominance of India. Forced to exist between their two giant neighbours, the smaller states have responded with a careful balancing act.

India's structural dominance in South Asia makes it a natural target of resentment among its smaller neighbours. Yet, there is no hope for regional economic cooperation in the absence of Indian leadership. The failure of India in countering China's rise has made it even more unlikely that such cooperation will evolve productively. As the two regional giants compete with each other in the near future, they will be more focused on their relative gains vis-à-vis each other than in the absolute gain that regional cooperation can bestow.

INDIA ENTERS THE 'GREAT GAME' IN CENTRAL ASIA

Major powers have competed for influence in Central Asia since the 19th century and that 'Great Game' seems to be back with a bang. The importance of the Shanghai Cooperation Organization (SCO) that has evolved into a forum for discussion on regional security and economic issues cannot be overstated in this context. It has become even more important post-September 11, 2001, because growing ethnic nationalism and Islamic fundamentalism is a major cause of concern for Russia, China and Central Asian states. In the post-9/11 environment, the SCO serves as a means to keep control of Central Asia and limit US influence in the region.

India's growing interests in Central Asia are well-recognised. There is a growing convergence between the US and Indian interests, especially their reluctance to see the region fall under the exclusive influence of Russia or China. India was worried in the 1990s when Russian influence in Central Asia weakened substantially with a commensurate rise in Chinese influence. This negatively impacted upon Indian threat perceptions which stabilised only after the growing US presence in the region since 2001. India views itself as a stabiliser and security provider in Central Asia and with its growing economic clout, an attractive economic power for the region. India's interest in securing reliable energy supplies and trade through Central Asia remains substantial.

Strong ties among the energy-exporting states of Central Asia, particularly Kazakhstan, Uzbekistan and Turkmenistan will go a long way in helping India achieve its energy security goals. It should be no surprise then that India's ties with the regional states are growing. Moreover, the imperatives of getting Afghanistan right are stronger than ever today when the situation is rapidly deteriorating.

India had opened its air base in Ayni, Tajikistan, in 2002 to guard against growing instability in the region, though nothing much has happened on that front for long. India's ties with regional states are growing and moderate Islam of the region makes it imperative for her to engage the area more substantively. Other powers, barring China, have recognised this reality and have sought to harness India towards achieving common goals. Russia, for example, supports Indian membership in the SCO and has talked about the possibility of India participating in the Collective Security Treaty Organization.

A great power competition in Central Asia, however, will make it harder for India to pursue its interests in the region. The country will have to work towards ensuring major power cooperation to bring some measure of stability to Afghanistan as well as the larger Central Asian region.

INDIA'S GROWING STAKES IN THE MIDDLE EAST AND EAST ASIA

India's engagements with the Arab states in the Middle East have gained momentum in the last few years, even as Iran continued to hog the limelight. India wants to secure energy supplies and consolidate economic and trade relations with the Gulf States, while these nations (Bahrain, Kuwait, Oman, Qatar, Saudi Arabia, and the UAE, or the members of the Gulf Cooperation Council) have adopted a 'Look East' policy which has allowed them to carve out a much more substantive relationship with India than in the past. India has far more significant interests to preserve in the Arab Gulf, and as tensions rise between the Sunni Arab regimes and Iran, India's larger stakes in the Gulf might lessen the possibility of healthy India–Iran ties.[9] At the same time, New Delhi's outreach to Tehran will remain circumscribed by the internal power struggle within Iran, growing tensions between Iran and its Arab neighbours, and Iran's continued defiance of the global nuclear order. Tehran's nuclear drive, its interference in neighbouring Iraq, and President Ahmadinejad's aggressive rhetoric are raising anxieties in Arab states about a resurgent Iran, forcing them to reorient their diplomacy accordingly. Reaching out to emerging powers such as India is one way to preserve the balance of power in the region. Indian interests in the Arab Gulf and Israel are significant and evolving, and India is carefully nurturing these ties.

As Sino-India competition intensifies, India is emerging as a serious player in the Asian strategic landscape as smaller states in East and Southeast Asia reach out to it for trade, diplomacy and, potentially, as a key regional balancer. The 'Look-East' policy initiated by one of the most visionary prime ministers India has ever had, P. V. Narasimha Rao, is now the cornerstone of India's engagement with the world's most economically dynamic region. India's Prime Minister Manmohan Singh has made it clear that his government's foreign-policy priority will be East and Southeast Asia, poised for sustained growth in the 21st century.

China is too big and powerful to be ignored by the regional states. But the states in China's vicinity are now seeking to expand their strategic space by reaching out to other regional and global powers. Smaller states in the region are now looking to India to act as a balancer in view of China's growing influence and America's anticipated retrenchment from the region in the near future, while larger states see India as an attractive engine for regional growth.

---

[9] Harsh V. Pant, 'India's Relations with Iran: Much Ado About Nothing', *Washington Quarterly* 34:1 (February 2011), pp. 61–74.

To live up to its full potential and meet the region's expectations, India will have to do a more convincing job of emerging as a credible strategic partner of the region. Neither India nor the regional states in East Asia have incentive to define their relationship in opposition to China. But they are certainly interested in leveraging their ties with other states to gain benefits from China and bring a semblance of equality in their relationships. Great power politics in the region have only just begun.

*

India is trying to figure out its position in the contemporary international system, and because the system itself is in a state of flux, the complexities facing the country are enormous. As was highlighted in the first edition of this volume, the loosening of the structural constraints imposed by the Cold War has given India greater flexibility in carving out its foreign policy. The changes in the structure of the international system have enabled India to pursue a 'multi-vector' foreign and security policy, allowing the country to strengthen its ties with all major global power centres, including the US, the EU, China, and Russia as well as expanding its profile in most regions of the world. But the search for India's rightful place in the global balance of power continues because India cannot continue for long with its multidimensional foreign policy without incurring significant costs. The really interesting issue here is how India will combine its rhetoric of nonalignment with the structural imperative of close ties with the US. So far there seems to have been no long-term strategic assessment of this in New Delhi.

This inability to think strategically remains Indian foreign policy's major vulnerability, and India's lack of capacity in dealing with its growing commitments is increasingly coming into sharp relief. It is often assumed that India has the necessary institutional wherewithal to translate its growing economic and military capabilities into global influence, even though the Indian state continues to suffer from weak administrative capacity in most areas of policy-making. In the realm of foreign and security policy, there was hardly any credible institutional capability to begin with. The personalization of foreign policy has always been a unique attribute of Indian policy-making, but the costs of this approach are rising by the day as the capacity of existing political leadership is failing to keep pace with growing demands on Indian foreign policy. There's a leadership deficit in India at the political level. The mystique of the Nehru–Gandhi dynasty is eroding by the day but it has not been replaced by an alternative national leadership. There are regional leaders who are doing well but their appeal remains geographically limited. The opposition parties, including the Bharatiya Janata Party (BJP), have failed to present an alternative leadership that is able to mobilise public opinion at a national level. None of the parties have leaders who seem capable of rising to the nation's many crucial challenges with the sense of urgency and the creative vision that is called for. It remains to be seen if the domestic political constraints will be powerful enough to overwhelm the structural factors in shaping the trajectory of Indian foreign policy in the years to come.

Bibliography

PRIMARY SOURCES

'A Cooperative Strategy for 21st Century Seapower', October 2007, at http://www.defenselink.mil/Blog_files/MaritimeStrategy.pdf.

'AFP: Indo-US nuclear pact not out of the woods: analysts', November 17, 2007, at http://afp.google.com/article/ALeqM5hB6CRtEOKNYNoBjfzYoIi0AGwT9w.

'ASEAN–India Joint Declaration for Cooperation to Combat International Terrorism, 2003', text available in Devare, *India and South Asia: Towards Security Convergence*.

Assessment by *Goldman Sachs*, at http://www2.goldmansachs.com/insight/research/reports/99.pdf.

Atlantic Council of the United States, *Defense Industry Globalization: A Compendium of Papers Presented at a Conference on: 'Defense Industry Globalization'*, Washington, DC, November 16, 2001.

BP Statistical Review of World Energy, June 2007, at http://www.bp.com/liveassets/bp_internet/globalbp/globalbp_uk_english/reports_and_publications/statistical_energy_review_2007/STAGING/local_assets/downloads/pdf/statistical_review_of_world_energy_full_report_2007.pdf.

Canadian Department of Foreign Affairs and International Trade, at http://www.dfait-maeci.gc.ca/nndi-agency/non-proliferation-en.asp.

Carnegie Endowment for International Peace, 'Address by the Defense Minister Pranab Mukherjee', Washington, DC, June 27, 2005.

———, 'India's Strategic Environment and the Role of Military Power', August 22, 2006, at http://www.carnegieendowment.org/events/index.cfm?fa=event Detail&id= 908&&prog=zgp&proj=zsa.

'China and India: A Rage for Oil', August 25, 2005, at http://www.businessweek.com/bwdaily/dnflash/aug2005/nf20050825_4692_db016.htm?chan=b.

Chinese Foreign Ministry's daily briefings, March 2, 2006, at http://www.china-embassy.org/eng/fyrth/t238267.htm.

CIA: The World Factbook 2006: India, 2006, at https://www.cia.gov/library/publications/the-world-factbook/geos/in.html.

CIA: The World Factbook 2007: India, 2007, at https://www.cia.gov/library/publications/the-world-factbook/geos/in.html.

CIA: The World Factbook, updated on November 15, 2007, at https://www.cia.gov/library/publications/the-world-factbook/index.html.

Comprehensive Revised Report with Addendums on Iraq's Weapons of Mass Destruction (Duelfer Report), Washington, DC, Government Printing Office, September 2004, at http://www.gpoaccess.gov/duelfer/index.html.

CRS Report for Congress (RL33407), 'Russian Political, Economic, and Security Issues and US Interests', Congressional Research Service, Washington, DC, October 19, 2006.

'Deepening Economic Doubts in India', Pew Research Center, Global Attitudes Project, September 10, 2012, http://www.pewglobal.org/files/2012/09/Pew-Global-Attitudes-Project-India-Report-FINAL-September-10-2012.pdf.

'Delhi Declaration', Signed by Saudi Arabia's King and the Indian Prime Minister, at http://meaindia.nic.in.

Draft Nuclear Doctrine, August 17, 1999, at http://www.indianembassy.org/policy/CTBT/nuclear_doctrine_aug_17_1999.html.

Economist Intelligence Unit Country Briefing, 'India', November 7, 2007, http://www.economist.com/countries/India/profile.cfm?folder=Profile%2DEconomic%20Data.

ESS, at http://www.consilium.europa.eu

EU on India, at http://ec.europa.eu/comm/external_relations india/intro/index.htm.

'Final Report of the *Counter-Terrorism International Conference*,' Riyadh, February 5–8, 2005.

Headquarters, Army Training Command (Shimla), *Doctrine for Sub Conventional Operations*, December 2006.

Human Rights Watch, '*Everyone Lives in Fear': Patterns of Impunity in Jammu and Kashmir*. New York and New Delhi: HRW, 2006, at http://hrw.org/reports/2006/india0906/.

Hydropower Development in India, 2006, at http://www.worldbank.org.in/WBSITE/EXTERNAL/COUNTRIES/SOUTHASIAEXT/INDIAEXTN 0,,contentMDK:20660353~pagePK:141137~piPK:141127~theSitePK:295584,00.html.

Index of Economic Freedom, at http://www.heritage.org/index.

India Data Profile (World Development Indicators Database), April 2007, at-http://devdata.worldbank.org/external/CPprofile.asp?PTYPE=CP&CCODG=IND.

'India Furthers Strategic Goals by Reaching out to Arms Markets', at www.stratfor.com, October 29, 2002.

'India: No troops to Iraq', July 14, 2003, at http://www.cnn.com/2003/WORLD/asiapcf/south/07/14/india.iraq/.

'India population to be the biggest', August 18, 2004, at http://news.bbc.co.uk/2/hi/in_depth/3575994.stm.

'India Rebuilding Air Base in Tajikistan: Diplomat', at www.DefenseNews.com, April 25, 2006.

India's Oil Import Bill Shoots to $44.64bn, May 10, 2006, at http://ns.rediff.com/money/2006/may/10oil.htm?q=bp&file=htm.

'India to Invest US$1 bln in Foreign Oil Equity', May 25, 2004, at http://www.atimes.com/atimes/South_Asia/FE25Df03.html.

'Joint India–US Statement', March 21, 2000, at http://www.indianembassy.org/indusrel/clinton_india/joint_india_us_statement_mar_21_2000.htm.

'Joint Statement between President George W. Bush and Prime Minister Manmohan Singh', July 18, 2005, at http://www.whitehouse.gov/news/releases/2005/07/20050718-6.html.

'Joint Statement of US, India on Terrorism, Bilateral Ties', November 9, 2001 at http://www.globalsecurity.org/military/library/news/2001/11/mil-011109-usia05c.htm.

'Mapping the Global Future', at http://www.cia.gov/nic/NICglobaltrend2020.html.

Ministry of Defence, *Annual Report 2005–2006*, New Delhi, at http://mod.nic.in/reports/.

———, *Annual Report 2006–2007*, New Delhi, 2007, at http://mod.nic.in/reports/welcome.html.

Ministry of Defence (Navy), *Indian Maritime Doctrine INBR 8*, Integrated Headquarters, New Delhi, 2004.

———, *Freedom to Use the Seas: India's Maritime Military Strategy*, New Delhi, May 2007.

Ministry of External Affairs, *Rebuilding Afghanistan: India at Work*. New Delhi: Government of India, 2005.

———, 'Statement by Indian External Affairs Minister K. Natwar Singh at SCO Council Heads of Government Meeting in Moscow', New Delhi, October 26, 2005, *FBIS SOV*, October 27, 2005.

———, 'Delhi Declaration', Joint Declarations & Statements, New Delhi, India, January 27, 2006.

———, 'Agreement between the Government of India and the Government of the United States of America Concerning Peaceful Uses of Nuclear Energy', New Delhi, August 1, 2007, at http://www.mea.gov.in.

———, Prime Minister Manmohan Singh's Comments on the Eve of his Departure to Attend the Sixth India–ASEAN Summit and the Third East Asia Summit Held in Singapore, November 21, 2007.

Ministry of Home Affairs, 'Census of India', at http://www.censusindia.net/religiondata/Religiondata_2001.xls.

National Security Strategy of the United States, September 2002, at http://www.whitehouse.gov/nsc/nss.pdf.

'New Delhi Declaration' (Signed by the Indian Prime Minister and the President of Iran on January 25, 2003), at www.meadev.nic.in.

'New Framework for the US–India Defense Relationship', June 28, 2005, at http://www.indianembassy.org/press_release/2005/June/31.htm.

Office of Counterterrorism, *Foreign Terrorist Organizations (FTOs) Fact Sheet*, Washington, DC, October 11, 2005.

'Oil and Gas', India Brand Equity Foundation, January 2006, at http://ibef. org/download/OilandGas_sectoral.pdf.
'Oil find in India's desert state', February 4, 2003, at http://news.bbc. co.uk/2/hi/business/2725969.stm.
'Operations', at www.ongcvidesh.com.
Planning Commission, Government of India, *Draft Report of the Expert Committee on Integrated Energy Policy*, December 2005, at http://planning commission. nic.in/reports/genrep/intengpol.pdf.
'Prime Minister Dr Manmohan Singh's interview with *Financial Times*', May 11, 2004, at http://meaindia.nic.in/interview/2004/11/05in01. htm.
Prime Minister's Office, 'PM Constitutes Energy Coordination Committee', July 13, 2005, at http://pib.nic.in/release/release.asp?relid=10163.
Quadrennial Defense Review Report 2006, February 26, 2006, available at http://www.defenselink.mil/qdr/report/Report20060203.pdf.
'Reforming the National Security System—Recommendations of the Group of Ministers', February 19, 2001.
Senate Foreign Relations Committee (#1a), 'Questions for the Record Submitted to Under Secretary Robert Joseph by Chairman Richard G. Lugar', November 2, 2005.
South Asia Regional Initiative for Energy Cooperation and Development, *Hydropower in South Asia—Potential Resource for Energy Exports*, at http://www.sari-energy.org/successdocs/IStudy SouthAsian HydroResources.pdf.
South Asia Terrorism Portal, at http://www.satp.org.
State of the Union Address, January 2002, at http://www.whitehouse.gov/ news/releases/2002/01/2002012-11.htm.
The High Commission of India, 'Brief on India–Sri Lanka Relations', Colombo, at http://www.hcicolombo.org/Ind_sl_bilateral.shtml.
'The Treaty of Mahakali', February 12, 1996, at http://www.nepaldemocracy. org/documents/treaties_agreements/indo-nepal_treaty_mahakali. htm.
The World Bank, 'Sustainable Development in a Dynamic World', in *World Development Report*. Washington, DC, 2003.
———, *2005 International Comparison Program: Preliminary Global Report Compares Sizes of Economies*, December 17, 2007, at http://go.worldbank. org/3YLCQ7L9K0.
United Nations Security Council Resolution 1441, November 2002, at http://daccessdds.un.org/doc/UNDOC/GEN/N02/682/26/PDF/ N0268226.pdf.
'United States, India Continue Cooperation against Terrorism: US–India Joint Working Group on Counterterrorism meets in Washington', April 22, 2006, at http://usinfo.state. gov/xarchives/display. html?p=washfile-english&y=2006& m=April&x= 200604221135 11 ABretnuH0.1901972.

United States National Intelligence Council, *Mapping the Global Future: Report of the National Intelligence Council's 2020 Project*, NIC 2004–13, Washington, DC, US Government Printing Office, December 2004.

USAID, *Regional Energy Security for South Asia: Regional Report*, USAID's South Asia Initiative for Energy, at http://www.sari-onergy.org/ProjectReports/Regional EnergySecurity_RegionalReport_Complete.pdf.

US Commission for International Religious Freedom, at http://www.uscirf.gov/home.html.

US Department of Defense, 'Quadrennial Defense Review Report 2006', February 6, 2006.

US Department of State, 'Background Briefing by Administration Officials on US–South Asia Relations', March 25, 2005, at http://www.state.gov/r/pa/prs/prs/ps/2005/438553.htm.

'US National Security and Nuclear Weapons: Maintaining Deterrence in the 21st Century', July 2007, at http://www.nnsa.doe.gov/docs/factsheets/2007/NA-07-FS-04.pdf.

Secondary Sources

Aaron, Sushil J., *Straddling Faultlines: India's Foreign Policy Towards the Greater Middle East*. Centre de Sciences Humaine (New Delhi), Occasional Paper No. 7, 2003.

Abbas, Hassan, *Pakistan's Drift into Extremism: Allah, the Army, and America's War on Terror*. London: M.E. Sharpe, 2005.

Abe, Nobuyasu, 'Challenges of the Second Nuclear Age: Preserving Multilateralism, Advancing Disarmament', Keynote Address at the Middle Powers Forum, New York, October 6, 2003.

Abedin, Mahan, 'The Iranian Intelligence Services and the War on Terror', *Terrorism Monitor*, Jamestown Foundation, May 20, 2004.

Acharya, Arabinda, 'India and Southeast Asia in the Age of Terror: Building Partnerships for Peace', *Contemporary Southeast Asia* 28, 2 (August 2006).

Ahmad, Naveed, 'The London Terror Plans: Pakistani-Afghan Connection', *Eurasia Insight*, August 23, 2006.

Aiyar, Mani Shankar, 'Asia's Quest for Energy Security', *Frontline* 23, 3 (January 28–February 10, 2006), at http://www.frontlineonnet.com/fl2303/stories/20060224002309000.htm.

Alexander's Gas and Oil Connections, 'Natural Gas Deal may Link Iran, India and Burma', June 29, 2004.

Alexander's Gas and Oil Connections, 'India Eyes Alliance With China and Uzbekistan for Oil Assets', December 8, 2005.

———, 'India to Join TAP Gas Pipeline', June 8, 2006.

Alibekov, Ibrahim, 'India Set to Expand Presence in Central Asia', *Eurasia Insight*, December 3, 2003.

Allison, Graham, *Nuclear Terrorism: The Ultimate Preventable Catastrophe*. New York: Henry Holt, 2004.

Al-Madani, Abdullah, 'Indo-Israeli ties: Arabs have None but Themselves to Blame', *Gulf News*, September 14, 2003.

Amir, Intikhab, 'The Waiting Game', *The Indian Express* (North American Edition), September 1, 2006.

Anas, A.Z.M., 'Bangladesh to Gain Little from FTA with India: WB Report', *The Financial Express*, December 6, 2006. http://www.bilaterals.org/article.php3?id_article=6610.

Andreyev, Alexei and Yevgeny Verlin, 'Geometry of Asian Security: Vajpayee Seeks to Improve Relations with Beijing, and Musharraf with Washington', Moscow, *Nezavisimaya Gazeta*, in Russian, June 25, 2003, *Foreign Broadcast Information Service, Central Eurasia*, June 25, 2003.

Aneja, Atul, 'Gas Pipeline Could be Extended to China', *The Hindu*, June 13, 2005.

Anklesariya Aiyar, Swaminathan S., 'Kush vs. Berry', *The Times of India*, October 10, 2004.

Arbatov, Alexi, 'Russia and NATO—Ten Years After', Paper prepared for the Conference on 'Russia—Ten Years After', Carnegie Endowment for International Peace, Washington, DC, June 7–9, 2001.

Associated Foreign Press, 'India, Iran Pledge Commitment to Build Gas Pipeline', February 24, 2006.

Aviation Week & Space Technology, 'India has Acknowledged Establishing an Air Base in Tajikistan', August 26, 2002.

Ayoob, Mohammed, 'South-West Asia after the Taliban', *Survival* 44, 1 (Spring 2002).

Ayrees, Alyssa, 'Regional Terror Goes Global', *Wall Street Journal*, August 18, 2006.

Bagchi, Indrani and Saibal Dasgupta, 'India Red-faced as China Gets Tough', *The Times of India*, May 27, 2007.

Bajaj, Vikas and Jim Yardley, 'Scandal Poses a Riddle: Will India Ever be Able to Tackle Corruption?', *New York Times*, September 15, 2012.

Bajpaee, Chietigj, 'India Held Back by Wall of Instability', *Asia Times Online*, www.atimes.com, June 1, 2006.

Bajpai, Kanti, 'Enhancing Ties Between India and Southeast Asia: An Indian View', in Satu P. Limaye and Ahmed Mukarram, eds, *India, Southeast Asia and the United States: New Opportunities and Prospects for Cooperation*. Singapore: Institute of Southeast Asian Studies, 1998.

———, 'Indian Strategic Culture', in Michael R. Chambers, ed, *South Asia in 2020: Future Strategic Balances and Alliances*. Carlisle, PA: Strategic Studies Institute, November 2002.

Bajpai, Kanti and Amitabh Mattoo, eds, *Engaged Democracies: India–US Relations in the 21st Century*. New Delhi: Har-Anand Publications, 2000.

Bakshi, Jyotsna, 'Russia's Post-Pokhran Dilemma', *Strategic Analysis* XXII, 5 (August 1998).

———, 'Prime Minister's Moscow Visit: Commentary', *Strategic Analysis* 29, 4 (October–December 2005).

———, 'India–Russia Defence Cooperation', *Strategic Analysis* 30, 2 (April–June 2006).

Banerjee, Soma, 'High on Energy, India Goes for Caspian Coup', *The Economic Times*, June 11, 2005.

Bannerjee, Indranil, *India and Central Asia*. Middlesex, Northolt: Brunel Academic Publishers Ltd., 2004.

Barber, Ben, 'US Plays the India Card', *Salon.com*, August 11, 2001, at http://archive.salon.com/news/feature/2001/08/11/india/index.html.

Barber, Benjamin R., *Fear's Empire: War, Terrorism, and Democracy*. New York: Norton, 2003.

Barman, Arijit, 'India Strikes LNG Import Deal with Qatar', 2003, at http://www.ndtvprofit.com/homepage/storybusinessreview.asp?id=15342&frmsrch=14txtsrch=LNGpercent2CQatar.

Basrur, Rajesh M., 'Nuclear Weapons and Indian Strategic Culture', *Journal of Peace Research* 38, 2 (March 2001).

Basu, Baidya Bikash, 'Trends in Russian Arms Exports', *Strategic Analysis* 23, 11 (August 2001).

Bedi, Rahul, 'The Military Dynamics', *Frontline* 19, 12 (8–21 June 2002), at http://www.hinduonnet.com/fline/fl1912/19120100.htm.

———, 'Indian Base in Tajikistan "Quietly Operational"', *Irish Times*, August 22, 2002.

———, 'India—Regional Focus: Power Play', *Jane's Defence Weekly*, July 13, 2005, at www4.janes.com/K2/doc.jsp?t

———, 'India develops Infrastructure on Chinese Border', *Jane's Defence Weekly*, July 18, 2007.

———, 'India Eyes Major Player Status', *Jane's Defence Weekly*, July 18, 2007.

Beehner, Lionel, 'The Rise of the Shanghai Cooperation Organization', Council of Foreign Relations, June 12, 2006.

Bello, Walden and Aileen Kwa, *G-20 Leaders Succumb to Divide and Rule Tactics*, August 10, 2004, at http://www.globalexchange.org/campaigns/wto/2946.html.

Ben-David, Alon, 'Israel Establishes Itself as Fifth-largest Arms Exporter', *Jane's Defence Weekly*, January 5, 2007.

Berlin, Donald L., 'The Indian Ocean and the Second Nuclear Age', *Orbis* 48 (2004).

———, 'India in the Indian Ocean', *Naval War College Review* 59 (Spring 2006).

Berman, Ilan, 'Israel, India and Turkey: Triple Entente?', *Middle East Quarterly* 9, 4 (Fall 2002).

Bertsch, Gary K., Seema Gahlaut and Anupam Srivastava, eds, *Engaging India: US Strategic Relations with the World's Largest Democracy*. New York: Routledge, 1999.

Bhadrakumar, M.K., 'India Plays Catch-Up with China, Russia', March 28, 2006, at http://www.atimes.com/atimes/South_Asia/HC28Df04.html.

———, 'Moscow Making Central Asia Its Own', *Asia Times Online*, August 24, 2006.

———, 'Putin Comes to India Riding on Russia's Resurgence', *rediff.com*, January 25, 2007.

Bhattacharya, Abanti, 'China's Foreign Policy Challenges and Evolving Strategy', *Strategic Analysis* XXX, 1 (January–March 2006).

Bhrbach, Roger and Jim Tarbell, *Imperial Overstretch*. London: Zed Books, 2004.

Bidwai, Praful, 'Ties with China Sour as Alliance with US Grows', *Inter Press Service*, July 6, 2007, at http://www.ipsnews.net/news asp?idnews=38444.

———, 'Five-Nation Naval Drill Presages "Asian NATO"?', *Inter-Press Service*, September 7, 2007, at http://www.ipsnews.net/news.asp?idnews=39175.

Blank, Jonah, 'Bridging US–India: A Defense Perspective', panel discussion, Center for Strategic and International Studies, Washington, DC, December 9, 2003.

Blank, Stephen, *Energy, Economics, and Security in Central Asia: Russia and Its Rivals*. Carlisle Barracks, PA: Strategic Studies Institute, US Army War College, 1995.

———, 'Central Asia, South Asia, and Asian Security', *Eurasian Studies* II, 3 (June 1995).

———, 'India's Rising Profile in Central Asia', *Comparative Strategy* XXII, 2 (April 2003).

———, *Natural Allies: Regional Security in Asia and Prospects for Indo-American Strategic Cooperation*. Carlisle, PA: Strategic Studies Institute, 2005.

———, *India: The New Central Asian Player*, Eurasia Insight, June 26, 2006, at http://www.eurasianet.org/departments/insight/articles/eav062606a.shtml.

———, 'India's Energy Options in Central Asia', Paper Presented at the Conference on Eurasian Pipelines, Columbia University, New York, November 12–13, 2007.

Blarel, Nicolas and Manjeet S. Pardesi, 'Price of Failure', *Daily News and Analysis*, November 13, 2007.

Bloomberg, 'Pakistan's Musharraf Says Relations with Afghanistan are Tense', March 6, 2006.

Blumenthal, Dan, 'Providing Arms: China and the Middle East', *Middle East Quarterly* 1?, ? (Spring 2005).

Boey, David, 'Sky's the Limit with S'pore–India Defence Pact', *The Straits Times*, October 17, 2003.

Bohlen, Celeste, 'Putting the Power Broker', *New York Times*, August 26, 2001.

Bokhari, Farkhan, 'Musharraf Urges US to Intervene in Afghan Dispute', *The Financial Times*, March 7, 2006.

Bose, Sumantra, *Sri Lanka, India and the Tamil Elam Movement*. Thousand Oaks, Calif.: Sage Publications, 1994.

Boucher, Richard A., 'The US–India Friendship: Where We Were and Where We're Going', Remarks at the Confederation of Indian Industries, New Delhi, April 7, 2006, at www.state.gov/p/sca/rls/rm/2006/4320.htm.

———, *US Policy in Central Asia: Balancing Priorities* (Part II) (Statement to the House International Relations Committee, Subcommittee on the Middle East and Central Asia), April 26, 2006, at http://www.state.gov/p/sca/rls/rm/2006/65292. htm.

———, 'Remarks at Electricity Beyond Borders: A Central Asia Power Sector Forum', Istanbul, Turkey, June 13, 2006, at http://www.state.gov/p/sca/rls/rm/2006/678 38.htm.

Bracken, Paul, *Fire in the East: The Rise of Asian Military Power and the Second Nuclear Age*. New York: Harper Collins, 1999.

———, 'The Second Nuclear Age'. *Foreign Affairs* 79, 1 (January/February 2000).

———, 'The Structure of the Second Nuclear Age'. *Orbis* 47, 3 (Summer 2003).

Brichieri-Colombi, Stephen, 'Geopolitics, Water and Development in South Asia: Cooperative Development in the Ganges–Brahmaputra Delta', *The Geographical Journal*, 169, 1 (March 2003).

British Broadcasting Corporation, 'Al Qaeda Statement: Full Text', November 17, 2003, at http://news.bbc.co.uk/2/hi/in_depth/3276859.stm.

———, 'India and Russia in Energy Talks', March 17, 2006, at http://news.bbc. co.uk/2/hi/sough_asia/4815588.stm.

Broad, William J., 'Facing the Second Nuclear Age', *New York Times*, August 3, 2003.

Broad, William J. and David E. Sanger 'Officials fear a second nuclear age with spread of technology'. *International Herald Tribune*, October 14, 2006.

Brooks, Stephen G. and William C. Wohlforth, 'Hard Times for Soft Balancing'. *International Security* 30, 1 (Summer 2005).

Brzezinski, Zbigniew, *The Grand Chessboard: American Primacy and Its Geostrategic Imperatives*. New York: Basic Books, 1997.

Buckley, Chris, 'China Likely to Swallow Anger over Indo-US N-deal', *Reuters*, August 29, 2007.

Bukharbayeva, Bagila, 'India Seeks Increased Engagement in Central Asia', *Associated Press*, November 6, 2003.
Bullion, Alan J., *India, Sri Lanka and the Tamil Crisis, 1976–1994: An International Perspective*. London: Pinter, 1995.
Burns, Nicholas, 'US–India Relations: The Global Partnership', lecture delivered at Carnegie Endowment for International Peace, Washington, DC, May 16, 2006, at http://www.carnegiee ndowment.org/events/index.cfm?fa=eventDetail&id=884&&prog=zgp&proj=znpp,zsa,zusr.
———, 'America's Strategic Opportunity with India', *Foreign Affairs* LXXXVI, 6 (November-December 2007).
Burr, Millard and Robert O. Collins, *Alms for Jihad*. Cambridge: Cambridge University Press, 2006.
Bush, George W., 'President Addresses Nation, Discusses Iran, War on Terror', at http://www.whitehouse.gov/news/releases/2005/06/20050628-7.html.
———, Graduation Speech at West Point, June 2002, at http://www.whitehouse.gov/news/releases/2002/06/20020601-3.html.
Business Standard, 'Tata Arm on Oil, Gas Hunt Abroad', April 10, 2006.
Business World, 'The rising "Soft Power" of China and India', May 30, 2005.
Calamur, Krishnadev, 'Indo-US Nuclear Deal Blasts Ahead', *Asia Times Online*, July 1, 2006., at www.atimes.com.
Cameron, Fraser, *US Foreign Policy after the Cold War*. London: Routledge, 2005.
Carlucci, Frank, Robert Hunter and Zalmay Khalilzad, eds, *Taking Charge: A Bipartisan Report to the President-Elect on Foreign Policy and National Security—Discussion Papers*. Santa Monica: RAND, 2000.
Cartwright, Jan, 'India and Russia: Old Friends, New Friends', *South Asia Monitor* 104 (March 1, 2007), Center for Strategic and International Studies, Washington DC.
Cha, Victor D., 'The Second Nuclear Age: Proliferation Pessimism versus Soviet Optimism in South Asia and East Asia', *Journal of Strategic Studies* 24, 4 (December 2001).
Chaliha, Kumar Amitav, 'India Moves on Central Asia', *Asia Times Online*, October 16, 2003, at www.atimes.com.
Chambers, Michael R., ed, *South Asia in 2020: Future Strategic Balances and Alliances*. Carlisle, PA: Strategic Studies Institute, November 2002.
Chaudhary, Amit, 'NTPC Scouts for Partners to Acquire Coal Mines Abroad', *The Hindu Business Line*, May 2, 2005.
Chaudhuri, Pramit Pal, 'It's time to look beyond Arafat: Israel to India', *Hindustan Times*, September 8, 2003.
Chellaney, Brahma, ed, *Securing India's Future in the New Millennium*. New Delhi: Orient Longman Limited, 1999.
———, 'The Quad: Australia–India–Japan–US Strategic Cooperation', *Asian Age*, July 3, 2007.

Chengappa, Raj, *Weapons of Peace*. New Delhi: HarperCollins Publishers India Pvt Ltd, 2000.

Cherian, John, 'The Defence Deals', *Frontline* 17, 21 (October 14–27, 2000).

———, 'The Deals in Question: A Look at the Defence Deals on the Table that have Figured in the Latest Scandal', *Frontline* 10, 7 (April 12, 2001).

China Brief, 'China Responds to the US–India Nuclear Deal', *China Brief* 6, 7 (March 29, 2006), at http://www.jamestown.org/publications_details.php?volume_id=415& issue_id=3670&article_id=237096.

Chubin, Shahram, 'Whither Iran?: Reform, Domestic Politics and National Security', Adelphi Paper 342 (London: International Institute for Strategic Studies, 2002).

Christenson, Thomas J., *Useful Adversaries: Grand Strategy, Domestic Mobilization, and Sino-American Conflict, 1947–1958*. Princeton: Princeton University Press, 1996.

Cohen, Stephen P., 'India and America: An Emerging Relationship', paper presented to the Conference on the Nation State System and Transnational Forces in South Asia, Kyoto, Japan, December 8–10, 2000.

———, *India: Emerging Power*. Washington, DC: Brookings Institution Press, 2001.

———, *The Idea of Pakistan*. Washington, DC: Brookings Institution Press, 2006.

Coll, Steve, *Ghost Wars*. New York: Penguin, 2004.

Conley, Jerome M., 'Indo-Russian Military and Nuclear Cooperation: Implications for the United States', INSS Occasional Paper No. 31, Proliferation Series, USAF Institute for National Security Studies, USAF Academy, Colorado Springs, Colorado, 2000.

Constable, Pamela, 'Pakistan's Awkward Balancing Act on Islamic Militant Groups, *Washington Post*, August 26, 2006.

Cordesman, Anthony H., *The India–Pakistan Military Balance*. Washington, DC: Center for Strategic and International Studies, May 2002.

———, *Saudi Arabia Enters the Twenty-First Century: The Political, Foreign Policy, and Energy Dimensions*. London: Praeger, 2003.

Cowell, Alan and Carlotta Gall, 'Pakistan is Accused of Terror Ties and Abuses', *The New York Times*, September 29, 2006.

Crenshaw, Martha, *India and the Sri Lanka Dilemma*, Case Study, Department of Government, Wesleyan University, November 2001.

Cronin, Audrey Kurth and James M. Ludes, eds, *Attacking Terrorism: Elements of a Grand Strategy*. Washington, DC: Georgetown University Press, 2004.

Curtis, Lisa, 'The Costs of a Failed US–India Civil Nuclear Deal', Heritage Foundation Web Memo 1688, November 2, 2007, at www.heritage.org/Research/AsiaandthePacific/wm1688.cfm.

———, 'India's Expanding Role in Asia: Adapting to Rising Power Status', *Backgrounder* 2008 (February 20, 2007).

Dadwal, Shebonti Ray, 'Energy Security: India's Options', *Strategic Analysis* XXIII, 4 (July 1999).

Dadwal, Shebonti Ray and Uttam Kumar Sinha, 'Equity Oil and India's Energy Security', *Strategic Analysis* 29, 3 (July–September 2005).
Das, Gurcharan, *India Unbound: The Social and Economic Revolution for Independence to the Global Information Revolution.* New York: Alfred A. Knopf, 2001.
———, 'The India Model', *Foreign Affairs* 85, 4 (July/August 2006).
———, 'Unshackling the Economy', *Foreign Affairs* 85, 4 (July/August 2006).
Datta, Saikat, 'Indo-Israeli Defence Deals Get a Big Push', *The Indian Express*, September 11, 2003.
Datta-Ray, Sunanda K., 'Suppose Russia, India and China could Really Get Together', *International Herald Tribune*, January 5, 1999.
Dawson, Peter M., *Liberal Hegemony, Democratic Peace, and United States Policy.* Newport, R.I.: Naval War College, 1996.
Denyer, Simon, 'India's "Silent" Prime Minister Becomes a Tragic Figure', *Washington Post*, September 4, 2012.
Desai, Stavan, 'On Our List, Gujarat Cops Who Didn't Act: Terror Suspect', *The Indian Express*, July 27, 2006.
Desai, Stavan, Anuradha Nagaraj and Sagnik Chowdhury, 'Cops Follow Aurangabad Arms Haul Trail, Arrest Four and Look for Key Lashkar Man on the Run', *The Indian Express*, July 15, 2006.
de Silva, K.M., *Regional Powers and Small State Security: India and Sri Lanka, 1977–90.* Baltimore: Johns Hopkins University Press, 1995.
Devare, Sudhir, *India and Southeast Asia: Towards Security Convergence.* Singapore: Institute of Southeast Asian Studies, 2006.
Dhoot, Vikas, 'Iraqi Trade Delegation in Town, Indian Businesses Line Up', *The Indian Express*, March 28, 2007.
Dixit, J.N., *India–Pakistan in War and Peace.* London: Routledge, 2002.
Dutta, Sanjay, 'Government to Set Up Energy Security Panel to Counter China', *The Times of India*, March 7, 2007.
Dyer, Gwynne, 'Containing China', *Walrus*, October, 2005, at http://www.walrus magazine.com/articles/2005.10-international-affairs-containing-china/.
Egreteau, Renaud, *Wooing the Generals: India's New Burma Policy.* New Delhi: Authors Press, 2003.
Einhorn, Robert J., 'The US–India Nuclear Deal', testimony before the International Relations Committee of the House of Representatives, October 26, 2005.
Elman, Colin, 'Horses for Courses: Why Not Neorealist Theories of Foreign Policy'. *Security Studies* 6, 1 (Autumn 1996).
Energy Security Insights, 1, 1 (March 2006), at http://www.teriin.org/div/esiissue 1march06.pdf.
Fair, C. Christine, *The Counterterror Coalitions Cooperation with India and Pakistan.* Santa Monica: RAND, 2004.
———, 'Indo-Iranian Relations: Prospects for Bilateral Cooperation Post 9-11', in *The 'Strategic Partnership' Between India and Iran.* Woodrow Wilson International Center for Scholars, Asia Program Special Report, No. 120, 2004.

Fair, C. Christine, 'Learning to Think the Unthinkable: Lessons from India's Nuclear Test', *India Review* 4, 1 (January 2005).
———, 'US-Indian Army-to-Army Relations', *Asian Security* 1, 2 (April 2005).
———, 'Indo-Iranian Ties: Thicker than Oil', Working Paper, Nonproliferation Policy Education Center, May 22, 2006, at http://www.npec-web.org/Essays/indo-iran_5_23_06.pdf.
———, 'Faltering Sri Lankan Peace Process: Sri Lanka's Drift Back into War', *International Journal of Peace Operations* 2, 3 (November–December, 2006).
———, 'India and Iran: New Delhi's Balancing Act', *The Washington Quarterly* 30, 3 (Summer 2007).
Fair, C. Christine and Peter Chalk, *Fortifying Pakistan: The Role US Internal Security Assistance*. Washington, DC: USIP Press, 2006.
Feldman, Noah, 'Islam, Terror and the Second Nuclear Age'. *New York Times Magazine*, October 29, 2006.
Foreign Affairs, 85, 4 (July/August 2006).
Frankel, Francine, ed, *Bridging the Nonproliferation Divide, The United States and India*, Washington: University Press of America, 1995.
Frankel, Francine and Harry Harding, eds, *The India–China Relationship: What the United States Needs to Know*. New York: Columbia University Press, 2004.
Frantz, Douglas, 'Around the World, Hints of Afghanistans to Come', *New York Times*, May 26, 2002.
Frieman, Wendy, *China, Arms Control and Non-Proliferation*. London: Routledge Curzon, 2004.
Gall, Carlotta, 'Musharraf Vows to Aid Afghanistan in Fighting Taliban', *The New York Times,* September 7, 2006.
Ganguly, Sumit, 'Between Iraq and a Hard Place: The Developing World and the New Oil Crisis', *International Executive* (January–February 1991).
———, 'India's Alliances 2020', in Michael. R. Chambers, ed, *South Asia in 2020: Future Strategic Balances and Alliances*. Carlisle, Penn.: US Army War College Stretegic Studies Institute, November 2002.
———, 'India's Foreign Policy Grows Up', *World Policy Journal* XX, 4 (Winter 2003–04), at www.worldpolicy.org/journal/articles/wpj03-4/ganguly.html.
———, *Energy Trends in India and China: Implications for the United States*. US Senate Foreign Relations Committee Testimony, 2005, at http://www.indiana.edu/~isp/media/sfr_7-26-05.doc.
———, 'Same the Nuclear Deal', *The Times of India*, October 26, 2007.
Ganguly, Sumit and Dinshaw Mistry, 'The Case for the US–India Nuclear Agreement', *World Policy Journal* 23, 2 (Summer 2006).
Ganguly, Sumit, Brian Shoup and Andrew Scobell, eds, *US-Indian Strategic Cooperation into the 20th Century: More than Words*. London: Routledge, 2006.
Garver, John W., 'The Future of Sino-Pakistani *Entente Cordiale*', in Michael R. Chambers, ed, *South Asia 2020: Future Strategic Balances and Alliances*. Carlisle, PA: Strategic Studies Institute, 2002.

Gentleman, Amelia, 'Russia Offers to Build Four New Nuclear Reactors for India', *International Herald Tribune,* January 25, 2007.
Gershman, John, 'Is Southeast Asia the Second Front?', *Foreign Affairs* 79, 4 (July/August 2002).
Ghose, Arundhati, 'Negotiating the CTBT: India's Security Concerns and Nuclear Disarmament', *Journal of International Affairs* 51, 1 (Summer 1997).
Ghoshal, Baladas, 'Some New Thoughts on India's Look East Policy', IPCS Issue Brief No.54, October 2007.
Gilpin, Robert, *War and Change in World Politics.* Cambridge: Cambridge University Press, 1981.
Glosserman, Brad, 'US Perspectives on East Asian Security', in N. S. Sisodia and G. V. C. Naidu, eds, *Changing Security Dynamic in Eastern Asia: Focus on Japan.* New Delhi: Institute for Defence Studies and Analyses, 2005.
Gokarn, Subir, 'Economic Policy Reforms: Implications for Energy Consumption', in Michael A. Toman, Ujjayant Chakravorty and Shreekant Gupta, ed, *India and Global Climate Change: Perspectives on Economics and Policy from a Developing Country.* Washington, DC: Resources for the Future Press, 2003.
Goldstein, Joshua S., *Long Cycles: Prosperity and War in the Modern Age.* New Haven, Conn.: Yale University Press, 1988.
Goldwyn, David L, ed, *Energy and Security: Toward a New Foreign Policy Strategy.* Washington, DC: Woodrow Wilson Center Press and The Johns Hopkins University Press, 2005.
Gopalakrishnan, A., 'Evolution of the Indian Nuclear Programme', *Annual Review of Energy and the Environment* 27 (November 2002).
Grare, Frederic, 'Energy Security for India', in Brahma Chellaney, ed, *Securing India's Future in the New Millennium.* New Delhi: Orient Longman Limited, 1999.
Grare, Frederic and Amitabh Mattoo, eds, *India and ASEAN: The Politics of India's Look East Policy.* New Delhi: Manohar, 2001.
Graver, John, *Protected Contest: Sino-Indian Rivalry in the 20th Century.* Seattle: University of Washington Press, 2006.
Gray, Colin S., *The Second Nuclear Age.* Boulder, CO: Lynne Reinner, 1998.
Grieco, Joseph, 'The Relative-Gains Problem for International Cooperation', *The American Political Science Review* 87, 3 (September 1993).
Griffin, Christopher, 'Containment with Chinese Characteristics: Beijing Hedges against the Rise of India', *Asian Outlook—AEI Online,* September 7, 2006.
Gulf Times, 'China, India for Joint Kazakh Oil Bid', June 11, 2006.
Hagerty, Devin T., 'Are We Present at the Creation? Alliance Theory and the Indo-US Strategic Convergence', in Sumit Ganguly, Brian Shoup, and Andrew Scobell, eds, *US-Indian Strategic Cooperation into the 20th Century: More than Words.* London: Routledge, 2006.

Hagerty, Devin T., ed, *South Asia in World Politics*. Lanham, MD: Rowman & Littlefield, 2005.
Haqqani, Husain, *Pakistan: Between Mosque and Military*. Washington, DC: Carnegie Endowment for International Peace, 2005.
———, 'India's Islamist Groups', *Current Trends in Islamist Ideology* 1, 1 (April 2005).
———, 'The Ideologies of South Asian Jihadi Groups', *Current Trends in Islamist Ideology* l, 1(April 2005).
Hasan, Mushirul, 'Dialogue Among Civilizations', *The Hindu*, New Delhi, January 29, 2003.
Hassell, John, 'An Update on the Great Game: Power Plays in the Graveyard of Empire', *San Diego Union-Tribune*, September 1, 2002.
Haté, Vibhuti, 'India's Energy Dilemma', *CSIS South Asia Monitor* 98 (September 2006).
Hazarika, Sanjoy, 'South Asia: Sharing the Giants–Water Sharing of the Indus, Ganges and Brahmaputra Rivers', *UNESCO Courier* 54, 10 (October 2001).
Herzig, Edmund, *Iran and the Former Soviet South*. London: Royal Institute of International Affairs, 1995.
Hindustan Times, 'What's Terror? India, Saudi Differ', January 27, 2006.
Hoagland, Jim, 'A Test of True Allies', *Washington Post*, November 8, 2001.
———, 'Staying On in Central Asia', *Washington Post*, January 20, 2002.
Holmes, James, 'China's Energy Consumption and Opportunities for US–China Cooperation', Testimony before the US–China Economic and Security Review Commission, June 14, 2007, at http://www.uscc.gov/hearings/200 7hearings/wr itten_testimonie s/07_06_14_15wrts/07_06_14_holmes_ statement.pdf.
Howard, Michael, 'What's in a Name? How to Fight Terrorism', *Foreign Affairs* 81, 1 (January/February 2002).
Hoyt, Timothy D., 'Military Force', in Audrey Kurth Cronin and James M. Ludes, eds, *Attacking Terrorism: Elements of a Grand Strategy*. Washington, DC: Georgetown University Press, 2004.
———, 'The War on Terrorism: Implications for South Asia', in Devin T. Hagerty, ed, *South Asia in World Politics*. Lanham, MD: Rowman & Littlefield, 2005.
Hu, Weixing, 'New Delhi's Nuclear Bomb: A Systemic Analysis'. *World Affairs* 163, 1 (Summer 2000), at http://findarticles.com/p/articles/mi_m2393/is_1_163.
Huntington, Samuel P., 'The Clash of Civilizations?', *Foreign Affairs* 72, 3 (Summer 1993).
———, *The Clash of Civilizations and the Remaking of World Order*. New York: Touchstone, 1997.
———, 'The Lonely Superpower'. *Foreign Affairs* 78, 2 (March/April 1999).

Hussain, Iwasbir, 'India and the Upcoming Druk Democracy', *Himal South Asian*, May 2007, at http://www.himalmag.com/2007/may/analysis_india_bhutan_relation.htm.

Hussain, Musahid, 'Pakistan's Quest for Security and the Indo-US Nuclear Deal', *Korean Journal of Defense Analysis* XVIII, 2 (Summer 2006).

IISS Strategic Comments, 'US–India Nuclear Energy Cooperation: Requirements and Implications', *IISS Strategic Comments* 11, 10 (December 2005).

Ikle, Fred Charles, 'The Second Coming of the Nuclear Age', *Foreign Affairs* 75, 1 (January/February 1996).

International Gas Report, 'Feasibility Study of Myanmar Pipeline Avoids Bangladesh', Issue 542 (February 2006).

International Herald Tribune, 'Al Qaeda Claim of Kashmir Link Worries India', July 14, 2006, at http://www.iht.com/articles/2006/07/13/news/india.php.

International Strategic Studies [*Guogji Zhanlue*], 'Future Directions of the Sino-Indian Border Dispute', November 2006.

Iqbal, Nadeem, 'Pakistan's Arms Industry Aims High', *Asia Times Online*, October 4, 2002.

Isachenkov, Vladimir, 'Russia, India Eye Deal on Nuclear Reactors', *Associated Press*, January 26, 2007.

Ispahani, Mahnaz, 'India's Role in Sri Lanka's Ethnic Conflict', in Ariel E. Levite, Bruce W. Jentleson and Larry Berman, eds, *Foreign Military Intervention: The Dynamics of Protracted Conflict*. New York: Columbia University Press, 1992.

ITAR-TASS News Agency (Moscow), 'India Planning to Join Shanghai Cooperative Organization', October 29, 2002.

———, 'Russia, India May Jointly Use Tajik military Airfield: Russian Defense Minister', December 5, 2005.

Jacob, Happymon, *Building a 'Strategic Oil Reserve' for India*, 2005, at http://www.observerindia.com/analysis/A018.htm.

Jaishankar, S., 'India–Japan Relations after Pokhran II', *Seminar*, Special Issue no. 427, 2000, at www.seminar.com.

Jane's Foreign Report, 'Electricity Relights Washington's Central Asian Policy', June 29, 2006, at http://www4.janes.com/subscribe/frp/doc_view.jsp?K2DocKey=/content1/janesdata/mags/ frp/history/frp2006/frp70038.htm@current&Prod_Name=FREP&QueryText=; *Janes's Intelligence Digest*, 'India's ASEAN Strategy', October 17, 2003.

Jane's Intelligence Digest, 'India's ASEAN Strategy', October 17, 2003.

Jha, Prakash Chandra, 'India Needs to Redefine its Relations with Nepal', *India Post*, June 11, 2007, at http://indiapost.com/article/perspective/498/

Jones, Owen Bennett, *Pakistan: Eye of the Storm*. New Haven: Yale University Press, 2002.

Jones, Rodney, 'India's Strategic Culture', *Science Applications International Corporation*, Washington DC, October 31, 2006.

Jones, Seth, 'Pakistan's Dangerous Game', *Survival* 49, 1 (Spring 2007).
Jung, Najeeb, 'Natural Gas in India', in Ian Wybrew-Bond and Jonathan Stren, ed, *Natural Gas in Asia: The Challenges of Growth in China, India, Japan and Korea*. New York: Oxford University Press, 2002.
Kakodkar, Anil, 'Energy in India for the Coming Decades', paper presented at the 'Inter Ministerial Conference on 'Nuclear Power for the 21st Century', organised by the International Atomic Energy Agency, Paris, France, March 21–22, 2005.
Kale, Sunila S., 'Current Reforms: The Politics of Policy Change in India's Electricity Sector', *Pacific Affairs* 77, 3 (Fall 2004).
Kalicki, Jan H. and David L. Goldwyn, 'Introduction: The Need to Integrate Energy and Foreign Policy', in Jan H. Kalicki and David L. Goldwyn, ed, *Energy and Security: Toward a New Foreign Policy Strategy*. Washington, DC: Woodrow Wilson Center Press and The Johns Hopkins University Press, 2005.
Kampani, Gaurav, 'India's Compellence Strategy: Calling Pakistan's Nuclear Bluff over Kashmir', Center for Nonproliferation Studies, June 10, 2002, at http://cns.miis.edu/pubs/week/020610.htm.
Kapila, Subhash, *United States War-Gaming on South Asia Nuclear Conflict: An Analysis*, South Asia Analysis Group, Paper no. 476, June 14, 2002.
Kaplan, Fred, *Daydream Believers*. New Jersey: John Wiley & Sons, 2008.
Karnad, Bharat, ed, *Future Imperilled: India's Security in the 1990s and Beyond*. New Delhi: Viking, 1994.
Katzenstein, Peter, 'Introduction: Asian Regionalism in Comparative Perspective', in Peter J. Katzenstein and Takashi Shiraishi, eds, *Network Power: Japan and Asia*. Ithaca and London: Cornell University Press, 1997.
Katzenstein, Peter J. and Takashi Shiraishi, eds, *Network Power: Japan and Asia*. Ithaca and London: Cornell University Press, 1997.
Kennady, Paul, 'The Eagle has Landed', *The Financial Times* (London), February 2, 2002.
Keohane, Robert O., ed, *Neorealism and its Critics*, New York: Columbia University Press, 1986.
Kerr, Paul, 'IAEA Board Seeks Strengthened Safeguards' *Arms Control Today*, July/August 2005.
Khalizad, Zalmay, et al., *The United States and Asia: Toward a New US Strategy and Force Posture*. Santa Monica, Calif.: Rand, 2001.
Khan, Amir Ullah, Mohammad Sadiq and Zafar H. Anjum, 'To Kill the Mockingbird', India China Economic and Cultural Centre, New Delhi.
Khan, Ashraf, 'Tribal Warlords Step Up Attacks on Chinese Projects: US and India Accused of Backing Militants in Province', *South China Morning Post*, March 16, 2006.
Klamper, Amy, 'The Thousand Ship Navy', *Sea Power*, February 13, 2007 at http://www.military.com/forums/0,15240,125158,00.html.

Klare, Michael T., *Blood and Oil: The Dangers and Consequences of America's Growing Petroleum Dependency*. New York: Metropolitan Books, 2004.
——, 'Containing China: The US's real Objective', *The Asia Times*, April 20, 2006.
Krepon, Michael, 'Are the Basic Assumptions Behind the Bush Administration's Nuclear Deal with India Sound?', Henry L. Stimson Center, March 15, 2006, at http://www.stimson.org/pub.cfm?id=276.
——, 'The US–India Nuclear Deal: Another Wrong Turn in the War on Terror', Henry L. Stimson Center, March 29, 2006, at http://www.stimson.org/pub.cfm?id=283.
——, 'India–US: Partners of Convenience', *Rediff.com,* September 25, 2006, at http://in.rediff.com/news/2006/sep/25mk.htm.
Krishnaswami, Sridhar, 'Indo-US N-deal "Win-Win": IAEA Chief', *Rediff.com*, May 25, 2006, at http://ia.rediff.com/news/2006/may/25ndeal.htm.
Kronstadt, K. Alan, *US-India Bilateral Agreements in 2005*, Congressional Research Service Report RL33072, September 8, 2005.
——, *India–Iran Relations and US Interests*, August 2, 2006, at http://italy.usembassy.gov/pdf/other/RS22486.pdf.
——, *CRS Report for Congress: India-Iran Relations and US Interests*, August 2, 2006, at http://fpc.state.gov/documents/organization/70294.pdf.
——, *CRS Report for Congress: India–U.S. Relations*. RL 33529 Washington, DC: Library of Congress, Congressional Research Service, updated October 2, 2007, at http://italy.usembassy.gov/pdf/other/RL33529.pdf.
Kuchera, Joshua, 'USAID Official Outlines Plan to Build Central-South Asian Electricity Links', *Eurasia Insight*, May 4, 2006, at www.eurasianet.org
Kumar, Nagesh, 'An Agenda for Safta's Dhaka Summit', *Financial Express,* November 8, 2005, at http://fecolumnists.expressindia.com/full_column.php?content_id=107951.
Kumaraswamy, P.R., 'India and Israel: Emerging Partnership', *Journal of Strategic Studies* 25, 4 (December 2002).
——, 'At What Cost Israel-China Ties?', *Middle East Quarterly* 13, 2 (Spring 2006).
Kupchan, Charles A., 'After Pax Americana: Benign Power, Regional Integration, and the Sources of a Stable Multipolarity', *International Security* 23, 2 (Fall 1998).
——, *The End of the American Era*. New York: Alfred A. Knopf, 2003.
Kux, Dennix, *India and the United States: Estranged Democracies, 1941–1991*. Wahington, DC: National Defense University Press, 1992.
——, *The United States and Pakistan, 1947–2000: Disenchanted Allies*. Baltimore: The Johns Hopkins University Press, 2001.
Kyodo News, 'India PM to Discuss Energy, Defence Contracts in Russia', December 2, 2005.

Lancaster, John, 'US Troops on Front Line of Expanding India Ties', *The Washington Post*, January 25, 2006.
Larkin, John, 'India and China Forge an Energy Tie; National Oil Companies to Work together to Bid for Select Assets Abroad', *The Wall Street Journal* (Eastern Edition), August 18, 2005.
Lavoy, Peter R., 'Pakistan's Nuclear Posture: Security and Survivability', at http://www.npec-web.org/Frameset.asp?PageType=Single&PDFF ile=20070121-Lavoy-PakistanNuclearPosture&PDFFolder=Essays.
Layne, Christopher, 'The Unipolar Illusion'. *International Security* 17, 4 (Spring 1993).
Leahy, Joe, 'Refining Hub will be the Largest in the World', *Financial Times*, November 23, 2007.
Levite, Ariel E., Bruce W. Jentleson and Larry Berman, eds, *Foreign Military Intervention: The Dynamics of Protracted Conflict*. New York: Columbia University Press, 1992.
Levitt, Matthew, *Targeting Terror: US Policy Towards Middle Eastern State Sponsored Terrorist Organizations, Post-September 11*. Washington, DC: The Washington Institute for Near East Policy, 2002.
Lieber, Keir A. and Daryl G. Press, 'The End of Mad? The Nuclear Dimension of US Primacy', *International Security* 30, 4 (Spring 2006).
Lieber Keir A. and Gerard Alexander, 'Waiting for Balancing: Why the World is Not Pushing Back', *International Security* 30, 1 (Summer 2005).
Limaye, Satu, *US-Indian Relations: The Pursuit of Accommodation*. Boulder, CO: Westview Press, 1993.
———, ed, *Asia's China Debate*. Honolulu: Asia–Pacific Center for Security Studies, Special Assessments, December 2003, at http://www.apcss.org/Publications/APSSS/ChinaDebate/ChinaDebate_Malik.pdf.
Limaye, Satu P. and Ahmed Mukarram, eds, *India, Southeast Asia and the United States: New Opportunities and Prospects for Cooperation*. Singapore: Institute of Southeast Asian Studies,1998.
Lisbonne-de Vergeron, Karine, *Contemporary Indian Views of Europe*, Chatham House Briefing, September 22, 2006.
Lober, Eric and Pramit Mitra, 'US–India Relations: Convergence of Interests', *CSIS South Asia Monitor* 84 (July 2005).
Lodgaard, Sverre and Maerli, eds, *Nuclear Proliferation and International Security*. Abingdon: Routledge, 2007.
Loudon, Bruce, 'India, China in Clash at Summit', *The Australian*, April 4, 2007.
———, 'Indian Troops to Fight the Taliban', *The Australian*, June 12, 2007.
Lowe, Robert and Claire Spencer, *Iran, Its Neighbors, and the Regional Crises*. London: Royal Institute of International Affairs, 2006.
Luce, Edward and Quentin Peel,. 'FT Interview Manmohan Singh', *The Financial Times*, November 8, 2004.
Luce, Edward and Ray Marcelo, 'Diplomacy: Why Energy Security is Top Priority?', *The Financial Times*, January 17, 2005.

Luft, Gal, *Iran–Pakistan–India Pipeline: The Baloch Wildcard* (Energy Security), at http://www.iags.org/n0115042.htm.

MacDonald, Juli A., *Indo-US Military Relationship: Expectations and Perceptions*. Washington, DC: Director, Net Assessment, Office of the Secretary of Defence, October 2002.

———, 'Rethinking India's and Pakistan's Regional Intent', in *Regional Power Plays in the Caucasus and Central Asia*, NBR Analysis 14, 4 (November 2003).

MacDonald, Juli A. and Bethany Danyluk, 'Pursuit of Energy Security can Enhance Its Relationship with the US', *Force*, September 2006.

Mahalingam, Sudha, 'Diversification and Energy Security', *The Hindu*, March 30, 2006.

Mahr, Krista, 'A Man in Shadow', *Time*, July 16, 2012.

Malhotra, Inder, 'After the Tehelka Bombshell: NDA Government Already a Lame Duck', *The Tribune* (Chandigarh), March 22, 2001.

Malik, Mohan, 'Eyeing the Dragon: India's China Debate', in Satu Limaye, ed, *Asia's China Debate*. Honolulu: Asia–Pacific Center for Security Studies Special Assessments, December 2003, at http://www.apcss.org/Publications/APSSS/ChinaDebate/China Debate_Malik.pdf.

———, 'Security Council Reform: China Signals Its Veto', *World Policy Journal* XXII, 1 (Spring 2005).

———, 'China and the East Asian Summit: More Discord than Accord', *Asia Pacific Center for Security Studies* (Honolulu), February 2006, at http://www.apcss.org/Publications/APSSS ChinaandEastAsiaSummit.pdf

———, 'China's Strategy of Containing India', February 6, 2006, at http://www.pinr.com/report.php?ac=view_report&reportid=434&language_id=1.

Mandelbaum, Michael, *The Fates of Nations: The Search for National Security in the Nineteenth and Twentieth Centuries*. Cambridge: Cambridge University Press, 1988.

Mann, James, *Rise of the Vulcans: The History of Bush's War Cabinet*. New York: Viking, 2004.

Manoharan, N., 'Consolidating Bilateral Ties: Rajapakse's India Visit', Institute of Peace and Conflict Studies, Article No. 1920, January 6, 2006, at http://www.ipcs.org/South_Asia_ articles2.jsp?action=show View &kValue=1933&country=1016&status=article&mod=a.

Matthew, Vinod, 'Videocon Bags Australian Offshore Exploration Block', *The Hindu Business Line*, April 4, 2006.

Maugeri, Leonardo, 'Oil: Never Cry Wolf–Why the Petroleum Age is Far from Over', *Science* 304, 5674 (May 2004).

———, *The Age of Oil: The Mythology, History, and Future of the World's Most Controversial Resource*. Westport, Conn.: Praeger Publishers, 2006.

Mavlanov, Ibrokhim, 'India's Economic Diplomacy in Central Asia', *Sapra India Bulletin*, March, 2006.

McDermott, Roger N., 'Tajikistan Diversifies Its Security Assistance', *Eurasia Daily Monitor*, September 22, 2004.

McGregor, Richard, Jo Johnson and Carola Hoyos, 'China and India Forge Alliance on Oil', *Financial Times*, January 12, 2006.

McMahon, Robert, 'Central Asia: Defence Minister Touts India's Potential Moderating Influence in Region', *Radio Free Europe Radio Liberty Features*, June 28, 2005.

Mearsheimer, John, 'Back to the Future: Instability in Europe after the Cold War', *International Security* 15, 1 (Summer 1990).

Meppen, LTC Kurt H., 'Central Asia and the Competition of National Interests: A Study of Colliding Interests', Unpublished Paper, US Institute of peace, June 2006.

Milhollin, Gary, 'The US–India Nuclear Pact: Bad for Security', *Current History* (November 2006).

Miller, Steven E., 'Skepticism Triumphant: The Bush Administration and the Waning of Arms Control', May 2003, at http://bcsia.ksg.harvard.edu/BCSIA_content/documents/Miller_Paris.pdf.

Mishra, Richa, 'Strategic Oil Reserves to Come Directly under Govt', *The Hindu Business Line*, April 2, 2006.

Mistry, Dinshaw and Sumit Ganguly, 'The US-India Nuclear Pact: A Good Deal', *Current History* 105 (November 2006).

Mitra, Amit, 'Global Coal Supplier Bullish on Indian Market', *The Hindu Business Line*, February 15, 2003.

———, 'Rising Coal Imports–Ports Need to Ramp Up Infrastructure', *The Hindu Business Line*, April 21, 2003

Mohan, C. Raja, *Crossing the Rubicon: The Shaping of India's New Foreign Policy*. London: Penguin, 2005.

———, 'Pipeline Diplomacy in South Asia', *Gulf News*, March 7, 2005.

———, 'Iran, Iraq to Figure in PM–Saudi King's Talks', *Indian Express* (New Delhi), January 24, 2006.

———, *Impossible Allies: Nuclear India, United States and the Global Order*. New Delhi: Indian Research Press, 2006.

———, 'India and the Balance of Power', *Foreign Affairs* 85, 4 (July/August 2006).

———, 'It's not about Uttar Pradesh', *Indian Express*, December 26, 2006.

———, 'India's Nuclear Exceptionalism', in Sverre Lodgaard and Maerli, eds, *Nuclear Proliferation and International Security*. Abingdon: Routledge, 2007.

———, 'Balancing Interests and Values: India's Struggle with Democracy Promotion', *Washington Quarterly* 30, 3 (July 2007).

Morarjee, Rachel, Farhan Bokhari and Jo Johnson, 'Pakistan "not involved" in Afghan insurgency', *Financial Times*, September 7, 2006.

Morgan, Dan and David Ottaway, 'Pipe Dreams: The Struggle for Caspian Oil', *The Washington Post*, October 4–6, 1998.

Morgan, John G. Jr. and Charles W. Martolgio, 'The 1,000 Ship Navy: Global Maritime Network', *Proceedings* (November 2005), at http://www.usni.org/magazines/ proceedings/archive/issues.asp?issue_year=2005.

Morgenthau, Hans, *Politics Among Nations*. New York: Knopf, 1973.

Mudiam, P.R., *India and the Middle East*. London: British Academic Press, 1994.

Mukherjee, Amit, 'IAF to Get 5th IL-78 Refueler Soon', *The Times of India* (Mumbai), Internet Version, September 29, 2004, *FBIS SOV*, September 29, 2004.

Mukherjee, Pranab, address to the Carnegie Endowment for International Peace, Washington, DC, June 27, 2005.

Mukherji, Joydeep and Takahira Ogawa, 'Will India be the First BRIC Fallen Angel?', Standard and Poor's, June 8, 2012, http://www.standardandpoors.com/spf/upload/Ratings_US/IndiaFirstBRICFallenAngel080612.pdf.

Mulford, David C., 'US–India Relationship to Reach New Heights', *The Times of India*, March 31, 2005.

Muni, S.D., *Pangs of Proximity: India and Sri Lanka's Ethnic Crisis*. Oslo, Norway: PRIO, 1993.

Musharraf, Pervez, *In the Line of Fire: A Memoir*. New York: Free Press, 2006.

Mustafa, Seema, 'New PRC Foreign Minister Hardens Border Dispute', *Asian Age*, August 4, 2007.

Nair, Brigadier Vijai K., VSM PhD, 'Challenges for the Years Ahead: An Indian Perspective', Paper Presented to the Annual National Defence University Asian-Pacific Symposium, Honolulu, March 2001, www.ndu.edu/inss/symposia/pacific2001/nairpaper.htm.

Narayanan, M.K., 'Asia's Global Foreign Policy and Security Interests', *Hampton Roads International Security Quarterly*, No. 2, 2006.

Narlikar, Amrita, 'Peculiar Chauvinism or Strategic Calculation: Explaining the Negotiating Strategy of a Rising India', *International Affairs* 82, 1 (January 2006).

Nath, Kamal, 'India-EU Strategic Partnership: Steps Ahead', speech delivered on January 14, 2005.

Nathan, K. S., ed, *India and ASEAN: The Growing partnership for the 21st Century*. Kuala Lumpur: Institute of Diplomacy and Foreign Relations, 2000.

Nayar, Baldev Raj and T.V. Paul, *India in the World Order: Searching for Major Power Status*. Cambridge: Cambridge University Press, 2003.

Nayar, K.P., 'The US Recognizes South Asia as India's Sphere of Influence', *The Telegraph* (Calcutta), April 5, 2006.

New York Times, 'US Strategy Plan Calls for Insuring No Rivals Develop a One Superpower World', March 8, 1992, at http://work.colum.edu/~amiller/wolfowitz1992.htm.

Noorani, A.G., 'Soviet Ambitions in South Asia', *International Security* 4, 1 (Winter 1979–80).

Nye, Joseph S. Jr., *Bound to Lead: the Changing Nature of American Power*. New York: Basic Books, 1990.

———, *The Paradox of American Power: Why the World's Only Superpower Can't Afford to Go It Alone*. Oxford: Oxford University Press, 2002.

Ollapaly, Deepa, 'India's Strategic Doctrine and Practice: The Impact of Nuclear Testing', in Raju G.C. Thomas and Amit Gupta, ed, *India's Nuclear Security*. Boulder, CO: Lynne Rienner Publishers, 2000.

———, 'Indo-Russian Strategic Relations: New Choices and Con-straints', in Sumit Ganguly, ed, Special Issue on 'India as an Emerging Power', *The Journal of Strategic Studies* 25, 4 (December 2002).

———, *US–India Relations: Ties That Bind?*, The Sigur Center Asia Papers No. 22, The Elliott School of International Affairs, The George Washington University, Washington, DC, 2005.

Opall-Rome, Barbara, 'Israel, China to Revive Ties', *Defense News*, December 15, 2003.

Organski, A.F.K. and Jacek Kugler, *The War Ledger*. Chicago: Chicago University Press, 1980.

Oxford Analytica, 'Pakistan: Instability Raises Nuclear Concerns', August 31, 2007, at http://www.belfercenter.org/files/Pakistan%20Nuclear%20Hassan%20Abbas.pdf.

Pachauri, R. K., 'Living with Coal: India's Energy Policy in the 21st Century', *Journal of International Affairs* 53,1 (Fall 1999).

———, 'The Pipeline of Peace', *The Indian Express*, New Delhi, January 21, 2003.

———, 'India, Iran Pledge Commitment to Build Gas Pipeline', *Associated Foreign Press*, February 24, 2006.

Page, Jeremy, 'Giants Meet to Counter US Power', *The Times* (London), February 15, 2007.

Pakkiasamy, Divya, 'Saudi Arabia's Plan for Changing Its Workforce', Migration Information Service, at http://www.migrationinformation.org/Feature/display.cfm?id=264.

Palat, Madhavan, 'Jettison Past Baggage', *The Times of India*, October 3, 2000.

Pan, Esther, 'India, China, and the United States: A Delicate Balance', Council for Foreign Relations, *Backgrounder*, February 27, 2006.

Pandian, S., 'The Political Economy of Trans-Pakistan Gas Pipeline Project: Assessing the Political and Economic Risks for India', *Energy Policy* 33, 5 (March 2005).

Pandit, Rajat, 'IAF May Follw US Air Force', *The Times of India* (Mumbai), Internet Version, October 28, 2005, *FBIS SOV*, October 28, 2005.

———, 'China's Growing Military Clout Worries India, US', *The Times of India*, April 10, 2007.

———, 'Indian Forces Get Foothold in Central Asia', *The Times of India*, July 17, 2007.

Pant, Harsh V., 'India and Iran: An "Axis" in the Making', *Asian Survey* (May/June 2004).

———, 'The Moscow–Beijing–Delhi "Strategic Triangle": An Idea Whose Time may Never Come', *Security Dialogue* 35, 3 (September 2004).

———, 'India–Israel Partnership: Convergence and Constraints', *Middle East Review of International Affairs* 8, 4 (December 2004).

Pant, Harsh V., 'India's China Policy: Devoid of a Strategic Framework', *South Asian Survey* 12, 2 (July–December 2005).

———, 'The US–India Nuclear Deal: The End Game Begins', *Power and Interest News Report*, January 27, 2006, at http://www.pinr.com/report.php?ac=view_ report&report_id=428&language_id=1.

———, 'Feasibility of the Russia–China–India "Strategic Triangle": Assessment of Theoretical and Empirical Issues', *International Studies* 43, 1 (January–March 2006).

———, 'The Indo-US Nuclear Deal: Much More Than Meets the Eye', *Royal United Services Institute Journal* 151, 2 (April 2006).

———, 'The Resurgence of the Taliban in Afghanistan', *Power and Interest News Report,* September 25, 2006, www.pinr.com.

———, 'Saudi Arabia Woos China and India', *Middle East Quarterly* 13, 4 (Fall 2006).

———, 'India and Bangladesh: Will the Twain Ever Meet', *Asian Survey* 47, 2 (March/April 2007).

———, 'The Emerging Balance of Power in the Asia–Pacific', *The RUSI Journal* 152, 3 (June 2007).

———, 'A Fine Balance: India Walks a Tightrope between Iran and the United States', *Orbis* 51, 3 (summer 2007).

———, *The China Syndrome: Grappling with an Uneasy Ralationship*. New Delhi: HarperCollins, 2010.

Pape, Robert A., 'Soft Balancing Against the United States'. *International Security* 30, 1 (Summer 2005).

Parthasarthy, G., 'Saudi-Pakistani Nexus on Terrorism', *The Tribune*, September 25, 2003.

———, 'Disturbing Signs Flow from across the Himalayas', *Pioneer*, July 1, 2007.

Pasha, A.K., 'India, Iran and the GCC States: Common Political and Strategic Concerns', in A. K. Pasha, ed, *India, Iran and the GCC States: Pol-itical Strategy and Foreign Policy*. New Delhi: Manas Publication, 2000.

Paul, T.V., 'The Systemic Bases of India's Challenge to the Global Nuclear Order', *The Nonproliferation Review* 6, 1 (Fall 1998).

———, 'Soft Balancing in the Age of US Primacy'. *International Security* 30, 1 (Summer 2005).

———, ed, *The Indo-Pakistan Conflict: An Enduring Rivalry*. Cambridge: Cambridge University Press, 2005.

Payne, Keith B., *Deterrence in the Second Nuclear Age*. Lexington, KY: University of Kentucky Press, 1996.

———, *The Fallacies of Cold War Deterrence and a New Direction*. Lexington, KY: University of Kentucky Press, 2001.

Peel, Quentin, 'India's Terms of Engagement', *The Financial Times*, November 11, 2004.

Peng, Wang, 'The US-Indian Nuclear Agreement: Cooperation or Threat?', *People's Daily*, August 11, 2007.

People's Daily online, Commentary, 'Nuclear agreement and big power's dream', August 30, 2007, at http://english.people.com.cn/90001/90780/91343/6251506.html.

People's Democracy, 'USS Nimitz Go Back!', XXI, 27 (July 8, 2007), at http://www.cpim.org/pd/2007/0708/07082007_aanainar.htm.

Perkovich, George, *India's Nuclear Bomb: The Impact on Global Proliferation*. Berkeley: University of California Press, 1999.

———, 'Bush's Nuclear Proliferation: A Regime Change in Non-Proliferation?', *Foreign Affairs* 82, 2 (March/April 2003).

———, 'Faulty Promises: The US–India Nuclear Deal', Carnegie Endowment for International Peace Policy Outlook No. 21, September, 2005.

Pickering, Thomas, 'US Policy in South Asia: The Road Ahead', Address to the Foreign Policy Institute, Johns Hopkins University, Washington DC, April 27, 2000.

Poulose, T.T., *The CTBT and the Rise of Nuclear Nationalism in India*. New Delhi: Lancer Books, 1996.

PTI, 'High-Level Tajikistan Defence Delegation Meets Fernandes', December 2, 2002.

———, 'India–China Bilatera Trade Touches $13.6 Billion', March 5, 2005.

———, 'India Loses to China on Myanmar Gas', *Rediff.com*, August 23, 2007, at http://www.rediff.com/money/2007/aug/23gas.htm.

Powell, Colin, Speech to the United Nations Security Council, February 5, 2003, at http://www.whitehouse.gov/news/releases/2003/02/20030205-1.html.

Pun, Santa B., 'Trading off a Jewel', *Himal South Asian*, November 2003.

Radio Free Europe Radio Liberty Newsline, 'Kabul Hopes for Strategic Ties with New Delhi, August 18, 2006.

Radyuhin, Vladimir, 'Russia Plays Energy Card', *The Hindu*, July 6, 2004.

———, 'Putin Visit: Chance for Course Correction', *The Hindu*, January 23, 2007.

Rag, Barnali, 'Issues Related to India's Energy Trading with Central Asian Countries', *RIS Discussion Papers* No. 69 (March 2004).

Raghuvanshi, Vivek, 'Indian Munitions Plants Fear Sales Losses, Seek Exports', *Defense News*, January 14–20, 2002.

———, 'India Eyes Markets Abroad', *Defense News*, May 20–26, 2002.

———, 'India Aims to Project Power Across Asia', *Defense News*, November 10, 2003.

———, 'India Embraces New War Doctrine', *Defense News*, November 8, 2004.

———, 'India Plans Weapons, Training to Project Power, *DefenseNews.com*, February 20, 2006.

———, 'India, Iran to Deepen Defense Relationship', *Defense News*, March 18, 2007, available at http://defensenews.com/story php?F=2620792&C=asiapac.

Rahman, Shaikh Azizur, 'India Strikes for Oil and Gas with Military Base in Tajikistan', *Washington Times*, September 2, 2002.
Rajan, D. S., 'China: Media Fears Over India Becoming Part of Western Alliance', *Saag.org*, Paper No. 2350, August 29, 2007, at http://www.saag.org/papers24/paper2350.htm1.
Rajesh, Y.P., 'India Says to have Missile Defence System in Three Years', *Reuters* (New Delhi), December 12, 2007, at http://www.reuters.com/article/latestCrisis/idUSDE L331120.
Ramachandran, R., 'Unclear nuclear identity', *Frontline* 16, 18, 28 August–10 September 1999, at http://www.frontlineonnet.com/fl1618/16180160.htm.
Ramachandran, Ramesh, 'Russian Wants India in Shanghai Pact', *The Asian Age* (New Delhi), January 3, 2006, *FBIS SOV*, January 3, 2006.
———, 'Helping US May Derail Border Talks', *Asian Age*, July 25, 2007.
Ramachandran, Sudha, 'India Gives Shanghai the Cold Shoulder', *Asia Times Online*, June 17, 2006, at http://www.atimes.com/atimes/South_Asia/HF17Df01.html.
Ramachandran, Sudha, 'India Promotes "Goodwill" Naval Exercises', *Asia Times online*, August 14, 2007, at http://www.atimes.com/atimes/South_Asia/IH14Df01.html.
Ramachandran, Sushma, 'Dahej LNG Terminal Commissioned', *The Hindu*, February 10, 2004.
———, 'Myanmar–India Gas Pipeline Proposal Runs into Problems', *The Hindu*, July 7, 2005.
Raman, B., 'Al-Qaeda, the IIF and Indian Muslims', South Asia Analysis Group, paper no. 1743, March 20, 2006.
———, 'Tawang: Some Indian plain-speaking at last!', *Saag.org*, Paper no. 2273, June 22, 2007, at http://www.saag.org/papers23/paper2273.html.
———, 'China and the 123 Agreement', *Indian Defence Review* (New Delhi) 22, 4 (October–December 2007).
Ramanna, M. V., 'Nuclear Power in India: Failed Past, Dubious Future', in Henry Sokolski, ed, *Gauging US-Indian Strategic Cooperation*. Carlisle, PA: Strategic Studies Institute, March 2007.
Ramazani, R.K., *Revolutionary Iran: Challenge and Response in the Middle East*. Baltimore: Johns Hopkins University Press, 1986.
Rangsimaporn, Paradorn, 'Russia's Debate on Military-Technical Cooperation with China', *Asian Survey* XLVI, 3 (May/June 2006).
Rashid, Ahmed, *Taliban*. New Haven: Yale University Press, 2000.
———, 'Afghan President Confronts Pakistani Counterpart over Suicide Bombers', *Eurasia Insight*, February 21, 2006.
Ray Choudry, Ranabir, 'India–Bangladesh FTA Prospects', *The Hindu Business Line*, April 16, 2007, at http://www.blonnet.com/2007/04/16/stories/2007041601450800.htm

Rediff.com, 'India's Oil Import Bill Shoots to $44.64 bn', May 10, 2006, at http://us.rediff.com/money/2006/may/10oil.htm?q=bp&file=.htm.

Reineberg, Hubert H., 'India's Electricity Sector in Transition: Can Its Giant Goals Be Met?', *The Electricity Journal* 19, 1 (January–February 2006)..

Reuters, 'India rebuffs Beijing on disputed border', *International Herald Tribune*, June 17, 2007.

Rice, Condoleezza, 'Campaign 2000–Promoting the American Interest', *Foreign Affairs* 79, 1 (January/February 2000), at http://www.foreignaffairs.org/20000101faessay5/condoleezza-rice/campaign-2000-promoting-the-national-interest.html.

———, 'Remarks with Indian Minister of External Affairs Natwar Singh Following Meeting', Department of State, Washington, DC, April 14, 2005, at www.state.gov/secretary/rm/2005/44662.htm.

———, 'Remarks of Secretary of State at the Senate Foreign Relations Committee on the US–India Civil Nuclear Cooperation Initiative', April 5, 2006, at http://foreign.senate.gov/testimony/2006 RiceTestimony060405.pdf.

Richter, Paul, 'In Deal with India, Bush has Eye on China', *The Los Angeles Times*, March 4, 2006.

RIS Policy Briefs, 'Energy Cooperation in South Asia: Potential and Prospects', No. 8, December 2003.

Rohde, David, 'The Afghanistan Triangle', *The New York Times*, October 1, 2006.

Ross, Robert, 'Balance of Power Politics and the Rise of China: Accommodation and Balancing in East Asia', *Security Studies* 15, 3 (July–September 2006).

Roy, Bhaskar, '123 Agreement and the People's Republic of China', *Saag.org*, Paper No. 2324, August 8, 2007, at http://www.saag.org/papers24/paper2324.html.

Rubin, Barnett R., *Afghanistan's Uncertain Transition from Turmoil to Normalcy*, Council Special Report No. 12, 2006.

Rubin, Barnett R. and Abubakar Siddique, *Resolving the Pakistan–Afghanistan Stalemate*, United States Institute of Peace Special Report No. 176, 2006.

Russell, Richard R., 'Oil for Missiles', *The Wall Street Journal*, January 25, 2006.

Sahgal, Brigadier Arun (Ret.) and Parama Sinha Palit, 'The "Singh Doctrine"', *Armed Forces Journal*, May, 2006.

Saikal, Amin, 'Iran's Turbulent Neighbor: The Challenge of the Taliban', *Global Dialogue*, 3, 2/3 (Spring/Summer 2001).

SAPRA India Bulletin, 'Astana to Meet Indian Energy Requirements', August 2005.

Saran, Shyam, 'Present Dimensions of the Indian Foreign Policy', address to the Shanghai Institute of International Studies, New Delhi, Ministry

of External Affairs Internet Version, January 12, 2006, *FBIS SOV*, January 12, 2006.
Sardesai, D. R. and Raju Thomas, ed, *Nuclear India in the Twenty-First Century*. New York: Palgrave-Macmillan, 2002.
Sarsembaev, Ilyas, 'Russia: No Strategic Partnership with China in View', *China Perspectives* 65 (May–June 2006).
Sartori, Silvia, 'How China Sees India and the World', *Heartland: Eurasian Review of Geopolitics* 3, Hong Kong: Cassan Press, 2005, at http://www. heartland.it/_lib/_docs/2005_03_chindia_the_21st_century_challenge.pdf.
Sasi, Anil, 'India to Wheel in Power from Abroad', *The Hindu Business Line*, August 12, 2006.
———, 'India Gets Power from Bhutan's Tala Project', *The Hindu Business Line*, August 17, 2006.
Sawhney, Pravin, 'India's First Airpower Doctrine Takes Shape', *Jane's International Defence Review* 30, 6 (June 1997).
Schaffer, Teresita C., 'India on the Move', *Survival* 49,1 (March 2007).
Schaffer, Teresita C., and Pramit Mitra, 'India as a Global Power?', *Deutsche Bank Research*, Frankfurt am Main, Germany, December 16, 2005.
———, 'The Bush Visit and the Nuclear Deal', *CSIS South Asia Monitor* 93 (April 2006).
Scheuer, Michael, 'Clueless Into Kabul', *The American Interest* I, 4 (Fall 2006).
Schweller, Randall L., *Deadly Imbalances: Tripolarity and Hitler's Strategy of World Conquest*. New York: Columbia University Press, 1998.
Scobell, Andrew, '"Cult of Defense" and "Great Power Dreams": The Influence of Strategic Culture on China's Relationship with India', in Malcolm R. Chambers, ed, *South Asia in 2020: Future Strategic Balances and Alliances*. PA: US Army War College, Strategic Studies Institute, November 2002.
Seiff, Martin, 'A Giant leap for Indian missile defence', December 1, 2006, at http://www.spacewar.com/reports/A_Giant_Leap_Forward_For_Indian_Missile_Defense_999.html
Sengupta, Jayashree, *EU–India Strategic Partnership,* Observer Research Foundation, at www.observerindia.com/strategic/st041108.htm.
Sengupta, Prasun K., 'Globalization of Security and its Regional Implications', *Asian Defence Yearbook*, *Asian Defence Journal*. Kuala Lumpur, 2001.
Sengupta, Somini, 'Indian Coalition Wins Dispute over Nuclear Pact', *New York Times*, November 17, 2007.
Sengupta, Somini, Scott Shane and David Rohde, 'Pakistan's Help in Averting a Terror Attack is a Double-Edged Sword', *The New York Times,* August 12, 2006.
Shahzad, Syed Saleem, 'Pakistan Reaches into Afghanistan', *The Asia Times,* October 3, 2006.

Shambaugh, David, ed, *Power Shift: China and Asia's New Dynamics*. Berkeley, CA: University of California Press, 2006.

Sharma, Anil, 'Indian Drive to Increase Arms Exports', *Asia Times Online*, November 6, 2002.

Sharma, Pranay, 'Terror & Truce Mix for Sharon', *The Telegraph*, September 9, 2003.

Sharma, Rajeev, 'India–China Border Row: No Headway Expected This Year', *Tribune*, June 8, 2007.

Sharma, Rakesh and Santanu Choudhury, 'India Cuts Back on Iran Oil Imports', *Wall Street Journal*, May 2, 2012.

———, 'China Jams DD, AIR Signals in Border Area', *Tribune*, June 26, 2007.

Shekhar, Vibhanshu, 'India–ASEAN Relations: An Overview', *IPCS Special Report* 39 (March 2007).

Shiva, Vandana, *Water Wars: Privatization, Pollution, and Profit*. Boston: South End Press, 2002.

Shukla, Saurabh, 'India, Israel tie up to combat terrorism', *Hindustan Times*, September 11, 2003.

Shukla, Vinay, 'India Pitches for Full Membership of Shanghai Cooperation Organization', *Press Trust of India* (New Delhi), October 26, 2005, *FBIS SOV*, October 26, 2005.

Sick, Gary, 'The Clouded Mirror: The United States and Iran, 1979–99', in Esposito and Ramazani, eds, *Iran at the Crossroads*.

Sikand, Yoginder, 'Intra-Muslim Rivalries in India and the Saudi Connection', Jamia Hamdard University.

Silu, Liu, 'Beijing Should Not Lose Patience in Chinese-Indian Border Talks', *Wen Wei Po* (Hong Kong), June 1, 2007.

Singh, Jaswant, 'Against Nuclear Apartheid', *Foreign Affairs* 77, 5 (September/October 1998).

Singh, Manmohan, Speech delivered at the third India–ASEAN Business Summit, October 21, 2004.

———, 'PM's Address at the China Academy of Social Sciences', Beijing, January 15, 2005, at http://www.pmindia.nic.in/lspeech.asp?id=644.

———, 'The New India', *The Wall Street Journal* (Eastern edition), May 19, 2005.

———, Speech delivered at the India–EU Business Summit, September 7, 2005, at http://pmindia.nic.in/speech.asp?id=189.

———, 'PM's Address to the Joint Session of the Diet', December 14, 2006, at http://pmindia.nic.in/visit/contentasp?id=142.

Singh, Manmohan and Wen Jiabao, 'A shared vision for the 21st Century of the Republic of India and the People's Republic of China', Beijing, January 14, 2008, at http://www.pmindia.nic.in/speech_14jan2k8-1.pdf.

Singh, Lt. Gen. R.K. Jasbir, ed, *Indian Defence Yearbook 2005*. New Delhi: Natraj, 2005.

Sinha, Yashwant, Speech delivered at the Institute of Defence Studies & Analysis, New Delhi, November 22, 2003.

Sirohi, Seema, 'Japan: The Sake is Warming', *Outlook*, August 27, 2007.

———, 'ASEAN: Ah, Singhapuram...China blocks India's attempts to join the powerful ASEAN plus', *Outlook.com*, December 3, 2007, at http://www.outlookindia. com/full.asp?fodname=20071203&fname=Asean +%28F%29&sid=1.

Sisodia, N. S. and G. V. C. Naidu, eds, *Changing Security Dynamic in Eastern Asia: Focus on Japan*. New Delhi: Institute for Defense Studies and Analyses, 2005.

Skosyrev, Vladimir, 'India and Pakistan on Verge of Détente. But Situation Could Be Complicated by US Arms Deliveries', Moscow, *Nezavisimaya Gazeta*, in Russian, August 10, 2005, *FBIS SOV*, August 10, 2005; Soderbeg, Nancy, The Superpower Myth. New Jersey:John Wiely & Sons, 2005.

Snow, Tony, Setting the Record Straight: Iraq is the Central Front of Al Qaeda's Global Campaign, at http://www.whitehouse.gov/news/releases/2007/05/20070503-6.html.

Sobhan, Farooq, 'Estranged Neighbours', *India Seminar* 557 (January 2006), at http://www.india-seminar.com/2006/557557%20farooq%20sobhan.htm

Soderbeg, Nancy, *The Superpower Myth*. New Jersy: John Wiley & Sons, 2005.

Sokolski, Henry, ed, *Gauging US-Indian Strategic Cooperation*. Carlisle, PA: Strategic Studies Institute, March 2007.

———, 'Negotiating the Obstacles to US-Indian Strategic Cooperation', in Henry Sokolski, ed, *Gauging US-Indian Strategic Cooperation*. Carlisle, Penna.: Strategic Studies Institute, March 2007.

Spector, Leonard S, 'US Nuclear Cooperation with India', testimony before the International Relations Committee of the House of Representatives, October 26, 2005.

Srinivasan, Rajeev, 'A Millennia-old Tussle', *Rediff.com*, November 22, 2002, at http://www.rediff.com/news/2002/nov/23chin.htm.

Srivastava, D., and P. Andley, *Great Power Dynamics: India, US and China*. Report of Panel Discussion, May 5, 2007, sponsored by Indian Army 15 Corps HQ, Srinagar, and Institute of Peace and Conflict Studies, New Delhi, at http://www.ipcs.org/Discussion Report_May07.pdf.

Srivastava, Leena and Megha Shukla, 'The Present Status and Future Prospects of Energy in India', in *Asian Energy Markets: Dynamics and Trends*. Abu Dhabi: The Emirates Center for Strategic Studies and Research, 2004.

Srivastava, Sanjeev, 'India's Air Force "Needs to Grow"', April 18, 2006, at http://news.bbc.co.uk/2/hi/south_asia/4919420.stm.

Srivastava, Siddarth, 'The Foundations of an Asian Oil and Gas Grid', *Asia Times Online*, December 1, 2005.

———, 'India Bets Big on Refining', May 5, 2006, at http://www.atimes.com/atimes/South_Asia/HE05Df03.html.

Stephenson, John and Peter Tynan, 'Will the US–India Civil Nuclear Cooperation Initiative Light India?', Henry Sokolski, ed, *Gauging US-Indian Strategic Cooperation*. Carlisle, PA: Strategic Studies Institute, March 2007.

Stobdan, P., 'Central Asia and India's Security', *Strategic Analysis* (January–March, 2004).

Stockholm International Peace Research Institute, *SIPRI Yearbook 2005: Armaments, Disarmament and International Security*. Oxford: Oxford University Press, 2005.

Subrahmanyam, K., 'Wanted Leaders with a Vision', *The Tribune* (Chandigarh), September 24, 2005.

———, 'The Lessons from Putin's Visit', *rediff.com*, January 29, 2007.

———, 'Don't Get Fooled By China', *The Times of India*, August 28, 2007.

Swami, Praveen, 'The Spreading Tentacles of Terror', *The Hindu*, August 31, 2003.

———, *India, Pakistan and the Secret Jihad*. London: Routledge, 2006.

———, 'The Road to Unimaginable Horror', *The Hindu*, July 13, 2006.

———, 'New Evidence on Mumbai Blasts Shows Up', *The Hindu*, August 1, 2006.

Swaminathan, R., 'India's Foreign Policy: Emerging Trends in the New Century', *Saag.org*, Paper No. 2194, April 5, 2007, at http://www.saag.org/%5Cpapers 22%5 Cpaper2194.html.

Synovitz, Ron, 'Afghanistan: US Reports "Breakthrough" on Afghan–Pakistan Security Cooperation', *Radio Fee Europe Radio Liberty Features*, August 25, 2006.

Talbott, Strobe, 'Good Day for India, Bad Day for Non-Proliferation'. *Yale Global Online*, July 21, 2005, at http://yaleglobal.yale.edu/display.article?id=6042.

———, *Engaging India: Diplomacy, Democracy, And the Bomb* (Revised Edition). Washington, DC: Brookings Institution Press, 2006.

Taylor, Paul D., ed, *Asia and the Pacific: US Strategic Traditions and Regional Realities*. Newport: Naval War College Press, 2001.

Tellis, Ashley J., 'South Asia: US Policy Choices', in Frank Carlucci, Robert Hunter and Zalmay Khalilzad eds, *Taking Charge: A Bipartisan Report to the President-Elect on Foreign Policy and National Security—Discussion Papers*. Santa Monica: RAND, 2000.

———, *India as a New Global Power: An Action Agenda for the US*. Washington, D.C.: Carnegie Endowment for International Peace, 2005.

———, 'Evolution of US-Indian Defence Ties: Missile Defence in an Emerging Strategic Relationship', *International Security* 30, 4 (Spring 2006).

———, 'Atoms for War? US-Indian Civilian Nuclear Cooperation and India's Nuclear Arsenal', Washington, DC: Carnegie Endowment, 2006.

Tellis, Ashley J., 'India in Asian Geopolitics', in Prakash Nanda, ed, *Rising India*. New Delhi: Lancer Publishers, 2007.

Tenet, George J., 'The Worldwide Threat: Evolving Dangers in a Complex World', Testimony of Director of Central Intelligence before the Senate Select Committee on Intelligence, February 11, 2003, at http://www.cia.gov/cia/public_affairs/speeches/dci_speech_02112003.html.

The Atlantic Monthly, 'Headlines Over the Horizon', *The Atlantic Monthly* 292, 1 (July–August 2003).

The Daily Excelsior, 'Al-Qaeda declares war, calls Kashmir "gateway of Jihad against India"', June 8, 2007, at http://www.jammu-kashmir.com/archives/archives2007/kashmir20070608d.html.

The Daily Star (Bangladesh), 'Current status of the Indo-US nuclear deal', November 24, 2007, at http://www.thedailystar.net/story.php?nid=12753.

The Energy and Resources Institute Press, New Delhi, *Defining an Integrated Energy Strategy for India: Ensuring security, sufficiency, and sustainability*, 2005.

The Financial Express, 'India, China May Jointly Bid for Energy Assets', July 8, 2006.

The Hindu, 'India and the Philippines Sign Extradition Treaty', March 14, 2004.

———, 'Uzbekistan, Azerbaijan can Join Pipeline Project: India', November 28, 2005.

———, 'Sea Bird Poised to Become Largest Naval Base: Officer', December 5, 2005.

———, 'Strategic Crude Reserve Gets Nod', January 7, 2006.

———, 'Ratnagiri Gas: India Looks to Oman for Fuel Supply', January 28, 2006.

———, 'India to Join US-Backed Gas Pipeline Project', May 19, 2006.

The Hindu Business Line, 'More Crude Imports from Saudi Arabia Soon: Aiyar', March 29, 2005.

———, 'India, Myanmar may Bypass Bangladesh for Gas Pipeline—Other Options to be Explored', July 7, 2005.

———, 'Tata Steel to Buy 5% Stake in Australian Coal Mine', July 19, 2005.

———, 'Iran Wants to Renegotiate 5-mt LNG Deal with India', August 5, 2006.

The Indian Express, 'And the Boys Go to Babylon', June 22, 2003, at http://www.indianexpress.com/india-news/full_story.php?content_id=26225.

———, 'Threat of Taliban Revival Brings Kabul, Delhi Closer', August 28, 2005.

———, 'PM Offers Helping Hand to Kabul, Karzai A Bridge to Entire Region', August 29, 2005.

The Indian Express, 'India says Iran has right to pursue nuke plan for civilian use', December 25, 2006.

———, 'Some Tears for Saddam, Left and Centre', December 31, 2006.

———, 'Pranab Says Can't Give Any Part of Arunachal', June 17, 2007.

The Los Angeles Times, 'Some ally: Pakistan has sold out Afghan and US interests by signing an agreement with tribesmen that aids the Taliban', November 6, 2006.

The Telegraph, 'Reliance in Pact for Oman Drill', March 13, 2005.

The Times of India, 'Singing Bush's Praise', April 13, 2001.

———, 'Iran, India show Solidarity with Iraq', January 28, 2003.

———, 'Tel Aviv worried about New Delhi's ties with Iran', September 11, 2003.

———, 'India a Growing Global Power', May 29, 2005.

———, 'PM Recalls Memorable Meeting with Castro', September 18, 2006.

———, 'Growing Chinese Economy Bad, Say Indians', July 5, 2007.

The Tribune (New Delhi), 'Saudi King Took Initiative in "Delhi Declaration"', January 27, 2006.

Thomas, Raju G. C., 'India's Energy Policy and Nuclear Weapons Programme', in D. R. Sardesai and Raju G.C. Thomas, ed, *Nuclear India in the Twenty-First Century*. New York: Palgrave-Macmillan, 2002.

Time Magazine, 'Iraq is Not Vietnam, But…', June 24, 2003, at http://www.time.com/time/columnist/karon/article/0,9565,460834,00.html.

Toman, Michael A., Ujjayant Chakravorty and Shreekant Gupta, ed, *India and Global Climate Change: Perspectives on Economics and Policy from a Developing Country*. Washington, DC: Resources for the Future Press, 2003.

Tomberg, Igor, 'Russia–India Energy Dialogue Traditions and Prospects', *Energy Daily*, February 7, 2007, at http://www.energy-daily.com.

Tønnesson, Stein and Åshild Kolås, *Energy Security in Asia: China, India, Oil and Peace*. (Report to the Norwegian Ministry of Foreign Affairs), April 2006, at http://www.prio.no/files/file47777_060420_energy_security_in_asia__final_.pdf?PHPSESSID=b8a30ac.

Vachhani, Ashish, 'India's Energy Security Dilemma', *The Hindu Business Line*, April 26, 2005.

Vajpayee, Atal Bihari, 'Next Steps in Strategic Partnership with USA', New Delhi, January 14, 2004, at http://www.mea.gov.in.

Varadarajan, Siddharth, 'Power Grids and the New Silk Road in Asia", *The Hindu*, July 11, 2005.

———, 'India, China and the Asian Axis of Oil', *The Hindu*, January 24, 2006.

———, 'New Delhi, Beijing Talk Nuclear for the First Time', *The Hindu*, November 22, 2006.

Vasudevan, Hari, 'Russia as a Neighbor: Indo-Russian Relations 1992–2001'. Lecture at the Conference on 'Russia—Ten Years After'. Carnegie Endowment for International Peace, Washington, D.C. June 7–9, 2001.

Virmani, Arvind, *India's Economic Growth: From Socialist Rate of Growth to Bhartiya Rate of Growth*, Indian Council for Research on International Economic Relations, Working Paper No. 122, February 2004, at http://www.icrier.org/pdf/wp122.pdf.

Vucetic, Vladislav, *South Asia Regional Energy Trade: Opportunities and Challenges*, October 1, 2004, at http://siteresources.worldbank.org/INTSOUTHASIA/Resources/Energy_a.pdf.

Wagner, Christian, 'From Hardpower to Softpower: Ideas, Interactions, Institutions, and Images in India's South Asian Policy', Heidelberg Papers in South Asian and Comparitive Politics, Working Paper No. 26, March 2005, p.11, at http://archiv.ub.uni-heidelberg.de/voltexserver/voltex/2005/5436/pdf/hpsacp26.pdf.

Walker, Martin, 'India's Path to Greatness', *Wilson Quarterly* XXVIII, 2 (Summer 2006).

Waltz, Kenneth N., *Theory of International Politics*. Reading, Mass.: Addison-Wesley, 1979.

———, 'A Response to My Critics' in Robert O. Keohane, ed, *Neorealism and its Critics*, New York: Columbia University Press, 1986.

———, 'Nuclear Myths and Political Realities'. *American Political Science Review* 84, 3 (September 1990).

———, 'America as a Model for the World? A Foreign Policy Perspective'. *PS: Political Science and Politics* 24, 4 (December 1991).

———, 'The Emerging Structure of International Politics'. *International Security* 18, 2 (Autumn 1993).

———, 'International Politics is Not Foreign Policy'. *Security Studies* 6, 1 (Autumn 1996).

———, 'Structural Realism after the Cold War'. *International Security* 25, 1 (Summer 2000).

Washington Times, 'Karzai Tells Neighbors to Stop Meddling', February 19, 2006.

Watson, Paul, 'Arms at the Heart of India–Israel Embrace', *Los Angeles Times*, September 9, 2003.

Weaver, Mary Anne, *Pakistan: In the Shadow of Jihad and Afghanistan*. New York: Farrar, Straus & Geroux, 2002.

Weinbaum, Marvin G., 'Afghanistan and its Neighbors: An Ever Dangerous Neighborhood', United States Institute of Peace, Special Report 162, 2006.

Weisbrode, Kenneth, 'Central Eurasia: Prize or Quicksand?', *Adelphi Paper 338* (London: International Institute for Strategic Studies, 2001).

Weiss, Stanley A., 'The Untapped Might of the Himalayas', *International Herald Tribune*, May 11, 2005.

Wenlei, Ding, 'Hardnosed Software Battle: India and China Square Up in IT Ring', *Beijing Review* 47, 12 (March 25, 2004).

Wimbush, S. Endors, 'India's Perspective', Central Intelligence Agency, *Russia in the International System: A Conference Report*, June 1, 2001, at www.cia.gov/nic/pubs/conference_reports/russia_conf.html.

Wishnick, Elizabeth, 'India Walks Central Asian Tightrope', at www.isn.ethz.ch.ch/ news/sw details.cfm?ID=7245.

Wohlforth, William C., *The Elusive Balance: Power and Perceptions during the Cold War*. Ithaca, NY: Cornell University Press, 1993.

———, 'The Stability of a Unipolar World'. *International Security* 24, 1 (Summer 1999).

Woodrow, Thomas, 'The Sino-Saudi Connection', *China Brief*, Jamestown Foundation, October 24, 2002.

World Bank, *World Bank Indicators 2006*. Washington, DC: World Bank, 2006.

Wybrew-Bond, Ian and Jonathan Stren, ed, *Natural Gas in Asia: The Challenges of Growth in China, India, Japan and Korea*. New York: Oxford University Press, 2002.

Yahoo India News, 'Muslims protest docking of USS Nimitz off Chennai port', July 4, 2007, at http://in.news.yahoo.com/070704/139/6hojm.html.

Yahya, Faizal, 'India and Southeast Asia: Revisited', *Contemporary Southeast Asia* 25, 1 (April 2003).

Yee, Amy, *Fuel for a Nation's Ambitions*, October 17, 2006, at http://www.ft.com/cms/s/6b21da38-5dfd-11db-82d4-0000779e2340.html.

Yergin, Daniel, *The Prize: The Epic Quest for Oil, Money, and Power*. New York: Simon and Schuster, 1991.

———, 'Ensuring Energy Security', *Foreign Affairs* 65, 2 (March/April 2006).

Zakaria, Fareed, 'Realism and Domestic Politics: A Review Essay'. *International Security* 17, 1 (Summer 1992).

———, 'Speak Softly, Carry a Veiled Threat'. *New York Times*, February 18, 1996.

———, *From Wealth to Power: The Unusual Origins of America's World Role*. Princeton: Princeton University Press, 1998.

Zhang, Dong, 'India Looks East: Strategies and Impacts', AUSAID Working Paper (September 2006).

Notes on Contributors

Stephen Blank is a Professor of Russian National Security Studies at the Strategic Studies Institute of the US Army War College in Pennsylvania. Dr Blank has been a Professor of National Security Affairs at the Strategic Studies Institute since 1989. He has published over 500 articles and monographs on Soviet/Russian, US, Asian and European military and foreign policies. He has published or edited 15 books focussing on Russian foreign, energy and military policies and on International Security in Eurasia. His books include *Russo-Chinese Energy Relations: Politics in Command* (London: Global Markets Briefing, 2006) and *Natural Allies?: Regional Security in Asia and Prospects for Indo-American Strategic Cooperation* (Carlisle Barracks, PA: Strategic Studies Institute, US Army War College, 2005). Prior to his appointment at the Strategic Studies Institute, Dr Blank was an Associate Professor for Soviet Studies at the Center for Aerospace Doctrine, Research, and Education of Air University at Maxwell AFB. He had also held the positions of Assistant Professor of Russian History at the University of Texas, San Antonio (1980–86), and Visiting Assistant Professor of Russian History at the University of California, Riverside (1979–80). Dr Blank's MA and PhD are in Russian History from the University of Chicago. His BA is in History from the University of Pennsylvania.

Stephen F. Burgess is Associate Professor, Department of International Security, US Air War College. He is also an Associate Director of the US Air Force Counterproliferation Center (CPC). He researches and publishes on South Asia, Africa, UN and counterproliferation and security issues. His South Asian publications have focussed on the growing strategic relationship between India and the US, between Pakistan and the US, and the role of Islamism in Pakistan and Bangladesh. His three books are *The United Nations under Boutros Boutros-Ghali, 1992–97*, *South Africa's Weapons of Mass Destruction* and *Smallholders and Political Voice in Zimbabwe*.

Fraser Cameron is a former European Commission advisor and a well-known policy analyst and commentator on EU and international affairs. He is Director of the EU–Russia Centre, Director of EuroFocus–Brussels, an Adjunct Professor at the Hertie School of Governance in Berlin, and Senior Advisor to the European Policy Centre (EPC) and the European Institute for Asian Studies in Brussels. Dr Cameron was educated at the Universities of St Andrews (MA) and Cambridge (PhD). He joined the European Commission in 1990, as an advisor in external relations, and he was Political Counsellor at the EU delegation in Washington DC from 1999 to 2001. Dr Cameron was seconded to the EPC in 2002 as Director of Studies. His books include *An Introduction to European Foreign Policy*, *The Future of Europe* and *US Foreign Policy after the Cold War* (all published by Routledge).

Manish Dabhade is an Assistant Professor of Diplomacy in the School of International Studies at Jawaharlal Nehru University (JNU), New Delhi. His areas of teaching and research include international security issues (theory and practice) with a special focus on great-power strategies in the post-Cold War era, nuclear proliferation in Asia, and India's foreign and security policy. He was awarded an MA in International Politics and an MPhil in Diplomacy by JNU and is presently pursuing his PhD from JNU.

C. Christine Fair is a senior political scientist with the RAND Corporation. Prior to rejoining RAND, she served as a Political Officer to the UN Assistance Mission to Afghanistan in Kabul and as a Senior Research Associate in USIP's Center for Conflict Analysis and Prevention. Prior to joining USIP in April 2004, she was an Associate Political Scientist at the RAND Corporation. Her research focuses upon the security competition between India and Pakistan, Pakistan's internal security, the causes of terrorism in South Asia and US strategic relations with India and Pakistan. She has authored and co-authored several books, including *The Madrassah Challenge: Militancy and Religious Education in Pakistan* (USIP, 2008), *Fortifying Pakistan: The Role of US Internal Security Assistance* (USIP, 2006), *Securing Tyrants or Fostering Reform?: US Internal Security Assistance to Repressive and Transitioning Regimes*

(RAND, 2006), *The Counterterror Coalitions: Cooperation with Pakistan and India* (RAND, 2004) and *Urban Battle Fields of South Asia: Lessons Learned from Sri Lanka, India and Pakistan* (RAND, 2004). She has written numerous peer-reviewed articles covering a range of security issues in Pakistan, India, Sri Lanka and Bangladesh. She is a member of the International Institute of Strategic Studies, London and is the managing editor of *India Review*.

Sumit Ganguly holds the Rabindranath Tagore Chair in Indian Cultures and Civilizations and is a Professor of Political Science at Indiana University in Bloomington. He has previously been on the faculties of James Madison College of Michigan State University, Hunter College of the City University of New York and the University of Texas at Austin. He is a member of the Council on Foreign Relations, New York and the International Institute of Strategic Studies, London. He has also been a Fellow and a Guest Scholar at the Woodrow Wilson International Center for Scholars in Washington, DC and a Visiting Fellow at the Center for International Security and Cooperation at Stanford University. His research and writing, focussed primarily on South Asia, have been supported by grants from the Asia Foundation, the Ford Foundation, the Carnegie Corporation of New York, W. Alton Jones Foundation and the United States Institute of Peace. He is the founding editor of both *India Review* and *Asian Security*, two refereed journals published by Taylor and Francis, London. Prof. Ganguly is the author, editor or co-editor of a dozen books on South Asia. His publications include the edited work (with Larry Diamond and Marc Plattner)—*The State of India's Democracy*.

Devin T. Hagerty is an Associate Professor of Political Science at the University of Maryland, Baltimore County. He was previously a Senior Lecturer in Government and International Relations at the University of Sydney, Australia. Hagerty was awarded a PhD by the University of Pennsylvania, an MALD by the Fletcher School of Law and Diplomacy and a BA by Rutgers University. He is the author of *The Consequences of Nuclear Proliferation: Lessons from South Asia*, as well as (with Sumit Ganguly) *Fearful Symmetry: Indo-Pakistani Crises in the Shadow of Nuclear Weapons*. His edited volume, *South Asia in World Politics*, was published in 2005. Hagerty is a co-editor of the journal *Asian Security*.

Timothy D. Hoyt is a Professor of Strategy and Policy at the US Naval War College, where he lectures on strategy, terrorism, counterinsurgency, weapons of mass destruction, military transformation, and contemporary conflict and he also teaches an elective course on South Asian security. He received his undergraduate degrees from Swarthmore College, and his PhD in International Relations and Strategic Studies from the Johns Hopkins University's Paul H. Nitze School of Advanced International Studies in 1997. Dr Hoyt's recent publications include chapters and articles on security and conflict in the developing world, the limits of military force in the global war on terrorism, the impact of nuclear weapons on recent crises in South Asia, the Irish Republican Army, the future of US-Pakistani relations and the new US maritime strategy. He is the author of *Military Industries and Regional Defense Policy* (Routledge, 2007), examining the role of military industry in the national security policies of India, Israel, and Iraq. He is currently working on several book-length projects, including an analysis of American military strategy in the 21st century and a study of the strategy of the Irish Republican Army from 1913 to 2005. He is also the Assistant Editor of the *Journal of Strategic Studies*.

Mohan Malik is a Professor at the Asia–Pacific Center for Security Studies in Honolulu, Hawaii. He is the author of *India and China as Global Powers: Back to the Future, Dragon on Terrorism, The Gulf War: Australia's Role and Asian-Pacific Responses*; co-editor of *Religious Radicalism and Security in South Asia*; and editor of *Australia's Security in the 21st Century, The Future Battlefield* and *Asian Defence Policies*. He has contributed numerous book chapters and published over 160 articles on Asian security issues in various journals, defence magazines and newspapers.

C. Raja Mohan is currently a Professor at the S. Rajaratnam School of International Studies, Nanyang Technological University, Singapore. Earlier, He was a Professor of South Asian Studies at the Jawaharlal Nehru University in New Delhi. He had also served as the Strategic Affairs Editor of the *Indian Express* in New Delhi and the Diplomatic Editor and Washington Correspondent of *The Hindu*. Mohan has a masters degree in Nuclear Physics and a PhD in International Relations. He was a member of India's National

Security Advisory Board during 1998–2000 and 2004–06. Dr Mohan Was a Jennings Randolph Peace Fellow at the US Institute of Peace, Washington, DC, during 1992–93. His recent books include *Crossing the Rubicon: The Shaping of India's New Foreign Policy* and *Impossible Allies: Nuclear India, United States and the Global Order*.

Deepa M. Ollapally is Associate Director of the Sigur Center for Asian Studies and Professorial Lecturer at the Elliott School for International Affairs, The George Washington University. Previously, she directed the South Asia programme at the US Institute of Peace and was an Associate Professor of Political Science at Swarthmore College. She had also been a Fellow at the International and Strategic Studies Programme at the National Institute of Advanced Studies in Bangalore, India. She is on the executive board of Women in International Security; and on the advisory council of Women in Security, Conflict Management and Peace, New Delhi. She is a well-known media commentator and has appeared on BBC, CNN, NPR, VOA and the Diane Rehm Show. She has received grants from the Ford Foundation, the Asia Foundation and the Rockefeller Foundation. Her publications include numerous journal articles as well as the books *Confronting Conflict: Domestic Factors and US Policymaking in the Third World* and *The Politics of Extremism in South Asia*. She holds a PhD in Political Science from Columbia University.

Harsh V. Pant is Reader in International Relations at the Department of Defence Studies at King's College London. He is also an Associate with the King's Centre for Science and Security. He joined King's after finishing his doctorate at the University of Notre Dame (USA). He holds a BA (Hons) from the University of Delhi, and MA and MPhil degrees from Jawaharlal Nehru University in New Delhi. His current research, focussed on Asia–Pacific security and defence issues, has been published by a number of academic journals and other publications. His recent books include *Contemporary Debates in Indian Foreign and Security Policy*, published in 2008, and *The Rise of China: Implications for India*, published in 2012.

Manjeet S. Pardesi is a PhD student at the Department of Political Science and a Graduate Assistant at the Center on American and Global Security at Indiana University, Bloomington. His research interests include war and strategy, great-power politics, and India's foreign and security policy. He obtained his MS in Strategic Studies in 2002 from the Institute of Defence and Strategic Studies (IDSS, now called the S. Rajaratnam School of International Studies), Singapore. After completing his MS, he worked as an Associate Research Fellow at IDSS and has lectured at the SAFTI Military Institute, Singapore. His articles have appeared in the *Air & Space Power Journal* (USAF), *The Fletcher Forum of World Affairs, World Policy Journal, India Review, Asian Security*, and *Defense and Security Analysis*.

Index

Abdullah bin Abdul-Aziz Al Saud, Saudi King, 256–57, 259, 270
Admiral Gorshkov (INS Vikramaditya), 199
Afghanistan, 75, 97, 138, 214; India relations, 210, 242, 248–49, 285–92, 326; humanitarian assistance, 142; military and intelligence presence, 135, 152; insurgency and Islamic terrorism, 88, 140–41, 200; NATO-led coalition, 249; Northern Alliance, 254; Pakistan, relations, 254, 286, 291–92; population, 232; Soviet invasion, 1979, 77, 257; United States-led coalition forces, 84, 200. *See also* Pakistan, Taliban
Africa Command (AFRICOM), 98
Afro-Asian summit, Jakarta, 2005, 244
Ahmadinejad, Mahmoud, 256, 258, 333
Ahmed, Mahmood, 200
Airborne Warning and Control System (AWACS), 118, 295
Aiyar, Mani Shankar, 123, 302
Aksai Chin, 175
Al Qaeda, 76, 85, 88, 144, 145, 242, 287
Al Qaeda and Associated Movements (AQAM), 74, 88, 90, 92, 97
Albright, David, 155
anarchy, 27, 81–82, 321
Andaman Nicobar Islands, 126, 282
Andijan massacre, 297
Anti-Satellite (ASAT), 319
Antony, A.K., 178

Apollo Group, 246
Arabian Sea, 202
Arab-Israeli conflict, 262, 266
Arafat, Yasser, 264
arms control concessions, 56, 66, 70
Arunachal Pradesh, 175, 177, 241. *See also* China
ASEAN (Association of Southeast Asian Nations), 18, 139, 219–20, 239, 305–08, 314–17, 318, 325; India–Bali summit (2003), 314–17; India Partnership of Peace, Progress and Shared Prosperity, 314; Plus Three (ASEAN Plus China, South Korea, Japan), 187
ASEAN Free Trade Area (AFTA), 305
ASEAN Regional Forum (ARF), 172, 187, 219–20, 305, 318
Asia Energy Union, 123
Asia–Europe Summit Meeting (ASEM), 172, 187, 210*n*
Asia–Pacific Economic Cooperation (APEC), 172, 187
Asia–Pacific region, Indian aspirations, 36–38
Atomic Energy Commission (AEC), 195
Australia, 117, 167, 187, 225; China military ties, 181; India relations, 305, 310, 318; US relations, 321
authoritarianism, 188–89
axis of evils, 75, 88, 90
Azerbaijan, 302

Baku–Tbilsi–Ceyhan oil pipeline, 122
ballistic missile programme, 236
bandwagoning, 27

378 ■ Indian Foreign Policy in a Unipolar World

Bangladesh, 181; China, relations, 165, 180, 246; strategic presence, 168; creation of, 1971, 236; India relations, 180, 231, 234, 246–47, 250; disputes, 238; energy cooperation, 121; free trade agreement (FTA), 239, 246–47; political, 121; water treaties, 240–41, 246; Islamic fundamentalism, 138, 143; least developed country (LDC) status, 247; population, 232; US policy, 143
Bangladesh, India, Myanmar, Sri Lanka, and Thailand Economic Cooperation (BIMSTEC), 172, 188, 239, 318
Barroso, José Manuel, 209, 223
Bay of Bengal, 108, 173, 305, 316, 321
Bengal Initiative for Multi-Sectoral Technical and Economic Cooperation (BIMSTEC), 139
Berlin Wall, fall of, 3
Bhabha Atomic Research Centre (BARC), 195
Bharatiya Janata Party (BJP), 49, 67, 82, 125, 192, 335
Bhutan, India relations, 238, 239, 245–46; energy cooperation, 112–13, 119; modernisation and democratisation, 245; population, 232
Bhutto, Zulfiqar Ali, 47
Biological Weapons Convention, 85
bipolarity, 26, 28
Birla group, 246
Blair, Tony, 209, 223
Blue Helmet mission, 158–59
Border Roads Organisation (BRO), 152
Bracken, Paul, 44–46
Brahmaputra river, 240, 241, 246

Brahmos, 199
Brazil, 117
Brazil, Russia, India and China (BRIC), 323
British Broadcasting Corporation (BBC), 223
bureaucracy, 24, 63–64, 81, 235
Burma. *See* Myanmar
Burns, R. Nicholas, 197, 278–79, 303
Bush, George W., 13, 43, 51–54, 57–61, 63–67, 68, 70–71, 75, 78–79, 132, 134, 140, 155, 157, 160, 203–04, 215, 217, 224, 242, 277, 279, 280
business freedom, 30

Cambodia, 181, 306; China India energy competition, 180
Canada and India relations, 155–56
capitalism, 188–89, 194
Carnegie Endowment for International Peace, Washington, 282
Caspian Sea, 303
caste conflicts, 90, 139
Castro, Fidel, 148
Caucasus region, 122
Central Asia, 255, 275; India, 13, 17, 277ff; defence and security policy, 293–99; energy policy, 299–303; Indian interest, 284–93; military and intelligence presence, 136; Russia, military alliance, 283; Central Asian Republics, India relations, 135–36, 284
Central Intelligence Agency (CIA), 2, 35, 36
Chemical Weapons Convention, 85
Cheng Ruisheng, 167
Chidambaram, R., 195
child labour, 216
China, 24, 36, 205, 208, 209; and Central Asia, relations, 278–79, 282, 297–98; economy/economic growth, 2, 34, 35, 39, 41, 166,

174, 225, 307, 311; European Union (EU) relations, 216, 218, 224; India diplomatic relations, 13, 14–15, 16, 19, 36, 38–39, 40, 41, 49, 51, 83, 116, 143–44, 163*ff*, 218–19, 235, 250, 272–73, 310, 312–13, 317, 322; in the 21st century, 174–82; border dispute, 163, 168, 174–78, 182, 186, 215, 235; competition, 14, 165, 170, 180; defence linkages, 18; economic/trade relations, 41, 88, 183, 187, 189–90, 207, 218, 305, 315; energy cooperation, 123–24, 180, 272; energy security spawns maritime rivalry, 180–82; geopolitical rivalry, 181, 190; joint military counterterrorism exercise, 305; perceptions, misperceptions, expectations and illusions, 164–74; perspectives on India, 164–70; nuclear competition, 178–80; security competition, 122–23, 138–39; US factor, 14, 143–44; war (1962), 39, 48, 163, 174, 235, 244, 305; water dispute, 241; energy consumption, 40; Iran, relations, 268, 272–73; and Japan relations, 219; Middle East, relations, 18, 255, 267, 276; Myanmar, relations, 294; non-proliferation, 39, 46–48, 50–51, 58, 87; nuclear test (1964), 48; nuclear-weapon state, 34; Pakistan, relationship, 17, 286, 313; military/nuclear assistance, 38, 39, 47, 170, 201; trade relations, 173–74; political system, 39; population, 34; rising power, 2, 8, 12, 18, 36–37, 52, 102, 111, 123, 137, 143, 149–50, 183, 186, 201, 210, 285, 306, 312–13, 319–20, 322; Russia relations, 83; military-technical cooperation (MTC), 201–03; trade relations, 207; Saudi Arabia energy relations, 259; security orientation, 201; size, 34; United States relations, 15, 52, 185–86, 203, 273; competition, 165; and India's quest for energy, 116–17
Christianity, 85
CIRUS reactor, 155
Clinton, Bill, 57, 60–61, 63–64, 70, 78, 131–32, 144, 195
coal energy, 106–07
Cold War, 2–3, 9–10, 11, 15, 17, 18, 19, 23, 28*n*, 37, 39, 45–46, 49–50, 55–57, 60, 61, 77, 83, 86, 124, 182, 185–86, 192, 195, 215, 231, 234, 235, 251, 260, 262, 266, 275, 305–07, 309–15, 322; end and rise of Indian multilateralism, 238–40; power politics, 101; United States' victory, 7
Collective Security Treaty Organisation (CSTO), 283, 285, 332
Commonwealth of Independent States (CIS), 300
communal conflict, 139
communications technology, 211
Communist Party of India (Marxist), 147, 222
Comprehensive Test Ban Treaty (CTBT), 62–63, 66, 70, 178
compressed natural gas (CNG), 108
confidence building measures (CBMs), 69, 161, 189, 316, 317
Congress, 55, 68, 71, 81, 104, 125, 192, 261, 268, 277
Cooperation to Combat International Terrorism, 316
Cray Supercomputer, 147
crisis management, 214
Curzon, Lord, 310

Dalai Lama, 170, 175–76
defence capabilities, 196, 205
defence expenditure, 9, 30, 34, 36–37
democratic institutions, democracy, 1, 2, 3, 35, 79, 165, 188–89, 213, 216, 224, 232
Deng Xiaoping, 69
dependency theory, 173
Dixit, J.N., 120
domestic politics, 3, 27, 69, 98, 264, 267; and nuclear diplomacy in a unipolar world, 67–72
domestic security, 303
drug trafficking, 255
Durand Line, 286

East Asia: and India, 18–19, 282, 305*ff*; economic integration and interdependence, 314–15; political relations, 313–14; security linkage, 315–18
East Asia Co-Prosperity Sphere, 188
East Asia Summit (EAS), 51, 167, 187, 282, 305
economic: development/growth, 19, 71, 88, 177, 189, 191, 224, 235, 268, 303, 310–11; disparities, 73
economic freedom, 30, 35, 42; globalisation and liberalisation, 183, 208, 224, 260; reforms, 34, 231; resurgence, 118; security, 181
economy, 1–2, 24–26, 29–30, 35, 40–42, 50, 82, 86, 99–100, 103, 115, 198, 222, 259, 307, 311
Einhorn, Robert, 154
El Baradei, Mohammed, 59, 157
electricity programme, 301
Enduring Freedom Operation, 75, 242
energy: consumption, 40, 100, 104, 107–8, 110, 115; cooperation, 121–22, 124, 279; demand, 268–69; policy in Central Asia, 299–303; pricing policy, 100, 103; profile of India, 105–10, 181; purchase of equity stakes overseas, 113–19; security, 15, 19, 51, 99*ff*, 125, 198, 276, 289–90; a foreign policy priority, 101–04; strategy, 110–18; sources and diversification of suppliers, 112–13
Energy Coordination Committee (ECC), 111
environmental considerations, 103, 107, 215
Essar, 246
ethnic and religious intolerance, 73, 90, 139
Eurasian Bank of Russia, 301
European Defence Policy, 8
European identity, 194
European Security Strategy (ESS), 212
European Union (EU), 29, 36, 136, 243; China, relations, 16, 216, 218, 224; European Community Economic (EEC) programme, 301; India, relations, 14, 16, 209*ff*, 329; background, 212–14; economic and trade, 220–23; free trade agreement (FTA), 209–10, 222 Indian response, 214–15; rhetoric and reality, 214–16; Generalized System of Preferences Scheme, 329; Hague Summit, 209; Japan relations, 216, 219; Russia relations, 216, 219, 224; Security Council over Iraq, 223; US relations, 216–17, 225
eurozone crisis, 324, 329

Farakka Barrage, 241
Fast Breeder Reactors, 109
federalism, 224
Fernandes, George, 296
fiscal freedom, 30

Fissile Materials Cut-off Treaty (FMCT), 62–63
food security, 100, 289
Foreign Direct Investment (FDI), 221–22, 329
foreign exchange reserves, 1
foreign policy of India: emerging themes and issues, 11–20; drivers in the Middle East, 265–75; quest for power and influence in East Asia, 18–19, 312–18
France, 8, 59, 71, 117, 210, 215; Dassault Aviation for Mirage, 151; non-proliferation norms, 50
free market democracy, 249–50

Gandhi, Indira, 236–38, 249
Gandhi, M.K., 81
Gandhi, Rahul, 324
Gandhi, Rajiv, 236–38, 249, 312
Gandhi, Sonia, 68, 324
Gang, Zhou, 167
Ganga–Mekong Cooperation Group, 318
Ganges, 240, 246
Gas Authority of India Limited (GAIL), 206
Gasprom, 206
gender discrimination, 216
General Agreement of Tariffs and Trade (GATT), 222
General Electric (GE), 147
geopolitical competition, 102, 118, 120, 281
Germany, 36; population, 35; attack on Russia (1941), 101
global war on terrorism (GWOT), 14, 19, 74, 75–80, 85, 94, 98, 140, 145, 161, 216, 242, 243, 320; ramifications for the Indo-US relationship and cooperation, 90–93
global warming, 58, 190

globalisation, 61, 82, 190, 211, 250, 304, 306
Gorbachev, Mikhail, 193
government effectiveness, 30
great powers, comparison, 24, 25, 29, 30–40, 41–42
Gross Domestic Product (GDP), 30, 34, 36, 99–100
Group of Eight (G-8), 1, 187, 204
Group of Six (G-6), 2
Group of Twenty (G-20), 210, 224
Gujarat: Muslims massacre (2002), 153
Gujral, I.K., 239
Gulf Cooperation Council, 333
Gulf War (1991), 103
Gwadar port, 292
Gyanendra, King, 244

Hamas, 274
Hawala system, 271
Hindu nationalism, 270
Hinduism, 85
Hizbollah, 274
Holland, 210
Hong Kong, 307
Hormuz Straits, 125, 181
human rights, 61, 213, 215, 224
Hussain, Saddam, 48, 57, 265, 267
hydroelectricity, 110, 112–13, 119, 122, 123, 301
hyperrealism, 80, 82–83, 89–90, 91, 93, 94. *See also* Nehruvianism, neorealism

India: as an energy outsourcing hub, 114–15; perspective on China, 170–74; and post-Cold War Asian tripolarity, 36–40; vision of the emerging world order, 80–83
Indian Ocean, 13, 23, 97, 118–19, 125, 126, 127, 181, 182, 293, 309, 316, 320

Indian Ocean Rim Association for Regional Cooperation (IOR ARC), 239
Indian Parliament, terrorists' attack (2001), 89, 161, 242
Indo-Tibetan Border Police (ITBP), 249
Indonesia, 183, 187, 223, 275; China military ties, 181; India relations, 306, 312, 314; maritime boundaries, 307; military relations, 293, 316
Indus, 240
inflation, 225
information-technology sector, 23, 87, 226, 246, 299
Intellectual Property Rights (IPR), 222
Inter-Governmental Group (IGG), 238
International: arms market, 263; community, 2, 23, 43–44, 56, 65, 76–77, 148, 157–58, 251, 275; competition, 4, 174; energy market,116; law, 224; markets, 100, 220; nuclear order, 12, 15, 44, 46, 52, 55–59, 68, 72; politics, 1, 2, 4–6, 12, 19–20, 25–26, 27–29, 304, 306, 310; relations/system, 3–6, 19–20, 23–24, 37, 44, 46, 52, 58–59, 69, 74, 75, 80, 81, 88, 89, 102, 116, 173, 189, 206, 208, 251–52; emerging structure, 7–11; security environment, 11, 39, 45
International Atomic Energy Agency (IAEA), 56, 59, 65, 68, 117, 157, 161, 179–80, 205, 259, 268, 270
International Conference on Counterterrorism, Riyadh, 2005, 258
International Criminal Court (ICC), 216

International Energy Agency (IEA), 115
Inter-Service Intelligence (ISI), 89–90, 200. *See also* Pakistan
investment freedom, 30
Iran, 39, 48, 68; China relations, 180–81, 269, 272; India relations, 18, 135, 160, 208, 252–56, 260, 265, 266, 268, 270, 272, 275, 287, 294, 333; cooperation, 40; energy cooperation, 107, 108, 112, 119, 122, 124, 210, 269, 290; military and intelligence presence, 135, 326; Islamic Revolution, 257; nuclear programme, 148, 160, 251, 258, 267–68, 272, 274–75; Pakistan relations, 254, 286; Palestine issue, 256, 262–66; proliferation, 69; Russia, relations, 268; sanctions against, 268; United Nations Security Council resolution, 267; United States relation, 79, 274, 280; assertions about terrorism, 144; tension, 120; weapons of mass destruction (WMD), 88; West relations, 254
Iran–Pakistan–India (IPI) pipeline, 119, 120, 123, 124, 205–06, 260, 269, 280, 290, 292, 300–01, 303
Iraq, 75–76, 214; India relations, 251; energy cooperation, 107; reconstruction, 270; United States War, 8, 75, 84, 205, 216, 225, 233, 255, 269, 274
Iraqi Freedom Operation (OIF), 76, 88
Islamic extremism and fundamentalism, 17, 83–85, 87–88, 89, 91–93, 138–39, 143, 205, 254, 258, 270, 274, 282, 298
Israel, 54, 252, 256; and China, defence cooperation, 181, 273; domestic politics, 265; economy,

263; India relations/Indian policy, 18, 88, 135, 136, 251, 260–65, 273, 275, 297
Ivanov, Sergei, 198, 206

Jamat-ul Dawa, 171
Jamnagar, 115
Japan, 18, 183, 187; China relations, 181–82, 185, 186, 219; defence expenditure, 34, 37; economy, 2, 35, 37, 166, 307; energy consumption, 40; European Union (EU) relations, 216, 219; India relations, 51, 195, 209, 218–19, 225, 305; Global Partnership Agreement, 313–14; security cooperation, 317–18; non-proliferation, 49; population, 35; size, 34; Saudi Arabia energy relations, 259; United States, relations, 319, 321
Jewish-Hindu axis against Islam, 265
Jiabao, Wen, 164, 175, 218
Jigme Khesar, King of Bhutan, 245
Jintao, Hu, 176, 203
Jordan, 266
Joseph, Robert, 155*n*
Judaism, 85

Kakodkar, Anil, 195
Kaluchak massacre, J & K, 161
Kargil War, 1999, 196, 239–40, 242. *See also* Kashmir, Pakistan
Karwar naval base, 126
Karzai, Hamid, 242, 248–49, 285, 288
Kashmir dispute, 37, 39, 97, 177, 214, 256, 257, 258, 262; infiltration, 88; Muslim separatists, 90; Pakistan-supported insurgency, 92, 140, 145, 161, 215, 231, 239, 242, 266, 286; United States policy, 153, 161, 243, 291

Kazakhstan: China India energy competition, 180; India, defence and security cooperation, 293, 296–99; energy cooperation, 122–23, 290, 302–03
KazMunaiGaz, 302
Kennedy, John F., 46, 78
Khan, Abdul Qadeer, 140
Khatami, Mohammed, 253, 268
Khomeini, Ayatollah, 48
Klebanov, Ilya, 196
Koirala, Girija Prasad, 245
Koizumi, 219, 314, 317
Kozyrev, Andrei, 193
Krepon, Michael, 154, 156
Kuwait and India energy cooperation, 107
Kyrgyzstan, India relations, energy cooperation, 122; security cooperation, 298

labour freedom, 30
Lashkar-e-Taiba, 154, 171, 271–72
left-wing radicalism and extremism, 139
Liberation Tigers of Tamil Elam (LTTE), 138
Light Combat Aircraft system, 147
Line of Actual Control (LAC), 177
Line of Control (LoC), 242–43
liquefied natural gas (LNG), 108, 112
Look-East policy, 18, 136, 167, 169, 174, 181, 187, 193, 305, 307–08, 314, 333
Loong, Lee Asen, 317
Lugar, Richard, 155*n*, 277

Ma Jiali, 167
Madagascar and China military ties, 181
Madrasa (Islamic school) education, 270–71

Mahakali River, 241
Malacca Straits, 97, 125, 181, 282, 321
Malaysia, 306; India, military and defence relations, 293, 316
Maldives, 238; China relations, 165, 181; strategic presence, 168; Indian operations, 159n; population, 232
maritime security, 95, 168, 320
market mechanisms, 104, 111, 194
Marxism-Maoism, 188
material power capabilities, 5–6
McMahon Line, 175
Mekong–Ganges Cooperation (MGC), 172, 188
mid air refueling, 118
Middle East, 79, 92, 96, 98, 101–03; China policy, 18; European Union (EU) relations, 216; Indian relations, 214, 233, 284, 321; foreign policy, 17–18; energy cooperation, 107, 112, 114, 124, 125–26, 210, 218, 290
military strength/capabilities, 19, 24, 26, 29, 30, 35, 37, 45, 82, 95, 117–18, 150
Millennium Development Goals, 213
missile defence test, 55
missile gap, 46
monetary freedom, 30
Mongolia, 183, 187; Chinese relations, 169
Mukherjee, Pranab, 177, 282, 291
Mulford, David, 149n
multialignment, 182–89, 190
multilateralism, 50, 56, 215, 222, 224, 238–41
multipolarity, 28, 202, 206
multi-vector policy, 334
Musharraf, Pervez, 140–42, 145, 148n, 200, 240, 242

Muslims in India, 150, 153–54, 254–56, 266–67, 270–71, 321
Myanmar (Burma), 225, 306, 312; China, relations, 165, 168–69, 180–81; India relations, 180–81, 210; border conflict, 215–16; energy, 112–13, 120–21, 124; maritime boundaries, 307, 308; military relations, 294; military dictatorship, 232

Nair, V.K., 294
Narasimha Rao, P.V., 3, 62, 104, 193, 333
Narayanan, M.K., 280
Narmada project, 110
Nathu La pass trade route, 175
National Democratic Alliance (NDA), 54, 125, 261
National Security Strategy document, US, 57
nationalism, 45–46
naval diplomacy, 316
Nazarbayev, Nursultan, 296
Nehru, Jawaharlal, 170, 193, 309; Nehruvianism, 80, 81, 85–86, 91, 93, 94
neoliberalism, 80, 81–82, 86–89, 91, 93, 94
neo-realism, 25
Nepal, 138, 142, 234; China, relations, 165; India relations, 210, 244–45, 247, 250; border disputes, 238, 239; energy cooperation, 112–13, 119; riverine cooperation, 241; role in democratisation process, 243, 244–45, 250; trade agreement, 239; Maoist insurgency, 243–44; population, 232; revolution, 143; United States policy, 143
New Zealand, 167

Next Step in the Strategic Partnership (NSSP), 2004, 64, 243
Nicobar Islands. *See* Andaman Nicobar Islands
Nigeria: India energy cooperation, 107
Nixon, Richard, 166, 186
non-alignment/Non-Aligned Movement (NAM), 39, 68, 148, 231–32, 310–11; to multi-alignment, 182–89
non-proliferation norms, 40, 43*ff*, 78, 154, 156, 179, 213, 215
North Atlantic Treaty Organization (NATO), 8, 58, 140, 194, 325
North Korea: India cooperation, 195, 210, 319; non-proliferation, 46–47
North–South Transport Corridor, 300
nuclear: autonomy, 65; control capabilities, 87; deterrence, 57; energy, 58, 140; nationalism, 62; politics in post-Cold War, 44; power, 109–10, 117; proliferation, 1, 45–49, 54; and the Asian balance, 49–55; technology, 157; tests (1974), 48, 60, 109; (1998), 23, 44, 60, 64, 69, 109, 165, 193, 195, 239; weapons programme, 82, 87, 132, 235–36; nuclear-weapon state status, 30, 34–35, 44, 68
Nuclear Non-Proliferation Treaty (NPT), 43, 47, 50, 55–57, 59–60, 68–69, 85, 109, 117, 179, 267, 269
Nuclear Suppliers Group (NSG), 66, 117, 140, 157, 172, 179–80, 197–98, 215, 314

Oil and Natural Gas Corporation (ONGC), 113–14, 270
oil and natural gas reserves, 30, 34–35, 40, 101, 107–8
oil imports, 103
Oman: China defence cooperation, 181; India energy cooperation, 108, 124, 114, 294
ONGC Videsh Limited (OVL), 113, 198
Organisation of Islamic Conference (OIC), 257, 266
over-regulation, 24

Pacific Ocean, 173, 182
Pakistan, 92, 181, 225; Afghanistan, relations, 254; and Central Asia, 295–97; China, relationship, 17, 165; military/nuclear assistance, 38, 39, 47, 170, 201, 250; strategic presence, 168; democracy, 140; domestic politics, 97; F-16, 146; India relations, 49, 97, 177, 195, 219–20, 310; conflict, 2, 152–53, 215, 234–36, 238, 239–40, 249, 254, 284; role of United States, 60–64; economic relations, 239; energy cooperation, 119–20, 121; Indus Water Treaty, 1960, 240; nuclear parity, 52, 54, 169; security competition, 138, 152–53; Iran relations, 254; Islamic ex-tremism, 85, 88, 89, 284, 330; missile development programme, 47; Most Favoured Nation (MFN) status, 239; nuclear proliferation, 44, 46–47, 60, 140, 218, 239; population, 232; Russia relations, 200–01; support to terrorism, 92, 140, 145, 161, 215, 231, 236, 239, 242, 266, 286–87, 291; United States relations/policy, 140–42; nuclear/military cooperation, 52–53, 142. *See also* Kashmir, Taliban
Palestine issue, 256, 262–66

Partition of Indian subcontinent, 235
Persian Gulf, 1, 96, 98, 102, 103, 181; India, relations, 255, 257, 265, 269, 272, 275, 278, 282, 288, 290; energy cooperation, 108, 119, 125
Pew Global Attitudes Project, 174
Pew Research Center, 325
Philippines, 306; China relations, 169, 181; India relations, 314; Extradition Treaty (2004), 317
Planning Commission, 113, 114, 115
plutonium reprocessing technologies, 58
political system, politics, 48, 188, 295; crises in oil-rich countries, 102; stability and competence, 24, 26, 29, 30, 31, 34–35
population, 34–36, 99
Portugal, 210
poverty, 189
power: global balance, 1, 12, 14–15, 19, 23ff, 36, 47–48, 50, 64, 68, 136, 150, 168; elements: a conceptual framework, 25–29; transformation from hard to soft, 7
Pressler Amendment Sanctions, 146
Pressurised Heavy Water Reactors, 109
Primakov, Yevgeny, 202
private sector, 114
Proliferation Security Initiative (PSI), 57, 58–59
property rights, 30
protectionism, 24
purchasing power parity, 30
Pushtuns, 286
Putin, Vladimir, 192, 194–200, 203–04, 206

Qatar, India energy cooperation, 108, 112

Qin Gang, 179

RAND Corporation, 252, 319
regional policy of India, 183, 224, 235–38, 243
regional security system in Central Asia, Chinese preponderance, 50–51
Reliance Industries, 114, 246
Reliance Petroleum Limited, 115, 270
resource endowment, 26, 29, 30, 35
Rice, Condoleezza, 1, 52–53, 78, 137, 151, 156, 166, 277
riverine cooperation, Indian leadership, 240–41
Rong Ying, 167
Rosoboron Service, 199
Russia, 8, 9, 17, 35, 59, 71, 117, 205, 254, 267, 278; Central Asia, China, triangle, 301; military alliance, 283, 297; China relations, 279, 301; trade, 207; China–India triangle, 172, 202–03, 283; China–Iran triangle, 184; European Union (EU) relations, 216, 219, 224; global navigation system (GLONASS), 200; hydrocarbon projects, 198; India, relations, 14, 15, 135, 192ff, 219, 279, 283–84, 290, 293, 299, 328; defence cooperation, 54, 198–99, 202, 262, 296–97; energy cooperation, 205; Iran relations, 268; MiG Corporation, 151, 196; nationalism, 45–46; non-proliferation, 58; nuclear-weapon state, 35; Pakistan, relations, 200–01, 286

SAARC (South Asian Association for Regional Cooperation), 139, 187, 188, 201, 231–32, 238–40, 249–50, 282, 330; Islamabad summit, 2004, 238, 240

SAARC Preferential Trading Arrangement (SAPTA), 238
Sakhalin 1 and 3 Projects, 198
Salafi movement, 258, 270
Saran, Shyam, 281–82
Saudi Arabia: financial assistance to Islamic organisations, 271; India relations, 18, 135, 251–52, 258, 266, 269–73, 275; energy cooperation, 107, 198; new found convergence, 256–60; Iran, relations, 257–58; Islamic extremism, 85, 92; Pakistan relations, 259; Wahhabi rule, 258
scientific and technological sophistication, 23
Seabird Project, 126
Sea Lines of Communication (SLOCs), 118
sea-lanes of control, 150
second nuclear age, 44–46; Asian factor, 45
security issues, 14, 50, 220, 308; perceptions of India, 138–40
self-help system, 26, 27, 321
Senate Foreign Affairs Committee, 151, 154
Shaksgam Valley issue, 178
Shanghai Cooperation Organisation (SCO), 50, 139, 172, 184, 187, 202, 203, 207, 282, 296, 300, 331
Sharon, Ariel, 260–61, 264
Shen Dingli, 167
Shengen Treaty, 222n
Shia-Sunni strife, 254
Shihai, Sun, 167
Siberia–China gas pipelines, 123
Sikkim, 231
Silk Route, 282, 302
Simla Agreement (1972), 38, 236
Singapore: China military ties, 181; economy, 307; India relations, 195, 305–06, 314; Comprehensive Economic Cooperation Agreement (CECA), 315; Free Trade Agreement (FTA), 315; security cooperation, 293, 317; United States relations, 321, 332–33
Singh, Jaswant, 62–63, 69, 131–32, 275, 284
Singh, Manmohan, 43, 65–68, 71, 73, 100, 103, 146, 147–48, 159n, 160, 164, 171, 190, 197–98, 206, 210, 217, 220, 244–45, 259, 288, 305n, 308, 314, 315, 332, 333
Singh, Natwar, 137, 300
Sinha, Yashwant, 295, 308
Sino, *See* China
social order, 73
socio-economic deprivation, 139
socio-economic process, 281
soft power diplomacy, 187–89
South Africa, 117; India relations, 294, 297
South Asia, 282, 300; and India/Indian dominance, 207, 231ff, 288; energy cooperation, 121–22; and Indo-US partnership since 9/11, 242–44; rivalries and conflicts, 286
South Asian Free Trade Area (SAFTA), 238
South China Sea, 181, 201, 316
South Korea, 219, 305, 306; China relations, 169; economy, 307; India, relations, 314, 317; United States relations, 319
Southeast Asia, 18, 282; and China, 298; India relations, 136, 278, 293, 306–07, 310
Soviet Union: China relations, 47, 182, 186; disintegration, 7, 26, 36, 39, 49, 50, 60, 61, 192, 196, 202, 208, 255, 260, 311, 322; India relations, 37, 61, 182, 235; economic, 184; Peace, Friendship

388 ■ Indian Foreign Policy in a Unipolar World

and Cooperation Treaty (1971), 39, 48, 77; security cooperation, 39, 47; nuclear proliferation, 45–46; South Korea nuclear cooperation, 47; United States relations, 45–46, 49, 135. *See also* Russia
Special Economic Zone (SEZ), 115
Spector, Leonard, 154
Sri Lanka, 181, 234; China, relations, 165, 180; strategic presence, 168; India relations, 180, 210, 247–48; disputes, 238; Open Skies Agreement, 248; peace process, 138, 159*n*, 231, 236–37, 243, 247, 249; free trade agreement (FTA), 239, 247
Standard and Poor's (S&P), 323
state(s): inter-state hierarchy, 6; and non-state actors, distinction, 86; relative position in international system, 5–6; rising powers and their foreign policies, 3–6; socialism, 61
status quo, 6
strategic implications, 20, 118–26
strategic reserves, creation, 115
strategic triangles, tilts and trilateral equations, 184–86
structural realism, a theory of foreign policy, 4, 10, 25
Subrahmanyam, K., 203
Sun Pharmaceuticals, 246
Sunni fundamentalism, 254

Taiwan, 170, 201, 225; China relations, 169, 181; economy, 307; United States relations, 319
Tajikistan, 187; energy cooperation, 122, 126; strategic, 135, 136, 293, 295–96, 298; Indian air base in Ayni, 332
Tajikistan–Afghanistan–Pakistan (TAP) pipeline, 119, 302–03

Talbott, Strobe, 62–63, 131–32
Taliban, 75, 90, 97, 140, 141, 144, 200, 242, 249, 254; Pakistani support, 286–87, 291
Tarapore power plant, 197
Tata Group, 114, 246
Tawang Monastery, 176
technical reforms in electricity sector, 111
technological development, 36, 45, 50, 59, 217, 220
technology transfer, 135, 196
territorial sovereignty, 17, 47, 231
terrorism, global terrorism, 12–13, 38, 39, 73, 75, 86, 90, 92–94, 97, 171, 190, 205, 214–17, 242, 260–62, 271, 292, 321; challenge, threats and nature of war, 83–85. *See also* global war on terrorism (GWOT)
Thailand, 306; China military ties, 181; India relations, 314; Free Trade Agreement (FTA), 315; maritime boundaries, 307; military relations, 293, 316
Tiananmen Square massacre, 1989, 179, 218
Tibet factor in Sino-Indian relations, 176–78, 182, 235, 241
Tibetan Autonomous Region, 175
'trade war', 326
Treaty of Rome, 16
tsunami (2004), 143, 248
Turkmenistan and India, energy cooperation, 122–23, 287, 290, 302
Turkmenistan–Afghanistan–Pakistan–India (TAPI) pipeline, 119, 122, 280, 292
Tyagi, S.P., 118, 171, 289, 294

Ukraine, 161
unipolarity, 28, 36, 37, 192–94, 322
United Kingdom (UK), 59, 117, 210, 215; non-proliferation, 50

United Nations (UN), 77–78, 88, 97, 98, 150, 211, 213, 214, 217, 223, 231, 273; General Assembly (UNGA), 258; peacekeeping operations, 158–59; Security Council (UNSC), 44, 76, 137, 138, 148–49, 165, 167, 171, 172, 179, 186, 215, 217, 219, 232, 233n, 267–68
United Progressive Alliance (UPA), 55, 261
Universal Declaration of Human Rights, 153
United States of America (USA), 24, 28–29, 36, 182, 255, 267, 276, 280; Afghanistan, conflict/relations, 84, 200, 254, 287; Bangladesh policy, 143; bureaucratic politics, 97; and Central Asia energy relations, 123; China, relations, 15, 32–39, 52, 169, 182, 185–86, 203, 273; competition, 165; energy relations, 124; and India, triangular relationship, 12, 15, 37, 168, 185–86, 311; strategic cooperation, 48; Commission on International Religious Freedom, 153–54; defence expenditure, 9, 34, 37; dominance and hegemony, 7–9, 15; economic power, 2, 34, 35, 41, 210; energy consumption, 40; European Union (EU) relations, 216–17, 225; foreign policy, 10, 13, 215, 219, 224, 253; Global Positioning System, 200; Hyde Act, 66n; India, relations, 14, 16, 17, 20, 36, 37, 39–41, 51, 74, 77–80, 90–93, 95, 97, 124, 195, 197, 203, 217, 224–25, 299, 283, 326; alliance against China, 66, 313; civilian nuclear cooperation, 12, 37–38, 40, 41, 43–44, 51–54, 60–67, 82, 87, 109, 111, 125, 133, 135, 145–48, 152–55, 166–69, 179, 197, 243, 277–78, 300–01, 321; convergence, 18–19, 38; cost and benefits of, 144–58; defence planning groups, 160; in East Asia, managing convergence and divergence, 318–21; embracing a new paradigm, 131ff; evolving appreciation of Indian threat environment, 140–44; Indian foreign policy, 11, 14; Joint Working Group on Counter terrorism, 95–96, 144; political, 67; strategic partnership, Indian perspective, 134–38, 186; sanctions against, 64; Iran relation, 79, 120, 274–75, 280; Iraq conflict, 8, 75, 84, 205, 216, 225, 233, 255, 269, 274; Japan, 319; and India triangular partnership, 172–73, 185; Middle East relations, 274; Missile defence initiative, 54–55, 274; Monroe Doctrine, 236; non-proliferation, 40, 56–57, 62–65, 78, 154, 180, 274; national security strategy, 138; nuclear power, 34, 45, 151–52; Pakistan relations, 140, 142, 161; strategic/nuclear cooperation, 47, 48, 52–53, 142, 217; perceptions, shift, 36; population, 34; Saudi Arabia energy relations, 259; size, 34; South Asia energy relations, 123–24; South Asia policy, 53; Soviet Union, relations, 49, 135; and China triangular relationship, 185; competition, 312; rivalry, 45–46; nuclear balance, 49; technology and weapon systems, 146–47; terrorists' attack on WTC (9/11),

52, 53, 73, 75, 77, 83–84, 90, 145, 200, 205, 242–44, 274, 286, 316, 319–20; unilateralism, 202, 233*n*, 237; victory in the Cold War, 7. *See also* global war on terrorism (GWOT)

USSR. *See* Soviet Union. *See also* Russia

uranium reserves, 117

Uzbekistan, 203; India, defence and security cooperation, 293, 296–99; energy cooperation, 290, 302–03

Vajpayee, Atal Bihari, 68, 79, 131–32, 149–50, 159*n*, 175, 240, 242, 293, 314

Videocon Industries, 114

Vietnam, 183, 187, 225, 306, 313; and China relations, 169; military ties, 181; and India relations, 293, 314

Waltz, Kenneth N., 27–29, 30, 41

Waziristan, 141, 286–87

weapons of mass destruction (WMD), 48, 55, 57, 59, 76, 83–84, 85, 87–88, 89, 91, 96

Wehrkunde conference, Munich, 2006, 280

West Asia, 282; Annapolis peace conference (2007), 251

western dominance, decline, 45, 163

World Bank, 30, 240

World Trade Organisation (WTO), 210, 222

World War I, 101

World War II, 16, 37, 50, 82, 83, 101, 185, 235, 309

Xinjiang: secessionism, 39

Yalta system, 50

Yang Jiechi, 177

Yaztrzgemsy, Sergei, 200

Yeltsin, Boris, 193, 196, 328

Yugoslavia: United States-led NATO strikes, 8, 194

Zoroastrianism, 85

For Product Safety Concerns and Information please contact our EU
representative GPSR@taylorandfrancis.com
Taylor & Francis Verlag GmbH, Kaufingerstraße 24, 80331 München, Germany

www.ingramcontent.com/pod-product-compliance
Lightning Source LLC
Chambersburg PA
CBHW050833230426
43667CB00012B/1986